DISCARD

DATE DUE

BRODART, CO.   Cat. No. 23-221

Kennesaw Mountain

CIVIL WAR AMERICA

Gary W. Gallagher,

Peter S. Carmichael,

Caroline E. Janney, and

Aaron Sheehan-Dean,

editors

EARL J. HESS

Kennesaw Mountain

SHERMAN, JOHNSTON, AND THE ATLANTA CAMPAIGN

THE UNIVERSITY OF NORTH CAROLINA PRESS

CHAPEL HILL

Set in Miller, Willow, and Copperplate
by Tseng Information Systems, Inc.
Manufactured in the United States of America

The paper in this book meets the guidelines for permanence
and durability of the Committee on Production Guidelines
for Book Longevity of the Council on Library Resources.

The University of North Carolina Press has been a
member of the Green Press Initiative since 2003.

Library of Congress Cataloging-in-Publication Data

Hess, Earl J.
Kennesaw Mountain : Sherman, Johnston, and
the Atlanta Campaign / Earl J. Hess.
p. cm. —
(Civil War America)
Includes bibliographical references and index.
ISBN 978-1-4696-0211-0 (cloth : alk. paper)
ISBN 978-1-4696-0212-7 (ebook)
1. Kennesaw Mountain, Battle of, Ga., 1864.
2. Atlanta Campaign, 1864. I. Title.
E476.7.H47 2013
973.7'371—dc23   2012037476

17 16 15 14 13   5 4 3 2 1

For Pratibha and Julie

Contents

Table and Maps

Illustrations

Preface

Six weeks after setting out from Chattanooga in early May, 1864, Major General William T. Sherman hit a massive roadblock while fighting his way toward Atlanta. Confederate general Joseph E. Johnston's Army of Tennessee was heavily fortified along a line that stretched across the Georgia countryside, anchored on the twin peaks of Kennesaw Mountain near Marietta. It was the ninth fortified position Johnston had created thus far in the campaign, and it proved to be the most difficult to bypass. For two weeks, from June 19 to July 3, Sherman tried to find a way to turn Johnston's left flank. Both armies were stretched to the breaking point in their extended positions as artillery duels, constant sniping, and a fierce battle or two erupted. As the two sides tested each other, heavy rains descended, and the dirt roads of Georgia became quagmires. Frustrated at the delay, Sherman decided to try a major frontal assault against three points of Johnston's line on June 27. The Federals who survived that day would remember the attack for the rest of their lives.

The assault of June 27 was a significant departure from Sherman's mode of operations during the Atlanta campaign. He had more often maneuvered parts of his massive force, an army group consisting of available troops from the departments of his Military Division of the Mississippi, in order to turn enemy flanks and force the Confederates out of their trenches. Sherman did mix attacks with his turning strategy at Dalton, Resaca, New Hope Church, and Pickett's Mill, but most of those assaults had been exploratory efforts to find and develop enemy lines and take advantage of opportunities that occurred. On June 27, the Federals knew what to expect and were hitting a heavily fortified, well-manned position. It was, in a way, an experiment, and Sherman arrived at the decision after many days of deliberation.

Sherman threw eight brigades of veteran troops, some fifteen thousand men, at three locations along the heavily fortified Confederate line on June 27. They failed to make a dent in the defenses, losing about three thousand casualties in the process. Only at one location, a small rise of ground that came to be called Cheatham's Hill, did the Federals stay close to the Confederate works after their attack. They dug new field works within yards of the Rebels. Here they stayed for the remainder of the Kennesaw phase of the Atlanta campaign, sniping, digging a mine with the intention of blowing up an angle in the Confederate works, and cooperating with their enemy in burying the many bodies of Union men killed in the attack. When Sherman resumed his practice of flanking Johnston out of his works, the Confederates evacuated the Kennesaw Line on the night of July 2 and retired a few miles to the next fortified position. The Chattahoochee River, the last natural barrier to Sherman's approach to Atlanta, lay only a short distance farther south.

The purpose of this book is to tell the story of Kennesaw Mountain in the Atlanta campaign. It is based on extensive research in archival collections and published primary sources. The work of previous historians who have written on the campaign is also incorporated for context. Special attention is devoted to the engagements at Kolb's Farm on June 22 and Sherman's assault on June 27. The battlefield itself presented a valuable resource for understanding the action around Kennesaw in late June and early July 1864. Although the area where Sherman's right wing tried to find and flank Johnston's left has been developed, the ground within the park is well preserved. The locations of the three attacks on June 27 are in a natural state, even if the site of the battle of Kolb's Farm is a mix of natural landscape and housing development.

The aim of this book is not only to describe the actions along the Kennesaw Line but to explain the significance of the Kennesaw phase of the Atlanta campaign and understand the outcome of operations along the line. By necessity, it is a study of high-command problems, decisions, and triumphs on both sides of no-man's-land. But it is also a story of common soldiers enduring and adjusting to the special rigors of continuous contact with the enemy, living within holes while spring weather did its worst overhead. The endurance of the Federal rank and file was most severely tested by the order to approach well-constructed earthworks filled with Confederate soldiers, and the attack of June 27 serves as an excellent case study of the experience of battle. The use of field fortifications on the minor tactical and the larger strategic level is a major feature of this story, and the failure of column formations to give the Federals an advantage in their risky assault is highlighted. Sherman's recurrent fights with newspaper correspondents came into play during the Kennesaw phase of the Atlanta campaign, and neither he nor Johnston could ever forget that higher-level authorities in Washington and Richmond kept watch over their every move. For Sherman, Kennesaw was a dangerous phase of his career, a time when he feared that weather conditions and Confederate fortifications had slowed his advance so much that Johnston might send reinforcements to General Robert E. Lee's army in Virginia. For Johnston, Kennesaw represented the best evidence he could muster to prove that his Fabian tactics were working to slow the Union advance into Georgia and were punishing the enemy with heavy casualties. There was much to be gained or lost for both commanders, depending on how this phase of the struggle for Atlanta came out.

"The most severe and trying experiences of the Campaign," remembered John C. Arbuckle of the Fourth Iowa, "were those we endured in the trenches in front of Kennesaw. For 26 days, 17 of which were days of continuous rain, we never had our clothes off, or a chance to wash." For Arbuckle, and for thousands of other men in blue and gray, Kennesaw Mountain loomed large in the lexicon of battle as much for its challenges to the campaigning life of the common soldier as for its threat of injury and death from bullets or shell fragments. "Such was our condition and personal appearance from grime, mud and burnt powder," Arbuckle concluded, "that we were all but a fright to ourselves."[1]

Kennesaw Mountain National Battlefield Park is one of the most valuable Civil War resources in the country. I first became acquainted with its riches in the summer of 1986 while traveling from West Lafayette, Indiana, to my first teaching appointment at the University of Georgia. On visiting the park, I was impressed by the remnants of earthworks preserved within its boundaries. Those earthworks in a sense haunted me, for they were the first major collection of these relics of Civil War military operations I had seen. During the course of my one-year stay at the University of Georgia, I made many trips to Kennesaw to study the system of fortifications, take field notes, and expose many photographs. This experience resulted in a major research project (still ongoing) to write books about Civil War field fortifications. It also eventually led to the writing of this battle book.

The significance of the ground enclosed within the Kennesaw Mountain Park cannot be overstated. It contains the most important collection of surviving Civil War earthworks in the Western Theater, remnants that are as important as those in the best battlefield parks of the Eastern Theater. It is remarkable that the large park at Kennesaw is perched so close to the con-urban expanse of Atlanta. If not for the veterans who initiated preservation efforts in the 1890s, and the efforts of those who followed them, the battlefield would likely be under concrete, houses, and commercial build-ings by now.

I wish to thank the staff members of all archival institutions represented in the bibliography. They all were generous and helpful in making their col-lections available to me. Especially helpful were Nan Card at the Ruther-ford B. Hayes Presidential Center in Fremont Ohio, and Debbie Hamm at the Abraham Lincoln Presidential Library in Springfield, Illinois. Greg Biggs also shared with me his thoughts on the June 27 attack.

I owe, as always, a special debt to my wife Pratibha for her love and support.

Kennesaw Mountain

One. The Road to Kennesaw

Sherman began the campaign against Atlanta with an army group consisting of troops from three different departments within his Military Division of the Mississippi. Major General George H. Thomas's Army of the Cumberland, the largest of the three field armies under his direct control, fielded more than sixty thousand men and 130 guns. Major General James B. McPherson's Army of the Tennessee brought more than twenty-four thousand men and 96 guns to the army group, with another corps on the way to bolster its ranks. Major General John M. Schofield brought more than thirteen thousand men from his Department of the Ohio, along with 28 guns. Although only one corps in strength, Schofield's command was designated the Army of the Ohio.[1]

On the opposing side, Confederate general Joseph E. Johnston mustered about sixty thousand men and 144 guns in the Army of Tennessee. His troops were dug in on high, dominating ridges around the railroad city of Dalton, Georgia, about thirty miles south of Chattanooga. The Confederates constructed only light earthworks atop Rocky Face Ridge to the west of town and Hamilton Ridge to the east because those ridges had narrow tops studded with rocky outcroppings. But the line that connected the two ridges across the valley between them had a deep trench and tall, thick parapets. The Confederates heavily fortified Mill Creek Gap, a passage in Rocky Face Ridge through which the railroad linking Chattanooga and Atlanta ran, and they had positioned troops at Dug Gap about four miles south of Mill Creek Gap.[2]

But Johnston had neglected to guard Snake Creek Gap, an important pass through Rocky Face Ridge about fifteen miles south of Dalton. Thomas had originated the idea to use Snake Creek Gap as a way to flank Johnston out of his position at Dalton, after a large demonstration he had led to the area to divert Confederate attention away from Sherman's raid against the rail center of Meridian, Mississippi, in February 1864. This demonstration

William T. Sherman (Library of Congress, LC-DIG-cwpb-06584)

had resulted in little more than a skirmish, but it revealed the usefulness of Snake Creek Gap to the Federals. Sherman adopted Thomas's plan and sent the Army of the Tennessee to attempt it. Unfortunately for the Federals, McPherson lost his nerve after passing through the gap and while approaching the Western and Atlantic Railroad, Johnston's vital supply line. Several miles from friendly troops, McPherson detected signs that the Confederates might be aware of his presence and were ready to turn on him. He retired to the gap and dug in, securing Federal possession of the passage. But McPherson failed to take advantage of his opportunity to cut Johnston's rail line. If he had continued advancing, the Army of the Tennessee might have secured Resaca, the next significant town on the line some fifteen miles south of Dalton. The Confederates were able to retire to Resaca on the night of May 12 and dig in to protect the town and the railroad. The operations around Dalton set up Sherman's tactical pattern; even though several units of Thomas's army conducted attacks and advanced up the steep slope of Rocky Face Ridge to occupy Confederate attention, Sherman placed his main hope for success on a turning movement.[3]

Perhaps because of his disappointment at McPherson's failure, Sherman opted for more vigorous attacks at Resaca and less emphasis placed on maneuver. When his army group moved up to confront the Confederates, he authorized some heavy assaults across the valley that separated the opposing armies. On May 14, those attacks were designed to hold Johnston's attention while pontoons were laid downstream from Resaca to enable McPherson to cross the Oostanaula River. But Sherman did not exploit the crossing the next day. Instead, Thomas and Schofield sent multidivision attacks against the Confederate center, and they repelled a couple of Confederate attempts to turn and strike the Federal left flank. Resaca developed into a slugging match, similar to an open-field battle despite the long lines of earthworks on both sides. The battle also saw intense artillery bombardments and heavy skirmishing, but only tentative Union efforts to cross the Oostanaula, which nevertheless worried Johnston into abandoning the town on the night of May 15. Sherman lost about four thousand men in two days of fighting at Resaca, and Johnston suffered three thousand casualties.[4]

The campaign entered a fluid phase after Resaca, as Johnston passed through Calhoun, seeking good defensive ground to make a stand. He briefly established a line across a wide valley just north of Adairsville on May 17, but he decided to evacuate the position that night after concluding that the ground was unsuitable after all. Johnston found a good position on top of a high ridge just east of Cassville, where his army began to dig in after an abortive attempt to strike one column of Sherman's advancing army group on May 19. Many Confederates considered the Cassville position the best yet in the campaign, but the ridgeline bent a bit and exposed a salient in the Rebel position to enfilading Union artillery fire. Rather than construct traverses to protect the men, two of Johnston's corps commanders argued for a pullout. Lieutenant General Leonidas Polk and Lieutenant General John B. Hood, whose corps lines met at the endangered salient, convinced Johnston to evacuate his position that night. Lieutenant General

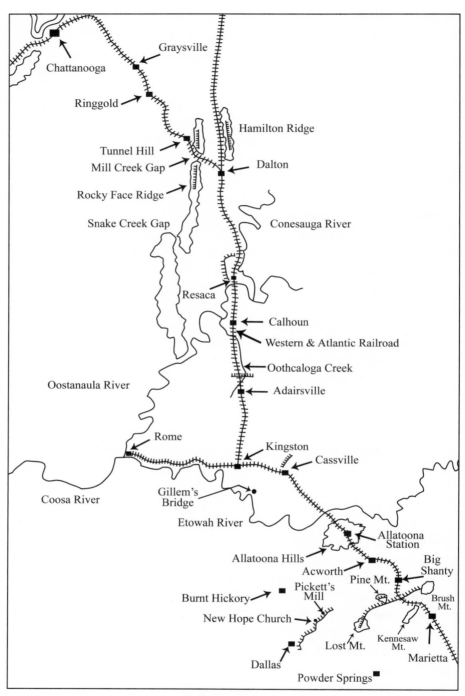

Dalton to Marietta

William J. Hardee favored staying, but he had missed the conference where the decision had been made. Sherman was preparing to flank the position anyway, but the Confederates had talked themselves into giving up a line that was stronger than some parts of the position they would hold with dogged determination at Kennesaw Mountain.[5]

NEW HOPE CHURCH–PICKETT'S MILL–DALLAS

Sherman altered his pattern when planning the crossing of the Etowah River and dealing with a rugged cluster of hills just south of the stream. The railroad ran through the Allatoona Hills, and Sherman knew from prewar travels in the area how difficult it would be to force the Confederates out of the region. He planned a huge flanking movement to the west, employing his entire force, cutting himself off temporarily from the railroad and hauling supplies along the way. Sherman hoped to reach Marietta in one move but was disappointed to encounter Johnston's army blocking his path twelve miles west of the town near a crossroads where New Hope Church was located. Major General Joseph Hooker's Twentieth Corps of Thomas's army attacked that position without knowledge of the terrain or enemy strength on the evening of May 25 and was repulsed. An attempt by Fourth Corps troops under Major General Oliver O. Howard to turn the Confederate right flank resulted in a fierce Union attack near Pickett's Mill on May 27, which also was repelled with heavy casualties. When McPherson aligned to Thomas's right, near Dallas, the Confederates launched an exploratory attack against his command on May 28 that was easily turned back.[6]

Stymied in his move toward Marietta, Sherman next sought to regain contact with the railroad and secure his supply line. Federal cavalry occupied Allatoona Station as the infantry began the slow process of moving battle lines to the left, even though separated from their fortified opponents by anywhere from a few yards to half a mile in the thick woods. Rain hampered the movement as well. It was not until early June that Sherman moved his command far enough to worry Johnston into abandoning the ten-mile-long New Hope Church–Pickett's Mill–Dallas Line on the night of June 4 and taking up a new position closer to Marietta. Johnston was forced to do this to protect his right flank and cover the northern and western approaches to the city.[7]

Sherman entered a different terrain when he crossed the Etowah River and tried to move directly toward Marietta. The landscape north of that

stream was typical Appalachian country—long, tall ridges divided by narrow valleys, both of which generally ran from northeast to southwest. The
gaps in these ridges were easily defended, but there was always another
gap farther away not covered by Johnston's men. The terrain north of the
Etowah favored Sherman's maneuver tactics because he could use the
valleys to move masses of troops, shielded by ridge cover.

The Federals left Appalachia when they crossed the Etowah River and
entered a flatter terrain covered with dense vegetation. The region was only
lightly developed—rugged roads, few farms, and almost a trackless forest.
As Sherman put it, the country "was very obscure, most in a state of nature,
densely wooded, and with few roads." It was difficult to maneuver large
masses of men, encumbered with wagon trains, in this environment. Sherman's operations against the New Hope Church–Pickett's Mill–Dallas Line
were slow and difficult as a result. The Federals consumed the time from
May 23 to June 7, more than two weeks, to close up on this line, to develop
its extent, and then to move away from it back toward the railroad. Meanwhile, Sherman rode along the lines almost every day and was amazed at
the extent of heavy skirmishing that took place and how deeply both sides
were digging in for protection. "I rarely saw a dozen of the enemy at any one
time," he recalled, "and these were always skirmishers dodging from tree to
tree, or behind logs on the ground, or who occasionally showed their heads
above the hastily constructed but remarkably strong rifle-trenches."[8]

Sherman continued to hope that his next move would enable his army
group to seize Marietta. When reporting Johnston's evacuation of the New
Hope Church–Pickett's Mill–Dallas Line to Major General Henry W. Halleck in Washington, he seemed confident of moving all the way down to
Kennesaw without obstruction. Taking it for granted that Johnston would
establish a defensive line anchored on the mountain, Sherman assured Halleck that he would "not run head on his fortifications"; rather, he would turn
Johnston's position at Kennesaw. Sherman consolidated his hold on the
railroad by turning Allatoona Station into a major supply depot, protected
by fortifications. Two divisions of the Seventeenth Corps arrived on June 8
to strengthen McPherson's army, and engineers rebuilt the railroad bridge
across the Etowah. When Sherman issued orders for the advance, which
was to begin on June 10, he instructed his subordinates to "continue until
some one of the columns reaches Kenesaw Mountain." Sherman warned
his generals, though, not to attack fortified positions without his approval.[9]

Joseph E. Johnston (Library of Congress, LC-DIG-cwpb-06280)

Johnston had no intention of giving up all the ground between New Hope Church and Marietta in one move. On June 5, he established a long line that stretched initially from Lost Mountain to Gilgal Church, the latter located at an important crossroads where the Sandtown Road from the north met the Burnt Hickory Road from the northwest. This junction was six miles west of Marietta. Lost Mountain rose like a castle in the landscape; it "swells from the plain solitary and lone to the height of six hundred feet," wrote Confederate division commander Samuel French in his diary. A short time after June 5, Johnston extended the line northeastward to include Pine Mountain and Brush Mountain. The former, at three hundred feet tall, became the center and salient of his line, while the latter, about the same height, anchored the right flank. Pine Mountain actually lay about a mile forward of the main Confederate line and was occupied by Major General William B. Bate's division of Hardee's Corps. Johnston's Mountain Line was about ten miles long, and his army was stretched nearly to the breaking point to hold it. Polk's Army of Mississippi (constituting essentially one of three corps in the Army of Tennessee), occupied the center. Polk's command was extended to only one rank in order to cover the ground assigned it.[10]

As the Federals approached the Mountain Line on June 10, the nature of the ground became apparent. In Sherman's view, "Kenesaw, the bold and striking twin mountain," lay in the background. Each of the peaks in the area, Lost, Pine, and Kennesaw, offered "a sharp, conical appearance, prominent in the vast landscape that presents itself from any of the hills that abound in that region." The position Johnston had created on those detached heights shielded Marietta and his rail line "perfectly."[11]

Sherman approached the Mountain Line with McPherson on the left, Thomas in the center, and Schofield on the right. One cavalry division each covered the flanks, and another protected his supply arrangements in the rear. McPherson's chief signal officer, Captain Ocran H. Howard, could see the Confederate signal station on top of Kennesaw Mountain when he reached Big Shanty on June 10. Howard managed to decipher Johnston's signal code within two days and fed the news to Sherman. Heavy rains delayed the Federal deployment in front of the Mountain Line and Sherman needed some time to examine it and come up with a plan. "We cannot risk the heavy losses of an assault at this distance from our base," he informed Halleck. Meanwhile, John C. Brown of the Ninth Iowa in McPherson's army

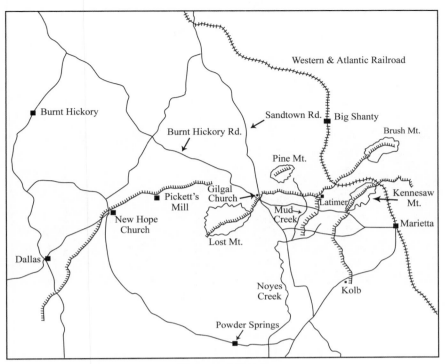

Closing on Marietta

was impressed by the sight of Kennesaw in the distance. At first sight, "it look very mutch like look out mountain" at Chattanooga, he thought.[12]

GILGAL CHURCH LINE

Johnston worried about the overly extended nature of his army's deployment on the Mountain Line. He sought a way to adopt a shorter version of the position. This would not only strengthen the line but allow him to mass troops for mobile operations against the enemy. Hardee also wanted to pull Bate's division off Pine Mountain and add him to the main line. Johnston and his staff consulted with Polk about these problems on June 13, and Polk was supportive. To work out the final details, Johnston, Hardee, and Polk went to the top of Pine Mountain to observe enemy positions on the morning of June 14. Sherman happened to be riding along the Union line in front of Pine Mountain that day and noticed a group of Confederate officers on the height. Giving a quick order for the artillery to fire at the group, Sher-

Lost Mountain from Kennesaw (Earl J. Hess)

man rode away. One round from Captain Peter Simonson's Fifth Indiana Battery caught Polk in the chest and killed him instantly.[13]

Sherman contemplated a major drive against the Mountain Line on June 15, ordering Thomas to prepare "a strong well-appointed column of attack" to strike between Pine Mountain and Kennesaw Mountain to break through the Confederate position. He believed that a ridge connected the two heights, which was the watershed of the area, with the ground south of the ridge flowing toward the Chattahoochee River. Sherman wanted Thomas to launch this attack at 2:00 P.M. on the 15th.[14]

But Johnston implemented his planned change of line before the Federals launched their advance. Bate's division evacuated Pine Mountain on the night of June 14. Gilgal Church now became the angle in the Confederate position. Hood's Corps and Polk's Army of Mississippi, the latter now led by Major General William W. Loring, continued to hold the Confederate center and right from Brush Mountain to near Gilgal Church, while Hardee's Corps held the line from Lost Mountain to Gilgal Church. The new Gilgal Church Line continued to block Sherman's approach to Marietta.[15]

Despite the altered enemy position, Thomas followed Sherman's instruction to make a major push between Pine Mountain and Kennesaw Mountain on the afternoon of June 15. That move now was in the nature of a reconnaissance in force to see where Johnston had gone. Howard's

Fourth Corps conducted the advance. Howard sent the division of Brigadier General John C. Newton to lead the way, supported by Major General David M. Stanley's division and Brigadier General Thomas J. Wood's division. Newton advanced at 3:00 P.M. with a heavy skirmish line ahead, but he found by late evening that enemy troops had erected strong earthworks in their new line not very far south. Howard chose not to attack, a decision supported by Thomas. The rest of the Army of the Cumberland moved up to align with Howard as Thomas ordered his artillery to pound the Rebel line.[16]

Sherman was disappointed that so little was accomplished by the Fourth Corps advance on June 15. He continued to envision the benefits if Thomas could break Johnston's line in the center. Sherman thought such a move had to be made, if it was made at all, by "the strongest army" in his group, "and where it will do most good. A break sufficient for me to pass the head of two columns about midway between Kenesaw and Pine Mountain will be best," he informed Schofield. If the Federals could push south of "the dividing ridge" that connected Kennesaw and Pine, Johnston's position "will be untenable." Such a major push proved to be impossible on June 15.[17]

The Federals concentrated on the salient at Gilgal Church on June 16. While Schofield worked his way from the west, Thomas nearly obtained an artillery crossfire on the salient from the east. Sherman again seriously thought about an attack on the enemy center while feinting on both flanks. "It may cost us dear," he admitted to Halleck, "but in results would surpass an attempt to pass around." He was conscious of the fact that Johnston had placed his army so that the Chattahoochee River was only fifteen miles to the south. If he could break the Confederate line, Johnston would have a good deal of difficulty retiring across the river under pressure and could lose much of his artillery, trains, and men to boot. To get a better understanding of the situation, Sherman went into the trenches on Howard's Corps front, talked to the men of the Thirty-Sixth Illinois, and took a look at the enemy line.[18]

MUD CREEK LINE

The pressure on Gilgal Church forced Johnston to retire his left wing on the night of June 16. Hardee evacuated the crossroads and Lost Mountain, falling back to Mud Creek, a stream that ran from north to south about four miles west of Kennesaw Mountain. This created Johnston's fourth position south of the Etowah River, the Mud Creek Line. The Confederate right wing

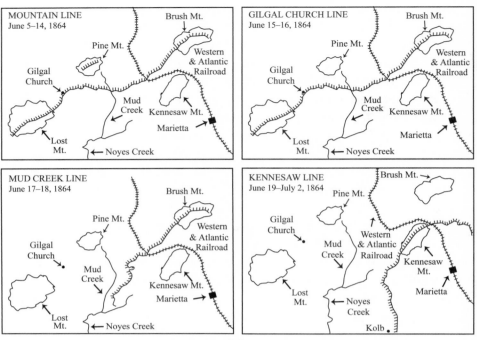

Four Confederate Lines

remained in place from Brush Mountain to Mud Creek, but the angle in the line now was an obscure bit of high ground just east of the headwaters of Mud Creek, near the Latimer House. The line here was forced into a very sharp angle, forming a pronounced salient that would be even more vulnerable to enemy crossfire than either angle at Pine Mountain or Gilgal Church. The salient, held by French's division, represented the junction of Loring's Army of Mississippi and Hardee's Corps.[19]

The Federals were impressed by the strength of the Confederate earthworks at Gilgal Church when they moved through the abandoned line. The complex of trenches, parapets, and obstructions seemed like "one vast fort" to Harvey Reid of the Twenty-Second Wisconsin. The men thanked their stars that Sherman had not ordered them to attack these formidable earthworks and were greatly encouraged that his flanking maneuvers seemed to force the Rebels so consistently out of their well-prepared defenses.[20]

Early on the morning of June 17, before Sherman realized that Johnston had pulled away only a short distance from Gilgal Church and Lost Mountain, he urged Thomas to follow up the Rebel retreat with a big push "between the two wings of the enemy." Sherman wanted to take advantage of

Confederate Fortified Lines from Dalton to Kennesaw Mountain

FIRST: Dalton, Rocky Face Ridge, May 8–12, 1864

SECOND: Resaca, May 13–15, 1864

THIRD: Adairsville, May 17, 1864

FOURTH: Cassville, May 19, 1864

FIFTH: New Hope Church, Pickett's Mill, Dallas, May 25–June 3, 1864

SIXTH: Mountain Line, June 5–14, 1864

SEVENTH: Gilgal Church Line, June 15–16, 1864

EIGHTH: Mud Creek Line, June 17–18, 1864

NINTH: Kennesaw Line, June 19–July 2, 1864

the fact that Johnston was on the move, hoping to hit him before he could settle into his next position. Thomas moved forward cautiously, however, with Howard swinging the Fourth Corps round to face east and advancing toward Mud Creek. A portion of Major General John M. Palmer's Fourteenth Corps, to Howard's left, held the line to the railroad, while McPherson extended it east of the track. Hooker's Twentieth Corps was advancing along Sandtown Road and reached a point five miles west of Marietta by the evening of June 17. Schofield stopped along Sandtown Road near the crossing of Noyes Creek, a crossing located south of the point where Mud Creek flowed into Noyes Creek. Sherman was disappointed that nothing more than marching and skirmishing took place on June 17. "I worked hard to-day to get over to [the railroad]," he reported to Halleck, "but the troops seem timid in these dense forests of stumbling on a hidden breast-work."[21]

Johnston had no intention of staying in the Mud Creek line for long. In fact, he was busy on June 17 planning to pull back to yet another position. The sharp angle of his line at Latimer's House was a trouble spot, and he dispatched his chief engineer, Lieutenant Colonel Stephen W. Presstman, to lay out a new line that incorporated the twin peaks of Kennesaw Mountain. It would be the last defensive position guarding Marietta. Johnston, however, decided to remain at Mud Creek another day, June 18, before moving to the Kennesaw Line.[22]

The weather began to severely hamper military operations in northwest Georgia. On the night of June 17, a severe rain set in for several days and filled the trenches of both armies with mud and water. Troops marching or bivouacking in the open were drenched, and the fields turned into bogs of red clay as chilly winds made everyone miserable. One result of this "hard pitiless rain" was that the number of men reporting sick in both armies rose significantly.[23]

As he contemplated operations for June 18, Sherman turned his mind toward finding and bypassing Johnston's left flank. He counted on Schofield to do that, while Thomas extended his line southward to keep connection with the Army of the Ohio. Sherman wanted his subordinates to move with caution while exploring the dimly known territory to the south. Once the Rebel position became clear, "or we are satisfied the enemy has lengthened his line beyond his ability to defend, we must strike quick and with great energy," he told Thomas. But Schofield reported that Noyes Creek was too deep near the Sandtown Road crossing, so Sherman authorized his command to bivouac for the day on June 18, with one division in line and another in column to screen his right flank.[24]

With time on his hands, Sherman updated General-in-Chief Ulysses S. Grant on his progress. He was satisfied with McPherson, despite the missed opportunity at Dalton, and could not ask more of Schofield. "My chief source of trouble is with the Army of the Cumberland, which is dreadfully slow," he admitted. "A fresh furrow in a plowed field will stop the whole column, and all begin to intrench. I have again and again tried to impress on Thomas that we must assail and not defend; we are the offensive, and yet it seems the whole Army of the Cumberland is so habituated to be on the defensive that, from its commander down to the lowest private, I cannot get it out of their heads."[25]

Of course, Sherman was exaggerating. The problem lay mostly with Thomas's old command, the Fourteenth Corps. Howard managed the Fourth Corps with a good deal of initiative, even if some of his division commanders tended to be cautious. When Sherman visited the Fourth Corps sector on June 17, he found that Howard's follow-up to the Confederate withdrawal was delayed because Stanley and Wood were arguing over which division should lead. "I'm afraid I swore, and said what I should not, but I got them started," Sherman reported. Hooker's Twentieth Corps consisted of eastern and western regiments that had never before served in the Army of the Cumberland and had not been influenced by Thomas's cautious style. Nevertheless, Sherman complained that the Army of the Cumberland "cannot keep up with my thoughts and wishes." Meanwhile, the rain fell "as though it had no intention ever to stop."[26]

Despite the rain, elements of Howard's corps managed to find a way to cross the swollen channel of Mud Creek on June 18. Aggressively pushing a heavily reinforced skirmish line, part of Newton's Second Division waded the waist-deep water of the stream, pressed back the skirmishers of Major General William H. T. Walker's division of Hardee's Corps, and lodged on the east bank. This took place in a steady rain that fell all day. Newton's success increased the pressure on French's division at the salient. The Federals now could obtain a better crossfire on the angle, and French lost 215 men on June 18. Guibor's battery suffered the loss of 13 men that day, more than it had lost during the entire siege of Vicksburg. Captain Thomas J. Perry's Florida Battery, of Hardee's Corps, became a target of vicious Union sniping fire that felled 10 percent of the unit's manpower. The Yankees fired through the embrasures of Perry's earthwork to cut and scar the faces of his guns and puncture canteens and blankets. As far as French was concerned, the Mud Creek Line was untenable. Thomas, on the other hand, was greatly heartened by Howard's progress. "General Sherman is at last very much pleased," he told his subordinate.[27]

JUNE 19

The pressure on French's division compelled Johnston to pull away from Mud Creek on the night of June 18. Loring laid out the procedure for French, a procedure proven by repeated experience thus far in the campaign. French would withdraw his artillery at dusk and start his infantry at 10:00 P.M. Each brigade was to leave one regiment behind in the trenches until the brigade was "well under way" and then pull out too. The skirmish line would remain in place until 2:00 A.M. French's men were slated to take position along the top of the twin peaks of Kennesaw Mountain, and that meant marching up the steep slope by the flank in single rank.[28]

Despite the heavy rain and thick mud, the Confederates began to withdraw from the Mud Creek Line on the night of June 18. "Oh, horrible! Most horrible!," complained Hiram Smith Williams in his journal. "There was no use in picking one's way. You might as well *wade* in at once. . . . You could find mud and water at all depths, and every consistency of thickness from two or three up to ten and twelve inches." The Confederates slipped and slid their way back to the Kennesaw Line by the morning of June 19. Loring positioned the Army of Mississippi on the heights in the center. Hood's Corps established a curving line to hold the relatively level ground to Loring's right, crossing the Bell's Ferry Road and a second, unnamed roadway farther east. Hardee positioned his corps to the left of Loring, straddling the Dallas and Marietta Road.[29]

French was responsible for holding the mountain, which consisted of not only two peaks but a smaller, conical rise called Pigeon Hill that was linked to the smaller peak. He put his left flank on the Burnt Hickory Road, which skirted the southern foot of Pigeon Hill and stretched his right to the top of Big Kennesaw Mountain. When Sergeant William Pitt Chambers of the Forty-Sixth Mississippi tried to survey the view on the morning of June 19, he found that the top of Little Kennesaw was literally enveloped in the clouds. "Nothing could be seen save a lead-colored mist that saturated one's clothing almost as quickly as a rain." The sky cleared off after a while, and then Chambers could see for miles. White-topped Federal wagons filled the open spaces in the landscape, and Union skirmishers were clearly visible.[30]

At first, their lofty perch fooled the Confederates into believing they were immune to Federal artillery. When the first round landed at the base of Little Kennesaw, William Pitt Chambers and his comrades "cheered derisively." But the next salvo struck halfway up the slope, and the third overshot the Mississippi line, which was fifty feet down from the top of the mountain and unprotected by earthworks. When the third salvo threw loose rocks all over the place, the Mississippians became alarmed and scrambled for shelter. One man was literally cut in two by a projectile on the fourth salvo. Now the Forty-Sixth Mississippi pulled back to the natural crest of the mountain where it found some protection behind rock ledges.[31]

Other parts of French's line also were hit by Union artillery fire as the day wore on. The same was true in Major General Edward C. Walthall's division, to French's right. Walthall's left flank rested at the top of Big Kennesaw Mountain. The men of Daniel Harris Reynolds's brigade in Walthall's division gathered rocks on Big Kennesaw to make breastworks because they had no tools to use. Federal gunners needed only half a dozen rounds to land shells squarely on the infantry line, scattering fragments of rock that were as deadly as fragments of iron. Reynolds's men received entrenching tools by 11:00 P.M. that night and used them until morning to dig in on the top of the height.[32]

The mountain provided a commanding perch for the Confederates, but it inhibited movement up to the line. In an effort to compensate, Loring directed his engineer, Captain W. J. Morris, to cut a military road along the eastern foot of Big Kennesaw, Little Kennesaw, and Pigeon Hill for easier movement around the heights. He also wanted him to cut paths from this road up the slope to each of French's and Walthall's brigades. The Federals had a commanding perch too. A Union signal officer atop Pine Mountain could see the Confederates moving about on Kennesaw, dodging artillery rounds, all day of June 19.[33]

When the Federals followed up their opponents' withdrawal from the Mud Creek Line, Sherman expected great things to happen. "Enemy gave way last night in the midst of darkness and storm," he reported to his wife early on the morning of June 19. Sherman continued to assume Johnston would fall back to the Chattahoochee and expected to walk the streets of Marietta later that day. He urged Thomas to push ahead and capture guns and trains. "There must be a pressure toward the railroad at all points," he asserted. Howard pursued that directive with his Fourth Corps along Burnt Hickory Road, capturing 250 stragglers, but running up against the left of French's division and the right of Walker's division of Hardee's Corps at Pigeon Hill. Palmer's Fourteenth Corps moved up to Howard's left and stopped near the base of Kennesaw, while Hooker's Twentieth Corps advanced along the Dallas and Marietta Road to find the bulk of Hardee's men confronting him. Fourth Corps troops "could plainly see swarms of rebels on top apparently very much interested in looking at us."[34]

The Federals spent June 19 adjusting their lines and skirmishing with the Confederates. On McPherson's front, the Federals occupied Hood's old defenses at Brush Mountain, which the Rebels had lived in since June 5. McPherson's men remodeled the works for their own use, constructing roads and bridges across Noonday Creek for easier movement up to their new position. Sherman's engineers managed to push a locomotive up to the lines and filled water within sight of the new Confederate line. The Federals gave a wild cheer to celebrate "the impudence of the trick," but it caused Confederate guns to open a furious bombardment. The range was too great to damage the locomotive, but Federal troops in nearby trenches received a pounding.[35]

Also on June 19, Schofield moved south along Sandtown Road as far as Noyes Creek only to find the bridge flooring was gone and the stream was too high to ford. Moreover, Brigadier General Lawrence S. Ross's brigade of Texas cavalry was in position on the east side with artillery, secure behind earthworks. One of Schofield's division commanders, Brigadier General Jacob D. Cox, noted that the stream was pronounced Nose's Creek by local blacks, and the Federals often spelled it that way in their dispatches. Johnston also spelled it Nose's Creek. By either name, the stream offered a substantial impediment to Schofield's efforts to find and turn the Confederate left flank. Sherman authorized Schofield to "remain quiet until the waters subside."[36]

Johnston saw Noyes Creek as an advantage to the Federals. He believed that Sherman could use the flooded waterway as a shield behind which to extend southward. To counter this threat Johnston decided on June 19 to extend his left by shifting Hood's Corps from the right flank. Initially planning to conduct this move early on the morning of June 20, Johnston postponed it to June 21. Major General Joseph Wheeler's Cavalry Corps of the Army of Tennessee, two divisions and one brigade strong, would fill much of the space to be vacated by Hood, while Loring would extend his army's line to meet Wheeler's troops. Johnston authorized Hood to rest his men on the night of June 21 near Marietta before continuing to the left wing.[37]

Although Sherman admitted to Halleck that "I was premature" in assuming the enemy had abandoned Marietta, the Federals closed up to the newly established Kennesaw Line with enough vigor to impress the Confederates. Hardee admitted to his wife that the Yankees moved so aggressively that he worried whether his men would be ready for them. Yankee skirmishers lodged so close as to be "inconveniently near to our main line," as Hardee put it. Johnston and Hood were enthusiastic about the prospects of their new position, but Hardee cautiously preferred to wait and see what developed. "My own convictions are, and have been for sometime, that we are drifting to the Chattahoochee and that we shall cross that stream in a week or ten days. Both Hood & myself expressed to Gen'l Johnston our desire to fight before reaching Atlanta, and that we would prefer to go there whipped rather than not to fight at all."[38]

Meanwhile, the Federals dug in as best they could on the soggy night of June 19. Fourth Corps pioneers tried to shovel the sticky mud of a cornfield into something that resembled a parapet. "If a man stood still in one place to shovel," wrote Chesley A. Mosman, "he would find himself stuck six inches in the sandy loam."[39]

JUNE 20

As Sherman gained more knowledge of the Kennesaw Line, he concluded that it was "unusually strong." The center rested on dominating heights, and the right flank was protected by Noonday Creek, the left shielded by Noyes Creek. Sherman reasoned, however, that as long as Johnston remained on the defensive, his left flank could be turned. Sherman also feared that the Confederates might launch an attack on his own left flank. McPherson guarded that wing with a compact line that straddled and protected the railroad, the vital communications link with Chattanooga. Sherman also feared cavalry raids on that rail line and was in the process of constructing defenses at key bridges between his army and his supply base at Chatta-nooga.[40]

On June 20, the Federal leader continued to waffle between attack and maneuver, with his mind on the latter more than the former. But the woods and the rain conspired to make coordinated moves along a ten-mile front difficult. As Howard remembered, the countryside around Kennesaw was "mostly wild, hilly, and rugged, and thickly covered with virgin trees, oak and chestnut, with here and there a clearing made for a small farm, or a bald opening that seemed to have come of itself." It was not good coun-try for maneuver, but the Federals continued to seek a way to bypass the enemy's left flank and avoid striking the high ground in Johnston's center for the time being.[41]

Moving to the south meant that Howard would have to shift troops to re-place Hooker, so Twentieth Corps units could move down to meet Schofield. These units had to move about two miles to accomplish that goal. To start the process, Wood's and Newton's divisions shifted south to relieve Briga-dier General John W. Geary's division and Brigadier General Alpheus S. Williams's division on June 20.[42]

While closing in on the Confederate line, Stanley's troops fought for con-trol of two small hills that lay in front of the Rebel position. At least one of the hills was "a commanding position," according to Fourth Corps staff officer Charles Henry Howard, and from it Confederate skirmishers were able to obtain "a destructive musketry fire" on a part of Stanley's line. The Federals also wanted to prevent their opponents from planting artillery on the heights. Oliver O. Howard took advantage of an order to demonstrate to draw attention away from Schofield's moves to the south and ordered a major effort to seize both hills on June 20. At 4:00 P.M., Brigadier General Walter C. Whitaker's brigade skirmishers advanced and drove back the skir-mishers of Walker's and Bate's divisions. They took one hill, while Colonel Isaac M. Kirby's brigade skirmishers took the other. Kirby's hill later be-came known as Bald Knob. A marshy ravine separated the two heights. Whitaker and Kirby began to move their main line to the hills and started to dig in.[43]

Three regiments of Hardee's Corps attacked on both fronts at 6:00 P.M. Whitaker had moved enough troops to the hill so that his men drove them off, and they did the same when the Rebels attacked again at dusk. At 8:00 P.M. a third counterattack captured part of the line held by five companies of the Thirty-Fifth Indiana. The Ninety-Ninth Ohio refused its flank and fired at these Confederates to contain the break. Then the Forti-eth Ohio counterattacked and drove them off the hill. It "was a very severe fight," with losses of 273 Federals.[44]

Kirby had more difficulty than Whitaker. He occupied Bald Knob, which was located near a salient in Johnston's Kennesaw Line known as the Horse-shoe, held by Brigadier General States Rights Gist's brigade of Walker's division. Yankee artillery on the hill could menace Horseshoe Salient. As Thomas later put it, Union possession of both hills seemed "to be a thorn in the side of the enemy." But Kirby had been slow to move more troops up to support his skirmishers on Bald Knob. When Hardee's men counterat-tacked up the hill, Kirby was not ready for them, and his skirmishers fell back partway down the western slope. A second Confederate push a half hour later was repelled, but Hardee still held most of the hill. As the heated fight ended, the Federals counted about 200 casualties and still had not secured the knob. This fact worried Howard. From Bald Knob, he feared the enemy might launch a larger attack on his line. "I was much annoyed," Howard remembered in his autobiography, "and as soon as Thomas and Sherman heard of the break they were also worried."[45]

Ironically, the Confederate generals on the other side of no-man's-land also worried that night. "The enemy approached as usual under cover of successive lines of intrenchments," reported Johnston with some degree of accuracy. The Seventy-Seventh Pennsylvania, for example, had built three lines of works in twenty-four hours because it moved forward in incre-ments on Stanley's division front. "We get a line of battle established and as soon as the enemy has discovered where it is," Hardee told his wife, "he ap-proaches all the weak points of it and commences a siege." Hardee did not know how long this could continue. Johnston had been all too ready, in his view, to evacuate lines when the enemy lodged "near enough to make his presence annoying." Hardee accurately described the situation for his wife. "How to whip Sherman is the problem to be solved, and our General has not yet been able to find a solution."[46]

Farther to the right of Hardee's Corps, where Loring's men held the heights in the center of Johnston's line, the Confederates continued to suf-fer from Union artillery fire on June 20. French adjusted his main line lower down the mountainside to better cover the slope with rifle fire, although he lost a number of men killed and wounded that day. Walthall's division, to French's right, was equally exposed to artillery fire, and Brigadier General Winfield S. Featherston's division, holding Loring's right, was even more

Confederates dragging guns up Little Kennesaw (Johnson and Buel,
Battles and Leaders, *4:271)*

exposed. All of Loring's units suffered because of a lack of entrenching tools to dig adequate works.[47]

The planting of Confederate artillery on top of the heights eased the suffering of the infantry only a little bit. The prospect of hauling guns up the steep slopes of Big and Little Kennesaw was so daunting that, at first, Confederate officers did not even try it. Major George S. Storrs, who commanded the battalion of three batteries attached to French's division, placed Captain James A. Hoskins's Mississippi Battery on top of Pigeon Hill and the other two batteries in reserve when initially taking up the Kennesaw Line on June 19. The next day, Storrs and two staff officers inspected Little Kennesaw and were impressed by the platform it offered, six hundred feet above the surrounding plain. Twenty guns could fit on its top, they concluded. Storrs then scouted a route up the slope opposite the enemy where he thought his men could pull the guns up by ropes. French authorized him to try it, despite the fact that army headquarters staff had already concluded it was too difficult. Storrs managed to pull his two reserve units (Captain Henry Guibor's Missouri Battery and Captain John J. Ward's Alabama Battery) up the hill. Brigadier General Randall L. Gibson's brigade of Hood's Corps provided manpower to haul up ammunition and dig gun emplacements. After Storrs's gunners staked out their positions, Gibson's Louisiana infantrymen constructed the parapets during the night of June 20.[48]

Storrs believed that Kennesaw Mountain offered the Confederates an opportunity to punish the enemy from artillery positions that could hit Union targets with plunging fire. Big Kennesaw was higher than Little Kennesaw, but its peak was not as level and therefore could accommodate only a handful of guns. By the morning of June 21, Storrs had placed nine pieces on top of Little Kennesaw.[49]

Far to the south of the big mountain, Schofield worked to carefully find his way toward Johnston's left flank on June 20. Sherman rode to Schofield's headquarters for a consultation and set 4:00 P.M. as the time for starting. The objective was to effect a lodgment on the east side of Noyes Creek that could be used as a bridgehead from which to extend southward. Cox advanced his division down Sandtown Road to find that the bridge over the creek had been partially dismantled by Ross's Confederate cavalrymen, who had taken the planks away. Nevertheless, members of the 103rd Ohio in Colonel Daniel Cameron's brigade crossed the creek by walking over the stringers and secured control of the bridge. Cameron quickly repaired the structure and moved his entire brigade across, advancing nearly three miles to the junction where the road to Marietta joined the Sandtown Road. This

Confederate artillery position on Little Kennesaw (Earl J. Hess)

was a key intersection, for it allowed Schofield to head east toward town along a road not yet covered by Hardee's line, or to head farther south to attempt a much wider flanking movement. Andrew J. Cheney owned a house near the junction, which Schofield used as his headquarters.[50]

JUNE 21

Schofield's promising success on June 20 was little noticed along the Kennesaw Line as officers continued to adjust their positions. Howard was determined to retake Bald Knob on June 21 and straighten his corps line as close as feasible to the Confederate position. Kirby's brigade was assigned the primary responsibility, with support from Colonel Richard H. Nodine's brigade of Wood's division to the right. Wood also planted four guns within supporting distance of the action, and Howard used the artillery position as his command post to personally superintend the attack. About midday, the guns opened a half-hour bombardment of the fortified Confederate skirmish line on top of the hill. When that ended at 12:45 P.M., Kirby sent the Thirty-First Indiana forward as skirmishers, supported by the Ninetieth Ohio. The Federals advanced 700 yards and then swept the Confederates off the hill. A company of pioneers armed with tools immediately followed Kirby's men and constructed earthworks in case the enemy counterattacked. Kirby praised "their almost superhuman efforts," which helped to secure the hill. Gist's men did not try to retake the place, and Howard moved the main line of his corps from 250 to 500 yards forward, posting a heavy skirmish line on Bald Knob.[51]

Nodine had assigned Colonel Frank Askew's Fifteenth Ohio to support Kirby's attack on the right. Before Kirby had started, Howard had offered advice to Askew, and then the colonel scouted the area and concluded that he should occupy a patch of woods near Bald Knob to prevent the enemy from assembling a force there to retake the hill. Askew then positioned two companies to go up Bald Knob to the right of Kirby's force, and two other companies to secure the woods. The rest of his regiment waited in reserve. Howard was so anxious to retake the hill that he hovered near Askew and urged him on when he thought the time was right. The Fifteenth Ohio performed its task to the letter, both supporting Kirby and taking control of the trees, capturing thirty prisoners in the process. Howard, in his excitement, rode up Bald Knob with his staff and waited until the pioneers had begun digging in before leaving. The Confederates did not like Askew's capture of the woods. They started a furious artillery bombardment and then sent the consolidated Fifteenth Tennessee and Thirty-Seventh Tennessee of Bate's division into the trees. Seven companies of the Fifteenth Ohio, with help from Forty-Ninth Ohio troops, repelled them. Askew lost fifty-four men in the attack of June 21.[52]

Federal operations south of Howard presented more difficulty than closing up on the enemy. Hooker was some distance from Schofield's position at Cheney's House and had but a loose connection with Howard's men to the north. He was convinced he did not have enough men to reach Schofield and maintain touch with Howard. Hooker's subordinates reported a fortified Confederate picket line one to one and half miles in front of his position, but they could not detect what, if anything, lay behind it. Hooker suggested that he slide his corps southward as Schofield moved east along the Powder Springs–Marietta Road, while Howard stretch his line to keep connection with the left flank of the Twentieth Corps.[53]

The suggestion was in line with Sherman's long-range plans, but Schofield was not yet ready to move east along that direct road to Marietta. He had too little information about the creek system and the exact location of Hooker's right flank. "In general," he told Cox, "let us find where the next corps is . . . with reference to ours, and the streams in question, then where the enemy is." Cox tried to map out the location of the streams and sent skirmishers to locate Hooker's picket line. They reported a large gap between the two corps, covered by Hooker's skirmishers. Sherman authorized Schofield to wait until the next day to make a move because rains fell nearly all the time on June 21.[54]

Sherman initially wanted Schofield to execute a wider turning movement against the Rebel left flank by continuing south on Sandtown Road rather than east toward Marietta. On the evening of June 21, though, Schofield pointed out to him that this would expose the Twenty-Third Corps unless Hooker could place troops on the Powder Springs and Marietta Road to protect his left flank. Even if Hooker could extend south to the road, his Twenty-Third Corps was not large enough to continue south and turn the Confederate flank. But if Hooker extended and then allowed the Twenty-Third Corps to advance eastward, the Federals could threaten the enemy flank in a concentrated way with both corps. It was a persuasive argument. Sherman arranged for the move as Hooker and Howard concentrated on firming up their connection and moving forward short distances to obtain better ground along their corps fronts for the rest of the day. Skirmishing continued under cloudy, rainy skies.[55]

On the Confederate side of the opposing lines, Johnston implemented his plan to shift Hood's Corps from the right to the left. Loring extended the Army of Mississippi so that his old division, now under Brigadier General Winfield S. Featherston, stretched out at least to the Bell's Ferry Road east of Big Kennesaw Mountain as Wheeler shielded Featherston's right flank during this move. While Wheeler never filed a report of his activities during late June, he probably dismounted his men and filled the rest of Hood's trenches. Hood's men left their position on the right early on June 21 and marched through Marietta, stopping for the night about two miles west of town to rest from duty in the trenches. Johnston told Hood that, when he moved out along the Powder Springs and Marietta Road to Hardee's left the next day, his job was to protect the railroad by preventing the enemy from moving east.[56]

While movements and fights took place along the southern portions of the line during the day of June 21, the Confederate guns on top of Little Kennesaw opened a bombardment that took the Federals by surprise. Storrs's gunners had a field day, chasing Union wagons out of the open fields and causing the Yankees to take down their tents. The Confederates even ran their pieces out of the works and down the slope a bit to obtain better fire on the line of Union earthworks near the foot of Kennesaw. They let the guns cool now and then so as to keep up the fun nearly all day. Confederate infantrymen were emboldened to cheer and wave their hats to celebrate their artillery's success, and many generals came by to observe and offer praise. But Storrs knew it would not last. The Federals were bound to position guns to counteract his fire the next day. That was why Storrs recommended that no more guns be hauled up to the top when Johnston's artillery chief, Brigadier General Francis A. Shoup, offered them.[57]

Elsewhere along Loring's line, inspectors complained of the poor state of defenses held by Brigadier General Claudius W. Sears's brigade of French's division. Sears offered a long list of explanations. His line was stretched to the breaking point, in a single rank, with wide intervals between each man as he tried to cover rough ground. He received only a small portion of the entrenching tools available to French's division, and his men had to wait until dark to work on the front portions of their earthworks or else risk their lives. His troops also were exhausted from heavy duty on the skirmish line, having had no opportunity to rest for a very long time. Undoubtedly many other brigade leaders in Johnston's army could have compiled a similar list of complaints.[58]

Sherman viewed the heights of Kennesaw as a looming fortress, anchoring the center of Johnston's position, a fortress that tended to split the Union line because it represented something of a salient. For that reason, the Federal commander wanted to operate only against one of his enemy's flanks rather than against both simultaneously. McPherson would continue to secure the railroad and the Union left at the same time. The Seventeenth Corps alone dug 20,000 linear feet of trenches from June 11 to 21, during its creeping advance along the railroad, plus 2,000 feet of corduroy road and 150 feet of bridging and six miles of military roads. McPherson was ready to shift his army to the right if efforts to turn Johnston's flank succeeded. But Sherman could not believe that his opponent intended to make a firm stand with the Chattahoochee River so close to his rear.[59]

Meanwhile, the rain continued to pour down on Georgia. "Rain, terrible rains," commented Brigadier General Peter J. Osterhaus, a Fifteenth Corps division commander, on June 18. He made similar comments in his diary over the next several days, including June 21. The Federals hardly had a moment to dry their clothes, skirmishing and sleeping in the open with a constant patter of moisture from the sky. Rations of whiskey helped keep them going. The Confederates, of course, suffered the same, standing in accumulated rain sometimes waist deep in the trenches. "We have entirely too much water falling for our business," commented Chesley A. Mosman, who commanded a pioneer company in the Fourth Corps. "It is about as bad for us as too much rain is for the farmer and I wish it would 'dry up.'"[60]

In fact, according to Sherman, June 21 was the nineteenth straight day of rain thus far "and the prospect of clear weather as far off as ever. The roads are impassable, and fields and woods become quagmires after a few wagons have crossed." With Secretary of War Edwin M. Stanton, Sherman could joke about the weather. If one took "the Flood as the only example in history, the rain squall is nearly half over." But Sherman knew how seriously the weather was delaying progress in his campaign. "I am all ready to attack," he assured Halleck, "the moment weather and roads will permit troops and artillery to move with anything like life."[61]

Two. Kolb's Farm

The morning of June 22 dawned clear, bringing in the first dry weather in many days. Sherman's plan for the day involved firming up his extreme right wing and advancing it closer to Marietta. Hooker's role in the operation involved extending the Twentieth Corps line southward to the Powder Springs and Marietta Road as Schofield moved the Twenty-Third Corps forward south of that road. The two commanders would link up somewhere near a farmhouse owned by Mrs. Kolb, about four miles from Marietta and almost due south of Hardee's line. Sherman insisted that Schofield maintain control of the intersection of the Powder Springs Road and the road to Marietta at Cheney's House, for he wanted to use the former to move farther south when Johnston abandoned the Kennesaw Mountain Line. Because of that directive, Schofield planned to advance only a portion of his command to the Kolb House while stringing the rest of it out diagonally to maintain connection between the forward unit and those holding the area around Cheney's. Sherman planned to ride along the line to visit McPherson, Thomas, and Hooker that day to keep tabs on progress.[1]

Hooker's scouts indicated that nothing more than Confederate skirmishers stood in the way along the Powder Springs and Marietta Road. His corps was arrayed with Major General Daniel Butterfield's Third Division on the left, connecting to Howard's Fourth Corps, then John W. Geary's Second Division in the center, and Alpheus S. Williams's First Division on the right. Butterfield and Williams had about 4,600 men each, while Geary's strength amounted to about 3,700 men.[2]

For Butterfield and Geary, the day involved limited movement. Geary's skirmishers had taken a small hill that seemed to command the area at 3:00 A.M., so he moved his main line about one mile to the spot at dawn on June 22. Hooker arrived to look the ground over and told Geary to hold the height at all costs. Later that morning, Butterfield moved up to align to Geary's left, and Williams moved up to align to his right. A "deep ravine and low ground" separated Geary's right flank from Williams's left, but otherwise the corps seemed to be in a good position. Geary extended his Second Brigade, commanded by Colonel Patrick H. Jones, toward the ravine to lessen the gap between his right flank and Williams's left. Jones placed the Thirteenth New York Battery on "a small knoll" between the hill and the ravine. Geary's men began to construct breastworks of rails and anything else they could find.[3]

Williams advanced his division to occupy two ridges south of Geary's position, the one on the right about two hundred yards farther east than the one on the left. He placed Brigadier General Thomas H. Ruger's Second Brigade on the right and Brigadier General Joseph F. Knipe's First Brigade in the center, both of them atop the forward ridge, while Colonel James S. Robinson's Third Brigade held the left atop the other height. Open ground stretching anywhere from 500 to 1,500 yards east lay before Knipe and Robinson, and before at least two of Ruger's regiments. A deep gully fronted Ruger's and Knipe's position, with ground rising from there eastward toward a belt of trees occupied by the Confederate skirmishers. But the Powder Springs and Marietta Road still lay "several hundred yards" to Williams's right flank. Williams placed Lieutenant Charles E. Winegar's Battery I, First New York Light Artillery, armed with three-inch rifles, on Robinson's brigade line. He also put Captain John D. Woodbury's Battery M, First New York Light Artillery, armed with twelve-pounder Napoleons, on Knipe's brigade line. Both batteries could sweep the open ground to the east with their fire. Hooker's careful advance had taken the Twentieth Corps line to near Kolb's farmhouse by about 2:00 P.M.[4]

Hooker's line was located about four miles southwest of downtown Marietta on farmland belonging to the Kolb family. The cleared area before the Twentieth Corps line extended about 1,000 yards east to west, and a couple of miles north to south. All of it lay north of the Powder Springs and Marietta Road. A small church, a schoolhouse, and some negro huts, "all of which give it something of the appearance of a small village," according to a newspaper correspondent, stood near Kolb's farmhouse. The home of Mr. Greer also stood near Geary's section of the corps line. In front of part of Ruger's brigade, near the road, a belt of trees extended from the Union position eastward about 350 yards to Kolb's house and the cotton gin near it. Many of the trees that still stood on the Kolb farm had been girdled in a slow process of deadening them for easier cutting. According to Rice C. Bull of the 123rd New York, "their dead limbs pointed in every direction made a weird appearance."[5]

While Hooker was moving east, Schofield shifted his entire command

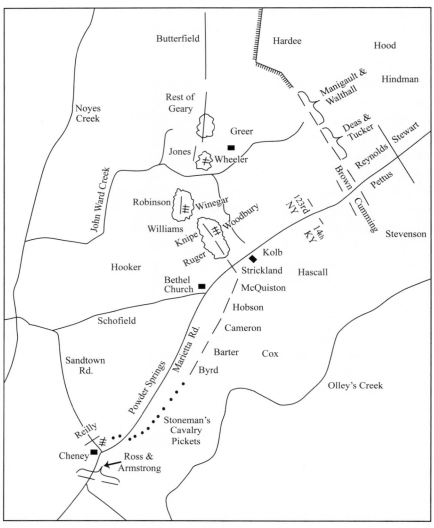

Kolb's Farm

across Noyes Creek early on the morning of June 22. He pushed Brigadier General Milo S. Hascall's Second Division of the Twenty-Third Corps eastward along the Powder Springs and Marietta Road as Cox's Third Division dug in to defend the vital intersection at Cheney's House. The two divisions were quite large, with Hascall marshaling about six thousand troops and Cox almost seven thousand men. Hascall reached a point due south of Hooker's right flank by about 2:00 P.M. and placed Colonel Silas A. Strickland's Third Brigade straddling the Powder Springs and Marietta Road. He arranged two other brigades at an angle to Strickland's right flank and heading toward Cheney's, facing south to protect the Union right flank. Colonel John C. McQuiston's Second Brigade of the First Division, temporarily acting with Hascall's division, connected its left to Strickland's right. Then Colonel William E. Hobson's Second Brigade of Hascall's division continued the line from McQuiston's right. All three of Hascall's brigades began to make breastworks of fence rails.[6]

Cox anchored his division's right flank at Cheney's House, but he was compelled to stretch out the rest of his command about one mile toward Hascall's right flank, which was located partway from Strickland's position toward Cheney's House. Two Confederate cavalry brigades attached to Brigadier General William H. Jackson's cavalry division of the Army of Mississippi, led by Brigadier General Lawrence S. Ross and Brigadier General Frank C. Armstrong, opposed Cox south of Cheney's House. Ross and Armstrong also covered the crossing of Olley's Creek, the next watercourse east of Noyes Creek that the Federals had to pass if they hoped to continue extending southward.[7]

Soon after Strickland established his line, the Federals pushed farther east along the Powder Springs and Marietta Road to determine exactly where and how strongly the Confederates were situated. Strickland sent forward the Fourteenth Kentucky south of the road as Knipe sent the 123rd New York north of the road in what amounted to a reconnaissance in force. Another ridge on the other side of the Kolb House seemed to be a desirable place to advance the Federal line, but no one knew if it was held in strength by the Confederates.[8]

Colonel George W. Gallup moved the Fourteenth Kentucky out with its left flank anchored on the road. He advanced Companies A and G as skirmishers, followed by the rest of the regiment as a reserve. After advancing three hundred yards across an open field, the two companies encountered Confederate skirmish fire coming from a belt of trees. Company A attacked with fixed bayonets and took the woods, along with about thirty Rebels from the Fifty-Eighth and Sixtieth North Carolina of Brigadier General Alexander W. Reynolds's brigade of Major General Carter L. Stevenson's division. After that, Gallup pushed his entire regiment through the belt of trees, crossed another cleared field, and halted at the edge of the next line of woods. His skirmishers soon reported that a strong Confederate battle line lay only eight hundred yards ahead. Gallup sent word back to Hascall and received an order to dig in and hold his position. While half of his Kentuckians gathered material for breastworks, the other half remained on line in case the enemy made a sudden appearance.[9]

Lieutenant Colonel James C. Rogers pushed his 123rd New York up to Gallup's left by this time, but he had first to negotiate the ravine that lay parallel to Williams's division line. The ravine was a "natural dugout," according to Rice C. Bull, and the regiment sheltered from Confederate skirmish fire in it for a short while during its advance north of the Powder Springs and Marietta Road. When the regimental skirmish line moved east of the ravine, it had to negotiate the obstruction posed by the Kolb homestead with its outbuildings and extensive peach orchard. Both the skirmish line and the main line of the regiment used the buildings as cover during the advance, pushing the Confederate skirmishers past the belt of timber and into the same woods that Gallup had taken cover in, aligning north of the Kentuckians. Bull reported that the Rebel skirmish line lay only two hundred feet away, and the Federals could hear the tramping of the Confederate main line several hundred yards farther east. It was obvious that preparations were underway for a fight. Testimony offered by the captured skirmishers also indicated that a battle could be expected very soon.[10]

Hooker had been very impatient for a further advance as soon as Williams assumed his new position along the Powder Springs and Marietta Road, but Williams felt uncomfortable moving east without a firmer connection to Geary's division. About 3:00 P.M. Williams rode forward to Kolb's house, where he found Hooker and learned that a Confederate attack was likely to occur. In fact, Hooker gave him the impression that Johnston's entire army was massing in his front. He ordered Williams to dig in and prepare for a defensive battle, and the division commander rode back to his men to make arrangements. From about 3:00 P.M. to 5:00 P.M., the Federals constructed rail breastworks and kept a watch on the terrain around them.[11]

Hooker also asked Thomas for help at 3:15 P.M., urging him to move the Fourth Corps line farther south so he could mass Geary and Butterfield near Williams and anchor the Union right flank more securely. Forty-five minutes later, Hooker told Thomas that Johnston's entire army was massing in his front (according to the prisoners), and that Schofield had but one division to the south of the Twentieth Corps to support him. "My line is too long to make an obstinate defense," he warned army headquarters.[12]

Thomas relayed Hooker's report to Sherman, but he did not place full faith in it. "I look upon this as something of a stampede," he wrote. But Thomas recognized that it was a plausible course of action for the Confederates to launch an attack on his right wing. He began to reposition a division of the Fourteenth Corps to relieve a division of the Fourth Corps so the line could shift farther south, but Thomas warned Hooker that he could not move so many units as would be needed to free up Geary and Butterfield. Thomas was convinced that Hooker's line would contract as it continued to advance east and that, with field works and Schofield to help, Hooker should be able to hold his position. If Johnston massed an overwhelming force in Hooker's front, the Confederates would be weak elsewhere, offering Sherman an opportunity to break through on McPherson's front, for example.[13]

When Schofield received word of the impending attack, he sent a message to Cox at 4:15 P.M. to move three brigades eastward and make connection with Hascall's right flank, which had not yet been done. Cox was to keep his last brigade at Cheney's House. In the worst-case scenario, Schofield wanted Cox to fall back to the crossing of Noyes Creek and hold that position at all hazards.[14]

HOOD PREPARES FOR ACTION

The Confederate force opposing Hooker's advance was not the whole of Johnston's army but only Hood's Corps. After resting his men near Marietta on the night of June 21, Hood began to move them in stages a short distance toward the west to align with Hardee's Corps and block the Union approach along the Powder Springs and Marietta Road. Major General Thomas C. Hindman's division took position on Hood's right at about 1:30 P.M., extending Hardee's line in the woods. Carter L. Stevenson received the order to move forward at 2:30 P.M., about the time that the Fourteenth Kentucky and the 123rd New York were pushing east on their reconnaissance. Stevenson advanced his division with a skirmish line deployed from Alexander W. Reynolds's brigade, which engaged the two Federal regiments as Stevenson established his line in the woods south of Hindman's position. Stevenson placed Brigadier General John C. Brown's Tennessee Brigade north of the road and Brigadier General Alfred Cumming's Georgia Brigade south of the road in his first line, with Reynolds's North Carolina and Virginia Brigade north of the road and Brigadier General Edmund W. Pettus's Alabama Brigade south of the road in his second line. Stevenson's formation straddled the Powder Springs and Marietta Road as all of his units began to make rail breastworks. Hood held Major General Alexander P. Stewart's division in reserve.[15]

Carter L. Stevenson (Library of Congress, LC-USZ62-126425)

Hood made a decision to attack soon after assuming his new position. Because the corps commander never fully explained his thinking in written form, one has to make assumptions about his motives and aims on June 22. The most likely reason was the advance of the Fourteenth Kentucky and the 123rd New York, which seemed to portend an aggressive move by the Federals along the Powder Springs and Marietta Road. Given responsibility for protecting this vulnerable sector, Hood apparently thought the best defense was a quick offense. He did not inform Johnston, much less seek his commanding officer's permission.[16]

The worst part of Hood's decision to attack was that he did not prepare adequately for the push. The terrain was new to everyone in his command, and exactly where and how strongly the enemy was positioned was equally unknown to them. Hood's move would essentially be a reconnaissance in force by two divisions that had just arrived on unknown ground. There was ample time to filter orders down the chain of command. Stevenson reported that "a good deal of time was occupied in getting and giving instructions and making the necessary preparations." He placed Cumming in charge of his first line, consisting of two brigades (Brown and Cumming), and Pettus in charge of his second line (also consisting of two brigades, Reynolds and Pettus). In Hindman's division, the brigade leaders were told to advance west by guiding to the left, toward the vital road.

But the Confederates did not take the time to advance their skirmish line to find out essential information about the terrain and enemy troop positions. It is true that Gallup's Fourteenth Kentucky and Rogers's 123rd New York occupied a forward position in the woods' edge quite close to Hood's Corps, but the Confederates could have advanced a heavy skirmish line to push them back. It is possible Hood deliberately avoided sending out the skirmishers, even though they could have driven close to Hooker's position and passed back valuable information, because he did not want to alert the enemy to his planned attack. If that was the case, the plan backfired. The Federals already knew full well what to expect from him. Hood would go in, but his men would go in blind and cold.[17]

THE BATTLE OF KOLB'S FARM

The Confederates began their attack at 5:00 P.M. with Stevenson's division moving on both sides of the Powder Springs and Marietta Road. Cumming's brigade constituted the first line of Stevenson's left wing, south of the roadway, and it encountered a great deal of trouble while moving through the woods. Trees and a dense undergrowth disrupted Cumming's formation. "The line thus became more irregular and broken every moment," as Stevenson put it. According to Gallup, Cumming's men "approached reluctantly and in much disorder, resembling a mob more than they did soldiery." The Kentuckians waited until their opponents were only thirty feet away before opening fire, and the first volley caused so much confusion in the Rebel ranks that Cumming retired firing. Few of the Confederate rounds took effect, however, because of wild aiming and because Gallup's men crouched behind rail breastworks.[18]

While Stevenson's left wing became stalled from the start, his right wing achieved quick success. Rice Bull could hear the sound of feet rustling among forest leaves as the Confederates approached the 123rd New York shortly after 5:00 P.M. When Brown's and Reynolds's brigades appeared, it became apparent that the lone Union regiment could not hold them back. Rogers ordered his New Yorkers to fire a volley and then pull away. They retired across open country and paused on the Kolb homestead to reload. But the Confederates were too close upon them, and Rogers's men continued moving west without firing. The Rebels called on them to stop and give up but, as they neared Williams's line, the New Yorkers broke up, and then it was "every man for himself." They had to dodge the first few rounds issuing from Williams's main line as they neared the division. The 123rd New York lost forty-eight men at Kolb's Farm.[19]

The retirement of the 123rd New York forced Gallup to pull away as well. When Stevenson's right wing moved westward north of the Powder Springs and Marietta Road, some Confederates fired into Gallup's left flank, alerting him to the fact that the New Yorkers had retired. Gallup ordered his regiment to break away by companies from the left. Each company was to face north to deliver fire on the Confederates as it moved by the left flank westward to escape. He stopped to re-form a proper line partway back to the main Union position and then sent his left wing back to Strickland while holding the right wing of four companies in place behind the crest of a small ridge to serve as a rear guard. Gallup tenaciously held here until Hascall sent a peremptory order to retire. There is no evidence, however, that Cumming pressed him in this position, but there was no need for Gallup to hold four companies in this forward, isolated position once the rest of his regiment had reached the main line. The Fourteenth Kentucky suffered sixty casualties at Kolb's Farm.[20]

The Federals who held the main line of Williams's division had enough opportunity to get ready for Hood's attack. In riding to each brigade leader to give instructions for the coming battle, Williams had barely reached Robinson's command when "the peculiar yell of the rebel mass was heard as they emerged from the woods and dashed forward." The Federal guns opened fire immediately, but the infantrymen of Knipe and Ruger waited until Brown and Reynolds reached the eastern edge of the ravine that ran parallel to Williams's position before they began to fire their muskets. Williams watched as some Confederates turned and retired, but most ran down into the ravine for cover. Some Rebels entered a grove of plum trees in front of Knipe's left wing, and Williams ordered the Union guns to direct their fire into the trees. At best, the Confederates made it to a point no more than fifty yards from the Union line before the attack broke apart.[21]

Even though only three Union batteries could reach the attacking Confederates north of the Powder Springs and Marietta Road, the guns pounded

Stevenson's men with great effect and essentially broke up Hood's attack before it even reached the Federal line. Stevenson reported that the Union artillery was "admirably posted," and "was served with a rapidity and fatal precision which could not be surpassed." Both brigades north of the road broke up, the men assembling mostly in the ravine to find some cover from the hail of projectiles. Most of Ruger's men had an elevated and clear view of the battlefield, and the ravine was close enough so that they could pelt the Confederates with musketry. "It was an episode of most murderous war," commented a man in the Third Wisconsin.[22]

The men of Knipe's brigade, in the center of Williams's division line, had a clear view of the battlefield as well. "It was a grand sight," as Captain William Merrell of the 141st New York remarked of Hood's attack. Knipe's men were in the process of building rail breastworks when the gray mass surged forward, but they grabbed their guns and were on line well before the danger neared. A section of Woodbury's guns was positioned near Merrell, and the artillery officer told the infantrymen to stand on the balls of their feet and avoid clenching their teeth so the concussion would not hurt them. Merrell was curious to know if this was really necessary. "I tried standing solidly on my feet, shutting my teeth together; but I never cared to try it again, for it seemed as though the top of my head blew off with the first discharge of the gun."[23]

The effect of Knipe's artillery and infantry fire was devastating. Merrell watched as the first round of projectiles seemed to demoralize the Confederates and cause many to huddle in the grove of plum trees "like frightened sheep." Other Rebels found shelter in the ravine and in "some deep washouts peculiar to the South," where they took potshots at the Federals. Merrell fired guns for four of his men, who reloaded them so fast that they put a ready musket in the captain's hand as soon as he had fired the previous one. One of the four men was hit in the forehead by a musket ball and died instantly, but the others continued to reload for Merrell. Knipe's brigade fired up to sixty rounds per man at Kolb's Farm, according to one account. A Confederate officer on a white horse tried to rally his men out of the ravine; he was shot, and the horse ran away. As Merrell recalled, whenever groups of Confederates tried to carry one of their wounded to the rear, "all would go down together." "I never saw such havoc among soldiers; they were almost completely annihilated," commented the New Yorker.[24]

Hindman's division went in about the same time that Stevenson attacked, but with even less effect. The division approached Robinson's brigade of Williams's division and the right end of Geary's line. Hindman's left wing, consisting of Brigadier General William F. Tucker's brigade and Brigadier General Zachariah C. Deas's brigade, was so pummeled by Union artillery fire across half a mile of open ground that it stopped before coming within effective musket range of the Federals. Walthall's brigade, led by Colonel Samuel Benton, also stopped early in its advance, while Brigadier General Arthur M. Manigault's brigade halted at the ravine that sheltered Stevenson's division. Hindman's attack was stopped entirely by Federal artillery, mostly Winegar's New York Battery; neither Robinson nor Geary opened infantry fire. Williams claimed that the guns fired no more than three rounds each before Hindman's troops stopped in their tracks. From Robinson's perspective, "It was a beautiful sight to see their columns shattered and fleeing in confusion."[25]

Despite their weak performance, Manigault was convinced that the men of Hindman's division could have accomplished something if not for the ravine that blocked their way. Its "boggy, miry margin on each side" was too much of an impediment for a coordinated advance. Manigault blamed Hindman, "who never led his division, but left it entirely to his brigadiers." The four brigade commanders had no idea what lay ahead. The lay of the land was as much of a mystery to them as was the exact Union position and strength. Manigault argued that Hindman knew of the ravine but told no one about it. Confederate officers, presumably from Hood's or Hindman's staff, had reconnoitered the ground on June 20 after Hood received orders to move to the spot. Moreover, if Hindman had sent out scouts to locate the Union line just before the attack, it would have yielded valuable information. In Manigault's view, the entire operation was misguided and mismanaged from the top down.[26]

The Federal guns continued to pound the Confederates for the rest of the day, mostly plunging rounds into the ravine but also shelling the woods into which much of Hindman's division had retired. Many Confederates recalled it as the heaviest shelling they had endured in the war. "The shot and shell [tore] through the timber, cutting down trees and large branches, which fell in our midst," remembered Manigault. "It was a terrific fire, and lasted until dark." A Confederate color-bearer stood behind the decayed trunk of a tree in the ravine and defiantly waved his flag. Although many Federal soldiers fired at him, he kept the colors waving until darkness.[27]

It was an unusual battle for the Federals, more easily won than they had reason to expect. Williams reported that his men, "after the first half-hour" of the fight, "considered the whole affair great sport. They would call out to the Rebels who had taken shelter in the . . . deep ravines in our front,

'Come up here, Johnny Reb. Here is a weak place!' 'Come up and take this battery; we are Hooker's paper collar boys.' 'We've only got two rounds of ammunition, come and take us.' 'What do you think of Joe Hooker's Iron Clads?' and the like." The Confederates did not take kindly to such taunts, and "generally answered with some very profane language and with firing of their guns."[28]

The Confederates had driven in Williams's skirmish line, which exposed the right flank of Geary's skirmish line, but Geary was able to keep his skirmishers in place because there was no close advance against his front. Captain William Wheeler's Thirteenth New York Battery delivered fire at Hindman's troops in the open field at a right oblique, contributing to their confusion, and swept the ravine with fire as well. Wheeler partially shielded himself by standing near a tree while observing the effect of his rounds, but he was "shot through the heart by one of the enemy's sharpshooters." Other than his loss, Geary suffered few casualties. His men had a magnificent view of events to the south. "It was a beautiful sight, for the spectator from a safe point of view to see," reported Stephen Pierson of the Thirty-Third New Jersey, "and we watched them with interest, at the same time keeping a sharp eye on our own front."[29]

Butterfield was not engaged at all on the afternoon of June 22, but Howard's troops skirmished heavily along the Fourth Corps line. When the Confederates attacked, Hooker's call for help led Thomas to ask Howard for more troops. He sent nine regiments that were not already holding trenches to Butterfield's position, so Butterfield could detach two of his brigades and send them to Williams. It soon became apparent, however, that those reinforcements were not needed. After dusk, Howard extended his corps line southward to more firmly support Hooker.[30]

The Twenty-Third Corps securely held the Union right flank during Hood's attack. Schofield had already ordered Cox to send three brigades forward to support Hascall. They arrived about the time that the Confederate advance was broken up by the Union guns. Schofield personally directed the placement of these three brigades. Colonel Daniel Cameron's Second Brigade connected with Hobson's right flank, while Colonel Richard F. Barter's First Brigade, First Division (temporarily acting with Cox's division), connected to Cameron's right. Colonel Robert K. Bryd's Third Brigade of Cox's command continued the line to the right of Barter. All three brigades continued the Union line south of the Powder Springs and Marietta Road, facing southeast. Cox kept Colonel James W. Reilly's brigade at Cheney's House. Reilly's men fortified the crest north of Cheney's, and

Twenty-Third Corps artillery was placed to sweep the valley of Olley's Creek toward the northeast. Schofield connected Reilly's unit with the rest of the corps near Kolb's Farm by deploying a screen of pickets from Major General George Stoneman's cavalry division, which was attached to the Army of the Ohio. Stoneman also held a position to the south of Cheney's House, at another crossing of Noyes Creek. Both Reilly and Stoneman were fronted by Ross's and Armstrong's Confederate cavalry brigades.[31]

EVENING OF JUNE 22

The attack ended well before dusk as the broken elements of Hood's command huddled in the ravine, enduring the torment of Union artillery rounds and small arms fire. Hooker was eager to launch a counterstrike "but the smallness of my force available for the service would not justify the movement," he reported. Williams believed he could have taken one thousand prisoners but dared not move forward with his single line of battle because of Hooker's belief, based on prisoner reports, that Johnston's entire army was massed in his front.[32]

The Confederates continued a covering fire from various positions during the evening of June 22 to divert Union attention from their comrades in the ravine. Returning this fire, the 150th New York of Ruger's brigade shot 140 rounds per man during the battle and its aftermath. Another regiment in Ruger's brigade, the Second Massachusetts, ran dangerously low on ammunition before the fight ended because it expended so many rounds on the hapless enemy.[33]

Those Rebels able to move began to leave the ravine soon after dark descended that evening. The Confederates evacuated most of their dead and wounded too. Williams sent out skirmishers to occupy the ravine, and they found five wounded Confederates who had been left behind. Stevenson tried to put the best face possible on the repulse, reporting that his men did not evacuate the ravine until Hood ordered it. He also reported that his men had been "in good spirits and perfectly willing to make the attempt" to advance out of the ravine soon after they had taken shelter there, but he decided not to take the chance. Stevenson expressed nothing more than wishful thinking, for the course of the battle at Kolb's Farm was entirely out of his control.[34]

The major part of the fight had lasted one and a half hours, from 5:00 to 6:30 P.M., with Confederate losses amounting to about 1,000 men. Stevenson alone suffered 807 killed and wounded on June 22. The Thirty-Second Tennessee lost its colonel and more than half of its enlisted men, while the Fifty-Fourth Virginia mustered only 150 men out of 450 who had started the attack. Brown's brigade reportedly lost 250 men. Several other regiments suffered heavily. An unidentified member of the Thirty-Ninth Georgia in Cumming's brigade reported that his regiment lost one-third of its number. He was wounded and lost his left arm, "then ensued my sufferings & long stay in hospital." The man apparently died, for his diary was taken up and used by Confederate surgeon W. H. Brooker.[35]

The Confederates brought in their wounded from the field all night. It was a dramatic and sad sight to Hiram Smith Williams, a pioneer in Hood's corps. "I never saw so many wounded men before," Williams confided to his diary, "they came out in gangs of ten, twenty and even more, besides the ambulances filled with those who were wounded too badly to walk. Poor fellows! All kinds and manner of wounds in the head, body, arms, legs. Oh, but it is sickening to look at them."[36]

For many wounded Confederates, a long and painful journey toward an uncertain future lay ahead. "I have met with a very sad fate," wrote William B. Calfee of the Fifty-Fourth Virginia to his father. "I was severely wound on 22nd in the right arm and also had it amputated the Same day." Calfee was transported to Kingston Hospital near Atlanta and was recovering well a few days after the battle. The Federals "give me a good one a Discharge at once for a man will not be worth much with his right arm off." Calfee had good reason to hope for recovery as long as "the gand green" did not begin to trouble the exposed flesh of his stump. Joseph Hamilton Bowman of the Thirty-Second Tennessee also was severely wounded at Kolb's Farm. He was sent to Montgomery, Alabama, where a group of twenty-five wounded men were farmed out to civilians in Lowndes County for care. Bowman developed gangrene and was bed-ridden for two months. He credited "the best of nursing by the citizens" for saving his life, although he lost "the use of rotary motion of right fore arm." But at least Bowman survived his ordeal and was discharged in February 1865. The major of the Fifty-Fourth Virginia died nearly a month after receiving his mortal wound at the battle of Kolb's Farm.[37]

The Federals were certain they had punished the Confederates a great deal, but they had to rely on indirect evidence to gauge the extent. Sherman reported that Hood left two hundred dead on the field, while Williams perused Atlanta newspapers that fell into Union hands to conclude that

Hood had lost more than one thousand men in the short battle. Prisoner statements led Geary to estimate Hood's losses much higher, as many as three thousand men.[38]

Federal casualties amounted to about three hundred troops, only one-third the number lost by Hood. One hundred eight of that number occurred among the two regiments that bore the brunt of the initial Rebel advance on the picket line, the Fourteenth Kentucky and 123rd New York. Knipe's brigade lost thirty-nine men (not counting casualties in the 123rd New York), and Ruger's brigade lost only twenty-eight men in the battle. Schofield's Twenty-Third Corps lost forty men, besides those who fell in the Fourteenth Kentucky.[39]

SHERMAN AND THE BATTLE OF KOLB'S FARM

Sherman remained largely unaware of the fight until after it ended. He conducted his planned ride along the line, waiting for Thomas to show up at a hill near the Wallace House only two miles from Kolb's Farm. This hill also was near the center of the line held by the Army of the Cumberland. While waiting for Thomas, Sherman sent a signal message to Hooker. "'How are you getting along? Near what house are you?'" Thomas was too busy to meet Sherman, but the latter stayed at the hill for the rest of the evening. It was already 5:30 P.M., and he could hear the sound of Twentieth Corps artillery but did not know a battle was underway. Not until four hours later, at about 9:30 P.M., did Sherman receive a message from Hooker. "'We have repulsed two heavy attacks and feel confident, our only apprehension being from our extreme right flank. Three corps are in front of us.'"[40]

Sherman was astonished, but he quickly discounted Hooker's report that Johnston was massing his entire army opposite the Twentieth Corps. He knew from his ride that day that the trenches in front of McPherson, Palmer, and Howard were still filled with Confederate troops. He also had given explicit orders for Schofield to cover Hooker's flank and knew that Schofield had received those instructions. Sherman sent a message to Twentieth Corps headquarters explaining all this. On the remote chance that Hooker was right, Sherman privately planned to "bring things to a crisis" the next morning with Johnston, fighting a climactic battle near Kolb's Farm.[41]

Schofield sent Sherman a more reliable message, written at 9:00 P.M., indicating that the fight was heavy for a while, but the Confederates were repulsed with considerable loss. He accurately reported that only Hood's Corps participated in the advance, "with the evident purpose of breaking our lines, yet their assaults were hardly strong enough for the force named."[42]

Thomas learned of the battle early enough to arrive on the scene a short while after the attack had been repulsed. He was heartened by what he saw. The Twentieth Corps had a good defensive position, as strong as any Howard's Corps had held during the past several days. Thomas also consulted with Schofield, who confirmed that all of Sherman's instructions for covering Thomas's right flank had been received and acted upon. "The enemy cannot possibly send an overwhelming force against Hooker without exposing his weakness to McPherson," Thomas informed Sherman. This message, and Schofield's dispatch, reassured Sherman that all was well on his right flank. Still, he had every intention of dressing down Hooker the next time he saw him for his reliance on the unverified reports of captured Confederates regarding enemy troop strength.[43]

Sherman had already discussed with McPherson a plan to have the Army of the Tennessee "leave a light force to cover" the Federal left and shift most of its manpower to flank Johnston's left. Now he anticipated the need to implement that plan on June 23, depending on developments at Kolb's Farm. For his part, McPherson reacted to Hood's attack by alerting Major General Grenville M. Dodge to have a division of the Sixteenth Corps ready to go to the right to help Hooker if needed.[44]

EVALUATING KOLB'S FARM

The Federals had every reason to feel good about the small battle that took place at Kolb's Farm on June 22. "The numbers were formidable," reported Alpheus Williams, "but the attack was indeed feeble." Hooker crowed more than anyone about how his men had handled the enemy. "Our artillery did splendid execution among them," he reported to Thomas's headquarters. The concentrated fire not only broke up Hood's formations but demoralized the Confederates. Hooker praised his command with superlatives. "The conduct of the troops throughout the day was sublime," he told Thomas. Williams agreed. "Altogether, I have never had an engagement in which success was won so completely and with so little sacrifice of life," he informed his family. "Considering the number of the enemy sent against my single division, the result is indeed most wonderful and gratifying."[45]

Along with the self-congratulation came wonder that the Confederates attempted to attack at all. "I cannot understand how Hood could commit such an error," wrote a newspaper correspondent of the *New York Herald*.

"If we were to select our own ground it could not be better chosen." Efforts to explain this "miserable failure," as Manigault put it, rightfully center on Hood. Still comparatively new to corps command, he failed to report the tactical situation to his superior and attacked without explicit approval from his commander. Later, Hood explained to Johnston that the Federals attacked him and he launched a counterstrike, which was stopped by the Union guns after his troops captured a line of enemy breastworks. Hood was guilty of exaggerating an advance by two Federal regiments into an "attack" on an entire corps of Confederate infantry, but for the time being Johnston accepted Hood's explanation for the battle. After the war, however, Johnston conversed with some officers who apparently were on the scene and developed a more accurate view of the battle. He then thought Hood had mishandled his attack by deliberately striking at the Federal artillery instead of seeking a weak spot in the Union position. It was unclear to Johnston if Hood had called off the attack when he realized it would not work, or if the men took it upon themselves to stop. Overall, Hood's relationship with Johnston was deteriorating by late June. Hood's engineer officer, Thomas L. Clayton, reported that his chief was "somewhat disappointed" in Johnston's treatment of the corps, seeming to favor Hardee and assigning Hood's command the worst positions.[46]

News of the battle spread rapidly along Confederate lines, and reports often gave incorrect impressions of the battle. The engagement came to be called several different names among Southerners, including the battle of Powder Springs Road and the battle of Mount Zion Church. All reports agreed that it was "a considerable" fight with heavy loss. Many Confederates thought Hood had done what was necessary to secure the army's left flank. Some of them believed that their comrades had driven the enemy two miles and captured twelve cannon and 1,700 prisoners, according to one report. Hood's own staff members believed the corps had been stopped by the fire of thirty Federal artillery pieces. Given the paucity of official reports about the battle, misconceptions of what was accomplished continued to surface for a long time to come. Only the survivors of the engagement knew the truth about Kolb's Farm. It was "a terrible battle," with "such terrible slaughter." As J. D. Harwell of the Twentieth Alabama sarcastically put it many decades later, Kolb's Farm was a place "where Genl Hood exhibited his Generalship."[47]

Hood remained largely silent on the subject of Kolb's Farm. He devoted only two paragraphs to the Kennesaw Mountain phase of the Atlanta Campaign in his memoirs and carefully avoided any mention of the battle of

June 22. Some historians have argued that Hood was motivated by a desire to seize the initiative and attempt to turn the Union right flank, while others have argued that he was motivated by a desire to implement the aggressive tactics he had learned under General Robert E. Lee's tutelage as a division commander in the Army of Northern Virginia.[48]

A simpler explanation for the Confederate attack at Kolb's Farm is to take Hood at his word. He believed the advance of the Fourteenth Kentucky and 123rd New York presaged a major attack by Schofield and Hooker. Hood wanted to launch a counterattack to hold the line south of Hardee's Corps and take advantage of any opportunities that might develop. On the surface this appears to have been a viable choice by Hood, but further analysis allows one to make a damning criticism of Hood's judgment in ordering this attack. He had enormous experience as a division commander in tough battles and surely knew that the advance of even a strong skirmish line did not necessarily presage a major attack. The Federals had skirmished vigorously at many places throughout the campaign thus far without a follow up assault. Most importantly, the best way to hold the line south of Hardee's Corps was to assume a good defensive position and dig in. That would have blocked Schofield and Hooker very effectively without the loss of irreplaceable Confederate troops. In the end, Hood's actions can best be explained not by a desire to turn Sherman's flank or to demonstrate to the Army of Tennessee how to fight via Lee's methods, but by Hood's faulty judgment about the best way to achieve the tactical goal set for him by Johnston.

The worst part of Hood's handling of the affair at Kolb's Farm was that he launched the attack with an appalling ignorance of what lay before his men, even though there was ample time to reconnoiter and learn details of the terrain. If he indeed meant to find and exploit weaknesses in the Union position, he spent no effort to first learn where those weaknesses might lay. Arthur Manigault formed his first negative opinion of Hood as a result of the battle at Kolb's Farm. The engagement "was a disgrace to the officer who planned it," and he thought "there could be no excuse" for the lack of intelligence that underwrote the entire operation. Later experience confirmed Manigault's opinion that Hood "was totally unfit for the command of a corps."[49]

After the war, Manigault found it strange that Hood had kept Johnston in the dark about the details of the affair at Kolb's Farm. The corps leader had "fought on this occasion on his own responsibility, was ashamed of the result, and did not give a correct statement" to his commander. Yet Manigault also faulted Johnston for remaining ignorant of the details, even if

Hood did not offer them. This was a criticism echoed by Richard McMurry, a modern historian who tends to look in a balanced way upon Hood's record in the Atlanta campaign.[50]

If anything, Hindman probably handled his command with less expertise than Hood. Both men came in for severe criticism by their subordinates. According to a veteran of the division, Hindman and Hood did not get along well together on a personal level. J. C. Higdon related a camp story about the battle of Kolb's Farm in which Hood gave directions to Hindman about placing the division, directions that Hindman did not like. When the division leader offered an alternative, Hood lost his patience. "'Gen. Hindman, why is it that I can never give an order but that you have some suggestion to make?'" Hindman replied, "'Because you never give me an order with any sense to it.'" If there is any truth to this interchange, it suggests that Hood's relations with his division leaders further complicated his handling of the corps.[51]

C. Irvine Walker, one of Manigault's staff officers, thought the failure at Kolb's Farm was attributable to poor generalship on the division level. He blamed "the incompetency of our Generals" and bemoaned the fact that the Army of Tennessee was "most sadly off for good Major Generals." Walker cogently summarized the battle for his wife-to-be. "The truth of the matter I believe is that we made an attack supposing the enemy to be not very strong, and when we struck their lines we found them much stronger than we anticipated, and retired without making an actual attack." Walker also minced no words when criticizing Hindman for "putting his Division in a very bad condition. He is utterly incapable to command a Corporal's guard, much less a Division." Other men also criticized Carter L. Stevenson for his handling of the attack, but without providing details as to what he failed to do.[52]

Despite the mistakes and the needless sacrifice of one thousand men, Hood effectively blocked Schofield and Hooker at Kolb's Farm. Jacob Cox believed that if the Federals had firmly established themselves some distance east of the farm before Hood arrived in the area, Johnston would have been forced to evacuate his Kennesaw Line on June 23. In the larger grand tactical picture, Sherman once again was stymied in his efforts to compel the enemy to leave their Kennesaw Line.[53]

Three. Sherman Decides to Strike

The Confederates worked all night on June 22 to clear the battlefield of their dead and wounded. They failed to find all of them before dawn forced an end to their mission of mercy. As a result, the Federals found quite a few bodies still in place when they moved forward to claim the field early on June 23. D. P. Conyagham, a correspondent for the *New York Herald*, described the battlefield for his readers. He found many Confederate dead behind a rail fence that ran along the small stream draining through the ravine. "The torn, bloody knapsacks, haversacks, blankets and frequent pools of blood around were ghastly evidences of how they suffered," Conyagham wrote. "The sluggish stream was actually discolored with blood, and several bodies lay there yet unburied." The correspondent found that heavy artillery fire had "piled their bodies over one another." He also discovered several Rebel dead around the Kolb House farther east. Edwin Weller of the 107th New York thought the Confederates had suffered enough to repay Hooker's men for the drubbing received at New Hope Church.[1]

Even though he could hear the Confederates using wagons to retrieve their dead and wounded during the night, Alpheus Williams counted at least sixty bodies in front of his division on the morning of June 23. George Gallup reportedly buried sixty-nine dead Rebels in front of his Fourteenth Kentucky alone.[2]

Sherman rode to the area early on June 23 to gauge the situation on his far right. He was still determined to reprimand Hooker for his intemperate report that all of Johnston's army opposed the Twentieth Corps the previous day. Sherman recalled in his memoirs that Thomas had earlier complained of Hooker's tendency to "'switch off,' leaving wide gaps in his line, so as to be independent, and to make *glory* on his own account." He further claimed that McPherson and Schofield had also voiced similar complaints of the Twentieth Corps commander. It was time to correct this tendency in Hooker.[3]

Sherman rode through Butterfield's division and found that it had not been engaged the previous evening. As he moved farther south, he saw burial squads from Geary's and Williams's divisions at work and found Schofield's command south of the Powder Springs and Marietta Road. Sherman met Hooker and Schofield near Bethel Church west of Kolb's House as a light rain fell. According to Sherman's own account, he showed Hooker's dispatch implying that the Twenty-Third Corps was not firmly holding the line south of his command to Schofield. "He was very angry," Sherman reported, "and pretty sharp words passed between them." Schofield argued that Hascall's division was farther forward than any of Hooker's men and offered to show Sherman how far east some of Gallup's dead had been left at the start of the engagement. Hooker pretended to be unaware of this as Sherman informed him that Johnston could not possibly have massed his entire army along the Powder Springs and Marietta Road.[4]

After this stormy interchange, Sherman rode away from the church with Hooker and told him privately that "such a thing must not occur again; in other words, I reproved him more gently than the occasion demanded, and from that time he began to sulk." Sherman thought Hooker's head had been turned by his performance in the battle of Lookout Mountain, during the Chattanooga campaign, and that he was jealous of the army commanders serving with Sherman because he believed he was their superior in "former rank, and experience." Hooker took his medicine without comment, and Sherman rode off to other parts of his long, extended line.[5]

Ironically, Schofield reported in his own memoirs that he was not present when Sherman met Hooker at the church. He did meet with Sherman sometime that morning and saw Hooker's dispatch, but never confronted the Twentieth Corps commander and thought Sherman was "unnecessarily alarmed" by the entire incident. He was in touch with Hooker before and after the fight on June 22, and there could have been no misapprehension on Hooker's part about the security of the right flank. Hascall was present at the meeting of Sherman and Hooker at the church, and Schofield thought his division commander probably got angry when he read Hooker's dispatch. Hascall was the one who argued that Twenty-Third Corps troops were in the most advanced position on June 22. Schofield knew that ill feelings between Sherman and Hooker had started before the engagement at Kolb's Farm; the two men had not gotten along well from the start of the Atlanta campaign, with Hooker jealous of Sherman's position and Sherman unable to cozy up to a subordinate who did not know his place.[6]

Schofield suggested that Hooker's alarmist dispatch on the evening of

June 22 was inspired by concern for the security of Schofield's right flank, not the flank of the Twentieth Corps. In other words, because Hooker believed prisoner reports that Johnston had massed his entire army on his front, he expected that the enemy would try to flank the entire Union line. Hooker, in Schofield's charitable interpretation of the dispatch, was worried about the safety of Cox's men at Cheney's House but failed to explicitly say so in the dispatch. Schofield did not worry, for he was always alert to such threats, having worked on the flanks of Sherman's army group for some time now while Hooker had little such experience. Sherman also was critical of Hooker for sending his dispatch to his own headquarters instead of working through the channels and sending it to Thomas. But Sherman had sent a message directly to Hooker requesting an update on progress, so Hooker was perfectly correct to write back. Howard, who was not present during the meeting at the church, also thought Sherman had acted a bit harshly toward Hooker in this fracas and explained it away by noting that the Twentieth Corps commander often became overly excited.[7]

Postbattle arguments among the generals came and went, but Federals of all ranks had to be ready for all contingencies on June 23. In Hascall's division, the front rank of men remained in position with guns ready, while the rear rank gathered rails and constructed a breastwork. Schofield reconnoitered for the rest of the day and reported to Sherman that the Confederate line extended well south of his position. It was apparent that the Rebels had constructed fortifications extending across the Powder Springs and Marietta Road and Olley's Creek. In fact, even if Schofield swung his entire command so as to extend the Union line opposite Hood's position, the Confederate fortifications would extend farther than he could deploy. It seemed impossible to match the enemy man for man in this sector in order to turn Johnston's left flank.[8]

The Confederates maintained their cavalry presence opposite Cox's position at Cheney's House even as Hood extended the main line southward from Hardee's Corps. Hood issued instructions to his division commanders to strengthen their position by constructing abatis in front of the breastworks and to be on the alert for a Union assault. Hood knew that great difficulties attended any attempt by Sherman to find and turn his flank, and he therefore worried that the Yankees might try a frontal attack. Hood also lectured his subordinates that, if the Federals drove in the Confederate skirmish line, they should quickly reestablish it so as not to allow the enemy to dominate no-man's-land. This had been a common failing in the corps, he observed, during previous engagements in the campaign. Hood's directive also indicates he could appreciate the value of effective skirmishing following the fight at Kolb's Farm.[9]

On the Fourth Corps sector, Stanley's and Newton's divisions skirmished heavily to snuggle up closer to the Confederate line on June 23. They advanced only short distances and lost substantially in the process. Stanley suffered sixty casualties that day and gained little for it. The operations proved to Thomas that the Rebel line was very strong. He also told Sherman that Howard's men were exhausted after "the continuous operations of the last three or four days."[10]

"We continue to press forward," Sherman informed Halleck on the night of June 23, "operating on the principle of an advance against fortified positions. The whole country is one vast fort, and Johnston must have full fifty miles of connected trenches, with abatis and finished batteries. We gain ground daily, fighting all the time." Confederate resistance near Kennesaw Mountain had been the most effective thus far in the campaign. The Federals had spent two weeks in advancing about three miles starting on June 10, and there was no clear prospect of faster progress in the foreseeable future. Hooker's men could hear the church bells in Marietta and the whistle of trains at the town's depot as Johnston received fresh supplies from Atlanta. Kennesaw Mountain also was in plain view of Twentieth Corps soldiers, who enjoyed seeing the muzzle flashes of Confederate artillery fire from its summit at night.[11]

While Sherman put the best face on the situation in reports to Washington, he felt frustrated at the slow progress of his advance since crossing the Etowah River. Ironically, Johnston also felt frustrated that he could not do more to stall the Yankees even further. "I have been unable so far to stop the enemy's progress by gradual approaches on account of his numerous army and the character of the country," he reported to Braxton Bragg, former commander of the Army of Tennessee and current adviser to President Jefferson Davis. Johnston urged a cavalry strike against Sherman's railroad as the best hope to turn the Yankees back, but he did not have enough mounted troops with the Army of Tennessee to attempt it. Johnston was forced to stretch his line to the breaking point to counter Sherman's attempts to find and turn his left flank, and he knew he could not continue to do so indefinitely. Meanwhile, the authorities in Richmond could not accommodate Johnston's plan to strike Federal logistics with mounted troops. The only available cavalry, that commanded by Major General Nathan Bedford Forrest in Mississippi, was being kept busy by repeated Union raids into the state from Memphis.[12]

Johnston's Kennesaw Line stretched for seven miles across the Georgia countryside and was the ninth fortified Confederate position of the campaign. The mountain upon which Johnston anchored his line dominated the surrounding countryside. Big Kennesaw rose 691 feet above the ground at its base, while Little Kennesaw was 400 feet tall and Pigeon Hill was 200 feet high. Big Kennesaw's peak was 1,808 feet above sea level. There was some difference of opinion about the exact name of the cluster of peaks that constituted the mountain. Samuel French referred to Big Kennesaw as "Great Kenesaw" and Little Kennesaw as "West Kenesaw." There also was some discussion about the origin of the mountain's name. One of McPherson's officers thought it had been named after a Cherokee Indian chief who had been killed on the eminence, but the National Park Service has reported that the name derives from the Cherokee word "Gah-nee-sah" which refers to a burial ground. Federal soldiers tried their best to spell the word phonetically. Joseph Miller of the Seventy-Eighth Ohio put it down as "Kaunausau," while James Naylor of the Eighty-First Ohio spelled it "Kinnesaw." Pigeon Hill derived its name from the fact that passenger pigeons stopped there during their annual migration at the turn of the twentieth century. The name, therefore, postdates the Atlanta campaign.[13]

Observing Federals offered many descriptions of the mountain that loomed in front of their lines. "It is an isolated mound," wrote a man in the Twentieth Corps, "and is traversed by a deep valley by which distinct peaks are formed." Some Yankees called it the "Twin Mountain," but it has been more technically termed a continuous geographic feature with breaks or depressions that formed three tops. The continuous mound was about two and a half miles long and more abrupt on the side facing the Federals than the side facing Marietta. Except for Little Kennesaw, which was largely denuded of trees, the rest of the mound had ample timber. Many Yankees compared it to Lookout Mountain. In fact, Oscar Jackson in the Sixteenth Corps thought it was more rugged and imposing than Lookout. "To see the clouds parting around it, drifting against its peak, is a grand sight and one I used to think had only been seen by poets anywhere," he wrote.[14]

Many of the Confederate earthworks along the Kennesaw Line are well preserved today, partly because of the red clay which adheres and compacts well, and partly because postwar efforts to preserve the battlefield were highly successful. The remnants of three one-gun artillery emplacements stand on top of Big Kennesaw, placed on and near the exact peak of

Big and Little Kennesaw (Earl J. Hess)

Confederate trench (Earl J. Hess)

the mountain. The connecting infantry trench adheres to the military crest religiously and has traverses only near the lower elevations. Storrs had managed to take nine guns up to the top of Little Kennesaw, and many of the one-gun emplacements used by the crews remain there today, along with covering infantry trenches. The Confederate line of works continues along the military crest of the saddle that connects Little Kennesaw with the much-smaller Pigeon Hill. The latter hill was also much rockier than the two Kennesaws, with a large rock outcropping covering its peak. The saddle connecting it with Little Kennesaw was only about two hundred yards from the peak of Pigeon Hill, and the gorge between the two peaks was covered with timber and briars. The Confederates dug their line by avoiding rock outcroppings, using logs as the base of their parapet. They used other logs to revet the embrasures and parapets of their artillery emplacements.[15]

"Johnston could not have found a stronger defensive position for his great army," thought Oliver Otis Howard. This "natural fortress" was a better stronghold than the Federals held at Gettysburg, "and quite impossible to take." The adjutant of the Thirty-Second Illinois thought Kennesaw "was the most perfect natural fortification Sherman's army ever encountered." Its slopes were so steep and rugged, it almost seemed as if there was no need for trenches to stop an assault. When Confederate pickets guyed their opponents by calling out, "'Come up and see us,'" the Federals retorted, "'We're coming, waiting only for our ladders.'"[16]

Kennesaw also was a superb artillery platform, offering a commanding view of the surrounding countryside. On the morning of June 22, before the fight at Kolb's Farm began, Samuel French rode to the top of Little Kennesaw and saw the Federal bivouacs located near the base of the mountain. He could even smell their breakfast cooking. "It was tantalizing, that breakfast, not to be tolerated," so French told Storrs to open fire with his nine cannon. The gunners reduced the powder charge so as to drop shells near the base of the slope, and it caused the Yankees to scamper for cover. All day the guns roared as W. L. Truman fired 167 rounds from his piece in Guibor's battery alone.[17]

But the Federals had no intention of simply taking punishment without retort. They assembled a formidable array of artillery and opened fire on the morning of June 23. Now, it became apparent that Kennesaw could serve as a good target as well as a good platform for artillery fire. Guibor's battery lost its commander and four other men that day in the rain of shells. The guns were silent on June 24, but French ordered them into action at

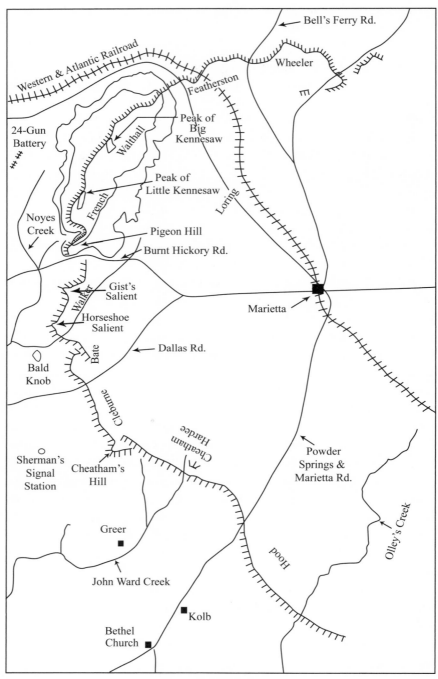

Kennesaw Line

Little Kennesaw and Pigeon Hill (Earl J. Hess)

10:00 A.M. on the 25th. That led to a furious return fire from at least forty Federal cannon lasting about an hour. The barrage sprayed the top of Little Kennesaw with shell fragments. One Union shell exploded an ammunition chest, as W. L. Truman estimated the enemy fired two thousand rounds at Little Kennesaw that day.[18]

While Sherman reported that the Confederate artillery did little harm to his lines, there is no doubt that it harassed his men. Everyone had to jump into the works, leaving camp equipment, tents, and animals exposed to shell fragments. The artillery exchange created a spectacle that touched the aesthetic sense of some Northerners. Henry Wright of the Sixth Iowa could never forget "the great cloud of white smoke rolling away from the enemy's guns on the crest of the mountain . . . floating away over the deep green of the forest covered hills, all tinged with the mellow glow of the setting sun."[19]

The fire of Storrs's guns on June 25 was hampered by the slow rate at which details hauled ammunition up from the base of the mountain. His crews had to cease fire during the exchange until the exhausted infantrymen managed to get more rounds to the top. This problem went beyond the logistical difficulties of resupplying guns on top of a mountain. Johnston reported that there was a general shortage of artillery ammunition in

Big Kennesaw from the east (Earl J. Hess)

the Army of Tennessee at Kennesaw, forcing his batteries to husband their reserves to repel an assault rather than expend it trying to counter the vigorous fire the Union guns laid down on the Confederate line.[20]

W. L. Truman noted a peculiar aspect of his position on Little Kennesaw Mountain. He claimed that Storrs's gunners could make it rain by simply firing up to ten rounds from each gun. Then "the clouds rush together with a low rumbling sound, and soon begin to pour out the rain upon us. When we stop firing, the rain will cease." This caused temporary springs to pop up on the mountainside about twenty feet down from the peak, providing fresh water for the gunners.[21]

The Federal works opposite Kennesaw Mountain became strong examples of field fortifications. The Confederate artillery fire, if nothing else, forced the Yankees to dig in for self-protection. While many Union batteries were placed in various locations, shielded by thick parapets, the Federals massed twenty-four guns in one location opposite the Kennesaw range on the night of June 22. This twenty-four-gun battery was ready to roar into action the next morning to counter Storrs's fire from Little Kennesaw.[22]

The area south of Kennesaw Mountain and north of Kolb's Farm was held by Hardee's Corps. Major General William H. T. Walker's division connected to French's left flank at Burnt Hickory Road, at the southern edge of Pigeon Hill, and extended southward along a low, irregular ridge that was mostly covered with timber. The irregularities forced Walker to bend his line to accommodate the terrain, forming both Gist's Salient and the Horseshoe Salient. The former was manned by the South Carolina troops of Brigadier General States R. Gist's brigade. Major General William B. Bate's division extended the line south of Walker's left flank and Major General Patrick R. Cleburne's division continued it south of the Dallas Road.[23]

Major General Benjamin F. Cheatham extended the Confederate line south of Cleburne's position. He sent Brigadier General Alfred J. Vaughan's Tennessee Brigade to start that process on the evening of June 19 and moved the rest of his division to prolong Vaughan's line on the night of June 20. While Vaughan occupied the same low ridge that Cleburne defended, Brigadier General George Maney's brigade took up a position to Vaughan's left that forced him to bend his line considerably. The ridge ended at a low hill next to a branch of John Ward Creek, but suitable ground south of the branch was located farther east. This forced Maney to place a portion of one regiment on the hill and the rest of his brigade along its border, facing south. Cheatham put the rest of his division south of the branch, and to the left and rear of Cheatham Hill, with a gap of 150 yards between the two wings of his command. A shallow salient was thus formed near the center of Cheatham's line.[24]

To make matters worse, Major Stephen W. Presstman and Confederate engineer officers had made a mistake while laying out the line in the dark. They staked it out a few yards farther up the slope of Cheatham's Hill than was required. As a result, the Confederate infantrymen could not fully see the ground in their front, partly shielded by the true military crest a few yards in front of their trench. It made the Confederate position less secure than it should have been. Men in the left regiments of Vaughan's brigade and the right regiments of Maney's brigade could not see more than twenty-five to forty yards ahead of their line. Farther right, the problem lessened to the point that Vaughan's men could see seventy-five yards away. Head logs placed on the parapet and abatis and other obstructions placed before the works were called for, but Cheatham's men would be busy for the next few days perfecting their trenches and skirmishing with Howard's Fourth Corps troops. As a result, many parts of the vulnerable line had none of these necessary adornments.[25]

The problem with the placement of the Confederate line at Cheatham's Hill became apparent when dawn of June 21 revealed the shape of the ground. Federal artillery began to pound the area early that morning, but there seemed little opportunity to correct the problem. Cheatham decided to stay and make the best of a bad situation. The angle in the line was often called the Devil's Elbow by the men who held it, while others called it the Dead Angle. The latter name derived both from the heavy casualties suffered there in the Federal attack of June 27 and from the fact that there was a considerable amount of ground not adequately covered by defending fire. In military parlance, that type of terrain was referred to as dead ground.[26]

To Maney's front, the low valley of another branch of John Ward Creek paralleled his line and that of Vaughan's brigade. A high ridge lay just west of the branch and some four hundred yards from the Rebel position. In short, the terrain seemed to offer the Federals some advantage in approaching the Dead Angle. Cheatham surveyed the terrain from afar on the morning of June 21 and decided that he should occupy the ridge with a skirmish line. This resulted in sporadic skirmishing with the Federals for the rest of the day, and Vaughan reinforced the skirmishers with a regiment from his brigade on June 22.[27]

Thomas was worried about all the skirmishing and ordered Howard to push the Confederates off this ridge on June 23. Fourth Corps artillery began pounding the position and Cheatham's main line from a distance of eight hundred to one thousand yards at about 1:00 P.M., tearing up the hastily constructed breastworks. The guns intensified their fire for half an hour before a reinforced skirmish line from Stanley's division moved forward at about 5:00 P.M. The Federals captured the ridge and forty Rebel prisoners, driving the rest away. Stanley's men then advanced across the valley and approached the Confederate main line. Cheatham witnessed all this and called on the consolidated First and Twenty-Seventh Tennessee of Maney's brigade, which held the angle, for assistance. He initially asked for one hundred men to volunteer to drive the Yankee skirmishers away, and the required number of troops began to cross the parapet. But a member of the consolidated regiment who was left behind yelled, "'Come on, boys, let us all go,'" and the entire unit moved forward together. It was able to stop and drive the enemy back but could not regain the ridge west of the creek valley. Vaughan sent the Fourth and Fifth Tennessee to hold the angle while Maney's men counterattacked. Hardee recalled both the bombardment and the skirmishing as among the heaviest he had seen during the campaign.[28]

The Federal guns continued firing on the morning of June 24, pounding the angle and partially enfilading Vaughan's left flank. Cheatham worried that his position would soon become untenable, that he might have to conduct a difficult withdrawal to a point three hundred yards to the rear under heavy fire. Fortunately for the Confederates, it seemed as if the Union gunners were unaware that their fire was having an effect, for they stopped after one hour. Cheatham concluded that they merely wanted to entice the Confederate guns to open and thus register their exact positions. He ordered his gunners to remain silent for the time and to mask their battery positions with brush. He also instructed brigade commanders to keep one-third of their men on watch in the trenches at all times. That night, Cheatham ordered his men to work on their fortifications, from the outside as well as the inside. Tools were issued, and the men willingly complied. The pounding had "knocked our works all into 'pi,' in fact, ruined them," commented a man in the First Tennessee. Logs, rocks, and spadefuls of red clay were put to use in an effort to make the fieldworks as strong as possible. The Confederates built their parapets seven feet tall and twelve feet thick, according to some accounts, with head logs along most of the length of the parapet and a firing step at the bottom of the trench. The men placed fence rails across the trench to catch a head log if Union artillery knocked it out of place, thus preventing it from falling on the troops. They dug cross ditches toward the rear so the men could shelter in them.[29]

Maney's men were less successful at placing obstructions before their line than they were in placing head logs on top of the parapet. In fact, most of Vaughan's line had ample abatis consisting of cut brush and tree limbs, while Maney's troops had little if any such advantage. Vaughan's troops had placed the abatis about thirty yards in front of their position, a good distance at which to force the attacking enemy to halt and receive short-range musketry. Vaughan's men had also cut some trees farther away from their line to clear a field of fire and create a slashing, with the felled timber pointing toward the approach of an enemy. The ground in front of Maney's position at the Dead Angle was much more open.[30]

The Confederates who defended this flawed segment of Johnston's line were tough veterans of many battles. Vaughan placed the Eleventh Tennessee on his left, connecting with Maney's brigade, and stretched the con-

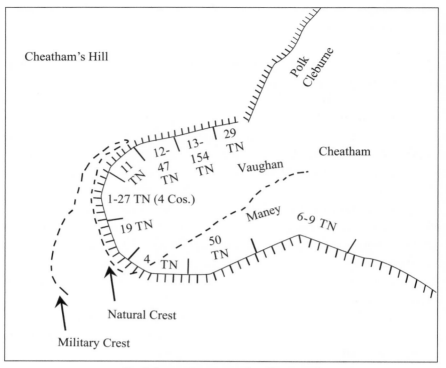

Cheatham's Hill

Polk

Cleburne

29 TN

12-47 TN

13-154 TN

11 TN

Vaughan

Cheatham

1-27 TN (4 Cos.)

19 TN

Maney

6-9 TN

50 TN

4 TN

Natural Crest

Military Crest

Confederate Troops on Cheatham's Hill

solidated Twelfth and Forty-Seventh Tennessee, the Thirteenth and 154th Tennessee, and the Twenty-Ninth Tennessee to the right. Four companies of the First and Twenty-Seventh Tennessee, of Maney's brigade, held the Dead Angle facing west, but the remainder of the brigade faced south. The First and Twenty-Seventh probably had no more than two hundred men on duty, and it was deployed in one rank with each man about two paces apart. It was, as one member of the First Tennessee put it, "rather a thin line." Maney deployed the Nineteenth Tennessee to the left of the First and Twenty-Seventh Tennessee, and then the Fourth Tennessee, Fiftieth Tennessee and the Sixth and Ninth Tennessee to complete the line north of the branch. South of the branch, Colonel John C. Carter's Tennessee Brigade continued the line and was able to lay down some oblique rifle fire on the area in front of Maney. But a more effective supporting fire could be laid down by a concentration of eight artillery pieces located on Carter's line that could enfilade the right flank of a Union column hitting the Dead Angle.[31]

The Confederates continued to strengthen their works on the night of June 25 as well. Those men positioned near the angle saw Cheatham, Hardee, and Johnston approach their position on the morning of June 26. The generals were worried about this flawed position, but Cheatham electrified the men's spirit by telling them, in the words of J. T. Bowden of the Twelfth Tennessee, that "we were going to be assaulted soon, that it was a weak place in the line, and that he didn't want a man to leave the ditches, that if they came so thick & fast we couldn't load & shoot, to catch them on our bayonetts & throw them to our rear, and that if we were over powered & captured, that he would go with us to prison." Talk like this had contributed to the devotion Cheatham's men felt toward him, and it worked beautifully to steel nerves weakened by Union artillery fire. According to a man in the First Tennessee, when Johnston told the troops that they could retire to a new line to the rear if pressed too heavily, the men refused. "Old Cheatham's boys were there & there to stay or die in the ditches," proudly asserted Bowden.[32]

The generals told Vaughan "that the safety of the army depended upon holding this position, and that it must be held if it required the sacrifice of every man in the regiments." As soon as the generals rode away on the morning of June 26, Colonel George W. Gordon of the Eleventh Tennessee began to coordinate a plan for infantry fire with neighboring units. He pointed out that some regiments could see in front of their neighbors' position better than the defending unit could, so they should fire obliquely to help each other in case of an attack. It was wise of Gordon to work out these plans well before the Yankees came.[33]

Cheatham carefully placed his available artillery, working with Colonel Melancthon Smith, who was chief of artillery in Hardee's Corps. The eight guns located south of the angle that Maney held consisted of Phelan's Alabama Battery of four Napoleons under Lieutenant Nathaniel Venable and Captain Thomas J. Perry's Florida Battery. To the north of the angle, two guns of Mebane's Tennessee Battery under Lieutenant Luke E. Wright were located about 175 yards from Maney's right flank, aimed so as to cross fire with the eight guns south of the angle and cover the immediate front of the Dead Angle.[34]

On the sector held by Cleburne's division, just north of Cheatham, the Confederates had no significant flaw in their position. The branch of John Ward Creek that separated Cleburne from the opposing Union line was merely a shallow depression filled with pine and blackjack trees. The ground was covered with leaves and pinecones, "which were like tinder" according to a member of Brigadier General Daniel C. Govan's Arkansas Brigade.

Govan's men cut blackjack saplings and laid them with sharpened limbs pointing toward the Federals in front of their trench. Cleburne stretched his available manpower thinly to cover the sector assigned his division.[35]

Skirmishing and artillery firing continued along Cleburne's line almost every day. "Sometimes it nearly amounts to a fight," reported Captain Sam Foster of Brigadier General Hiram B. Granbury's Texas Brigade, "then it eases off to the same old bang, bang, bang, like water droping off the eaves of a house. The bullets go zip zip over our breastworks day and night, making the men bow their heads." Federal dead left in no-man's-land from the skirmish fight of June 23 began to smell bad in the warm weather.[36]

Other than the danger posed by the Dead Angle, Johnston's Kennesaw Line was a formidable position. The Confederates endured heavy artillery fire and skirmishing all along the line for days, but deep trenches helped them to survive. The weather had finally dried up after nearly two weeks of heavy rain, but the effects of living in damp, muddy trenches were still being felt. Johnston reported that three hundred of his men reported sick every day as of June 26. Living conditions in the works produced a high demand for soap, with infrequent issues of the necessary article along the Union line and even less frequent issues along the Confederate position. Members of the Seventeenth Corps near Big Kennesaw Mountain often heard Rebel bands play in the evening. For days, the opposing armies seemed locked in an almost fraternal intimacy across the Georgia countryside.[37]

SHERMAN MAKES A DECISION

Although the Confederates had attacked at Kolb's Farm on June 22, Sherman knew he could not count on them to repeat that performance very often. The only alternatives open to him were to assault the front of Johnston's line or continue trying to find and turn his left flank. "Either course had its difficulties and dangers," Sherman later reported. Long after the confrontation at Kennesaw had ended, he tried to argue that it was important his own men learn that he could do more than merely flank a dangerous enemy out of a strong position. "An army to be efficient must not settle down to a single mode of offense, but must be prepared to execute any plan which promises success. I wanted, therefore, for the moral effect to make a successful assault against the enemy behind his breast-works, and resolved to attempt it at that point where success would give the largest fruits of victory." The decisive point seemed to be Johnston's left center. A strong Federal column penetrating the Confederate line there could possibly reach the railroad near Marietta and crack the Army of Tennessee in two.[38]

Many of Sherman's soldiers preferred the safer mode of flanking strong positions to save lives. Federal moves thus far in the confrontation at Kennesaw Mountain had indicated that flanking was Sherman's preferred mode of operation as well. Joseph Miller of the Seventy-Eighth Ohio in the Seventeenth Corps thought his commander intended to continue the least risky course of action. "Gen'l Sherman dont appear to be in any hurry about driveing Johnson away it appears as though he would rather besiege them than loose a lot of men by chargeing their works." The men in blue were keenly aware that, as James Naylor of the Eighty-First Ohio put it, Johnston had taken up the strongest position of the campaign since Rocky Face Ridge. But there were other Federal soldiers who tended to think along Sherman's developing line of reasoning that an attack might be necessary. Edwin C. Obriham of the Ninth Iowa in the Fifteenth Corps concluded that "we will have to carry the rebel works by an asault or we will never get them out of this place."[39]

Sherman indicated his firm resolve to attack on June 24, when he told Thomas that he wanted to force Johnston to stretch his line as thinly as possible before striking. He consulted with his three army commanders, and they supported his conclusion that the Federals "could not with prudence stretch out any more," in Sherman's words. "I ordered a general assault with the full cooperation of my great lieutenants," he recalled years later. In evaluating the reasons for the attack at Kennesaw, Howard compared Sherman's decision with Lee's at Gettysburg. Outflanking had also seemed a moot alternative to the commander of the Army of Northern Virginia when he had ordered attacks on Little Round top and Cemetery Ridge.[40]

Sherman's order for the attack, issued on June 24, involved a feint by McPherson against the Confederate left while the Army of the Tennessee's real assault was taking place against the left wing of Loring's Army of Mississippi. Thomas was to strike Hardee's Corps near the center of the Army of the Cumberland's line, and Schofield was to continue feeling for the Confederate left flank and attack Hood near the Powder Springs and Marietta Road. McPherson's skirmish line also was to be ready to ascend the heights of Kennesaw and take advantage of any opportunity. Sherman modified these instructions a bit on June 25, calling off the proposed attack by the Army of the Ohio and instructing Schofield to move Cox's division southward to find a crossing of Olley's Creek. This would, Sherman hoped, force

Johnston to draw more troops from the real points of McPherson's and Thomas's attacks.[41]

PREPARATIONS

Sherman's directive led to a flurry of activity during the next two days as his subordinates prepared for the assault. McPherson planned to make the main effort with Brigadier General Morgan L. Smith's division of the Fifteenth Corps and Osterhaus's division of the same corps in support. Smith commanded essentially the same division that Sherman had led in the battle of Shiloh. As Sixteenth Corps troops relieved Osterhaus, the two divisions were to pull out of the line on the afternoon of June 26 and replace Brigadier General Absalom Baird's division of the Fourteenth Corps, Thomas's leftmost unit opposite Little Kennesaw and Pigeon Hill. Blair would extend his Seventeenth Corps line farther to the right to cover the ground vacated by Morgan L. Smith and use Brigadier General Mortimer D. Leggett's division, supported by Brigadier General Kenner Garrard's division of cavalry, to threaten Johnston's right flank. As brigade commander Manning F. Force told a correspondent, Leggett's instructions were "to 'make a demonstration' to threaten Marietta[;] it was to be only a feint, but it must drive in the rebel skirmish line, and the order stated that we could not have reinforcements." McPherson also ordered that all skirmishers of the Sixteenth and Seventeenth Corps should press forward and try to get to the top of the mountain. Pioneers armed with entrenching tools were to move in behind the attack columns to dig in and hold all ground gained. "As little change as possible should be made in the appearance of things along our line," McPherson's order continued, "and the movements made with as much caution and as little noise as possible."[42]

Major General John A. Logan, commander of the Fifteenth Corps, finetuned the attack instructions. He decided to place Osterhaus in the center of the corps line, while Morgan L. Smith occupied the far right of his corps (and of McPherson's Army of the Tennessee). He also detailed Brigadier General Charles C. Walcutt's brigade of Brigadier General William Harrow's division to cooperate with Smith in the attack, and Osterhaus to be ready to help both Smith and Walcutt as needed. Captain Chauncey Reese, McPherson's chief engineer, selected the point of attack—the place where the Confederate line crossed Pigeon Hill and continued south on morelevel land. Although Reese did not explain his choice of targets, he and other officers knew that the Confederate line did not continue directly south from Pigeon Hill because of a sizable open field that lay next to the hill. The Rebel trench line was set back a couple of hundred yards farther east to take advantage of some woods. This small break in the enemy line may well have been seen as a vulnerable spot worth attacking. Logan's formation would straddle Burnt Hickory Road to compass both sides of the break in the Confederate line. Also, from the perspective of the Union line, Pigeon Hill seems a far less formidable terrain feature than do the two Kennesaws. It is possible the Fifteenth Corps officers assumed they could take it. Staff officers selected the best route for Morgan L. Smith and Osterhaus to take while getting into position for the assault.[43]

Thomas's Army of the Cumberland was responsible for launching two attacks, and Thomas designated one to be undertaken by Howard's Fourth Corps and the other by Major General John M. Palmer's Fourteenth Corps. Hooker planned to support the attack with oblique artillery fire and by moving his skirmish line forward to press Hood's men. Schofield's Army of the Ohio had its objective well set—to move south along Sandtown Road, cross Olley's Creek at almost any cost, and advance toward the railroad. The primary purpose was to divert attention from the attacks, but Cox was to take advantage of any opportunity that presented itself to achieve more than that limited goal. While Haskell's division contributed to the effort with diverting artillery fire, Stoneman would cover Cox's right flank with cavalry units.[44]

Preparations for the attack aroused a good deal of attention. The men could see and hear that something was in the air. Sherman, Thomas, Howard, and Stanley visited a battery emplacement that Lieutenant Chesley Mosman's pioneers were working on in Stanley's division sector, opposite Little Kennesaw and Pigeon Hill. One of the pioneers reportedly overheard Sherman say, "'Flanking is played out.'" A Fourteenth Corps division staff officer also heard rumors of a pending attack. "It is understood that Sherman says he will flank no more, but move directly on their works."[45]

To be in closer communication with his subordinates Sherman instructed his operatives to place a field telegraph line connecting him with McPherson, Thomas, and Schofield. He chose a hill near the center of Thomas's line, used pioneers to clear the hilltop of trees, and planned to make it his command post for the operation. As the Signal Corps strung the wire, infantrymen who were ignorant of its importance cut trees that fell on it. Sherman ordered Thomas to send patrols out to make sure this did not happen anymore. Captain Ocran H. Howard, McPherson's chief signal officer, reported that the telegraph was finished barely in time for the attack. It replaced the system of flag signals that he had operated before the wire was stretched, having established signal stations on Pine Mountain and Brush Mountain. Even though some distance to the rear, these stations maintained contact with observation points close to the front that were high enough to enable signalers to see each other.[46]

Sherman allowed Thomas to select the exact point of his attack, and Thomas allowed considerable latitude to his subordinates in deciding this important issue. Howard took advice from his division and brigade commanders and then chose the line held by Cleburne's division as the "least objectionable" target. Although no one said so, this target probably was chosen because the Federals had captured the ridge that lay only four hundred yards from Cleburne's and Cheatham's position on June 23, offering a fairly close starting point for Thomas's advance. Howard, Palmer, and Thomas "were for hours closeted together" to plan the attack. Howard ordered a column formation, stacking one regimental battle line behind the other to form a column of division, as the tactical manual called it. This would better conceal the formation before the attack and during the initial advance, Howard reasoned. If the men broke through, they could deploy into battle lines to exploit their success. Support units would remain in deployed lines. In this, Howard was also acting in accordance with prevailing tactical theory of the day. Dennis Hart Mahan, the influential professor at West Point, agreed with French theorists that columns were the best formation for attacking fortified positions. When Fourth Corps surgeons received orders to prepare for a large flow of wounded very soon, they cleared field hospitals by sending most of the sick to Big Shanty for transport north.[47]

Palmer also did a good deal of scouting to find a suitable place for his Fourteenth Corps troops to attack, and he chose Cheatham Hill. But Palmer later admitted that he had little faith in the enterprise. After scouting the position all morning with an orderly, dodging Confederate fire, Palmer "reported to General Sherman that this whole army could not carry the position." According to the corps leader, Sherman responded "that Joe Johnston must not consider any part of his line safe, and ordered the assault."[48]

JUNE 26

June 26 dawned as a dry, intensely warm day, good weather to resume operations. Schofield moved Colonel James W. Reilly's brigade of Cox's division down the Sandtown Road from Cheney's House and drove Confederate skirmishers across Olley's Creek. There, at the crossing, he reported that Reilly was confronted by at least a brigade of Confederate cavalry, plus artillery, on the other side of the valley. Reilly tried to cross the creek by advancing the 100th Ohio and the 104th Ohio, plus two guns of the Twenty-Third Indiana Battery, close to the bridge to draw Confederate attention. He then sent the Sixteenth Kentucky, 112th Illinois, Eighth Tennessee, Fifteenth Indiana Battery, and the other two guns of the Twenty-Third Indiana Battery on an obscure private road to cross the creek upstream. But the flanking column was stopped by a swamp and failed to achieve its purpose. Nevertheless, Sherman wanted Schofield to make a lot of noise in that area to draw Rebel troops from other parts of Johnston's line. Schofield did more than merely make noise. He moved Colonel Robert K. Byrd's brigade of Cox's division across Olley's Creek one mile north of the Sandtown Road crossing, and farther upstream than Reilly's abortive flanking maneuver. Then Byrd dug in on good defensive ground. "All right," Sherman responded when he learned the news. "Be careful of a brigade so exposed, but I am willing to risk a good deal." Byrd was in position to clear the Sandtown Road crossing the next day.[49]

Officers on all levels of command in the Fourth, Fourteenth, and Fifteenth Corps were busy preparing for their role in the attack during the course of the day and night of June 26. Benjamin T. Smith, a division-level orderly, saw corps commanders Howard, Hooker, and Palmer, along with division commanders Geary and Stanley, ride along the line of Union earthworks while reconnoitering. The group was so large that it drew the fire of Confederate skirmishers. Logan marshaled 5,500 men for the assault, while Howard positioned 5,000 of his Fourth Corps troops and Palmer 4,000 of his men in the Fourteenth Corps. These troops, totaling 14,500, represented the main strike force, but they were supported by many more in reserve.[50]

Logan had to rearrange the position of two-thirds of the Fifteenth Corps to place Morgan L. Smith in a good place to launch the attack, with Osterhaus in close support to his left. Some Fifteenth Corps units marched a total of five miles on the night of June 26 to accomplish that goal and did not finish until dawn of June 27.[51]

Harrow received an order to send Walcutt's brigade to help Morgan L. Smith and relayed the instruction to Walcutt. The brigade leader consulted with Smith, who told him he should strike into the gorge separating Little Kennesaw from Pigeon Hill. Some officers of Walcutt's command sensed that something was up when they saw high-ranking officers scouting the terrain, but official word of the pending operation was not divulged to the rank and file until late on the night of June 26. After maneuvering to gain a position from which to attack, word finally was given to everyone in Walcutt's brigade by about 9:00 P.M. When he learned what was to take place, Captain Charles W. Wills of the 103rd Illinois compared the ground to Lookout Mountain and gave up most of his confidence that the attack would succeed. He concluded his diary entry with the sentiment, "'good-bye, vain world,'" and then went to sleep.[52]

On the far Union left, Leggett prepared to demonstrate by advancing his skirmish line and scouting for a good position for his artillery. After dusk, Leggett moved his entire division up to the new line, cutting a road toward the new artillery position to place his guns. The area was cluttered with thick woods and rocky outcroppings, making it difficult to reposition the troops. Sixteenth Corps units replaced Osterhaus's division near McPherson's center, settling in with artillery and a strong skirmish line.[53]

Thomas had much the same work to do as McPherson, juggling units about because the place selected for his attack was held by a division that was not slated to conduct the assault. Stanley's division of the Fourth Corps held the Union line opposite Cheatham's Hill and Cleburne's division, but for reasons that are not clear, Howard chose Newton's division to make the assault. Rumor among Stanley's men had it that their division commander told Howard he would lose half his command and fail to break through, and did not want to make the charge. Newton, on the other hand, expressed confidence in the enterprise. Whether there was any truth to the rumor is difficult to know, but it is possible that Howard felt more confidence in Newton, who had also served in the Army of the Potomac during the early part of the war.[54]

Newton had to move his division to Stanley's sector on the night of June 26 and position it for the attack. Orders went out for the maneuver late in the afternoon, but some regiments did not start moving until 3:00 A.M. of June 27. Newton had some of the best troops in the Army of the Cumberland, which may be another reason Howard trusted the division to make this dangerous assault. Everyone was impressed by Brigadier General Charles G. Harker and the brigade he had long commanded. Described by one admirer as "a small but very handsome man, and all sunshine," the New Jersey born Harker had been a West Point cadet when Howard had taught mathematics at the academy. The corps leader remembered him as one of the most promising young men there. Harker had lived up to that promise. He commanded the Sixty-Fifth Ohio before assuming control of a brigade that saw action at Perryville, Stones River, and Chickamauga. He drilled his command until it outperformed every other unit in the corps and infused it with a high degree of discipline and self-confidence. Newton positioned his men to strike at Cleburne's front the next day.[55]

Thomas also moved Davis's division of the Fourteenth Corps all the way from the far left of the Union line to take position next to Newton, where it could assault Cheatham's Hill. Davis had maintained connection with McPherson's troops as a reserve, and now McPherson had to extend some of his own men into the space vacated by the division. Because they had the longest route to take, Thomas started Davis's troops after dusk on June 25 and allowed them to bivouac behind Stanley's line for the night. The men continued to rest all day of June 26 as their commanders scouted out the terrain. Still trying to live down the shooting of his superior, William Nelson, in September 1862, Davis was not daunted by the prospect before his troops. He could see that the Confederate line formed something of a salient and that the terrain before Cheatham's Hill was comparatively open. Baird's division took position to support Davis as needed, after it was replaced near Little Kennesaw by Morgan L. Smith.[56]

Davis's men had a difficult time marching through the countryside on the night of June 25, maneuvering through thick woods and crossing innumerable ravines. They took a roundabout course to avoid being seen in the glittering moonlight by the Confederates. Most of Davis's regiments marched about three to five miles, but it took all night to make that distance. The men rested as best they could on June 26, although they were not allowed fires for cooking and the weather was quite hot.[57]

THE GENERALS AND THE MEN

Sherman steeled his nerves on June 26 to convince himself that the decision to attack was the right one. "He is afraid to come at us," he told his wife about the enemy, "and we have been cautious about dashing against his breastworks, that are so difficult to understand in this hilly & wooded Country. My lines are ten miles long, and every change necessitating a larger amount of work. Still we are now all ready and I *must* attack direct or turn the position. Both will be attended with loss and difficulty but one or the other must be attempted. This is Sunday and I will write up all my letters and tomorrow will pitch in at some one or more points." Ellen Sherman was near to giving birth to another child, and Sherman wondered if he would be the equal of Willie, the nine-year-old son who had died of illness the previous September. "I would gladly surrender all the honors & fame of this life if I could see him once more in his loving confidence & faith in us, but we must now think of the living & prepare them for our exodus, which may be near at hand."[58]

Staff officers and brigade and regimental commanders had little time to muse about anything on the night of June 26. They were busy locating artillery, positioning units, and issuing rations and extra ammunition. When they did catch a few moments to think and converse, the subject of the attack often was attended with some degree of misgiving. Dodge recalled that this was a major topic of discussion in a conference of higher-ranking officers in the Army of the Tennessee. "Logan criticized the order saying that when it came to the killing, his command always got in." McPherson, according to Dodge, was "nettled" by Logan's petulance. He agreed that the chances of success were slim and suggested replacing Logan's men with one of Dodge's divisions. Logan's pride now took control of his emotions. "No, I do not want anyone to make a charge in front of me except my own division," he declared. McPherson went on to caution Logan about his doubts regarding the wisdom of the attack and the slender chances of success. "So much the more reason that we should put our energies and hearts into carrying it out, so that it shall not fail on account of our disapproval," he told his subordinate. Dodge recalled this instance as the only time he heard anyone in the Army of the Tennessee criticize an order.[59]

One of Davis's men, Nixon B. Stewart of the Fifty-Second Ohio, learned of the coming attack from a schoolmate of his, Captain Gordon Lofland on Morgan L. Smith's staff. The two happened to meet on the evening of June 26, and Lofland felt compelled to tell his friend of the operation. "'If successful, it will doubtless be the destruction of Johns[t]on's army,'" he told Stewart. "'Goodbye, and may you come out all right.'" As he rode away, Lofland called out, "'Let me hear from you when it is over.'" Stewart did not feel any particular sense of foreboding, but he seemed more appreciative of the small things in life after meeting Lofland. "There was such a beautiful sunset that evening," he recalled. "The trees and woods seemed touched and set on fire."[60]

The next day, a Confederate soldier rifled the pockets of a dead Federal soldier who had participated in Sherman's attack and found a diary. "Tomorrow we charge Kennesaw Mountain," its last entry read, "and will take it like a d-n."[61]

Four. The Fifteenth Corps Attack

The sun rose in a clear sky early on the morning of June 27, and the temperature began to climb with it. Before long it was very warm and became uncomfortably hot before the day was out. Sherman advised McPherson to have plenty of orderlies at Army of the Tennessee headquarters to carry messages to all parts of his line. "Keep me well advised, as I must work the flanks according to the progress in the center," he told his friend and subordinate. Signal officers also maintained a close watch on developments from posts along Logan's sector.[1]

Federal guns roared into action at 6:00 A.M.; fifty-one pieces alone were arrayed along McPherson's front. As they pounded the enemy, Logan superintended the preparations for his corps attack. Three brigades made ready to go in. Brigadier General Charles C. Walcutt's Second Brigade of Harrow's Fourth Division, with 1,500 men, aimed at the saddle between Pigeon Hill and Little Kennesaw. To his right, Brigadier General Giles A. Smith's First Brigade of Brigadier General Morgan L. Smith's Second Division, with 2,000 men, aimed directly at Pigeon Hill. Still farther to the right, south of Burnt Hickory Road, Brigadier General Joseph A. J. Lightburn's Second Brigade of Smith's division, with 2,000 men, aimed at the flat land south of Pigeon Hill. McPherson's army threw only 5,500 troops into the attack. Walcutt was scheduled to advance first, and the other two brigades would set out when they heard the sound of firing.[2]

Federal officers tried to prepare their men for the ordeal to come. Giles A. Smith required the presence of the top three officers in each of his regiments to attend a conference at brigade headquarters. They assembled "under a hickory tree" at 7:00 A.M. Captain Alvah Stone Skilton of the Fifty-Seventh Ohio remembered what Smith told them. "'This column has been selected as a *forlorn hope* and we are expected to carry the enemy's works in our front.'" According to Skilton, Smith warned that their men would have to hold whatever ground they occupied at the end of the attack until help arrived. "'Gentlemen this will be serious business and some of us must go down,'" Smith told them. In case any regimental commanders were shot, the brigade leader designated who should take over in each regiment so there would be no confusion when the bullets started to rain. "'May God Bless and protect you all,'" Smith concluded.[3]

By the time the officers returned to their regiments, there was no more than half an hour to tell the men and prepare for the attack. Everyone gulped down some food, and each company commander detailed one man to guard the knapsacks and haversacks of his comrades. The mood was quiet and resigned among members of the Fifty-Fifth Illinois as some troops gave their precious belongings to the chaplain or "wrote brief notes and placed them in their knapsacks." Captain Jacob M. Augustine, who commanded the Fifty-Fifth that day, wrote a note and stuffed it in one of his books. "Our division takes the lead. Now may God protect the right. Am doubting our success," it read.[4]

Morgan L. Smith noted that his men started the attack precisely as planned, at 8:00 A.M., after two hours of intense bombardment. Walcutt's brigade set out and immediately drew Rebel fire, which was the signal for the other two brigades to begin. Because Lightburn's movements shaped what happened not only on his own front but on that of Giles Smith's as well, we will look at what happened to those two Fifteenth Corps brigades before discussing Walcutt's attack.[5]

LIGHTBURN

Joseph Andrew Jackson Lightburn had been born in Pennsylvania but moved with his family to western Virginia. He was a member of the convention that set in motion a movement to separate the mountainous western counties from the seceded state of Virginia and eventually create West Virginia. Lightburn also commanded the Fourth West Virginia and led a brigade in the Fifteenth Corps at Vicksburg and Chattanooga. Although he had served in the regulars during the Mexican War, he was not a West Pointer.[6]

Lightburn's men awoke early and deposited their knapsacks at the brigade's bivouac area before moving a mile to the right to form just behind the Union line of earthworks, south of Burnt Hickory Road. They made two lines with the Fifty-Third Ohio on the right of the first line, and the Eighty-Third Indiana and Thirtieth Ohio arrayed to its left. On the second line, the

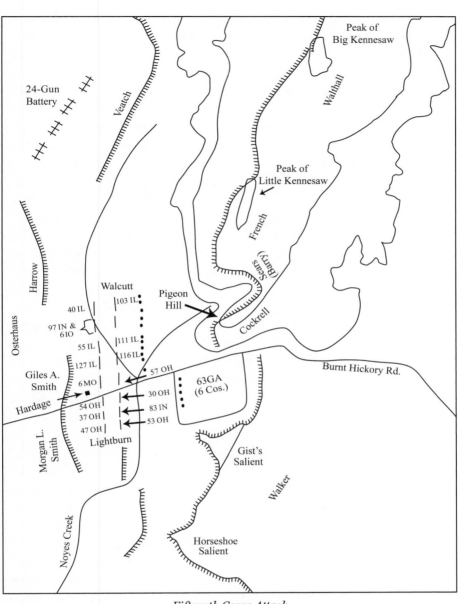

Fifteenth Corps Attack

Forty-Seventh Ohio anchored the right with the Thirty-Seventh Ohio and Fifty-Fourth Ohio to its left.[7]

The brigade began to advance shortly after 8:00 A.M. to the sound of bugles. Lightburn's men crossed earthworks that had been constructed by the Army of the Cumberland several days before and which were now held by Osterhaus's division. Initially the men passed over an open field at the double quick, pelted by Confederate artillery fire the whole way. The brigade stopped to re-form at the edge of a thickly timbered bottomland that bordered a shallow branch before plunging into the trees. The bottomland, which girdled a branch of Noyes Creek, proved to be a difficult obstacle because of the tangled brush. Struggling through at least 150 yards of this matted jungle, Lightburn's men neared the edge of another open field before discovering a fortified Confederate skirmish line. Because of the vines, bushes, and pine trees in the bottomland, the Federals had been able to catch glimpses of this Rebel position only when they were twenty to thirty yards away from it.[8]

The Confederate skirmish pits were held by members of the Sixty-Third Georgia of Brigadier General Hugh W. Mercer's brigade, Major General William H. T. Walker's division in Hardee's Corps. The Georgians were surprised to see the Federals approach, "they creaped up on us before we were aware," as an unidentified member of the regiment put it. He had just come off duty from his vidette post about thirty yards inside the timbered bottomland when the Yankees made their appearance and "came right to our ditches." Lightburn's line was disorganized by the struggle through the bottomland, but there was no opportunity to re-form. The Federals threw themselves onto the Georgians, with the Fifty-Third Ohio bearing the brunt of the short but intense struggle that followed. Hand-to-hand combat erupted, the only instance of this rare type of fighting that the Fifty-Third experienced in its war service. The men of both sides used bayonets and clubbed muskets. "Never did men show more gallantry," reported an officer of the Fifty-Third Ohio, "shooting the enemy, and beating them over their heads with the butts of their guns." In fact, sixteen members of the regiment completely destroyed their muskets by using them in this way. One large Confederate was about to smash Colonel Wells S. Jones with his gun, but Jones had the presence of mind to order him to stop and give up. The Rebel obeyed him.[9]

Members of the Forty-Seventh Ohio came upon the scene just before the brief fight ended, and they helped the Fifty-Third Ohio consolidate control of the Rebel skirmish line. The Forty-Seventh men apparently had no bayonets to use in this fight but relied entirely on their muskets to substitute for clubs. It was an uneven struggle, to be sure. Only six companies of the Sixty-Third Georgia held the pits with the other four in reserve. This regiment had seen little active service since its organization, having performed garrison duty along the Atlantic coast. It had reached Johnston's army only six weeks before the confrontation at Kennesaw Mountain. The veterans of Hardee's Corps tended to call these men "'holiday soldiers.'" It had an effect on them. "Stung by this unmerited epithet," wrote Hardee's staff officer Thomas Benton Roy, many Georgians fought to the last in their skirmish pits rather than run away. Others, however, retreated hastily. "Our company went off it seemed to me like a flock of sheep," reported William O. Norrell of Company B, "though they had the company of other portions of the Regt." The four reserve companies started forward to help their comrades but could not reach them in time to take part in the struggle.[10]

The Sixty-Third Georgia lost heavily in this short fight. About forty men were killed and wounded, and another forty were taken prisoner. After hearing a report that the Federals managed to get past the right flank of the Georgians' skirmish line, Walker blamed the defeat on French's division. "I lost over 100 of my skirmishers yesterday," he berated French on June 28, "they were flanked and attacked by a line of battle. They were butted and bayoneted from the pits." French rightly pointed out that his line of responsibility started at the southern foot of Pigeon Hill. Lightburn's approach lay entirely south of that point. The Confederate skirmish line fell because the Federals brought an overwhelming force to bear on it, not because of a failure by French's skirmishers to hold their line.[11]

But the failure of Walker's skirmishers to maintain their position permitted Lightburn to maneuver and threaten French. After taking the skirmish pits, the Fifty-Third Ohio re-formed and continued to advance. The men managed to move two hundred yards across the open area south of Pigeon Hill before they realized they were receiving fire from both flanks as well as from the front. Jones now called on them to stop and lie down for protection behind a slight crest which offered comparatively little shelter. The men returned the fire as best they could, but with little effect. To the left of the Fifty-Third, the Eighty-Third Indiana and Thirtieth Ohio came up to extend the forward position of Jones's command.[12]

Lightburn's second line apparently did not come up to support the first line at this time, although the accounts are not entirely clear on that point.

Pigeon Hill and the open field (Earl J. Hess)

On the far left of Lightburn's second line, the Fifty-Fourth Ohio separated into two wings with the left advancing northward and the right moving east into the open field to within fifty yards of Walker's main line before stopping.[13]

Lightburn's advance proved the fallacy of Federal expectations that the area south of Pigeon Hill was a vulnerable sector of the Confederate position. Despite the loss of the skirmish line, Rebel troops had no difficulty stopping Lightburn's brigade in the middle of the open field. In fact, the Federals were in a vulnerable position and saved themselves only by lying prone behind the slight rise of ground in the middle of the field.

But Lightburn's exposed position in the open field south of Pigeon Hill gave the Federals an opportunity to threaten French's leftmost unit, Brigadier General Francis M. Cockrell's Missouri Brigade. The left wing of the Fifty-Fourth Ohio moved north against the flank of Cockrell's skirmish line north of Burnt Hickory Road. By rushing the skirmish reserve to that point, Lieutenant Colonel Thomas M. Carter, who commanded Cockrell's skirmish line that day, was able to temporarily stop the Ohioans. But then Giles A. Smith's Yankees advanced against Carter's front with overwhelming force. Smith pushed forward on Carter's left wing, forcing the Rebel skirmishers to give way. At the same time, the left wing of the Fifty-Fourth

Ohio of Lightburn's brigade swept northward along the base of Pigeon Hill.[14]

Carter could not prevent the left wing of Cockrell's skirmish line from collapsing, but he managed to hold the right wing in place for a time. This stalled Smith's advance on his front until the Fifty-Fourth Ohioans began to penetrate the area behind Carter's right and in front of Cockrell's main line. Carter now told the men of his right wing to fall back as fast as possible. Many of them tried to burst through the Federal formation and were captured in the process. Other Confederate skirmishers decided to move northward, toward the gorge between Pigeon Hill and Little Kennesaw, with Ohioans only thirty or forty paces behind them in pursuit. Cockrell lost forty-one men on his skirmish line that morning.[15]

Samuel Gibbs French was one of the more capable division commanders in Loring's Army of Mississippi. Born in New Jersey, he graduated from West Point in 1843 and was wounded while serving in the artillery at the battle of Buena Vista. His marriage into a Mississippi planter family sealed French's loyalty to the South, which led to service in Virginia, North Carolina, and Mississippi before the Atlanta campaign.[16]

French tried his best to shore up Cockrell's brigade and protect the division's left flank. He and his staff had perched on a large rock between the Rebel artillery on top of Little Kennesaw Mountain and the main Confederate line a short distance down the western slope. From there, they saw the appearance of Lightburn's brigade in the edge of the open field south of Pigeon Hill, and they caught glimpses of the hand-to-hand struggle at the skirmish pits. French ordered several of his guns to move to the western extremity of Little Kennesaw and lay down fire on the open field.[17]

W. L. Truman of Guibor's Missouri Battery clearly saw the line of blue as Lightburn's formation crossed the open ground. Three guns of the battery were wheeled into position to hit that formation, sending their rounds over Cockrell's men on Pigeon Hill. "We plunged the shells among them, as fast as we could load," Truman recalled years later. "I saw their flag go down three times, and as often picked up and kept in front, it was to me an awful sight, to witness so many men being killed and wounded." Colonel Ellison Capers of the Twenty-Fourth South Carolina, in Walker's line just south of Mercer's brigade, credited the "raking artillery fire" from Little Kennesaw Mountain with playing a large role in stopping Lightburn's advance. Cockrell sent a staff officer to ask Mercer for help, but, as French was careful to report, neither Mercer nor Walker ordered his available artillery to help French's guns lay down fire on the enemy.[18]

If Logan's attack had any chance of success, it seemed to lay in the coopera-tion of Smith's and Lightburn's brigades around Pigeon Hill. Giles Alex-ander Smith held ample credentials for the task. The younger brother of his division commander, Morgan L. Smith, the two had been born in up-state New York. A businessman and hotelkeeper in Ohio and Illinois, Giles served as a captain in his brother's regiment, the Eighth Missouri, and later replaced Morgan as colonel of the unit. He commanded a brigade at Chickasaw Bayou, Arkansas Post, and Vicksburg and was wounded at Mis-sionary Ridge.[19]

Smith formed his brigade in two lines about one hundred yards in front of the works held by Osterhaus's division and just behind the Federal skir-mish line. His men were located north of Burnt Hickory Road. The Fifty-Seventh Ohio held the right of the first line, with the 116th and 111th Illi-nois to the left. In the second line, the Sixth Missouri anchored the right as the 127th Illinois and Fifty-Fifth Illinois deployed to the left. The ground ahead was obscured by vegetation, and no one in Smith's brigade knew much about what to expect before they reached the Confederate line six hundred yards ahead.[20]

The Federals moved forward a little after 8:00 A.M. and found the terrain worse than they had imagined. Smith traversed the same branch of Noyes Creek that had proved such an obstacle for Lightburn. The underbrush was so dense and matted that his men had to "crawl almost on their hands and knees through the tangled vines." It helped a bit when they pulled the bushes aside to create room to worm through. The brigade was preceded by a skirmish line, but it moved so slowly because of the vegetation that the skirmishers nearly merged with Smith's main formation. Nevertheless, the skirmishers emerged from the bottomland and engaged Cockrell's skir-mishers near the foot of Pigeon Hill. The main force of Smith's brigade managed to negotiate up to 200 yards of jungle before entering a narrow open space in front of the hill, where they stopped briefly to re-form their ranks.[21]

Now the combined weight of Smith's skirmishers and his main line, along with the advance of the left wing of the Fifty-Fourth Ohio of Lightburn's brigade, forced Cockrell's skirmishers to give way with heavy losses. The Federals managed to strip away the protective cover of the Confederate position on Pigeon Hill.[22]

After a short halt, Smith's main line moved forward to reach the foot of

Giles A. Smith (Library of Congress, LC-DIG-cwpbh-00495)

Pigeon Hill. From the perspective of Lieutenant George W. Warren of the Fifth Missouri on top of the hill, they appeared as "a solid line of blue emerging from the woods, a hundred yards below us." Smith's troops then began to ascend the slope. The hill had many rocky outcroppings, covered with a thin layer of felled trees described by one observer as "stunted, scraggy oaks." The obstacles broke up the Union formation, and soon a swarm of blue-coated men were scrambling among the rocks and trees. "There could be no concert of action and little leadership," commented the historian of the Fifty-Fifth Illinois; "each had to climb or shelter himself and fight as he best could." Cheering to keep up their spirit, the Federals suffered from rifle fire delivered by Cockrell's Missourians from their secure works located near the top of Pigeon Hill, where they could command the entire slope. Cockrell's men rested their musket barrels on the rock and dirt parapet

Cockrell's trench on Pigeon Hill (Earl J. Hess)

that sheltered them and took steady aim. Also, Confederate batteries to the north poured in a searing cross fire.[23]

It was impossible to maintain formation or momentum going up the cluttered slope of the hill, especially with heavy fire pouring into the Federals from two directions. As losses mounted, the attack came to a halt with the leading edge of Smith's brigade (about sixty men) lodged only fifteen to thirty yards short of Cockrell's main line. Many officers were shot down at this close range as they scurried about to encourage their men. Even enlisted troops sometimes exposed themselves to boost their comrades' morale. George W. Crowell of the Fifty-Fifth Illinois jumped atop a tree trunk to swing his hat and was shot down almost immediately.[24]

The Yankees failed to close in on the Rebel position on some sectors held by the Missouri Brigade. On the far left of his line, Cockrell reported that the enemy did not climb up the slope at all. That was because the Fifty-Seventh Ohio, the rightmost regiment on Smith's first line, did not extend that far south. The Fifty-Seventh approached Colonel James McCown's consolidated Third and Fifth Missouri, the second regiment from the left of Cockrell's line, and lodged twenty-five paces away. The Confederates could hear Union officers encourage their troops. Moreover, Walcutt's brigade by now was penetrating the gorge between Pigeon Hill and Little Kennesaw Mountain, putting pressure on the far right of Cockrell's line.[25]

Francis Marion Cockrell commanded one of the elite brigades of the Confederate army in the West. His Missourians had been in active service since the early days of the war in their state, initially as part of Major General Sterling Price's Missouri State Guard before their transfer to Confederate national service. They were tough veterans of Wilson's Creek, Pea Ridge, Corinth, and the siege of Vicksburg. Cockrell had been born in Missouri and had practiced law in addition to serving as a Missouri militia officer. He had shared with his troops all the trials of battles in Missouri, Arkansas, and Mississippi before the Atlanta campaign.[26]

Cockrell barely had room on Pigeon Hill for his brigade. Because of the size of the crest and the presence of a large rock outcropping, he could plant only one battery on the hill. The guns were silent because of the weight of Union artillery fire that had descended on Pigeon Hill for two hours before the attack. But Cockrell's infantrymen were firing so heavily that many units ran out of ammunition. James McCown called for volunteers to bring more cartridges to his consolidated Third and Fifth Missouri, and W. J. Ervin and his brother, John A. Ervin, ran across the top of the hill to the rear. They knew that a supply of ordnance was located near the eastern base of the hill. The officer in charge of the ammunition, however, insisted on a written requisition, but there was no time to go back for one. W. J. Ervin offered his loaded musket instead and persuaded the officer to give the brothers three thousand cartridges. Each one carried a box on their shoulder and shared the weight of a third box between them. The brothers managed to cross the top of Pigeon Hill unhurt, dodging Union artillery rounds, before reaching their regiment.[27]

From his command post on the western slope of Little Kennesaw Mountain, French could not see Smith's Federals as they struggled up the slope of Pigeon Hill. He therefore was surprised to receive a message from Cockrell at about 9:00 A.M. that the Missouri Brigade needed help. French ordered Matthew Ector to send two regiments from his position on the west slope of Little Kennesaw. A bit later, a second message for aid arrived, and French personally escorted more troops from Ector's command toward the left. The firing continued at a high pitch of intensity. "So severe and continuous was the cannonading," reported French, "that the volleys of musketry could scarcely be heard at all on the line."[28]

Smith's attack was like the surge of an ocean wave against a rocky shore. It reached a high tide close to the target, but there was little opportunity to stay there. Cockrell reported that the Fifty-Seventh Ohio remained close to his line in front of McCown's Third and Fifth Missouri for only about fifteen or twenty minutes. Colonel Americus V. Rice was "severely wounded in the right leg, the left foot, and forehead," reported Lieutenant Colonel Samuel R. Mott. As the Federals to the left of the Fifty-Seventh began to retire, Mott assumed command of the regiment. Because he happened to be on the left wing, Mott told the men there to stay down and remain in place. Companies G, B, E, K, H, and A did so, but the other four companies on the right wing began to fall back because their position had less shelter from Cockrell's musketry.[29]

The four companies on the regiment's right wing retired with great difficulty, and Captain Alvah Stone Skilton improvised a method to get the regimental flag back down the slope. He was taking shelter about fifteen feet behind, and lower than, where the color-bearer lay. Skilton told the man to pass the flag to him low to the ground, and then he furled the colors by twisting the staff. Skilton then clambered down slope during a comparative lull in the firing. Near the base of Pigeon Hill, he gave the flag to Sergeant Samuel Winegardner and told him to display it as a rallying point for the regiment. It took a full hour for the Fifty-Seventh to assembly near Winegardner's position, in part because Mott still held the left wing at high tide for some time. During that period, members of the regiment carefully brought their injured colonel down the hill. When Rice reached the base of the slope, Skilton improvised a stretcher by tying blankets between two muskets and assigned men to carry him to the Union line. The next day, Federal surgeons amputated one of his legs "above the knee." Rice had barely recovered from a serious wound received at the siege of Vicksburg a year before.[30]

Samuel Mott was greatly puzzled by the withdrawal of the Fifty-Seventh Ohio's right wing, so he went down the slope to find out why it had abandoned the rest of the regiment. There he learned that Giles A. Smith had authorized the fallback by sending an orderly with word to retire. The orderly had passed on the order to someone in the right wing, whether before it had begun to fall back or after is unclear. But the orderly apparently declined to approach the regiment's left wing to deliver Smith's message. The only thing Mott could do was to climb back up the hill and bring his men down. He had to leave Company A in place, however, because it was lodged closer to Cockrell's line than any other part of the regiment. The men of Company A were forced to stay until dark, only ten to fifteen steps from the Missouri Rebels.[31]

Although Mott did not mention it in his report, he apparently stayed on the slope with Company A for the rest of that long, hot day. He and the men of Company A endured a grueling experience, exposed to the sun without food or water, and under the gaze of watchful Confederates the whole time. Dusk brought a welcome chance to escape the ordeal. The men broke off one by one and made their way down Pigeon Hill.[32]

On the far left of Giles A. Smith's second line, the Fifty-Fifth Illinois lodged close to the Rebel position with no support to its right or left. When a bugle sounded retreat, Captain Jacob M. Augustine misinterpreted the call and stood up, moved ahead a couple of steps, and called out, "'Forward, men!'" Augustine presented "for one moment the grandest figure in the terrible scene," wrote the historian of the Fifty-Fifth Illinois. But then he was shot in the left breast. At this close range, the bullet passed through his body. "His fall visibly disheartened the regiment," reported the regimental historian, "though a few men got closer under the rebel parapet, any attempt at further forward movement ceased." Captain Francis H. Shaw took charge of the regiment and brought it down the slope. Two men carefully took Augustine down the hill as well. The captain was awake the whole time, giving orders for his men to lay down a covering fire to protect those who still had not retired from their forward position. Augustine died an hour after his brother, Lieutenant Henry Augustine, reached his side. One of the two men who had carried the captain down the hill, Joseph Putnam, was shot in the thigh while looking for a stretcher to take Augustine to the main Union line. Putnam bled to death because the ball not only broke the thighbone but cut an artery as well.[33]

Some members of the Fifty-Fifth Illinois remained longer on the slope than others and made their way back during the course of the day. One of the last to come away was Charles Merrill, who stopped near the base of Pigeon Hill to look back at the enemy and was shot through the heart for his trouble. Perhaps it was the color-bearer of the Fifty-Fifth Illinois who so impressed Major Charles Dana Miller of the Seventy-Sixth Ohio, in Osterhaus's division. Miller reported seeing a man bring a Union flag down Pigeon Hill to the rear, cradling the color with his left arm because his right was "shot away with the blood streaming from his ragged stump. He held the colors erect until they reached their former position, then laid down and died."[34]

The heat of the morning caused much suffering among the wounded. It is possible, as contended by the historian of the Fifty-Fifth Illinois, that the moist, hot air contributed to the early death of some wounded Federals before the surgeons could attend to them. Medical personnel could not save Captain William C. Porter, who had been hit in the left thigh and was carried from the slope by two of his men. Porter died from loss of blood at 4:00 P.M. that day. He had married only a few months before during his veteran furlough. Soon after his men buried him, a Rebel shell landed so close to the grave as to nearly move his body out of it. It seemed as if the Confederates were "begrudging him his six feet of Southern soil."[35]

Giles A. Smith's men continued to suffer from enemy fire even after they retired from the slope of Pigeon Hill. Lieutenant William D. Lomax and Sergeant James W. Kays of Company K, Fifty-Fifth Illinois, were both hit by the same bullet while passing a canteen between them. The ball penetrated Kays's left thigh and smashed into Lomax's right hip, but both men survived.[36]

While many survivors of the attack retired to the main Federal line, others remained near the base of Pigeon Hill to begin digging a new line much closer to the enemy. The same was true of Lightburn's brigade after it retired from its high tide in the open field south of Pigeon Hill. Lightburn's men assembled at the captured Confederate skirmish pits on the east edge of the timbered bottomland. Here, Captain Aaron B. Chamberlain of the Thirtieth Ohio was decapitated by a Confederate shell, which exploded a second later and took off both of his arms as well. The Thirtieth fell back across the wooded bottomland and tried to re-form on the west edge of the trees, but here the rain of Confederate artillery was even worse. While trying to form a line, a shell drilled right through the color-corporal and tore off the arms of the color-sergeant and the legs of another man. When it exploded in the process, fragments wounded several other men too. The shaken regimental commander ordered his men to fall back to the main Union line "by small squads" and re-form behind the works. Colonel Augustus C. Parry of the Forty-Seventh Ohio was "severely wounded in the leg" while his regiment retired to the Federal line.[37]

But the Thirty-Seventh and Fifty-Fourth Ohio of Lightburn's brigade secured control of the eastern side of the bottomland before the Confederates advanced skirmishers to retake their former position. The Federals were joined by the Fifty-Third Ohio, which retreated from its high tide by standing up and cheering as if the men intended to charge. They fell back instead and reinforced the developing Union position at the former Rebel skirmish pits. Along some parts of Walker's division line, the Federals safely dug in only one hundred yards in front of the main Confederate position, and it proved impossible for Mercer to establish a picket line. The Thirty-Seventh Ohio, Fifty-Third Ohio, and Fifty-Fourth Ohio were relieved by other Union troops at 11:00 that night.[38]

Smith's brigade had tested Cockrell's position on Pigeon Hill and found it secure. McCown's Third and Fifth Missouri, holding the part of the line most severely pressed, had fired sixty rounds per man in the hour-long fight. McCown was able to deliver such a concentrated fire, amounting to one round per minute per man, because the Ervin brothers had brought forward extra ammunition. Cockrell counted thirty dead Federals left behind along his brigade front, including several officers, because they were "so close to my lines that they could not be carried off." The Missourians also recovered several Federal wounded and one or two unwounded prisoners. Information gathered from the prisoners and found in the memo books on the dead Federals indicated to Cockrell that he had fought members of the Fifteenth Corps. The Missouri Rebels and Fifteenth Corps troops had met each other along the siege lines at Vicksburg as well. Cockrell had repelled Smith's attack by his own resources, before the reinforcements from Ector arrived. He lost 109 men in the battle, with McCown's consolidated regiment losing 36 of that total.[39]

WALCUTT

The brigade that started the Fifteenth Corps attack was commanded by a descendant of veterans of the American Revolution and the War of 1812. Charles Carroll Walcutt had been born in Ohio, but he graduated from the Kentucky Military Institute three years before the firing on Fort Sumter. As an officer in the Forty-Sixth Ohio, Walcutt received a bullet in the shoulder at the battle of Shiloh and carried it for the rest of his life. The injury did not prevent him from participating in the Vicksburg siege and the battles for Chattanooga. He was one of the best brigade commanders in Logan's corps.[40]

Early on the morning of June 27, Walcutt brought his troops to a position several hundred yards behind the Union line, where they deposited their knapsacks and other personal belongings, keeping only a canteen full of water and their weapons. Alert Confederate gunners noticed the movement and began to target the brigade when it formed in front of the line. Rebel skirmishers also took potshots at Walcutt's formation, hitting several men before the advance started. Walcutt formed his units in two lines, like the other Fifteenth Corps brigades, with the 103rd Illinois on the far left of the first line and the Fortieth Illinois to its rear in the second line. Captain Joshua W. Heath deployed the Forty-Sixth Ohio as skirmishers in front of the brigade. Heath's men immediately answered the skirmish fire of the enemy, but they could not keep bullets from sailing on to continue striking soldiers in Walcutt's main line.[41]

Walcutt wasted little time in forming, so the exposure to enemy fire was kept to a minimum. But the waiting time was long enough for Captain Charles W. Wills of the 103rd Illinois to scrawl a thought and an emotion in his diary just before setting off. "If we are successful with a loss of only half our number in this mountain charging," Wills mused, "I will think our loss more than repaid. I believe we are going to thoroughly whip Johnston to-day, and if we fail I do not care to live to see it."[42]

Heath led the Forty-Sixth Ohio forward at 8:00 A.M. and overwhelmed the Confederate skirmish line fronting Walcutt's brigade. Estimates of the number of Rebel prisoners taken range from 50 to 120, and Heath's men also killed quite a few of the enemy. An observer later noticed 5 Confederates lying so close to their lieutenant as to nearly touch each other near the skirmish pits, which indicated how intense the fighting must have been. After clearing the way, Heath's men ascended the rugged slope of the gorge between Pigeon Hill and Little Kennesaw until coming to rest about fifteen yards from the Confederate works. Here, according to an officer of the Forty-Sixth Ohio, their progress was stalled "by the perpendicularity of the rocks."[43]

Walcutt started his main formation soon after the skirmishers set out, with the sound of a bugle signaling the beginning of the attack. "A column never charged more gallantly or with greater determination," Walcutt wrote of his men. The troops had to negotiate the same branch of Noyes Creek that fronted Lightburn and Giles A. Smith, "covered with a dense undergrowth of oak and vines of all kinds," Charles Wills wrote, "binding the dead and live timber and bush together, and making an almost impenetrable abatis." It was impossible to maintain a tight formation in this environment so the men were largely on their own.[44]

After crawling for nearly three-quarters of a mile through the vegetation, the Federals emerged onto the comparatively open area at the foot of the mountain. There apparently was no effort to stop and re-form the brigade; every regimental commander operated as best he could with the men he had under his control as the brigade continued, "broken and scattered," up the slope.[45]

Charles Wills spoke for all when he later reported that no one had a very clear idea of what they were supposed to do, other than advance straight ahead until hitting the enemy works. But the 103rd Illinois entered an area where the Confederate line curved to accommodate the gorge. As Wills's company advanced, it entered the gorge but could not catch sight of the Rebel works until the enemy position suddenly became apparent to their right about sixty yards away. Wills now realized his company was moving parallel to the trench, not directly toward it. One of his men pointed to the Rebels and asked, "'Look there, Captain, may I shoot?'" Wills took a moment to examine the situation. He noticed that a deep ravine lay between his company and the Confederate line, and he saw a mass of Rebels moving up the slope of the gorge in front of the line. Undoubtedly, these were the dispersed skirmishers of Cockrell's brigade escaping from the combined pressure of Lightburn and Giles A. Smith. The right wing of the 103rd Illinois had seen the Rebel position and had redirected its line of advance to attack it, but the three left companies (K, G, and B) had not noticed it and were still advancing parallel to the enemy. Wills thought that the Confederates had "no excuse for not annihilating" the three companies at such a short range.[46]

Wills ordered his company to turn right and attack the line, in concert with the right wing of the 103rd Illinois. The men did their best. They ran down the slope of the deep, narrow ravine and two-thirds of the way up the opposite slope before they realized the strength of the Rebel position. Wills's company ground to a halt, lying prone on the ravine slope for protection. The Federals opened a heavy fire to keep the Rebels crouching in their trench. Wills and his men had reached their high tide.[47]

Their story was similar to that of most members of Walcutt's brigade. After struggling through the tangled bottomland, the Federals advanced up the slope in isolated groups, receiving intense rifle fire as soon as they came within sight of the Confederate earthworks. The slope of the gorge and the northern side of Pigeon Hill was steep and covered with outcroppings and ledges of hard rock. Over much of the rise, felled trees added to the obstacles encountered by the Federals. Yet many groups managed to plant themselves quite close to the target. Lieutenant Colonel George W. Wright brought many men of the 103rd Illinois within thirty yards of the works, where the regimental flag was prominently displayed. Also, Lieutenant Colonel Rigdon S. Barnhill of the Fortieth Illinois was killed about thirty feet from the enemy trench.[48]

Charles Wills admitted that his company had no chance of taking the Rebel position unaided. In fact, his men were "so scattered that we only presented the appearance of a very thin skirmish line." But, Wills thought that supporting units could have added enough weight so that his men would have had a chance of penetrating the enemy position.[49]

The right end of Cockrell's brigade and the left end of Sears's Mississippi Brigade (commanded by Colonel William S. Barry) bore the brunt of Walcutt's advance. Because of their curving line along the military crest of the gorge, the Confederates got the Federals in a crossfire. In French's words, the blue line "seemed to melt away, or sink to the earth, to rise no more." Yet many elements of Walcutt's command "gained a hold nearer my main line in front of the left of General Sears' brigade than I had reason to expect," as French complained to Loring the next day. The right wing of Barry's command was not hit by Walcutt, yet the men there stood ready for anything and endured skirmishing and artillery fire the rest of the day. The Forty-Sixth Mississippi lost five men on June 27 even though it was not directly engaged in repelling the attack.[50]

The fragments of Walcutt's brigade which lodged close to the Rebels remained in place about forty-five minutes before orders filtered through to pull back. George Wright was severely wounded in the leg, and Charles Wills had to take charge of the 103rd Illinois. He moved to the center of the regiment in time to hear the order to retire. Wills passed the word up and down the line and superintended the withdrawal. The regiment fell back as it had advanced, in fragments, and Wills had difficulty assembling the men near the tangled bottomland. He started with about thirty troops, placing them near the Sixth Iowa, but other fragments soon showed up as something resembling a brigade line took shape. The men started to construct breastworks while they waited, within about two hundred yards of the enemy, and held the works before returning to the main Union line after dusk. The 103rd Illinois had left about a dozen of its dead in the gorge. The Fortieth Illinois also left behind the body of it commander, Rigdon Barnhill, when it fell back.[51]

OSTERHAUS AND THE REST OF HARROW

McPherson had arranged for many other units of his army to provide support for the Fifteenth Corps brigades that conducted the attack. Osterhaus's First Division sent a heavy skirmish line forward to the right of Lightburn's brigade south of Burnt Hickory Road. Colonel James A. Williamson's Brigade provided Lieutenant Colonel Samuel D. Nichols's Fourth Iowa. Nichols started at the sound of a bugle call and worked his way through the tangled vegetation of the branch valley. He met Confederate skirmishers on the eastern edge of the underbrush and pushed them back to the main Confederate line, "using the bayonet freely," as Williamson put it. Brigadier General Charles R. Woods's brigade also pushed a skirmish line out to the left of Walcutt's brigade, taking the Confederate skirmish line. Osterhaus's division captured about one hundred prisoners in these spirited fights.[52]

To Osterhaus's left, and well to the left of Walcutt's brigade, the rest of William Harrow's Fourth Division advanced its skirmish line as well. Led by Lieutenant Colonel John M. Berkey of the Ninety-Ninth Indiana, Harrow's skirmishers also captured the Rebel skirmish pits, but they could not ascend the steep slope of Little Kennesaw Mountain. The Federals took shelter for the rest of that long day wherever rocks and trees offered some protection. Theodore F. Upson of the 100th Indiana crowded together with fifteen comrades behind one huge rock that was twenty feet tall until dusk offered them a chance to retreat in comparative safety.[53]

DODGE

Although Samuel French reported that his skirmish line "did not give way," the truth was that the Federals dominated the skirmish fighting on his division front on June 27. Major General Edward C. Walthall's division, positioned on Big Kennesaw Mountain to the right of French, also fared poorly in the skirmish fighting to dominate no-man's-land. Major General Grenville M. Dodge's Left Wing of the Sixteenth Corps advanced a skirmish line at 8:00 A.M. It consisted of three regiments, the Ninth Illinois and Sixty-Sixth Illinois from Colonel August Mersy's brigade of Brigadier General Thomas W. Sweeny's Second Division, and the Sixty-Fourth Illinois from Brigadier General John W. Fuller's brigade of Brigadier General James C. Veatch's Fourth Division.[54]

The Sixty-Fourth and Sixty-Sixth Illinois, which Dodge referred to as "my skirmishing regiments," were armed with Henry repeating rifles. All three regiments stretched out along a frontage of two brigades. The Federals advanced halfway across no-man's-land before receiving a heavy enfilading fire. They continued, driving the opposing skirmishers away and advancing up the slope until coming to rest only thirty yards from the main Rebel position. According to Fuller, "the steep and rocky face of the mountain was an obstacle of itself more formidable than a line of men." Nevertheless, the Sixteenth Corps skirmishers provided an inspiring show to all observers in the

Union line. "It was a beautiful sight," remembered Dodge, "to see the movement as the two lines went up—the enemy's falling back and ours moving up. The line of fire was distinct and it was very interesting."[55]

The skirmish line of the Seventeenth Corps, to the left of Dodge's force, failed to keep pace with the Sixteenth Corps skirmishers, exposing their flank dangerously, so the Sixty-Sixth Illinois refused its left wing to guard against a flanking move by the enemy. Dodge sent two regiments from his main position to support the three advanced Illinois units. One regiment went to their left and another to their right to extend the flanks down the mountainside and connect to the main Union line near the foot of the slope. Some members of the Sixty-Fourth Illinois reportedly attempted to scale the main Confederate line and were killed on the parapet, while others were shot down "within a few yards of the works." Dodge reported that the Illinoisans tried to close in on the Rebel main line to retrieve some Henry rifles that had been dropped by fallen comrades. They failed to do that but did manage to keep the Confederates from getting the prized weapons, which had magazines large enough to hold sixteen rounds.[56]

Walthall arrayed his division with Brigadier General Daniel H. Reynolds's brigade on the left, covering the western slope of Big Kennesaw, and Cantey's brigade (led by Colonel Edward A. O'Neal) on top of the mountain. Brigadier General William A. Quarles's brigade covered the eastern slope, its right resting on the Marietta and Big Shanty Road. Walthall's men endured the heavy Union artillery bombardment that preceded the Union skirmish advance. Dodge's effort was so strong that it seemed to Walthall as if the Federals were conducting a general attack. The broken nature of the ground also made it difficult for observers on top of Big Kennesaw to accurately gauge the strength of Dodge's advance, although the noise of heavy firing to right and left of the eminence contributed to the impression that Sherman was throwing his all into the fight.[57]

On Reynolds's front, only one section of the skirmish line was driven in by Dodge's skirmishers. In the process, Major L. L. Noles of the Twenty-Fifth Arkansas was killed and half a dozen other men were shot. Reynolds also lost about half a dozen men in his main line owing to Union artillery fire, but he reported finding fifty Federal casualties along his brigade front at the end of the day. O'Neal's brigade bore the brunt of Dodge's skirmish advance and lost about eight men in the fight. Dodge pointed out in his report that his men accomplished their basic goal, to keep the Confederates occupied so as to draw attention away from the Fifteen Corps attack.[58]

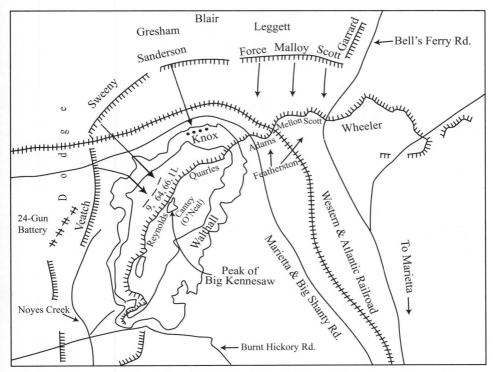

Sixteenth and Seventeenth Corps Demonstrations

BLAIR

Major General Francis Preston Blair Jr. mounted a vigorous effort with his Seventeenth Corps to skirmish against the Confederate position on Big Kennesaw Mountain and to demonstrate on Sherman's far left flank. Brigadier General Walter Q. Gresham shifted his Fourth Division to the right when Giles A. Smith evacuated that part of the line to take position from which to launch his attack on Pigeon Hill. Gresham rested his right at Dodge's left flank and connected his left with Brigadier General Mortimer D. Leggett's Third Division of Blair's corps. Gresham advanced his skirmish line at 8:00 A.M. On the right, Colonel William L. Sanderson's First Brigade contributed fourteen companies under Major Henry C. Ferguson of the Twenty-Third Indiana and Major Warner L. Vestal of the Fifty-Third Indiana as its contribution to the skirmish line. Ten of those companies advanced toward the Confederates, while the remaining four tried to maintain contact with Sixteenth Corps skirmishers to the right.[59]

Ferguson and Vestal advanced their men cautiously because the Confederate skirmish position was obscured by undergrowth. In fact, the Federals were only a few yards away when the defending Rebels began to fire. Some of the Yankees reportedly were almost on the parapet of the pits when this happened. The Confederates opened "a murderous fire of musketry" and forced the Federals to retire, leaving several of their sixty-five killed and wounded comrades behind. To the left, nine companies detailed from the Eleventh Iowa and Sixteenth Iowa of Colonel William Hall's Third Brigade advanced in concert with Sanderson's brigade skirmishers. They met similar resistance and retired as well.[60]

Confederate major Samuel L. Knox was responsible for bluntly repulsing Gresham's skirmishers through his inspired leadership. The right wing of his First Alabama, consisting of 188 men, had held the skirmish line in front of Quarles's brigade since the evening before. These five companies met the advance of twice their number on the morning of June 27. Heavy fire from the center of Knox's skirmish line forced many of the Federals to bunch in front of only one and a half companies on Knox's left center. Knox was therefore able to direct the fire of less-threatened sections of his line to this concentration and thus "brought my whole strength to bear upon them." Knox reported that the enemy mostly got no closer than 20 yards from his line, but in places they made it to within ten feet. A few daring Yankees got into the skirmish pits where they were compelled to surrender. Gresham's skirmishers tried to re-form only 30 yards away but found it impossible. They then tried to re-form 150 yards away behind "a slight sassafras hedge." Knox directed his men to fire on this area, which "soon resulted in confusing and dislodging" them. Quarles feared for the security of his skirmish line and held two regiments ready to reinforce Knox, but that proved to be unnecessary. Quarles gave full credit to Knox for the sterling performance of his skirmishers that day. Praising this officer, who had attended Oglethorpe University with poet Sidney Lanier before the war and who had endured the siege of Port Hudson, Quarles described his fight on June 27 as "the most brilliant affair it has ever been my fortune to witness."[61]

Knox reported capturing sixteen Yankees, among them Captain Hezekiah B. Wakefield of the Fifty-Third Indiana, when they jumped into the skirmish pits and were subdued. Knox suffered only six losses on the skirmish line, but he believed his opponents lost three hundred men. That was surely an exaggeration, but Quarles inflated it even more until he offered the suggestion that Gresham had suffered five hundred casualties in the skirmish fight on the morning of June 27. Knox's men picked up twenty-seven abandoned muskets in front of their line when another regiment sent skirmishers out to relieve them from duty.[62]

Gresham's demonstration was a bloody failure, but Blair instructed Mortimer Leggett, his other division commander, to continue distracting Confederate attention. Leggett had placed his Third Division more to the left early on the morning of June 27, planting his left flank on top of a hill that lay about one hundred yards from the Bell's Ferry Road. That left flank was anchored by Colonel Robert K. Scott's Second Brigade, with Colonel Adam G. Malloy's Third Brigade in the center and Brigadier General Manning F. Force's First Brigade on the right. Leggett formed his division in two lines and connected his skirmish formation with that of Brigadier General Kenner Garrard's cavalry division of the Army of the Cumberland, which occupied a refused position to his left. Leggett's assignment was to draw attention away from the real attacks elsewhere, but the division leader reported that his men were ready to do more than just make noise. They "expressed great eagerness to go into the rebel works," he wrote.[63]

The division advanced at 8:00 A.M., preceded by a skirmish line which pushed the Confederate skirmishers back along the entire division front. On both right and left, the Federals began to receive enfilade fire so Leggett changed his formation from double to single line so as to cover more front. The division had completed this change and was taking shelter in the captured Rebel skirmish pits when three batteries of Confederate artillery obtained a crossfire on the formation. The division remained in place for a long while, Malloy losing nineteen men from this crushing barrage.[64]

Leggett finally moved his men from the captured skirmish pits in stages. At about noon, he pulled Malloy's small brigade back to the division's former position, before he had shifted it to the left early that morning. In late afternoon, Leggett pulled Scott's brigade away and moved it farther to the right, to its old position. Here, Scott advanced directly toward the Confederates to conduct a second demonstration. His men lodged about fifty yards from the Rebel skirmish line where they fired away for more than an hour before falling back. Scott reported that his loss was "considerable."[65]

Force held his brigade in the captured Rebel works all day, a grueling experience because of effective Rebel artillery. "We had to lie there and take their shells and grape and canister, to lie still in such shelter as the ground afforded," Force informed a friend. "Two shells exploded simultaneously in one regiment, wounding two officers, and ten men." A soldier in the Thirty-First Illinois quipped "'that rouses my patriotism'" every time a round came near him. He was instead hit by a skirmisher's bullet but had the presence of mind to cut out the ball with his pocket knife and hobble back to the Union position where a surgeon amputated the leg. Despite the terrible pounding of artillery, Force's cook brought his dinner to the forward line, and the brigadier dined under fire. He finally withdrew his men near dusk when descending darkness offered some degree of cover.[66]

Loring's division, now led by Brigadier General Winfield Scott Featherston, opposed Leggett's demonstration on June 27. Featherston had Colonel Thomas Moore Scott's brigade on his right, his old Mississippi Brigade under Colonel Thomas A. Mellon in the center, and Brigadier General John Adams's brigade on the left. Adams covered part of the eastern slope of Big Kennesaw Mountain, while the rest of the division was positioned along the relatively level countryside. Leggett mostly pressed Scott's brigade and the right wing of Mellon's brigade in his advance. Featherston was able to hold his main line with effective fire by Captain James J. Cowan's Mississippi Battery and Captain Alcide Bouanchaud's Louisiana Battery, plus the fire of several other artillery units. At the end of the day, after the Federals retired, Featherston's men reclaimed their skirmish pits and found the shallow graves of several Federal dead left behind. Rumors circulated for many years that seven Yankee regimental commanders were killed on Featherston's front on June 27, but there was no basis in fact for such stories. Nevertheless, Featherston continued to believe that Leggett intended to make a serious attack on his position rather than just a demonstration. Leggett reported losing no more than sixty men in his division, but he took satisfaction in knowing that he fulfilled his limited objective to keep the enemy's attention away from the Fifteenth Corps area of attack.[67]

The cavalrymen who held the far end of Sherman's line skirmished during the course of the day on June 27. Kenner Garrard's division of Federal horsemen, reporting to Thomas's headquarters, held a refused line off from the left flank of Leggett's division. It was unable to do more than make noise against Major General Joseph Wheeler's Cavalry Corps of the Army of Tennessee because, as Garrard complained, Wheeler had all the advantages of position and numbers.[68]

CONCLUSION

McPherson's Army of the Tennessee was more active than were the other two field armies with Sherman on June 27. Not only did Logan launch a vigorous assault with three of his best brigades, but the rest of the Fifteenth Corps, the Sixteenth Corps, and the Seventeenth Corps mounted significant and wide-scale demonstrations along the entire line. No wonder that Loring got the impression McPherson was unleashing a general attack on the Army of Mississippi.[69]

But the result of all this activity merely proved two salient points. The Federals were able to dominate no-man's-land (for the most part) with aggressive and effective skirmishing. Only on Gresham's division front along the Seventeenth Corps sector did the Confederates hold their own on the skirmish line. Knox blunted his blue-clad opponents and broke the connection between Gresham's skirmishers and their neighbors to the right, the skirmish line thrown forward by Dodge. But everywhere else along the line of Loring's army the Confederate skirmishers were driven back to the main line, and often times with considerable loss. The Federals tended to best their gray-clad opponents in skirmishing throughout the Atlanta campaign, and June 27 was no exception to the general rule.

The other salient point developed by McPherson's operations was that there were no weak points in Loring's main line that were open to Federal exploitation. The setback of the main line just south of Pigeon Hill, where Hardee's Corps joined the left flank of Loring's Army of Mississippi, held as firmly as did Cockrell's brigade on top of Pigeon Hill. The Federals could control no-man's-land and lodge close to the Rebel main trench, but they failed to make any dent in the main enemy position. Good works located on the best ground in the area, and fully manned by alert veterans, amply explain why McPherson could not break or dislodge the main position of Loring's army.

Five. The Fourth Corps Attack

At about the same time that Logan's Fifteenth Corps troops started their advance along Burnt Hickory Road, elements of Howard's Fourth Corps also started their attack two miles to the south of Pigeon Hill. Howard's men aimed at an obscure sector of the Confederate line, shielded by a shallow stream lined with heavy vegetation. The Rebel line ran along level ground, in contrast to the line Logan futilely assaulted that morning. But the Federals had secured a position on the ridge only four hundred yards from the Confederate line on June 23; that ridge seemed to offer a good place from which to start the Fourth Corps assault.

John Newton and his Second Division were responsible for making the Fourth Corps attempt to break Johnston's Kennesaw Line. He moved his men about one mile in the early morning hours of June 27 to the sector held by Stanley's First Division, on the far right of the Fourth Corps line. Brigade commanders Harker and Kimball were at Newton's headquarters when the order to form their commands was issued. Howard identified the point of attack and instructed the brigades to form in columns. According to Kimball's postwar recollection, both he and Harker protested, believing that lines would be more appropriate, but Newton told them that the order had already been issued by corps headquarters and there was nothing to do but obey them. Howard, for his part, explained that he relied heavily on Newton's advice to pinpoint the target and form the troops in columns. In light of the bloody affair to come, everyone seemed interested in shifting responsibility for the details of the Fourth Corps attack onto someone else.[1]

Newton had some difficulty finding places to assemble his three brigades for the attack. Initially, he wanted to form Wagner and Kimball in one long column of regiments, but Wagner was unable to obtain ground far enough forward because clusters of Federal "shelter-trenches" were in the way. Moreover, Kimball could not find room sufficiently in the rear "owing to the irregularity of the ground." As a result, Newton placed Kimball en echelon to the left and rear of Wagner, while Harker formed his brigade to the right of Wagner. Intervals of about one hundred yards existed between each of the three brigades to allow for the troops to deploy into lines, if necessary, before hitting the target. Within each brigade column, the individual regiments were already in battle lines, one behind the other. The distance between the regimental lines was closed en mass, as the terminology of the day put it. In short, the regimental lines were as close to each other as the distance between the two ranks of the regimental line itself.[2]

The division began forming in the space between the main Union line and the fortified skirmish position at 6:00 A.M. Brigade leaders assembled their regimental commanders and gave them instructions for what was to be done. The regimental leaders then assembled their company commanders to impart these instructions.[3]

Harker organized his brigade with the Fifty-First Illinois in the lead, then the Twenty-Seventh Illinois, followed by the Sixty-Fifth Ohio, and, bringing up the rear, the Sixty-Fourth Ohio. For some reason, Harker formed his command in a very narrow column with a front of only two companies. His formation was not only narrow but quite long as a result. John K. Shellenberger recalled that his regiment, the Sixty-Fourth Ohio, counted off to form eight companies of equal strength, and he assumed the other regiments in Harker's brigade did the same thing. If so, that meant Harker's column consisted of sixteen lines stacked one behind the other. There is no evidence that Wagner or Kimball did this; they opted instead for the traditional column of division as prescribed in the tactical manual—one regimental battle line behind the next, with a frontage of ten companies.[4]

Newton arranged for a heavy skirmish line to precede his troops and assigned Colonel Emerson Opdycke of the 125th Ohio to lead it. "'You will have heavy work to do,'" Newton told Opdycke at 7:45 A.M. "'I want you to clear the front of the attacking columns, go smack up to the rebel works and pass over them if possible, before the attacking column comes up; if not pass over with them, protect their deployment; but if the Columns are knocked to pieces and cannot get up, then you must protect their retreat.'" Newton's bluntly worded instructions clearly spelled out the typical role of skirmishers in Civil War military operations.[5]

Opdycke chose his own regiment as one of those to compose the skirmish line. His men had been up since 3:00 A.M. and had moved to Stanley's division sector just before dawn. Opdycke explained to them their assignment as the rising sun melted off some fog that had accumulated during the night, exposing the Federals to the view of Confederate skirmishers. To escape their fire, Lieutenant Colonel David H. Moore deployed the 125th Ohio in intervals, each man four feet from his neighbor, and moved them into the skirmish pits of Grose's brigade. When told what was about to happen, Grose's men ventured the opinion that "no troops could cross the interval between the lines," which was hardly encouraging news for Opdycke's men. Moore took charge of the regimental left wing, and Major Joseph Bruff superintended the right wing.[6]

Newton's troops had only a dim understanding of what lay ahead in the Georgia woods. They aimed at a sector of the Confederate line held by Cleburne's division. Brigadier General Lucius E. Polk's brigade held the left, with Brigadier General Mark P. Lowrey's brigade to Polk's right. Brigadier General Daniel C. Govan's brigade was positioned to the right of Lowrey. While Brigadier General Hiram B. Granbury's brigade on Cleburne's right flank was not targeted, Vaughan's brigade of Cheatham's division, to Cleburne's left, marginally came within the sector hit by the Federals. If there was any need to exploit success or protect failure, Stanley's division was there to help.[7]

The terrain did not favor the Federals; in fact, it was far worse than that which confronted Logan's Fifteenth Corps farther north. One of Howard's staff officers was astonished at the thick vegetation that lay between the Fourth Corps position and the Confederates. The country "is so thickly wooded, and the topography is such that it is almost impossible to tell anything about the enemy's works," which could not be seen until one was nearly on them. Felled timber constituted "an almost impassable abatis," in the opinion of a member of Kimball's brigade. Colonel David Moore reported that the distance between his skirmish line and the target was not more than four hundred paces, but the shallow valley of a small stream that ran parallel to and about fifty paces from the Federal line was the only spot where a man could find any shelter from bullets. It was no more than twenty feet deep and was a branch of John Ward Creek that flowed in a southerly direction. The ravine was choked with briars, small trees, and undergrowth, and was about two hundred yards wide. Once across this forbidding no-man's-land, an abrupt ascent several inches high lay at least twenty yards from the main Confederate line of works. Beyond that ascent, the Federals would encounter obstructions. The abatis was less strong in front of Vaughan's brigade, but along Cleburne's division sector it was thick. The Confederates had also driven sharpened stakes into the ground to sup-

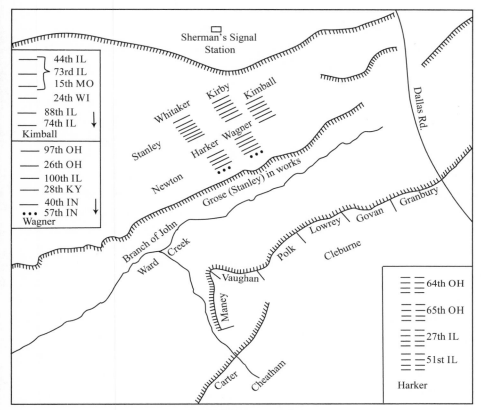

Fourth Corps Attack

plement the tree limbs. There were head logs on top of the parapet along at least a portion of the Confederate line.[8]

Howard marshaled seven batteries to bombard the Rebel position for fifteen minutes, beginning at 8:00 A.M. A member of Butterfield's division of the Twentieth Corps, a short distance to the south, witnessed some of those guns in action that morning. They were firing from the bald top of a rise of ground, and "kept up a constant roll of thunder" as return Confederate fire kicked up clouds of dust when the rounds fell nearby. Howard termed the bombardment "a heavy cannonade." Sherman had asked Thomas to keep him minutely informed of developments, and the army commander did so; he telegraphed Sherman at 8:00 A.M. that the "movement of my troops against the enemy's works has commenced."[9]

Opdycke's skirmish line set out at 8:00 A.M. when the guns opened up, and it advanced under the dubious cover of their fire. The troops received scattering musketry, which was "harmless" for a minute as the Yankees crossed the shallow ravine between the lines. Soon after, the skirmishers came across the Confederate picket line and captured nearly all of its occupants. Moore sent the prisoners back to the Union position under the escort of walking wounded or simply told them to make their way back if no one was available to guard them. "I could not spare well men from the ranks," he reported. The Federals continued forward after taking the line of pickets, "exposed to a withering fire" until they hit the tangled abatis fronting the main Confederate position. There Opdycke ordered his men to stop and lay down to wait for the attacking column to catch up.[10]

Harker led his brigade forward soon after the skirmishers started, but the men had difficulty pushing across the fortified Union skirmish line and through the tangled landscape of the branch valley. According to an officer of the Third Kentucky, the men tried to move forward on the double quick. They marched down a sharp descent before crossing the ravine valley, jumping across the narrow stream, and continued up the slope toward the main Rebel line. The slope was gentle until the abrupt ascent, and the main Confederate line loomed ominously beyond.[11]

As members of the 125th Ohio lay flat on the ground at the foot of the abatis, firing at the Rebels only a few yards away, the head of Harker's column neared its position. The Confederates concentrated "a tornado" of rifle fire at the formation. As often happened with columns, the successive lines to the rear gave impetus to the front, and the head of Harker's formation (the Fifty-First Illinois) continued moving into the teeth of this fire until it reached the abatis. Then the men in the first regiment stopped and lay down among the skirmishers, and some of the troops that followed broke formation to the right and left to do the same thing. The rest of the Federals took cover behind the abrupt ascent.[12]

All forward movement ended, although a few individuals crawled their way through the entanglement and climbed the parapet only to be shot down before they reached the top. The color-bearer of the Fifty-First Illinois planted his flag on the Rebel parapet as his comrades huddled at the abatis. The historian of the 125th Ohio also claimed that the flag of the Twenty-Seventh Illinois was taken to the Confederate parapet, but not enough men could get that far to effect a lodgment on the Rebel works. The rest of the men in the brigade opened with their muskets but could not suppress enemy fire. The Confederates were too well protected by their fortifications.[13]

From the Confederate perspective, it seemed as if Cleburne's musketry "literally mowed them down." One of Newton's orderlies later described the plight of his comrades in Harker's brigade. "The cross fire was terrible, a rebel bullet was liable to go through three men in line. It was a veritable death trap, like the famous charge of the six hundred at Balaclava in the Crimean war." Colonel Luther P. Bradley's Fifty-First Illinois hit the abatis between two Confederate artillery positions, but the Rebel gunners had to angle their pieces so much that they blew the revetment out of the embrasures when they fired. "'My God!,'" yelled one of Bradley's men when the revetting material came sailing over, "'they are shooting sticks of wood at us.'" The Federals were no more than forty yards from the guns.[14]

John K. Shellenberger argued that forming the brigade in such a long, narrow column inside the Union skirmish line had been a mistake. The men had difficulty crossing the skirmish trench and became disordered. Rather than halt on the outside to re-form, the regiments in the lead simply moved to the attack. They were, in part, impelled forward by the advance of Wagner to the left and by the need to get across the valley as fast as possible. But this meant that Harker's already long, narrow column became stretched out even longer as it crossed the valley in clusters rather than as a unit.[15]

By the time the Sixty-Fourth Ohio, at the tail of Harker's column, negotiated the Federal skirmish trench and crossed the shallow valley, all forward movement had ended. Shellenberger found the bulk of the brigade huddling behind the scant protection of the abrupt ascent. Brave individuals now and then tried to inspire their comrades to move on, but they invariably were shot soon after rising. This led to the utter collapse of their efforts as those brave enough to rise and follow them now dropped back behind cover. As Shellenberger put it, the situation demanded a trusted leader who had the authority "to carry the men forward in mass."[16]

Charles Harker tried to fill that role and get the advance of his brigade started again. He had insisted on riding into action on a white horse and was compelled to jump the steed across the Union skirmish trench. Harker managed to negotiate the tangled environment of the valley and rode around the right flank of the brigade. As he went forward, up the slope, his horse literally "lifted him above the line of battle." Harker sent an aid to the rear with word that the enemy's fortifications were "formidable." He then continued with his adjutant, Captain Edward G. Whitesides of the 125th Ohio, riding by his side. The pair rode along the abrupt ascent in full view of the Confederates, but as yet neither one was hit.[17]

When he reached the center of the brigade line, Harker took off his hat and yelled, "Forward, men, and take these works." The troops started to rise up, and Harker faced his white horse toward the enemy when a bullet smashed into his right arm, breaking it, and went on to penetrate his breast. Whitesides also was hit, and Harker's white horse fell, pierced by bullets as well. All the men who had started to get up quickly took cover again.[18]

"Whenever anything difficult was to be done," Howard recalled, "anything that required pluck and energy—we called on Harker." The only thing that Howard ever heard in the way of a complaint about his subordinate was "that if Harker got started against the enemy he could not be kept back." This trait cost Harker his life.[19]

The Federals held their position another fifteen minutes as Luther P. Bradley took charge of the brigade. Bradley saw that the Fourteenth Corps units to the right had failed to break through, and he "reluctantly gave the order to retire." The Federals dragged as many of their wounded back with them as possible. Bradley sent word to the rear that the "head of his column is all smashed up and disorganized," in the words of Fourth Corps staff officer Joseph S. Fullerton. As Harker's troops fell back, many Confederates rose up in their trenches to get a better shot at them. Some members of the Fifty-First Illinois who had lodged too close to the Rebel works were taken prisoner by the Confederates, who could now expose themselves for the duration of the Yankee retreat. That retreat turned into a harrowing experience for those who tried to get away. "Our men rushed back like an immense herd of infuriated buffaloes," complained John W. Tuttle of the Third Kentucky, "running over and trampling each other under foot. I was run over and badly bruised but very glad to get off so well."[20]

Chesley Mosman witnessed the retreat of Harker's brigade from a position between Newton's division and Davis's division to the south. The Federals were in a "great deal of confusion" as they streamed back across the Union earthworks. "'What are you doing?'" called out one of Mosman's comrades to an officer in Harker's command. "'Trying to rally my men,' was the reply as he made a flying leap, clearing our works and the ditch inside as well, a distance of over 20 feet." Another of Harker's officers stopped with Mosman's group to catch his breath. When asked where was his regiment, the officer heatedly replied, "'I don't know and I don't care. I am ashamed that I belong to it.'"[21]

The emotional reaction to the repulse bubbled up the chain of command to Howard himself. The corps commander rode up to Mosman's group and asked what regiment held this part of the line. When told it was the 59th Illinois, Howard asked, "'Can you hold these works?'" No one replied, so the general asked again with much more emotion in his voice. Then several men responded affirmatively. When Howard asked who commanded their brigade and found out it was William Grose, he felt reassured. "The General was terribly in earnest and evidently feared a counter charge by the enemy," Mosman concluded.[22]

Moore's 125th Ohio covered the retreat as best it could by stopping at the captured Confederate skirmish pits. The Federals remained there for half an hour before fresh regiments from Stanley's division relieved Harker's command.[23]

Harker's failure, in John Shellenberger's view, lay in forming his command inside rather than outside the Union line of earthworks. If not for the disruption caused by traversing the Federal skirmish trench, the brigade could have retained its cohesion and crossed the Confederate works in one mass. Shellenberger, however, ignored the obstacles posed by the vegetation in the shallow valley, the Confederate abatis, and most importantly the stopping power of Cleburne's hardened veterans firing from behind amply made earthworks.[24]

The Federals managed to carry the wounded Harker to safety during the retreat. On the way, Opdycke came across his commander and "talked a few hurried words with him." While lying in the field hospital, Harker was joined by Edward Whitesides. Harker had given Whitesides all of his money and some other personal belongings just before the attack, to be disposed of in case he fell. He had also told him to wait until the last regiment in the brigade column, the Sixty-Fourth Ohio, had started to advance before he moved forward. Whitesides obeyed his orders and then tried to catch up with Harker on horseback. He was among members of the Third Kentucky when a Rebel bullet smashed into his thigh. It first went through Whitesides pocket, mangling keys and "smashing his little ivory handled knife, which turned the ball down into the thigh, carrying the knife into the wound." Whitesides slid off his horse to examine the injury but thought it was not so bad. When he tried to remount, his horse was killed. By now, the injury incapacitated Whitesides, but comrades managed to carry him to the rear. The staff officer wound up in the field hospital lying next to Harker. The general greeted him with the plaintive question, "'Is that you, my dear boy?'" Harker died quietly at one o'clock that afternoon. Members of the

Fifty-Eighth Indiana constructed a coffin so his body could be sent North. Eventually, Harker was buried at his birthplace, Swedesboro, New Jersey.[25]

WAGNER

To the left of Harker's brigade, George Day Wagner led his command forward in concert with his colleague. Born in Ohio, his family of farmers moved to Indiana where the young Wagner served in both houses of the state legislature as a Republican. He became colonel of the Fifteenth Indiana and led a brigade at Shiloh, Stones River, and Missionary Ridge. His effective performances on the battlefield proved that politicians could be good soldiers as well.[26]

Wagner assembled his brigade in a traditional column of division, a stack of regimental battle lines. He placed the Fortieth Indiana in front, followed by the Twenty-Eighth Kentucky, 100th Illinois, Twenty-Sixth Ohio, and last the Ninety-Seventh Ohio. Wagner assigned Colonel John W. Blake to superintend the movements of the first two regiments and Colonel John Q. Lane to oversee the last three. The Fifty-Seventh Indiana took position on the skirmish line in front, under Opdycke's general supervision. Lieutenant Colonel Willis Blanch started the Fifty-Seventh forward at the sound of a bugle call and immediately received "a very heavy fire" from the main Confederate line. His men made slow headway through the brush in the valley before the head of Wagner's column caught up with them, and the two forces merged into one, continuing forward.[27]

The brigade column received the same "terrific and deadly fire of artillery and musketry" as soon as its head crossed the Federal skirmish pits. The men pushed through the trees and underbrush as best they could. Wagner recalled seeing Captain Absalom Kirkpatrick of the Fortieth Indiana waving his sword at the head of the column and asking him as he passed by, "'where shall I strike the enemy's lines?'" There could be no answer to that question other than to continue moving straight ahead.[28]

On the other side of the imposing earthworks, the Confederates of Cleburne's division were more than ready for the attack. The men had stockpiled up to sixty cartridges, laying them on the ground for ease of use. The head of Wagner's column climbed the abrupt ascent and approached the outer edge of the abatis. Some Federals dropped their guns to tear the tree limbs apart while their comrades fired at the works a few yards away. Meanwhile, the Confederates poured musketry into the packed mass. One Rebel later recalled that he fired at least seventeen rounds "and I hit a man every

George D. Wagner (Library of Congress, LC-USZ62-101448)

time," as he told a newspaper reporter. A fifteen-year-old soldier next to him used a shotgun. According to a newspaper correspondent who signed himself J.W.M., the head of Wagner's column "struck an entire battery fairly in the teeth, and his alignments were blown to pieces."[29]

The Federals could not penetrate the abatis so they stayed just outside the obstruction for several minutes. Confederate fire "mowed us down by the hundreds," wrote George W. Parsons of the Fifty-Seventh Indiana. Those brigade men who had gone beyond the abrupt ascent now fell back to its slim protection, crowding with their comrades who had not ventured beyond the slight crest. Retreat was a relief not only to the Yankees but to at least one Confederate who had grown sick of watching the slaughter. "I was glad to see the column retreat," he recalled years later. "It looked too much like cold blooded murder to kneel there and take dead aim on a man so near you that you could see the color of his eyes and hair."[30]

George W. Parsons had surged to the Rebel abatis in the ranks of the Fifty-Seventh Indiana and lodged there for protection. He thought he might have to stay all day, but then the brigade began to fall back, and the Confederates raised a deafening cheer. That was when Parsons made a run for safety. "I jumped to my feet and started and I think I made as good time as ever a hoosier did until I got back to wher our men were." Parsons correctly indicated that the retreat was a free for all; even though regimental and company officers tried to keep their men together, it proved impossible to do so. The historian of the Fifty-Seventh Indiana believed the regiment suffered more in its retreat than in the advance. The Confederates "rose from behind their works, fearless of danger from the retreating foe, and fired with greater precision than when the column advanced."[31]

Two of the three brigades in Newton's division had been bluntly repulsed, but the high command was as yet unaware of it. Thomas sent a message to Sherman at 9:30 A.M. that Howard reported his men were "doing well." The two generals had already exchanged several telegrams about small matters, the silencing of a particular Confederate battery, for example. Sherman also had informed Thomas that "McPherson's musketry fire well advanced." The news seemed to be encouraging. "All well," Sherman telegraphed Thomas at 9:50 A.M. "Keep things moving."[32]

KIMBALL

Before Wagner fell back, and while his men were still trying to deal with the impenetrable abatis, Opdycke sent a message to Newton suggesting that it was time for Kimball to advance. He thought this fresh brigade could move obliquely to the right and pass through Wagner's brigade to enter the obstruction and hit the Rebel works. It is difficult to understand why such an intelligent officer believed Kimball could succeed where Wagner had failed, but the people at division headquarters liked the idea, and Newton ordered Kimball to go in along Opdycke's suggested line of advance.[33]

Nathan Kimball had already led a brigade against a strong Confederate position under fire. A year and a half before, he had been wounded while attacking the stone wall at the foot of Marye's Hill at Fredericksburg, losing heavily and gaining nothing for the effort. Born in Indiana, Kimball had attended what is now DePauw University for two years and had then taught school in Missouri and later practiced medicine. He also served as a captain in the Second Indiana during the Mexican War. Kimball commanded the Fourteenth Indiana in Virginia, defeating Stonewall Jackson at the battle of Kernstown, and went on to campaign in many other operations, including Antietam, the siege of Vicksburg, and the capture of Little Rock, before assignment to a brigade command in the Fourth Corps.[34]

Kimball had barely finished forming his brigade in column of division, the ranks closed en mass, before Wagner began his advance. He had the Seventy-Fourth Illinois first in the column, followed by the Eighty-Eighth Illinois and the Twenty-Fourth Wisconsin, with the three other regiments (Forty-Fourth Illinois, Seventy-Third Illinois, and Fifteenth Missouri) making up the rest of the column. The Thirty-Sixth Illinois constituted the brigade skirmish line under Opdycke's general supervision. Kimball's men had dropped their knapsacks before forming but now had to wait until the drama of Wagner's attack played itself out before moving forward.[35]

Kimball responded to Newton's order of attack as soon as he received it at about 9:00 A.M. His men advanced with fixed bayonets and "a yell that could not be equaled," according to the historian of the Seventy-Third Illinois. But Kimball wisely advanced straight ahead, to the left of Wagner's position, and made no attempt to pass through Wagner's broken ranks. Kimball's men were punished by heavy Confederate fire as soon as the head of his column crested the Union skirmish line. They pushed forward across the valley and up the ascent until near the dense abatis. Here the Seventy-Fourth Illinois deployed into battle line and tried to penetrate the entanglement. Taking heavy losses, a handful of the regiment managed to get through the cut brush and limbs and touched the Confederate parapet. The men were all shot or taken captive, with at least twelve members of the regiment falling into Rebel hands. Colonel James B. Kerr was mortally wounded and became a prisoner while trying to penetrate the obstructions.[36]

According to the historians of the Thirty-Sixth Illinois, Kimball's brigade remained at its high tide for thirty minutes. Only that regiment, which was on the skirmish line, and the Seventy-Fourth Illinois, which led the column, lodged at the edge of the abatis. Colonel Silas Miller of the Thirty-Sixth Illinois was shot through the right shoulder and Lieutenant Colonel George W. Chandler of the Eighty-Eighth Illinois was killed. Besides the Thirty-Sixth and Seventy-Fourth Illinois, the other regiments were strung out in the brigade column some distance to the rear. The second regiment in the column, the Eighty-Eighth Illinois, remained at the edge of the woods a few yards from the abatis. Major Arthur MacArthur of the Twenty-Fourth Wisconsin, the third regiment in the column, estimated that his unit was stuck about three-fourths of the way across no-man's-land for half an hour. His men were subject to enemy fire but could not return it for fear of hitting their comrades in front. Kimball's men took considerable losses from artillery and rifle fire as they waited, lying prone on the ground and taking advantage of any shelter that was available.[37]

When Wagner's brigade had fallen back from its earlier attempt to penetrate the Confederate position, it had re-formed behind the abrupt ascent and in the shallow ravine partway between the opposing lines. His regiments formed a ragged battle line and waited for orders. Then word arrived to make a second attempt to advance and support Kimball's attack. Wagner's men gamely obeyed, advancing roughly in concert with Kimball, "but met with such a terrific fire from the enemy that they were compelled to fall back," as Wagner reported. They apparently stopped well short of the tangled abatis. On the way back, Wagner noticed that "a heavy fire" slammed into his flank from the south. He accurately concluded this was a sign that Harker's brigade had failed in its effort to take the enemy works and had retired. Harker had started his attack one hundred yards to the right of Wagner, and the woods extended a bit farther toward the Confederate line between the positions of the two brigades. The sound and impact of enemy fire were the only clues to Harker's progress, or lack of success. The Confederates, Wagner now feared, "were coming out of their works and striking me on the flank." This time, his troops retired all the way back to the main Federal line after suffering additional losses. The color-bearer of the Twenty-Sixth Ohio, for example, was killed, and his flag displayed the rips and tears of fifty-six bullets that had passed through the cloth.[38]

With no support to right or left, there was no need for Kimball to remain near the Rebel abatis. Newton ordered him to pull back, and his men did so at about 10:00 A.M. Many members of the Seventy-Fourth Illinois who had thus far survived the attack were now shot down as they moved back. The Confederates "were swarming on the top of their works in their eagerness to kill the Yankees," wrote A. M. Potter. Many of the Federals who were close to the abatis simply gave up rather than risk a shot in the back. Colonel Joseph Conrad positioned his Fifteenth Missouri to cover the withdrawal. It is possible that the Thirty-Sixth Illinois also performed such a role. At any rate, Confederate troops noted that for some time after the retreat a number of Federals remained at the edge of the woods, partly shielded by the abrupt ascent, and sniped at the Rebel line. The Confederates could hardly see the Federals, but they returned the fire at random into the trees.[39]

David S. Stanley held his division ready to support Newton's advance. He placed Grose's brigade in the Union works opposite the point of attack, while forming Whitaker's brigade and Kirby's brigade in columns of regiments just behind the Federal entrenchments. Whitaker had orders to help Harker if called on, and he moved the Forty-Fifth Ohio, Fifty-First Ohio, and Twenty-First Kentucky into the captured Confederate skirmish pits as soon as Harker's men cleared those works of Rebels. Kirby had orders to help Wagner and Kimball if the need arose. Grose's men were subject to intense artillery fire but suffered no casualties because of the protection afforded by their field works. Kirby also was annoyed by fire. "We are in a hot place," wrote J. M. Raymond of the 101st Ohio, "and life is hardly worth the asking, as stray bullets are constantly flying over and around us." Stanley's division suffered few casualties compared to those in Newton's attack columns, but one of his best artillery officers, Captain Samuel M. McDowell of Company B, Independent Pennsylvania Battery, was killed just before Harker's men began to advance.[40]

Thomas J. Wood kept two brigades of his division ready to support Newton if the need arose. The rest of his men tried to cover the works vacated by Newton's command. Some of the units had to stretch their manpower out in thin lines to accomplish that goal. Colonel Samuel F. Gray's Forty-Ninth Ohio, for example, held the works vacated by Wood's division and did so in a very thin line. With several brigades of the corps massed nearby, however, there was little danger in keeping so few men in the works. The massed formations could quickly maneuver to meet any Rebel counterstrike.[41]

THE CONFEDERATE DEFENDERS

Cleburne's men turned back the Fourth Corps attack with comparative ease. No more than a handful of Federals penetrated the obstruction in front of their works, and they were easily subdued. Newton's advance bore mostly on only two brigades of Cleburne's division, Polk's and Lowrey's, and to some degree on Vaughan's brigade of Cheatham's division to the left. Granbury's and Govan's brigades on Cleburne's right wing were not pressed at all except by Federal skirmish fire. Govan's men, at least, opened fire obliquely to the left on Wagner and Kimball as the Federals advanced toward Lowrey. The attack of the three Federal brigades lasted about two hours, from 8:00 to 10:00 A.M. Although Cleburne, Polk, and Lowrey were among the very best division and brigade leaders in Johnston's army, there was very little scope for their talents in repelling the Federal attack. For the Confederates, it was a soldier's battle; all that was required was rapid, effective shooting, while the well-placed earthworks and the abatis took care of the rest.[42]

At some point during the heavy firing, and near the end of the attack, the dry abatis caught fire. The obstruction was thick enough for the flames to spread steadily until quite a few wounded Yankees were in danger. Several of them burned, and a courageous Rebel officer could not bear it. Lieutenant Colonel William H. Martin of the First and Fifteenth Arkansas in Polk's brigade shouted, "'Boys, this is butchery.'" He mounted the parapet and used a handkerchief to signal a truce with the Federals. Major Luther M. Sabin of the Forty-Fourth Illinois in Kimball's brigade accepted the offer, and the firing died down along some length of the line.[43]

The truce extended down to Polk's brigade, where Captain Robert Davis Smith reported that the dried leaves scattered across no-man's-land had caught fire. Smith indicated that the truce on Polk's sector began a half hour after the last Federal attack. He did not hesitate to take advantage of the cease-fire to gather ninety Federal rifles that had been dropped on the ground; seven of them, he wrote, were Henry rifles. Even Colonel Martin apparently took advantage of the truce to gather abandoned Yankee guns. An invoice found in his service record indicates that the First and Fifteenth Arkansas acquired forty-one rifles of 58 caliber. The invoice clearly states that the weapons were picked up on the battlefield sometime before June 30. The only real opportunity for Martin's men to have done so was during the truce of June 27.[44]

George W. Parsons of the Fifty-Seventh Indiana also commented on an opportunistic motive the Confederates may have had for initiating the truce. The fire was burning brush and sticks in front of the Confederate earthworks, and a few Rebels worked to stamp the fire out while the Federals gathered their wounded. The obstruction was one of the most valuable parts of the Confederate defensive system at Kennesaw. "If it had not been to save thare works," Parsons concluded, "I do not think that they would have allowed us to carry our wounded off the field."[45]

To most Federals, it made little difference if their enemy called the truce for either humanitarian or ulterior reasons. They were grateful for the opportunity to save their injured comrades from the flames and thanked the Confederates in word and deed. Colonel John I. Smith of the Thirty-First Indiana in Kirby's brigade of Stanley's division offered a brace of pearl-handled pistols to Martin in appreciation of his Samaritan act. The truce

Truce on Fourth Corps sector (Southern Battlefields, *46*)

lasted just long enough to move the wounded out of harm's way, and then the firing was allowed to continue. Martin's brief moment of fame endured in the memory of those who survived the Fourth Corps attack, and Martin himself survived the war. When his wife died, the Confederate veteran traveled to Honduras to make money for his daughter's welfare. One day, while traversing a river on a small boat, the boom swung around and struck him on the head, knocking him into the water where he drowned.[46]

The Fourth Corps had tried its best only to demonstrate that there were no weak spots in the Confederate position. Some of Newton's men remained in the captured Rebel skirmish pits for a while until Stanley's troops relieved them. Then Newton's division resumed its former position minus a large number of good men.[47]

Newton's division also proved that columns were rarely effective in conducting attacks on strong enemy positions. Shellenberger's comment that a column was like a battering ram well expressed the emotion-laden perception of that particular formation, with the idea that concentrated mass could physically break through a line like a giant hammer. But the reality was far different. The heads of columns easily collapsed when they hit resistance, either causing the rest of the column to collapse too or at least forcing it to a standstill. All three brigades failed to bring their full strength to bear on the enemy at the critical moment as a majority of men in Harker's, Wagner's, and Kimball's commands came up to the abrupt ascent after the head of the column had already stopped. Or, they lay on the ground all the way back toward the Union line after all hope of penetrating the Confederate position had ended, having had no opportunity to contribute to the success of the advance. Columns of attack all too often represented a poor use of manpower.

In the worst-case scenario, when a column collapsed like an accordion, the danger posed to individuals when the rear lines collided with the forward lines was real and deadly. "'Damn these assaults in column,'" a newspaper correspondent overheard one of Wagner's men complain, "'they make a man more afraid of being trampled to death by the rear lines than he is of the enemy.'"[48]

Six. The Fourteenth Corps Attack

The third attack by Sherman's army group on the morning of June 27 was the smallest, but it involved some of the best troops in Thomas's Army of the Cumberland. Two Fourteenth Corps brigades of Jefferson C. Davis's Second Division started from the same ridge that Newton used, but from a location a bit south of Newton's position, and they aimed squarely at the angle in the Confederate line on Cheatham's Hill.

The men of McCook's and Mitchell's brigades had spent two nights resting in a wooded area, unaware that they were to play a bloody role in the attack. When officers aroused them from sleep at 4:00 A.M. on June 27, they instructed their men to eat breakfast before setting out two hours later. As the troops moved a short distance forward, regimental commanders gathered at brigade headquarters for instructions. The rank and file knew that trouble was afoot when they were told to leave their camp equipment and baggage behind. Haversacks, canteens, and sixty rounds of ammunition were all they would need for the task ahead. The morning already was warm, portending one of the hottest days of the campaign thus far.[1]

The conference of regimental leaders was brief but full. McCook told Lieutenant Colonel Allen L. Fahnestock that the Eighty-Sixth Illinois would take place as the second regiment in a brigade column of division. When the first regiment, the 125th Illinois, reached the Confederate line, Fahnestock was to move his men by the left flank so as to clear the front unit and then close up on the works. According to Fahnestock, McCook urged him to have his men "shove down the head logs on the rebels" in order to disconcert the enemy. As soon as he had a chance to do so, Fahnestock called a conference of his company commanders and explained to them what was expected of the regiment.[2]

Mitchell and McCook assembled in a field just behind the Federal skirmish line and close to the shallow valley that separated the Union position from the Confederates. Both brigades formed columns of regiments.

McCook placed the 125th Illinois in front because its colonel, Oscar F. Harmon, was the ranking regimental officer. The Eighty-Sixth Illinois was next, then the Twenty-Second Indiana, and last the Fifty-Second Ohio. Each regiment stood ten paces behind the one in front and fixed bayonets. McCook also placed the Eighty-Fifth Illinois in front as a skirmish line. He controlled nearly 1,800 men in his brigade. Looking to the left, many of McCook's men realized that a gap the size of a brigade front existed between their ranks and those of Harker's command in the Fourth Corps. This circumstance occurred because all of the Fourth and Fourteenth Corps units were attacking in columns instead of brigade lines, in contrast to the Fifteenth Corps units. While many survivors of June 27 tended to blame Oliver Otis Howard for choosing columns instead of lines, Jefferson C. Davis also opted to send his troops into this risky attack in columns as well.[3]

MCCOOK'S BRIGADE

By now, everyone was aware that they were preparing for a major assault on the enemy fortifications. While the ranks were forming, officers dismounted and sent their horses to the rear for safekeeping. In all three corps attacks that morning, only Harker and Whitesides in Newton's division were mounted. While standing with their men, some of McCook's officers began to converse with their colleagues about the prospects ahead. Fahnestock talked with Harmon and Captain William W. Fellows of the 125th Illinois, assuring the two that he would rather surrender than see his regiment return unsuccessfully from the attack. It was rather bold talk that contrasted sharply with the feelings of James Lewis Burkhalter of the Eighty-Sixth Illinois. Burkhalter had so little faith in the success of the enterprise that he made a decision not to tell his men the details of what to expect for fear of depressing them. This violated Fahnestock's explicit orders, but Burkhalter thought it was the best course.[4]

The mood among the rank and file was tense and foreboding. "There was an ominous stillness in the ranks," recalled Major James T. Holmes of the Fifty-Second Ohio. "Here and there was a talkative, restless, profane old soldier." Holmes heard one such man in the Twenty-Second Indiana, placed just in front of the Fifty-Second, who had fought in many previous engagements. "'Aye! God, Jim, that hill's going to be worse'n Pea Ridge. We'll ketch hell over'n them woods.' This was uttered in a low tone with mysterious nods toward the opposite ridge." The mood grew worse when a Confederate skirmisher took shots at the Union line. One ball hit a man in

Dan McCook (Library of Congress, LC-USZ62-104988)

the Fifty-Second Ohio at random, causing a great deal of suffering. "I can see him writhe on the ground," Holmes remembered of the incident.[5]

McCook put on a brave front. The brother of two Union generals and cousin of another, he hailed from the famous "Fighting McCook" family of Ohio. He had been Sherman's law partner in Leavenworth, Kansas, before the war. McCook had seen action at Wilson's Creek as a captain in the First Kansas, and he had commanded the Fifty-Second Ohio since July 1862, moving up to a brigade command soon after that. His tenure with the brigade resulted in much campaigning but comparatively little fighting. The troops were engaged at Perryville, missed Stones River, and were but lightly engaged at Chickamauga.[6]

The attack on June 27 gave McCook a rare opportunity to shine on the battlefield, and he seemed to be eager for the trial. His superior officers, Thomas and Davis, took post just to the rear of the brigade at "a small earthwork" on the main Union line, and McCook walked back to consult with them. After a short conversation, he started back toward his command. Either Thomas or Davis called out to McCook, "'Don't be rash, colonel, don't be rash.'" The young man responded by reciting a stanza from the English writer Thomas Babington Macaulay's "Horatius." Macaulay had translated the poem from an ancient Latin text. It dealt with the legendary figure of Publius Horatius Cocles, who, sometime in the period 509–504 B.C., held off an invading Etruscan army at the Sublician Bridge over the Tiber River until other Romans could destroy the crossing. McCook remembered verse twenty-seven of Macaulay's seventy verses.

> Then out spake brave Horatius,
>   The Captain of the gate:
> "To every man upon this earth
>   Death cometh soon or late.
> And how can man die better
>   Than facing fearful odds,
> For the ashes of his fathers,
>   And the temples of his Gods."[7]

James T. Holmes, standing with McCook's old regiment at the end of the brigade column, heard the colonel's oration as he walked past. "It was a heathen refrain, but impregnated with love of country and kith and kin and duty owed to them all." Yet, in Holmes's mind, the stanza also drove home how desperate was the work ahead, making a deep impression on his mind just before the attack began.[8]

THE TERRAIN

Long after the war, survivors of McCook's charge measured the ground over which they had advanced on the morning of June 27. The brigade formed 675 feet behind the fortified Union skirmish line. After crossing that trench, McCook's men would have to move 166 feet down slope to reach the branch that flowed southward into John Ward Creek. From the stream to the edge of the woods on the east side of the bottomland was another 572 feet, and

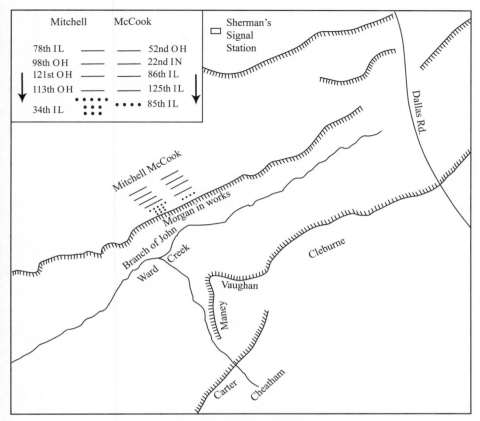

Mitchell	McCook
78th I L	52nd O H
98th O H	22nd I N
121st O H	86th I L
113th O H	125th I L
34th I L	85th I L

Sherman's Signal Station

Dallas Rd.

Mitchell McCook

Morgan in works

Branch of John

Ward Creek

Vaughan

Maney

Cleburne

Carter

Cheatham

Fourteenth Corps Attack

the Federals still had to march up slope another 330 feet to hit the Confederate earthworks. The total length of McCook's charge amounted to 1,743 feet, or 581 yards.[9]

McCook's brigade had to negotiate a downhill slope to a wide, marshy bottomland, grown up in pasture grass and about four acres in extent. The Confederates placed their fortified skirmish line in the wood's edge on the east margin of this bottomland. The ascending slope toward their main line of works was at least partly wooded, especially on the left wing of McCook's column. Waiting for them in the trenches stood the men of Vaughan's Tennessee Brigade.[10]

Thomas's artillery opened fire at about 8:00 A.M., the scheduled time for all three assaults to begin on the morning of June 27. Pieces on Hooker's Twentieth Corps front contributed to the bombardment. William Clark McLean of the 123rd New York had a clear view of the batteries in action.

"The gunners worked in their shirtsleeves and looked like workmen in a furnace," he reported. "The sweat pouring from them and the fire and smoke from the guns made it look like a modern Mount Sina."[11]

The guns alerted the Confederates to the fact that trouble was on its way. Before then, June 27 had started as a comparatively hot, lazy morning. After breakfast, the men of the 1st Tennessee within the angle on Cheatham's Hill "arranged their blankets across the poles over the ditch as a protection against the beaming sun." Soon after, their skirmishers sent back reports that the Yankees were massing troops. When the shower of Union artillery began to descend, the Confederates were relieved to see that their improved fortifications withstood the pounding very well.[12]

THE ADVANCE

McCook's men started as soon as the guns opened fire.[13] Colonel Caleb J. Dilworth's Eighty-Fifth Illinois, leading the brigade as skirmishers, crossed the Union skirmish trench held by members of Brigadier General James D. Morgan's brigade and raised "a prolonged cheer" as it moved swiftly down the slope into the valley. Each regiment in the brigade column in turn did the same thing, the men holding their arms at right shoulder shift. After clearing the Federal line, McCook's men continued at quick time until they were in the valley and then shifted to double-quick as they began to cross the bottomland. Some troops of Morgan's brigade misunderstood their orders and thought they were to attack with McCook. One company actually started out to follow, but officers were able to stop it in time.[14]

Confederate artillerists began to fire at McCook's column as soon as it moved down the slope into the valley. James Holmes of the Fifty-Second Ohio thought they did little damage because the Federals were moving downhill, "each step changed the range by reason of the descent." Moving double-quick across the marshy bottomland disarranged the Federal ranks a bit, and a thin skirt of small trees and vines lay along both sides of the branch in many spots. The Eighty-Fifth Illinois, on a run, preceded the column far enough to capture the thin line of Confederate skirmishers on the eastern edge of the bottomland by the time the 125th Illinois crossed the branch.[15]

At the end of McCook's column, not more than halfway down the slope toward the stream, Lieutenant Colonel Charles W. Clancy felt the sting of a bullet just below his left knee. He dropped off to examine the injury, believing his leg was shattered, but saw that the ball had bored a hole through the overturned flap of his boot and had only numbed his leg. Using his sword as a cane, Clancy began to hobble along after his regiment.[16]

Crossing the branch somewhat disarranged the line of the Fifty-Second Ohio. When it quickly re-formed and continued pushing forward, the regiment lost its first member killed in the attack. About ten paces short of the captured Confederate skirmish line, a man "pitched forward to the ground, both hands stretched out with his rifle in the right." James T. Holmes recognized him as Corporal Isaac Newton Wycoff, a former student of his in Richmond College, Ohio. Wycoff died later that day.[17]

Holmes had no time to think of Wycoff as the regiment closed in on the thin skirt of trees within which the Confederates had planted their skirmish line. Enemy fire from the main line thickened with each step. "I remember a queer thought that passed through my mind as the balls whizzed and zipped above and around us striking the grass, the ground and an old stump," wrote Holmes. "They seemed to come so thickly that my thought was, 'If I should hold out my hand I could catch several of them—a handful—immediately.'"[18]

Then Holmes saw a man near him who "suddenly whirled about, with a face as white as death's and the purpose plainly written on it to take flight." He raised his sword and yelled "'Stop, Joe,'" and the man quietly turned around and did his duty for the rest of the day. Holmes knew him as a good, reliable soldier on every previous occasion, and Joe never exhibited fear again during the rest of the war. But decades later, when Holmes helped him to obtain a pension and reminded him jokingly of June 27, the man "was utterly incredulous" because he could not recall trying to run away at all.[19]

Despite all that was happening, Holmes glanced to the left as his regiment crossed the meadow and saw the right flank of Harker's brigade to the north. Harker was mostly crossing the little valley where it was more narrow and wooded, but his right flank appeared near the northern end of the cleared area that McCook crossed. Holmes could plainly see the Fourth Corps troops and observed for a minute as Harker rode boldly forward, directing his brigade.[20]

McCook received a thickening hail of bullets as his men crossed the open bottomland, but he also became more easily aware of the heavy artillery fire directed at his command from the south. Cheatham had much earlier placed eight guns south of the endangered hill that was the target of the Fourteenth Corps troops. They were Phelan's Alabama Battery, commanded by Lieutenant Nathaniel Venable, and Captain Thomas J. Perry's Florida

Federal approach to Cheatham's Hill (Earl J. Hess)

Battery, both planted within the sector controlled by Carter's Tennessee Brigade just south of Cheatham's Hill. These pieces were able to sweep the valley, and McCook's only recourse was to move quickly across the marshy expanse. The closer his men got to the Confederate line of works, the less they would be exposed to this artillery fire.[21]

But, of course, the closer they moved toward the works the more they became exposed to the Confederate infantry. The gray-clad troops were led by a veteran of many battles. Alfred Jefferson Vaughan Jr. was a graduate of Virginia Military Institute and had worked as a civil engineer, surveyor, and farmer before the war propelled him to the command first of the Thirteenth Tennessee and later a brigade. His men waited anxiously for a clear sight of the approaching enemy amid the din of artillery fire and the scattering skirmish fire that occurred as the Eighty-Fifth Illinois took the picket line. J. T. Bowden of the Twelfth Tennessee remembered the sight of his comrades "craning their necks away above the head logs looking for some thing to shoot at." Soon Vaughan's brigade opened fire directly to the front, even though Bowden still could not see anything. He glanced to the left and caught sight of a "solid mass of Yankees" only about 100 feet in front of the line held by the Eleventh and Twenty-Ninth Tennessee, immediately to the left of the Twelfth Tennessee. Bowden remembered the instructions of Colonel George W. Gordon of the Eleventh Tennessee, who had suggested

View from Cheatham's Hill (Earl J. Hess)

that individual regiments fire obliquely if the enemy appeared before neighboring units. Bowden consulted with his captain, Johnnie B. Jones, who acted on that advice and directed the fire of his company toward the left.[22]

The sight of McCook's solid column ascending the slope impressed everyone who saw it. A member of the First Tennessee, clinging to the angle on Cheatham's Hill and not directly targeted by McCook, admired the Federal approach. They "marched up quietly without any huzzas or noise, with their bayonets gleaming in the bright sun. They were fine-looking fellows and brave ones at that."[23]

McCook's front stretched from near the angle northward to cover much of Vaughan's sector. Cheatham estimated that the Yankees were sixty yards away before his infantry opened fire. As the Federals continued to close on the works, Lieutenant Luke E. Wright's two-gun section of Mebane's Tennessee Battery, located in a redoubt on Vaughan's right wing, opened fire at close range and devastated their ranks. The artillerists had kept the guns hidden as much as possible by piling brush in front of them. Now, Wright had a rare opportunity to pummel a dense enemy column at short range.[24]

The rest of McCook's brigade was making its way up the slope, and the front regiment already was hitting the Confederate works when the last unit, the Fifty-Second Ohio, came into the skirt of timber shadowing the eastern side of the bottomland. The Ohioans paused a few moments to lay down and catch their breath. "A perfect shower of lead swept just over us," recalled James T. Holmes. Walking wounded from regiments farther ahead began to stream back through the ranks of the Fifty-Second. After a pause, the regiment rose up and began to climb the slope. As it ascended, the backward surge of wounded and frightened troops increased with each passing step. "Men came rushing down the slope in crowds breathing hard through fear and physical exhaustion," Holmes continued. "The tide of retreat swelled until I thought at one moment my part of the regiment, the left wing, would be swept away by the throng."[25]

Company officers strove to maintain order as the Fifty-Second Ohio continued to move up the eastern slope of the valley, losing casualties along the way. "Up and up and up, we went through death and wounds to within seventy-five feet of the blazing, smoking line," Holmes dramatically put it. Enfilading artillery fire and direct musketry continued to thicken with each step forward. "It was dreadful, deadly work," Holmes wrote. "The very air quivered with insistent mortality."[26]

What happened to McCook's brigade was summed up by Styles W. Porter of the Fifty-Second Ohio when he confided to his diary that the attack brought his comrades to the Confederate works, and "there we stuck." As the regiment came within close range of the enemy trench, "with one accord the line halted, crowded and began firing," as Captain Frank B. James put it. McCook's column collapsed into a roughly formed mass of men. Only the Fifty-Second Ohio, according to its surviving members, maintained something like a regimental battle line as it closed up on the rear of this mass before it came to rest only twenty-five yards from the Rebel line. In essence, as phrased by Nixon B. Stewart, "we were all in the front line at that point." Bringing up the rear, the Fifty-Second Ohio had lost eighty-five men (four of them color-bearers) out of three hundred engaged. Fifteen minutes had elapsed between the time Corporal Wycoff went down until the regiment ended the advance twenty-five yards from the blazing Confederate line.[27]

To the credit of the brigade, most of the men remained within close range of the objective and sought ways to crest the defenses. Adjutant Lansing J. Dawdy of the Eighty-Sixth Illinois noticed that ample abatis lay in front of the angle on Cheatham's Hill but none north of it. That gave him an opportunity to try a quick penetration of the Rebel line. He called on the prone men of Company A to rise up and advance. A man near Sergeant J. H. Brubacker openly "said it was hopeless and hesitated," but at least twenty men of the company tried to follow Dawdy. They slowly moved forward, firing as they went, and the group was essentially all shot down. Brubacker noticed two of them, who were close friends, emotionally supporting each other. They "reached behind one of the men that separated them and clasped hands as though bidding each other good bye." Both friends were killed in the hail of short-range musketry. Dawdy recalled that Company A lost twenty-three men out of forty engaged in the battle, most of them in this abortive attempt to cross the works. Dawdy himself was shot about twenty feet north of the angle and ten feet short of the Confederate line.[28]

Some Union color-bearers moved close enough to plant their flags on the enemy parapet. As J. T. Bowden put it, they "stuck their flag up to our noses." This portended an effort to cross the works but the Confederates were ready. "Just as it looked like they were going to come over the works, we began to yell, Come on," Bowden recalled.[29]

McCook fearfully exposed himself to urge his troops on. He saw that another surge of men began to move forward and waved for them to follow him. Then the intrepid officer made his way up the parapet. Most of the men who followed him dropped from the incessant enemy fire before they could close on their commander.[30]

S. M. Canterbury of the Eighty-Sixth Illinois managed to reach the parapet and lay down near McCook to take cover. The brigade leader continued to stand fearlessly on the parapet, one foot resting on a head log. He used his sword to parry efforts by the Confederates to bayonet him. Canterbury reached up and grabbed his coat, telling him "'Colonel Dan, for God's sake get down, they will shoot you.' He turned partly around, stooping a little, and said to me, 'G—d d—n you, attend to your own business.'" Just then McCook was shot by a Confederate soldier who pointed the muzzle of his musket only a foot from the colonel's body. "Had I not pulled on his coat, I believe he would have fallen inside the rebel works," Canterbury concluded.[31]

Canterbury probably played loosely with the facts, embellishing what was for the brigade a traumatic moment in the loss of their beloved commander. Surgeon M. M. Hooton of the Eighty-Sixth Illinois, who treated McCook later that day, testified that the officer briefly told him what really happened. "'I had just placed my left hand on the head log and turned to Capt. [William W.] Fellows and called to him to tell Col. [Oscar F.] Harmon to bring the right wing up double quick. The next thing I knew the men were carrying me down to the ravine, and someone put some water on my face.'"[32]

Yet another perspective on the wounding of McCook was provided by an officer of a Confederate unit opposing the brigade. He told Samuel A.

Harper of the Fifty-Second Ohio during the burial truce on June 29 that McCook held a sword in his right hand and his hat in the left while he called out "'Surrender, you damn traitors.'" Two members of the Eighty-Sixth Illinois confirmed that they saw McCook in this pose, saying something similar to those words. The brigade leader also encouraged his men to "'Stick to them boys, I am wounded,'" as he was carried away.[33]

Whatever the exact particulars, McCook paid dearly for his bravado. A Rebel ball entered his right chest a few inches below the collar bone and lodged in his body after penetrating the top of his lung. He was shot about eighteen feet north of the angle of the Confederate line on Cheatham Hill.[34]

Colonel Oscar Harmon of the 125th Illinois took charge of the brigade, but he was shot little more than five minutes later. Harmon died almost instantly, and later in the day his body was transported to the rear. James T. Holmes characterized Harmon as "one of nature's noblemen, a quiet, vigilant, effective officer, who never lost his head." Holmes considered him to be a similar type of man as Abraham Lincoln, his fellow Illinoisan. Another acquaintance, Major James Connolly of Baird's division staff, carefully laid out Harmon's body when it arrived at the rear. Captain William Fellows also was shot soon after McCook fell and only a few feet from his commander. Fellows served on McCook's staff as brigade inspector. Like Harmon, Fellows was killed almost instantly.[35]

For a few minutes of frenzied turmoil, the Federals remained close to the Confederate works, in some places separated only by the width of the parapet. The combatants were close enough so that the Confederates began throwing rocks onto their opponents "with telling effect," according to Leroy Mayfield of the Twenty-Second Indiana. Allen Fahnestock recalled that not only stones but axes, spades, and chunks of wood came flying across the parapet onto the heads of nervous Union soldiers.[36]

Meanwhile, the Federals planted several flags in the loose dirt at the foot of the parapet. A Rebel officer was killed trying to take possession of one such color. Along the sector held by the Twenty-Ninth Tennessee, a Confederate enlisted man made a grab for a Union flag and was fired at. The bullets missed, and he took the color safely into the Confederate line, "waved it & talk about the 'rebel yell.' You never heard one to beat it," recalled J. T. Bowden. Captain A. A. Lee of the Eighty-Sixth Illinois managed to get close enough to grab an axe from the hand of a Confederate soldier and brought it back as a trophy.[37]

During the few minutes that McCook's brigade remained close to the Confederate line, many of the men were shot. Johnson Brown of the Fifty-

Second Ohio described the death of comrade James Beard to his cousin. Beard was "a good soldier" who "stood up to it like a man." He was next to Brown when a bullet smashed into his mouth. "I think he did not struggle but very little," Brown reported. In the same regiment it seemed to James Holmes that men "gave up their lives everywhere. . . . You could not say or think who would die or be maimed the next instant." Holmes remembered the "sickening sound" made by minie balls as they thudded into human flesh for the rest of his long life. As Alfred Tyler Fielder of the Twelfth Tennessee put it, his men were "Mowing them down with awful slaughter."[38]

The irregular formation of the brigade as it lay close to the Rebel line placed the left wing about ten yards farther away from the works than the right wing. Apparently most of the efforts to climb the parapet had taken place on the right. All the men were lying down after McCook's fall, many of them taking cover behind the bodies of their comrades. Those to the rear had opportunities to return fire. When the Rebels rose in their trenches to depress the muzzles of their weapons and hit those Yankees who were lying close to the works, Federals at the rear of the brigade were able to fire at them as the tips of their hats appeared above the head log.[39]

Destiny seemed to dictate the fate of many that day. R. J. Stewart of the Fifty-Second Ohio had told John Moore the evening before that he expected to die. "'I don't want to be wounded,'" he confided to Moore. "'I want to be shot through the heart,'" and die instantly. He got his wish. Moore saw Stewart's body with a bullet hole in the breast lying only twelve feet from the Confederate line.[40]

Not long after McCook fell and fifteen to thirty minutes after reaching high tide, the brigade began to move away from the Confederate works. Styles W. Porter phrased it bluntly when he wrote, "somehow we lost our grit." But the men did not fall back to the starting point of their attack. They discovered the advantage of the slight crest a few yards away from the enemy and used it as a shelter. The crest would, at the very least, allow them the opportunity "to recover breath and wits" as Holmes put it. The right wing, lodged a bit closer to the Confederates, broke up and fell back quicker than the rest. Initially the center and left wing held fast but then crawled back too. Survivors reported that the fall back covered anywhere from thirty to one hundred feet, lodging the Federals from twenty-five to sixty yards from the enemy.[41]

McCook was taken away when the brigade crawled back to the crest of the hill. Three men carried the badly wounded officer to the rear. One of them was John S. Cochennour, a member of Morgan's brigade who had joined

McCook's attack, and another was J. T. Seay of the Eighty-Fifth Illinois. About one hundred feet from the Confederate works, Julius Armstrong of the Fifty-Second Ohio saw the group pass by and hurriedly exchanged a word with the colonel. McCook told him "that he was disabled, but that the fight must be continued."[42]

The group came upon McCook's colleague, Colonel John Mitchell, whose Second Brigade had gone in to the right of McCook's. Mitchell and his staff were standing near a tree about seventy-five yards in front of the main Union line, on the other side of the branch valley. According to Cochennour, McCook angrily berated Mitchell. "'If I live, I will have you court-martialed,'" he said. McCook was furious that Mitchell had stayed behind instead of leading his brigade to its fate. Mitchell ignored the threat and calmly told one of his staff members, "'We will have to have Morgan.'" He meant that Morgan's brigade ought to be called into action to support those men already engaged, but that thought was never acted on.[43]

Colonel James W. Langley of the 125th Illinois also had not gone in with his command, but he had a good excuse. Langley was serving on the staff of Fourteenth Corps commander John M. Palmer. He broke away from his duties to ride forward and see how his regiment fared in the attack and came across McCook on the way. The wounded colonel's voice "was weak and he spoke with difficulty and seeming pain." But McCook managed to communicate with Langley. "'Tell Gen. Thomas and Gen. Palmer that we did all we could to break the rebel line, I was on their works when I fell and others were with me, but it was impossible.'"[44]

While McCook was carried to the rear, other men moved Harmon's body back as well. Palmer, who had seemed to one observer earlier that day to be "deeply flushed," also rode forward to get a closer view of the assault. When he encountered McCook and Harmon, he knew with certainty that the attack was a failure.[45]

As the men of McCook's command settled into place behind the crest of the hill, Colonel Caleb J. Dilworth of the Eighty-Fifth Illinois assumed command of the brigade. He consulted with Allen Fahnestock about what to do, and the two came to the conclusion that to renew the attack was suicidal. To attempt a fallback to the starting point of the attack might be nearly as deadly. There seemed no choice but to remain where they were and dig in. The crest offered scant protection, but it was enough to make such a plan feasible. Holmes later estimated that "a man lying flat on the ground was an inch or two below the rebel line of fire." An illustration of just how tenuous that terrain feature was in protecting the Federals lay in the case of Captain

Samuel Rothacker of Company G, Fifty-Second Ohio. As he lay flat behind the crest, with his head resting on his hands, the brim of his "big black military hat was shot through just by the band within a half inch of his head."[46]

Dilworth and the regimental commanders tried to separate their units as much as possible to impose order on the mass of men huddling behind the crest. They also bent back the two flanks of the brigade a bit.[47]

Not every survivor of the attack had an opportunity to fall back with the others. Nixon Stewart of the Fifty-Second Ohio estimated that perhaps one-half of that regiment continued to lay close to the Rebel earthworks. The men were too exposed to do anything but crawl back as best they could, hoping the Confederates would not be able to hit them. Stewart himself lay only ten feet from the parapet near the stump of a chestnut tree. When Joseph E. Watkins of the Twenty-Second Indiana rose up to run toward the rear, the Confederates shot and killed him almost instantly. Watkins fell across Stewart's feet. Colonel Clancy of the Fifty-Second Ohio also stood up to run back, but he soon caught his foot in the belt of an abandoned officer's sword. This probably saved his life, for it caused him to lunge crazily into the brigade formation, offering a poor target to the Confederates. Stewart waited for at least forty minutes, nervously wondering what he should do, before he drummed up enough courage to reach safety.[48]

By the time Stewart rejoined his comrades, the brigade was throwing up dirt to make crude earthworks. They did so without tools of any kind for several hours to come. It is doubtful any of McCook's men realized it at this time, but they were doing something comparatively unique in the Civil War, digging in within close range of the enemy after a failed assault. Unlike the other units in the attack at Kennesaw, the Fourteenth Corps men remained within a stone's throw of the Confederates. It had not been planned but came about through circumstance. If the Confederate engineers had not placed Cheatham's line a few yards behind the military crest of the hill, the Federals would not have had an opportunity to remain so close. This happy opportunity, which undoubtedly saved many Union lives, also gave McCook's men the chance to argue that they were not really repulsed. In the words of Allen Fahnestock, the brigade "maintained the position gained and fortified [it] from twenty-five to sixty yards from the rebel works."[49]

MITCHELL'S BRIGADE

Colonel John Grant Mitchell roused his Second Brigade at the same time that McCook's men woke up that morning. Born in Ohio, Mitchell graduated from Kenyon College only two years before the firing on Fort Sumter and practiced law. He served as a captain in the Third Ohio before becoming colonel of the 113th Ohio in the summer of 1862. Mitchell led a brigade in the heroic defense of Snodgrass Hill at Chickamauga but saw no action in the fighting at Chattanooga. Like McCook's brigade, Mitchell's command had seen much campaigning but comparatively little combat thus far in the Atlanta campaign.[50]

Mitchell's men disposed of their knapsacks, baggage, and cooking utensils by piling the material as officers detailed sick men to guard it. The brigade then moved to the staging area and formed a column of regiments. The 113th Ohio stood first in the column, followed by the 121st Ohio, then the Ninety-Eighth Ohio, with the Seventy-Eighth Illinois bringing up the rear. The Thirty-Fourth Illinois deployed as skirmishers in front. While the regiments forming the column fixed bayonets, Lieutenant Colonel Oscar Van Tassell placed Companies A and B of the Thirty-Fourth Illinois as a first line of skirmishers without bayonets. He further placed Companies F and I five paces behind the first line with fixed bayonets. The other six companies of the regiment constituted the skirmish reserve.[51]

While waiting for the signal to start, members of the rank and file noticed their officers gathering in knots and engaging in earnest conversation, "telling each other what they wish to have done in case the worst happens." F. M. McAdams recalled that "it gradually dawns upon us in the ranks, that we are to carry his works by assault." Ironically, there were some staff officers nearby who lay bets on whether the skirmishers could take the Confederate skirmish line. When members of the Thirty-Fourth Illinois heard about it, they became angry that anyone could doubt their ability.[52]

Mitchell instructed Colonel Henry B. Banning to move his 121st Ohio, placed second in the brigade column, off to the right as soon as the 113th Ohio reached the enemy's main line. Mitchell further warned Banning that once he had extended to the right of the 113th Ohio, he would probably see that his own left flank was even with an angle in the Confederate line of works. This would require him to conduct a left wheel in order to close up on the reentering line of the Confederate trench. But Mitchell also wanted every regiment behind Banning's to conduct a similar move and extend the brigade formation in a continuous line to the right. In short, while approaching the target in a column of regiments, Mitchell planned to deploy a line of battle when his command came within short range of the objective.[53]

In order to facilitate this tricky move, Mitchell aligned his regiments in a form slightly different from that used by McCook. Banning's regiment formed so that its two right companies extended farther to the right than did Lieutenant Colonel Darius B. Warner's 113th Ohio. Mitchell instructed Banning to make the right flank of his third company the guide of his regiment, keeping alignment with the right flank of Warner's regimental line directly in front. Banning's two right companies were instructed to guide left, so as to keep closed in on the rest of the regiment. The other two regiments behind Banning were instructed to do the same thing. As a result, Mitchell's brigade formed slightly en echelon to make it easier to deploy into line at the proper time.[54]

Mitchell was poised to strike at Maney's brigade of Cheatham's division, which held the Confederate line from the angle in the works and along the reentering line. Cheatham spread the word early in the morning that the enemy would attack this day and encouraged his men "to hold the works at all hazards." Because of the heat, members of the First Tennessee had stretched their blankets across the trench to provide shade. They quickly took them down as soon as the Federal artillery opened fire at 8:00 A.M.[55]

The Yankees began to advance as soon as the guns opened up. Companies A and B of the Thirty-Fourth Illinois sprang forward, "yelling like so many Comanches," as William C. Robinson put it. They were followed by Companies F and I as a first line of reserves. The skirmishers received Confederate artillery fire as soon as they crossed the Union skirmish trench. Edwin Payne noticed that one round tore off the saddle from an artillery horse nearby but did no harm to the horse at all. The first line of skirmishers had no difficulty overrunning the Confederate skirmish line, taking several prisoners. The Rebel skirmishers occupied a line of pits big enough for four men each, and the line was farther from the main Confederate position on Mitchell's right than on his left. This made it more difficult for the Rebel skirmishers to escape, and Payne reported that all but half a dozen of them were taken prisoner. The Federal skirmishers continued forward and were the first men of Mitchell's brigade to close on the enemy line.[56]

With the onset of the artillery bombardment, Mitchell's brigade started the attack at about 8:00 A.M. The men began at the double-quick and moved swiftly down the valley of the branch that separated the opposing forces. The slope and the branch disrupted the formation of the 113th Ohio at the head of the column, but the men continued to move forward "with ardor and the highest courage," according to one of the regimental captains. Members of Williams's Twentieth Corps division off to the south caught glimpses of Mitchell's column as it moved through the open space of the valley. "It was a grand sight to see them charge across the field," reported William Clark McLean of the 123rd New York.[57]

As members of the First Tennessee huddled in the angle, waiting for the enemy, Captain W. D. Kelly of the Rock City Guards rose up to see farther down the slope. He caught sight of Mitchell's skirmishers as they approached and yelled "'Up, up men; they are charging us!'" Kelly's troops steeled themselves for the onset, lifting away a small tree that had fallen across the trench. The Federal advance was slowed a bit by numerous saplings and underbrush that the Confederates had cut "and cross-lapped in a manner that made it impossible to keep in line," reported F. M. McAdams of the 113th Ohio. It was also difficult "to advance singly, with any rapidity." Moreover, rifle fire from the front and artillery fire from the eight-gun battery to the south exacted a toll on the advancing Federals. The Confederate guns had an enfilading fire on the formation, causing some of Mitchell's men to crowd to the left toward McCook's command.[58]

Captain Toland Jones of the 113th Ohio remembered that the Confederate fire intensified when his men reached a point halfway up the slope of Cheatham's Hill. As the regiment neared the enemy position, Banning moved his 121st Ohio by the right flank to clear the 113th Ohio and prepared to execute a left wheel. Everyone could see that a substantial abatis fronted the angle and the reentering line, and that the Confederates occupied a deep trench behind the abatis. In fact, as Jones put it, the Rebels had prepared their position "with all the appliances of the most skillful engineering."[59]

Companies A, B, F, and I of the Thirty-Fourth Illinois, constituting Mitchell's skirmishers, halted about twelve to fifteen rods from the main Confederate line and waited for the brigade to catch up. Warner's 113th Ohio came forward a few short minutes later, many of his men "crowded up to the works only to be shot down," wrote F. M. McAdams, while "a few climbed upon their works and were made prisoners." Most of Warner's troops, however, found shelter wherever they could on the uneven ground or behind stumps, and then they opened fire. Warner was hit and badly wounded in the right arm while urging his men forward. A lieutenant of the 113th Ohio was overcome with heat prostration, and ten out of nineteen officers in the regiment were either killed or wounded. Mitchell later argued that it was impossible for a large number of his troops to penetrate the abatis and mount the works.[60]

Banning found that the scenario described to him proved to be accurate;

the angle in the Confederate works lay just before the right end of Warner's 113th Ohio line. Banning moved his 121st Ohio by the right flank as the brigade column was still advancing. As Mitchell had instructed, he began to conduct a left wheel when his left flank came to rest only a short distance from the Confederate works in an attempt to close up on the reentering line. Ironically, the Rebels in that reentering line waited until Banning had nearly completed his wheel before they opened fire on the closing enemy. The losses of the 121st Ohio were appalling. The captain of Company B was mortally wounded, the captain of Company G was killed, and the captain of Company E was wounded in the ankle, an injury which later proved mortal. Banning's major, who exercised control of the regiment's left wing, was hit by three bullets and died before the end of the day. Company I lost twenty-nine out of fifty-six men engaged that day, and lost its commander owing to a wound in the knee. Every sergeant in Company B was either killed or wounded. All of this destruction took place within a few short minutes after the regiment completed its left wheel and snuggled close up to the reentering line.[61]

THE CONFEDERATE STRUGGLE FOR CHEATHAM'S HILL

Brigadier General George Earl Maney had not been able to pack troops in the vulnerable angle on Cheatham's Hill. Born at Franklin, Tennessee, and a graduate of the University of Nashville, Maney served in the Mexican War and practiced law before the war offered him a chance to command the First Tennessee. He had a great deal of experience in battle from Shiloh to Chattanooga and apparently felt comfortable with posting only 180 men of the consolidated First and Twenty-Seventh Tennessee in the angle. Some parts of the line had no head logs because Union artillery had knocked them down during the past couple of days. "We had the word passed to us to hold the works at all hazards," commented a member of the First Tennessee, "and it did look as if we would be pushed back by sheer force."[62]

The Confederates mounted one of the most inspired defensive actions of the war at the angle. George B. Allen of the Rock City Guards excitedly jumped onto the parapet and shouted to encourage his comrades. He paid for it with his life. Colonel Hume R. Feild, who commanded the consolidated regiment, encouraged his men by yelling, "'Give them the bayonet, if they come over.'" After a few minutes of rapid firing the gun barrels grew so hot that "we could hardly hold on to them." The Confederate veterans shifted into a frame of mind that transformed them into killing machines.

"There was no time to think, action, under such circumstances, becomes intuitive, mechanical," recalled an anonymous member of the Rock City Guards.[63]

Colonel Feild joined in the shooting spree. He "sat astride of a stringer that supported a head log while his men below passed loaded guns up to him." Then a Federal soldier who managed to penetrate the abatis confronted the colonel at such close range that their musket barrels overlapped. The Federal shot first, and his bullet grazed Feild's head. The colonel fell off the stringer, unconscious, and landed among his men in the trench. Fortunately for the combative officer, he regained consciousness a few minutes later but found that his left side was temporarily paralyzed. "'Well, they have got me at last,'" he told Sam R. Watkins, "'but I have killed fifteen of them; time about is fair play, I reckon.'" The colonel was very lucky that the bullet only grazed his skull, and he later regained the full use of his muscles.[64]

Pressed hard by what seemed like an overwhelming force of the enemy, each defender of Cheatham's Hill felt "the whole responsibility of the Confederate government was rested [sic] upon his shoulders," as Sam R. Watkins put it. His comrades "had to keep up the firing and shooting them down in self-defense," continued Watkins. "It was, verily, a life and death grapple, and the least flicker on our part, would have been sure death to all. We could not be reinforced on account of our position, and we had to stand up to the rack, fodder or no fodder."[65]

Watkins fired 120 rounds that day and reported that his gun barrel became "so hot that frequently the powder would flash before I could ram home the ball, and I had frequently to exchange my gun for that of a dead comrade." Several men of the First Tennessee began to grab rocks and sticks and throw them across the parapet onto the Federals, and the Yankees returned the favor as well. At one point in this frenzied combat, Watkins looked up and saw the stars and stripes floating almost in his face. John Branch of the Rock City Guards, the company next to Watkins, shouted "'Look at that Yankee flag; shoot that fellow; snatch that flag out of his hand!'"[66]

Watkins's life was saved by William A. Hughes, his messmate and close friend. When three Federals approached the parapet Watkins fired and killed two of them with one round. The third man was enraged and had Watkins at a disadvantage. Hughes, however, reached up and grabbed the muzzle of the Yankee's gun, "receiving the whole contents in his hand and arm, and mortally wounding him." Later, when carried away "all mutilated and bleeding," Hughes told his stretcher-bearers to give his gun, blankets, and clothing to Watkins.[67]

There was little time then to contemplate the meaning of Hughes's sacrifice. For Watkins and all the other Confederates at the angle, the fight continued for what seemed like ages. "The sun beaming down on our uncovered heads, . . . and a solid line of blazing fire right from the muzzles of the Yankee guns being poured right into our very faces, singeing our hair and clothes, the hot blood of our dead and wounded spurting on us, the blinding smoke and stifling atmosphere filling our eyes and mouths, and the awful concussion causing the blood to gush out of our noses and ears, and above all, the roar of battle, made it a perfect pandemonium. Afterward I heard a soldier express himself by saying that he thought 'Hell had broke loose in Georgia, sure enough.'"[68]

The press of Yankees at the angle was tremendous, so the adjutant of the First Tennessee ran toward the left along the reentering line and told the consolidated Sixth and Ninth Tennessee to move in that direction. His own regiment was nearly out of ammunition. The men obeyed immediately, moving by the right flank through the trench. Although there were as yet few enemy troops facing them, the move was conducted amid a shower of balls, which caused the Tennessee men to stoop low as they hurried toward the angle. They also had to stoop in order to go under the braces that lined the trench, placed there to catch a head log in case it fell off the parapet.[69]

The embattled members of the First and Twenty-Seventh Tennessee saw help on its way but felt insulted, according to Sam Watkins. They assumed it was because someone thought they could not stand up to the pressure. "'Go back! go back! we can hold this place, and by the eternal God we are not going to leave it,'" some of them shouted. But the members of the Sixth and Ninth Tennessee took position behind the First and Twenty-Seventh to add the weight of their fire to the volume already issuing from the angle.[70]

The firing was so intense for a while that it affected the men's weapons. A man of the Ninth Tennessee showed Captain James I. Hall that his rifle was "choked and rendered useless by melted lead. The thin shaving of lead pared off from the minie ball by the grooves of our rifles when melted, ran down into the tubes of the guns when held in an upright position." Hall quickly understood the problem and called on his men "to reverse their guns" before reloading to allow the melted lead to drain out of the muzzle. Hall saw "small round pellets of melted lead" roll out of the guns when they did as he ordered.[71]

The Federals could not remain long in their exposed position just outside the Confederate earthworks; they had to either cross the parapet or retire. Colonel Banning's 121st Ohio suffered enormously because of the eight-gun battery to the south, on Carter's brigade sector. The other regiments behind him in the column, the Ninety-Eighth Ohio and Seventy-Eighth Illinois, had failed to extend their line and wheel left to close on the Rebel works to his right, as ordered. No one offered any criticism of those two regiments for their failure; it was asking too much of them to do so. Only the 113th Ohio, 121st Ohio, and Thirty-Fourth Illinois actually closed in on Maney's entrenchments. Banning therefore ordered his men to move a bit to the right and then fall back about twenty paces to take advantage of the crest of the slope where they could obtain some protection. The slope ran along the northern edge of the smaller side branch that flowed westward into the main branch of John Ward Creek, which divided the opposing lines.[72]

Warner's 113th Ohio also fell back from the angle a bit after Banning's 121st Ohio did so to its right, and after McCook's brigade had done so to its left. The men retired through the ranks of the Ninety-Eighth Ohio, causing Companies B and G of the Ninety-Eighth to fall back with them before orders were issued within the regiment to retire. The entire brigade very soon followed the example and assembled just beneath the crest.[73]

George Phipps, the color-bearer of the Thirty-Fourth Illinois, had a desire to plant his flag on the Confederate works and had moved forward to do so. But Lieutenant Joseph Teeter of Company I stopped him and ordered the foolhardy sergeant to fall back with the rest. Phipps was hit by a ball as he started to do so. Teeter rescued the flag as other men carried the wounded man away and brought the colors to Van Tassel. The regimental commander carried them to the crest, the staff on his left shoulder and the colors draped across his right shoulder.[74]

Cheatham was aware of the danger at the angle, and he arranged for reinforcements to help Maney. Brigadier General Jesse J. Finley's brigade rushed forward for a mile on the double-quick but arrived just after the Federals fell back. According to Sergeant Washington Ives of the Fourth Florida, the brigade had been issued brand new Enfield rifles the night before the battle, and "the boys were disappointed in not getting to shoot." Finley deployed a battle line just to the rear of the angle for the time being.[75]

The fight at the angle lasted anywhere from twenty minutes to an hour, according to estimates by embattled Confederates. The actual time surely must have been closer to twenty minutes given the exposed condition of the attacking Federals. A member of the Thirty-Fourth Illinois estimated that the battleground itself was quite small. Mitchell's brigade probably covered no more than a thousand square feet of Georgia soil at the height of its assault on Maney's works.[76]

Mitchell's men dug in just behind the crest of the branch, using bayonets to break up the red clay and tin cups to scoop it into something like a parapet. They were forty paces to one hundred yards from the Confederate works. The Rebels could see them digging in and recognized that the crest provided essential cover for the Yankee position. Nevertheless, the repulse offered some degree of consolation to those privates who had earlier been critical of the placement of Cheatham's line. As a member of the First Tennessee put it, "a good many of the 'high privates'" had already given their opinion that "our works were too far beyond the crest of the hill for us to successfully defend them." Cheatham felt that he was too weak to attack the Federals and dislodge them from their close position, but he also felt certain his men could continue holding the works indefinitely.[77]

FEDERAL SUPPORT

James D. Morgan's brigade of Davis's division continued to hold the main Union line opposite the angle during the frenzied attack of June 27, having relieved Brigadier General Walter C. Whitaker's brigade and the Seventy-Seventh Pennsylvania of Colonel William Grose's brigade of the Fourth Corps early that morning. With McCook and Mitchell lodged a few hundred yards away, perilously close to the enemy, Morgan maintained his position for the rest of the time that Sherman spent at Kennesaw Mountain. Morgan suffered casualties despite his support role. Also, Colonel Charles M. Lum of the Tenth Michigan reported that "many of our men had to be restrained by their officers to keep them from joining the charging force" when Mitchell started the attack. Morgan's men also watched as stragglers from Mitchell's column came back and crossed the Union line on their way to the rear.[78]

Thomas had arranged for ample reserves to be available to Davis if the need arose. Brigadier General Absalom Baird's division of the Fourteenth Corps, which replaced Davis's division when Davis pulled out of his works to assemble for the attack, was ready to go in. In fact, about half the men of the 105th Ohio mounted the parapet because they had the idea that they were supposed to join in the attack, and they had to be called down into the trench. Baird's troops later stared at a stream of wounded men from Davis's command heading back to the main Federal position. Their wounds were dressed in makeshift stations near the line before transport to the rear.[79]

Hooker stood ready to advance Williams's division of the Twentieth Corps along the Powder Springs and Marietta Road if called upon to divert Confederate attention from Cheatham's Hill. Geary's division, closer to the scene of the Fourteenth Corps attack, also made ready to go in. Geary massed his command, forming a column of brigades, as Williams sent a brigade to occupy Geary's works. At 8:00 A.M., when the triple attack began, Geary advanced eastward and easily captured the Confederate skirmish line, taking many prisoners. He deployed his division along the eastern edge of the woods that separated him from the main Confederate line, bending back both flanks because of his advanced and exposed position. Hooker's artillery, and that of Palmer's Fourteenth Corps, kept up a nearly constant fire during and long after the attack, as many men in the Twentieth Corps wondered if they would suddenly be called on to move forward against the Rebel works. That order, however, never arrived.[80]

END OF A MORNING'S WORK

It is possible, as J. T. Bowden of the Twelfth Tennessee believed, that no more than a thousand Rebel soldiers held the sector of Cheatham's line that was hit by McCook's and Mitchell's brigades. The Federals brought about four thousand veteran troops against that sector. If this level of disparity in numbers is accurate, it is a sterling testament not only to the staying power of Cheatham's Tennessee troops but to the value of heavy fortifications in compensating for scarce manpower.[81]

But that did not mean the Confederate victory was easy. "When the Yankees fell back, and the firing ceased," wrote Sam Watkins, "I never saw so many broken down and exhausted men in my life. I was as sick as a horse, and as wet with blood and sweat as I could be, and many of our men were vomiting with excessive fatigue, over-exhaustion, and sunstroke; our tongues were parched and cracked for water, and our faces blackened with powder and smoke, and our dead and wounded were piled indiscriminately in the trenches. There was not a single man in the company who was not wounded, or had holes shot through his hat and clothing." But the survivors of the bloody fight for the angle had held the ill-placed position, even if the enemy glared at them only a few yards away behind the crest that Cheatham's works should have been placed on from the start.[82]

McCook's and Mitchell's troops conducted the closest, most intense action of the day and came nearer a breakthrough than had the Fifteenth or Fourth Corps men. And yet, that statement is valid only as a form of comparison, for the Fourteenth Corps attack never penetrated Cheatham's line. Columns worked no better for Davis than they had for Newton, and the use of multiple lines by Morgan L. Smith and Walcutt in the Fifteenth Corps was no solution either. Well-placed and effectively designed earthworks that were adequately manned provided the key to Confederate success that morning.

But Davis's men did accomplish something no other Federals had on June 27. They remained within short range of the main Rebel line and fortified a forward position. Fifteenth Corps troops had no terrain feature in their line of advance that would have allowed them to do this. Fourth Corps troops had the thin protection of the abrupt ascent along the east side of the shallow branch valley, but they chose not to utilize it for more than temporary protection. Fourteenth Corps troops had the same feature on their line of advance, but it was more pronounced because of the slightly higher elevation of Cheatham's Hill. In short, the terrain offered more protection to Davis's men than to Newton's. Moreover, Davis's troops chose to take advantage of it; they could have done what Newton's men did and fallen back all the way to the Union line.

Because they chose to stay close to the target, McCook's and Mitchell's men imparted at least a modicum of reason to argue that their attack was not a complete failure. They also created an opportunity for the Federals to continue operations against the salient on Cheatham's Hill through means other than an attack, such as siege approaches. Their close-in position could have allowed Sherman to shift the long confrontation at Kennesaw away from flanking or attacking and toward siege operations, if the commanding general had any inclination to do so.

Seven. The Residue of a Long Day

While the Fifteenth, Fourth, and Fourteenth Corps conducted fierce attacks against the Confederate center, Schofield's Army of the Ohio quietly worked on Johnston's left flank all morning of June 27. Sherman's double approach—experimenting with assaults combined with a tried and true method of seeking to turn the enemy's flank—held promise of results in one way or another. While everyone's attention was focused on the bloody dramas at Pigeon Hill, Cheatham's Hill, and the line between those two heights, Schofield created a small but significant advantage for the Federals with minimal loss and little fanfare.

In Sherman's plan, Schofield was to move down Sandtown Road early on June 27, cross Olley's Creek, and head for the railroad if at all possible. If that were not feasible, he was to secure a position from which further advances could be made. Sherman sought any information about the unknown terrain south of Johnston's army, any advantage of position he could use to further his goal of prying the Confederates from their line of heavy entrenchments. Schofield entrusted this assignment to Brigadier General Jacob D. Cox's Third Division, which had not been engaged during the past few days. Moreover, Cox controlled the area around Cheney's House near the junction of the Powder Springs and Sandtown Roads, one of several intersections that would play a role in Sherman's flanking maneuvers. He was well placed to cross Olley's Creek while Brigadier General Milo S. Hascall's Second Division extended Hooker's line. Hascall would divert Confederate attention with artillery fire while Cox made his move, and Major General George Stoneman's cavalry division of the Army of the Ohio was to cover Cox's right flank.[1]

Schofield had to deal with Brigadier General William H. Jackson's cavalry division of Loring's Army of Mississippi. Jackson placed Brigadier General Lawrence S. Ross's Texas Brigade in his center, straddling Sandtown Road just south of the crossing of Olley's Creek. Ross maintained his headquarters at the house of Mr. Shaw, only a quarter of a mile from the creek.

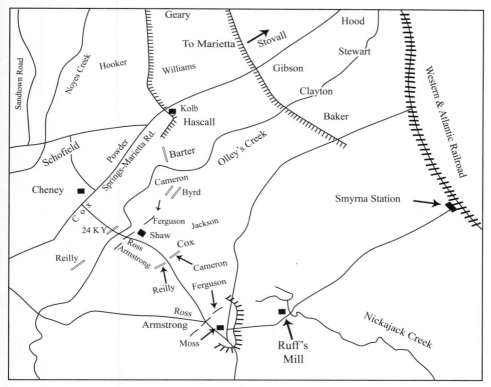

Operations South of Kennesaw

Brigadier General Frank C. Armstrong's Mississippi Brigade was positioned to the left of Ross, representing the extreme left unit of Johnston's army, while Brigadier General Samuel W. Ferguson's Alabama and Mississippi Brigade held the line to the right of Ross's troopers.[2]

Sherman hoped to keep abreast of Schofield's progress from his command post on Signal Hill, a height near the center of Thomas's sector. The telegraph line that John C. Van Duzer had stretched for thirteen miles along the rear of the Federal army group worked well all day; it kept Sherman in touch with all of his subordinate commanders much faster and more easily than relying on couriers. At one point during the day, Sherman noticed a good deal of smoke coming from one part of the contested line and wondered what it meant. Schofield was able to inform him that artillery rounds had set fire to dry leaves between the opposing positions and that it did not affect operations.[3]

Cox put together an effective plan to cross Olley's Creek and push on south in careful stages. The troops of Colonel Robert K. Byrd's Third Brigade had already crossed the stream the previous day and established a small foothold on the other side, in an area not adequately covered by the Confederate cavalry. They had constructed a crude bridge at this crossing one mile north of the Sandtown Road bridge. Colonel Daniel Cameron's Second Brigade was to cross the bridge early on June 27, while Byrd covered the maneuver. Cameron had orders to move south along a ridgeline to drive the Confederates from in front of Colonel James W. Reilly's First Brigade. Reilly had already divided his brigade the day before in an unsuccessful effort to cross the creek near Sandtown Road. Three regiments and most of his artillery had been stopped by a swamp while seeking an alternate crossing a short distance upstream, as two regiments advanced along Sandtown Road. Reilly would continue trying on June 27 and planned to meet Cameron if he got across. In addition, Cameron sent his Twenty-Fourth Kentucky to reinforce Reilly's 100th Ohio and 104th Ohio at the Sandtown Road crossing.[4]

The plan worked beautifully, in part because Cox was up early and rode from one brigade to another for several hours to make sure they started according to plan. The operation began at 4:00 A.M., four hours before the triple attacks started much farther north. Little more than light skirmishing took place as the Confederate cavalrymen discovered that three Federal brigades were coordinating their advance. Cox pushed his subordinates relentlessly. "I find they move too timidly when the commanders are left to their own responsibility," he candidly wrote to Schofield. "I have told them they must have their work substantially accomplished before 8 o'clock." The reason Cox specified that hour was to entice Johnston into diverting his attention to the south just before the three attacks against his center took place. Unfortunately for the Federals, it did not have that effect.[5]

While Byrd took a new position on a ridge near the creek, Cameron advanced south and threatened Ross's troops near Sandtown Road. At the same time, Reilly's flanking column found a way to march past the swamp and cross Olley's Creek upstream from Sandtown Road. Three regiments, the Eighth Tennessee, Sixteenth Kentucky, and 112th Illinois, pushed aside Confederate skirmishers and effected a lodgment on the other side. Also at the same time, Colonel John S. Hurt's Twenty-Fourth Kentucky advanced along Sandtown Road in two lines, supported by the 100th Ohio and 104th Ohio, and scampered across the bridge even though the planks had been taken up by the Confederates. The timing of these advances was perfect, and Ross fell back along with the other two Confederate brigades. Then Cox advanced Cameron and Reilly forward along the Sandtown Road past Shaw's House and to a high ridge a mile south of Olley's Creek. Byrd remained at his post a mile to the left of this new position taken up by Cameron and Reilly. Colonel Richard F. Barter's First Brigade of the First Division in Schofield's command, which was temporarily assigned to Cox, now deployed north of Olley's Creek so as to provide a link between Byrd's brigade (which was south of the stream) and Hascall's division north of it. When the dust settled by about 8:30 A.M., Cox's division occupied an extended line covering four miles of ground. His losses had been light so far. Hascall fulfilled his part of the program with intense artillery fire and by advancing his skirmishers several times, losing about one hundred men during the course of the day.[6]

The Federals pushed Jackson's division back in part because a mile long gap had existed between Ross's brigade and that of Ferguson to his right. Ferguson relied on Colonel Horace H. Miller to fill the gap as best he could with his Ninth Mississippi Cavalry, but Miller was unable to hold on. He fell back under pressure from Cameron. This forced Ross to send his Ninth Texas Cavalry to Miller's aid. Ross could ill afford to lose the Ninth Texas in light of the pressure soon exerted by Reilly. Even though the Confederates operated on foot and behind light earthworks, they were compelled to fall back that morning in the face of Cox's advance. Ross retired half a mile from his first position by a little after 8:00 A.M. He counted on Ferguson to protect his right flank if he hoped to remain there very long. But soon word arrived that Ferguson could not maintain his position, and the Confederates fell back even farther.[7]

This second retreat opened the way for Cameron and Reilly to move ahead and secure the ridge one mile from Olley's Creek. They set out toward that ridge shortly after Cox heard the sound of the Union artillery bombardment that started the triple attacks farther north. By the time those three assaults ground to a bloody halt, Cameron and Reilly were beginning to dig in on the high ridge.[8]

This ridge represented the watershed between Olley's Creek and the next stream barring Sherman's path, Nickajack Creek. It was irregular in shape, separating into knobs. A crossroad skirted the foot of the ridge, running from the area of Marietta to join Sandtown Road. "The importance of the position was evident as soon as seen," Cox wrote, and he made sure his men securely held it. Cameron's brigade deployed to Reilly's left and also dug entrenchments. Reilly placed a lunette for artillery and a regiment of infantry on a detached hill nearby so as to command the crossroad toward Marietta more effectually. Cox ordered Byrd to maintain his position but stretch his right flank enough to connect with Cameron's left. Long stretches of his division's position were held only by a line of pickets, but he counted on being able to cover those sectors with oblique artillery fire. Cox had to be careful; all of Jackson's cavalry division was now assembled a mile away, where the next important crossroads, near the Moss House, was located.[9]

Cox's new position was situated so that he could see Hood's fortified line to the northeast, at least wherever the tree cover allowed such a long view. It was clear that Hood's line extended south of Olley's Creek across the knobby ridge at least a mile from Hascall's right flank. The ridge was too irregular and wooded to allow Cox to advance along it toward the main Confederate line. Cox also advised his commander that he did not feel comfortable moving farther south along Sandtown Road without support, and he advised shifting Hascall's division to help him. Schofield agreed and informed Sherman a bit after noon on June 27 that Cox could not advance farther without exposing his division. Cox's position, however, would threaten Johnston as much as one could hope.[10]

Sherman readily agreed with his subordinate's view. Less than one hour after hearing from Schofield, Sherman told him not to push Cox any farther south. At 4:10 that afternoon, he further informed Schofield to hold all that he had gained "and remain on the defensive." Sherman told Thomas at the same time that "Schofield has gained the crossing of Olley's Creek on the Sandtown road; the only advantage of the day." Schofield remained proud of his men's achievement on June 27 in the face of the bloody repulse suffered by other corps.[11]

Sherman was eager to grasp any sign of success in the operations of June 27 and looked on Cox's advance as one step in a lengthening series of moves to deal with Johnston's strong position at Kennesaw Mountain. He little feared that the Confederates would attack Cox but wanted to accumulate more supplies so as to cut himself off temporarily from the railroad and push large numbers of troops along the Sandtown Road. That would take a few days. "Make your position very strong," Schofield told Cox that evening. "I regard it as the key to the next movement."[12]

For the rest of the day, the Federals merely held on to their new positions. There was a considerable amount of skirmishing on the afternoon and evening of June 27 as Ross sent forward a skirmish line to locate the new Federal position and test its strength. Ross also sent scouts to pass around to the rear of Cox's position and report all they could discover. Stoneman did little more than cover Cox's right flank and send out a skirmish line to confront Armstrong's cavalry brigade, to Ross's left. Schofield complained to

John M. Schofield (Library of Congress, LC-DIG-cwpb-05934)

Sherman that Stoneman's division was too weak to do more than play a defensive role in the operations, a message that prompted the commander to contemplate a more aggressive, offensive role for the horsemen.[13]

For his part, Johnston was alarmed by Schofield's progress on the left of the Kennesaw Line. He sought ways to strengthen Jackson's cavalry division by requesting the commander of the Georgia Militia, Major General Gustavus W. Smith, to dispatch as many infantry as he could spare along with a battery to help the troopers. The militiamen, most of whom were ill-suited for active campaigning, poorly trained and equipped, would have to cross the Chattahoochee River and move three miles to Jackson's position near the Moss House. Johnston did not want the militia to become heavily engaged in combat but to give the impression to Sherman that infantry were cooperating with the cavalry. He hoped they could offer "a demonstration calculated to deter the enemy" from trying to reach the Chattahoochee. Smith put the wheels into motion, but it would be a few days before the militiamen took the field.[14]

The true value of Schofield's operations on June 27 lay in the area of position, topography, and knowledge of the unknown countryside south of Kennesaw. The actual advance was minimal, only two miles, but Cox could gather information about the lay of the land from the high ridge his men occupied that day. The comparative ease with which Cox pushed the dismounted Rebel cavalrymen also boded well for continuing this line of advance in the future. Meticulous planning and brisk execution, along with a surprisingly lax defensive attitude by Jackson, had accounted for the Federal success. Schofield's men proved something that Sherman should have already well known; flanking was more effective than butting one's head against strong Confederate earthworks. They also offered Sherman something to take his mind off the heavy casualties suffered by the Fifteenth Corps, the Fourth Corps, and the Fourteenth Corps that morning.[15]

THE GENERALS

Thanks to the field telegraph, Federal commanders were in close touch with each other all morning. Thomas informed Sherman as early as 10:45 that the attacks along his sector had failed. Harker had gotten within twenty paces of the Confederate line before his repulse, Wagner suffered severe losses, and so did McCook, while Mitchell still held on to a line of Rebel works. "The troops are all too much exhausted to advance," Thomas concluded, "but we hold all we have gained." Fifteen minutes later, Thomas informed Howard and Palmer to re-form their units and report more fully about their condition. He also urged them to prepare for another strike if Sherman so ordered.[16]

Sherman responded to Thomas's report at 11:45 by telling him that McPherson's men were unsuccessful in their attack on Pigeon Hill, but they were still lodged closer to the Rebel line than when they had started. "I wish you to study well the position, and if it be possible to break the line do it; it is easier now than it will be hereafter. Hold fast all you make." Nearly two hours later, with no word from Thomas, Sherman again urged him to determine whether another attack was feasible. He exaggerated a bit by saying that "McPherson's men are up to the abatis and can't move without the direct assault. I will order the assault if you think you can succeed at any point."[17]

Thomas responded within five minutes after this last telegram arrived from Sherman's command post at Signal Hill. He relayed the views of Davis and Howard that it was extremely unlikely another attack would succeed. The Confederate works were of formidable size and strength, with parapets six to seven feet high and nine feet thick, according to reports. Davis and Howard suggested holding on as close as possible to the target and planting guns at short range to pound the fortifications. Thomas agreed. "From what the officers tell me I do not think we can carry the works by assault at this point to-day, but they can be approached by saps and the enemy driven out."[18]

Forty-five minutes later, Sherman replied to Thomas's message by questioning whether it was worthwhile to engage in the tedious and time-consuming mode of conducting siege approaches. Could not Johnston's men build many more lines of works by the time Thomas completed one sap? This brought an immediate response from Thomas, who reiterated his view that attacking should be avoided; it would not work and cost far too many good men. Conducting regular approaches was the only alternative he could suggest. "We have already lost heavily to-day without gaining any material advantage; one or two more such assaults would use up this army."[19]

This exchange of views gave rise to the assertion that Sherman wanted to renew the attack after the first bloody failure, and that Thomas decisively put his foot down to stop it. Henry Stone, a member of Thomas's staff who tended to write bitterly about Sherman after the war, promoted that viewpoint and gave his old commander credit for stopping the carnage. "General Thomas, especially, spoke his mind with unwonted vigor and positiveness." That is not an entirely accurate portrayal of events, however, for it is clear Sherman wanted to find out only whether another attack was justified. He easily conceded to his subordinate's viewpoint when it was expressed. Sherman's only concern was that siege approaches would not work any better than a direct attack, and that comment, not a stubborn insistence on launching another strike, was what brought on Thomas's rather testy assertion that further assaults "would use up this army."[20]

Ironically, Thomas formally asked his subordinates for their opinion on whether a renewal of the attack was feasible *after* he had already relayed to Sherman their informal views at 1:40 that afternoon. At 1:45 P.M., word arrived at Howard's headquarters that the army commander wanted Howard to canvass his division commanders on that subject. This was forty minutes before Thomas's frustrated assertion to Sherman about destroying the army if further attacks were ordered. It would be sometime later that all of his subordinates managed to send in their reports.[21]

Howard asked his division commanders to give him their opinion. Newton responded quickly with a view that it was useless to try again, and Howard relayed that opinion to Thomas by 2:40 P.M. It took another hour for the other division leaders in the Fourth Corps to offer their views to Howard. Hooker responded by strongly arguing that no further attacks ought to be made. He thought regular approaches or flanking the enemy were the proper alternatives. Pressed by the problems encountered by his two brigades, Davis did not respond to Palmer's request for his views until 10:30 that night. While he relayed Dilworth's opinion that McCook's brigade could carry the enemy works in its front, Davis painted a more negative picture of the situation by noting that both brigades needed the support of fresh troops if any further action was contemplated. Palmer endorsed Davis's views by noting that he had spoken with Mitchell, who emphatically told him "his men are too much exhausted to do anything at present."[22]

As Hooker noted, Sherman did have an alternative to attacking or conducting siege approaches, and Sherman was more fully aware of that third alternative than any of his subordinates except Schofield. "Satisfied of the bloody cost of attacking intrenched lines," he recalled in his memoirs, "I at once thought of moving the whole army to the railroad at a point (Fulton) about ten miles below Marietta, or to the Chattahoochee River itself." By about 6:00 P.M., Sherman began to inform his subordinates of his idea to temporarily abandon the railroad and move his entire force along the route pioneered by the Twenty-Third Corps. It would be a grand flanking movement similar to what he had conducted after crossing the Etowah River. "The question of supplies will be the only one," he told Thomas. Sherman anticipated having to wait "a few days" until more material could be stored up to make the move feasible.[23]

"Are you willing to risk the move on Fulton, cutting loose from our railroad?," Sherman asked Thomas at 9:00 P.M. "It would bring matters to a crisis, and Schofield has secured the way." Thomas was interested and asked how far the troops would have to march and if there were any natural obstacles along the way. Sherman assured him the distance was about ten miles and that only Nickajack Creek had to be crossed. Thomas agreed that the plan was "better than butting against breast-works twelve feet thick and strongly abatised." But Sherman warned and in a gentle way chastised Thomas for his slowness by asserting, "Go where we may we will find the breast-works and abatis, unless we move more rapidly than we have heretofore." Thomas issued instructions that night to his corps commanders to ready for the move as much as they could. He told them to "adopt any means in your power to move with the greatest celerity."[24]

ON THE LINE

The survivors of the failed attacks tried to make the best of their situation for the rest of June 27. Along the Fifteenth Corps sector, the men of Lightburn's, Giles A. Smith's, and Walcutt's brigades generally remained at the captured Confederate skirmish pits for the day. Toward evening, Walcutt's troops were treated to what one of them called the "prettiest artillery fight I ever saw," as nearly a dozen guns exchanged fire over their heads. Dusk finally offered some degree of relief to those wounded men who had suffered while lying between the lines. Osterhaus's division relieved the Fifteenth Corps brigades that had conducted the attack and continued to hold the position formerly occupied by the Rebel skirmishers for the duration of its stay at Kennesaw. Pioneers had already begun to reverse the pits to face the mountain, aided by infantrymen supplied with a few entrenching tools. Federal skirmishers kept up a constant fire at French's and Walker's line. "It is dangerous to step out from our works," reported Samuel McKittrick of the Sixteenth South Carolina. "Their Sharpshooters are ready to pick us out." But Fifteenth Corps commander John A. Logan did not consider the new position of much value except "that it reduces the distance to be traversed" if Sherman decided that another attack was necessary.[25]

As dusk approached, McPherson's battered units tried to settle down to a state of normality fronting Kennesaw. Giles A. Smith's and Walcutt's brigades dug a new line of works as medical officers worked hard to care for the injured. Wounded men had begun to trickle back to field hospitals by late morning. According to Captain Edward B. Moore of the Fifty-Fourth Ohio, who missed the attack because he was in one of those hospitals recovering from illness, the wounded "came in one steady stream" from noon until dark.[26]

Confederate guns opened up an intense bombardment of the Federal positions that lasted all afternoon. French directed this barrage in order to push Federal troops as far back toward their own line as possible and help Cockrell reestablish his skirmish line. Walker hesitated to advance his skirmish line to support Cockrell's desire to move his skirmishers forward; the open field south of Pigeon Hill was too exposed. But the Federals pulled back toward their own line at any rate, suffering from French's artillery. When a six-gun battery began targeting the right flank of Osterhaus's division, William Augustus Renken of the Twenty-Ninth Missouri reported that it gave "us the very Devil for a while, . . . the Shelling was the most Spirited I ever saw & would have been distructive had we no good fortifications." From the perspective of Lightburn's brigade, the Rebel artillery "swept our position in every possible direction—men's heads, arms etc were blown off & scattered over the earth." Guibor's battery on top of Little Kennesaw continued the fire at a steady pace all evening, letting off five rounds every ten minutes, while other batteries kept up a much more intense rate of fire.[27]

The experience of June 27 along the range of the Kennesaws differed according to one's position. For Samuel G. French, the action "became a pageantry on a grand scale." From William Renken's position as an observer in Osterhaus's division, "It did look horrible[;] I occupied a place where I could see the whole affair I don't see how men could Live in such a murderous fire." As far as Renken was concerned, the attack was "an other Chickasaw." He referred, of course, to the first battle in which Sherman ordered assaults on a strong Confederate position atop high ground, at Chickasaw Bluffs in late December, 1862, which was the opening of Grant's long campaign against Vicksburg.[28]

Along the Fourth Corps sector, the survivors of Newton's division pulled back to the rear of the Federal position at about noon. Howard had examined the ground earlier that day and recommended to Thomas that the troops hold a forward position, but that was not possible. A brief and little-noticed truce took place on the Fourth Corps sector sometime during the afternoon of June 27. This occurred after the famous truce initiated by Lieutenant Colonel Martin, and it allowed the Federals to gather at least some of their dead. Despite that interlude of compassion and understanding, there were scares and alarms along the corps front during the day. The Confederates, however, made no effort to advance and take advantage of the drubbing they had delivered to Newton's division. Captain John W. Tuttle of the Third Kentucky in Harker's brigade spent a long night "listening to the shrill panther-like screech of the sharpshooters balls."[29]

The survivors of McCook's and Mitchell's brigades of the Fourteenth Corps had the most dangerous experience during the rest of that long day.

Lodged only a few yards from the enemy, desperately trying to increase the thin ground cover that offered them safety, they worked hard to improve their position. The Federals had no tools so they made do with bayonets, cups, and tin plates while lying as flat as possible to avoid Rebel bullets. "Sticks and stones and brush and chunks of wood were pushed between their heads and the enemy's works," recalled James T. Holmes. After an hour, the Federals had enough of a parapet so they could "raise their heads from the ground with some safety," according to Lieutenant Colonel John S. Pearce of the Ninety-Eighth Ohio.[30]

It took a while for regimental officers to sort out positions after the confused fallback from the Confederate parapet. In McCook's brigade, the Eighty-Fifth Illinois held the right and connected with Mitchell's left flank, while the Twenty-Second Indiana held the left. The 125th Illinois occupied the center of the makeshift earthworks as the Eighty-Sixth Illinois and Fifty-Second Ohio lay a short distance to the rear in reserve. Mitchell's troops constructed their works a bit farther from the Confederates than McCook's men had. Moreover, Mitchell never personally joined his brigade during the day. After the men fell back from their high tide, Colonel Banning of the 121st Ohio sent a written description of the brigade's position to his commander at the rear. Mitchell replied with a dispatch ordering him to dig in and refuse his right flank, "if I could do it without too great a sacrifice." Banning took charge, ordering half the brigade to keep up fire at the enemy, while the rest scratched out an earthwork. Banning's men constructed two lines to the rear of the front line, both of them as long as a regimental front, or about five hundred feet. Like Dilworth, who now commanded McCook's brigade, Banning wanted to rotate regiments in and out of the front line and needed reserve positions for them to occupy.[31]

CHEATHAM'S HILL

The battlefield atop Cheatham's Hill presented a horrible sight soon after McCook's and Mitchell's commands fell back from their high tide. The bodies of dead Federals lay within a few yards of the works, and some were actually lying on the parapet. The ground between the contending lines was littered with wounded men, some of whom tried to crawl back to the crest where their comrades were hastily throwing up dirt, but many of the wounded lay where they were, waiting for darkness.[32]

The Confederates tried to take in as many Yankees as they safely could, calling on those near to crawl over the parapet and into their trench. A number of men who were not wounded but who had been stranded by the retirement of their comrades decided to give up. Sergeant John W. Baltzly of the Fifty-Second Ohio had found some degree of shelter in a shallow ditch carved out at the foot of the parapet, but he soon realized Confederates to the right of his location had an opportunity to see and fire at him if he tried to make his way toward friends. Baltzly then gave himself up and crossed the parapet into Confederate hands. J. L. W. Blair of the First Tennessee recalled a young Federal soldier wearing a straw hat who was hiding near the Rebel works behind a rock. "We invited him to come in, and he very promptly accepted our invitation."[33]

Quite a few wounded Federals also sought aid within Rebel lines during the day. Adjutant Lansing J. Dawdy of the Eighty-Sixth Illinois lay wounded only ten feet from the parapet and about twenty feet north of the angle. He stayed there for five hours after the attack before finally signaling to the Confederates that he wanted aid. They managed to help him across the parapet, and four Rebels carried Dawdy on a stretcher four hundred yards to the rear of the angle where a field hospital did thriving business. In another example, seventeen-year-old Newton H. Bostwick of the Fifty-Second Ohio was badly wounded in the shoulder. He tried to cross the parapet but failed, and Sergeant Major James A. Jennings of the First Tennessee "reached over the head log to help the boy," as Nixon B. Stewart of the Fifty-Second Ohio put it, when a bullet from the Federal line plunged into Bostwick's neck. Surprisingly, both Jennings and Bostwick survived the exposure necessary for crossing the parapet. Jennings even kept in touch with Bostwick for some time after, sending food to him in the hospital in Macon, Georgia, until the young Federal was exchanged. But there were limits to the opportunities of good Samaritans among the Confederates to help their injured enemies. Major John Yager of the 121st Ohio lay wounded close to the line and called out to the Rebels for help. They could not safely reach him, and Yager died that night.[34]

The fire that threatened the Federal dead and wounded on the Fourth Corps sector apparently spread toward the Fourteenth Corps position as well, although there was not a significant accumulation of dried leaves to cause a major problem for McCook's and Mitchell's wounded. Both Federals and Confederates near the angle could hear the cries of wounded Fourth Corps troops who feared the flames would reach them. Two Rebels of Vaughan's brigade went out to try and rescue a wounded Yankee as fire neared his position, but they were both wounded by Union gunfire. Vaughan saw it happen and became angry, ordering his men to stay put and "let them burn if they didn't appreciate the saving of their own men," as J. T. Bowden of the Twelfth Tennessee put it. Sam Watkins remembered that several men of his regiment also were shot when they tried to offer aid to the wounded.[35]

To be fair, the Confederates of Maney's and Vaughan's brigades did not let the Federals out of their earthworks to rescue their own wounded. They kept up a pretty steady fire at any one who exposed himself, leaving the wounded to the mercy of individual, brave Confederates whose sense of humanity overcame their instinct for survival.[36]

Both sides on top of Cheatham's Hill kept up a pretty strong fire across no-man's-land all day and evening of June 27. Allen Fahnestock owned a Spencer rifle; he loaned it and 120 cartridges to Fife Major Alonzo P. Webber of the Eighty-Sixth Illinois, who took post behind a tree and fired every round that day to give some cover to wounded Federals so they could crawl back to the line. Webber admitted that he inadvertently killed a wounded Yankee as the man was being pulled across the Confederate parapet. Webber later received a Medal of Honor for his work, and Fahnestock gave him a duplicate Spencer rifle as a memento of the day. A sixteen-year-old black man named Tom, who acted as a servant for Sam Pyle and Joe Swan of the Fifty-Second Ohio, picked up an abandoned gun and fired it during the day.[37]

The constant exchange of gunfire had its effect. James T. Holmes recalled with sadness the sight of some poor wounded Federal, able to stand up and walk from the entrenched position across the valley toward safety in the main Union line, being struck "by a death shot" partway there, and evening brought little relief from the firing. Members of the Eighty-Fifth Illinois heard a noise in the Confederate line just after dusk and came to, ready to repel an attack. This was followed by a crashing Confederate volley that killed Captain Charles H. Chatfield of Company D and wounded several men, but there was no enemy advance.[38]

The Federals needed entrenching tools to make proper defenses, but it took hours for them to reach Cheatham's Hill. Soon after the attack had stalled, Dilworth sent Captain E. L. Anderson, the brigade adjutant general, to ask Davis for spades and shovels. Anderson could not find Davis, so he reported to Thomas, who had trouble believing, at this early stage of events, that McCook's and Mitchell's men could remain only a few yards from the smoking works. Only when Davis sent in his separate report that the troops were able to stay where they were did Thomas consent to forward tools, but they did not arrive until nearly dusk. By then, as Holmes put it, "there was no mean row of works along our line." The men used their implements to improve the shelter during the long night of June 27. The tools were distributed right after the Confederate volley that had killed Captain Chatfield, an occurrence that heightened the enthusiasm with which the Eighty-Fifth Illinois used them to raise the parapet. By morning, Holmes described the works as "formidable."[39]

The Confederates spent the night of June 27 improving their own works on Cheatham's Hill, replacing head logs where needed, clearing out the trench of wounded and debris. Many injured Federals now took advantage of darkness and the enemy's preoccupation with the entrenchments to crawl away toward their friends. Captain Joseph Major of the Eighty-Sixth Illinois had been knocked unconscious by a rock during the attack; he lay all day in the hot sun until recovering his senses after dusk. Two Confederates crawled out in the deepening shadow and robbed him of everything they could find, but Major later "came rolling into our lines," as Nixon Stewart put it. Several other wounded Federals rolled rather than crawled over the space of no-man's-land to find safety within Union lines. Otho W. Loofborrow of the 113th Ohio, however, had been unhurt when he was taken in by the Confederates sometime that day, probably very late in the evening. He managed to give his captors the slip and "came bounding into our lines" after dark.[40]

Several Federals took advantage of the darkness to venture into no-man's-land and secure their own wounded. "It was a dangerous and grewsome [sic] undertaking," commented Edwin Payne of the Thirty-Fourth Illinois. "It was necessary to use the utmost silence, and to creep close to the ground amongst the dead to find any that were living." F. M. McAdams and three comrades of the 113th Ohio took blankets and crawled forward under cover of darkness. They waited and listened for the sounds of groans before locating Sergeant Henry C. Scott. They managed to get him to the rear. Scott was very grateful, but he died the next day. McAdams went out again later that night with four comrades and found Corporal Peter Baker. Several other wounded Federals were rescued by their friends that night.[41]

LOSSES

The butcher's bill for June 27 amounted to 3,000 Federals killed, wounded, and missing. Two-thirds of that total occurred among the three attack columns, which consisted of 15,000 men in eight brigades, but the rest took place in all other Federal units which came under fire that long day. Logan's Fifteenth Corps lost 586 men, while Newton's division of the Fourth Corps suffered 654 losses. Davis's division of the Fourteenth Corps counted 824 casualties that day. Confederate losses were very modest by comparison. They amounted to about 700 killed, wounded, and missing.[42]

The huge difference between Union and Confederate losses testified to the effectiveness of well-made earthworks. Sherman admitted to Halleck that his men "inflicted comparatively little loss to the enemy" because the Confederates "lay behind . . . well-formed breast-works." In fact, for years to come, Johnston tried to minimize the accounting of his losses as much as possible. In his memoirs, published in 1874, he argued that the army lost only 522 men on June 27. Cleburne's division suffered only 11 casualties in this reckoning, while Cheatham lost 195 troops. Johnston was not the only man who tried to minimize Rebel losses; a correspondent to the *Memphis Appeal* asserted that they amounted to a mere 153 men altogether. Federal staff officer Henry Stone reported that Johnston lost 220 men, "about one twelfth of Sherman's" losses, but Stone had an agenda to criticize Sherman at every opportunity.[43]

Johnston had an incentive for minimizing his own losses compared to Sherman's, for Kennesaw Mountain was the most impressive defensive victory during his tenure as commander of the Army of Tennessee. Given that Johnston enjoyed no offensive victory of any kind during that time, he had to make the most of Kennesaw. Johnston already was under fire from Richmond for giving up so much territory without a general battle. He had every incentive to demonstrate that his Fabian policy had inflicted high casualties on the enemy while he suffered comparatively little.

Johnston waited until he had the opportunity to write an article for the *Century* magazine entitled "Opposing Sherman's Advance" to open full score on this issue. He discounted Sherman's report of losses as too low, arguing that most of the firing took place at short range and that Sherman's veterans would not have given up the attack unless they had lost quite heavily. "I have seen American soldiers (Northern men) win a field with losses ten times greater proportionally." Johnston argued that most of the Federals who fell at Cheatham's Hill lay very close to the Confederate position for two days and thus could be counted. Testimony from Rebels on the scene would indicate that total Union losses on June 27 must have been at least 6,000 men. Johnston noted that 10,126 Union soldiers were buried at the National Military Cemetery near Marietta and suggested that Federal losses on June 27 were greater than generally admitted in order to create such a large cemetery.[44]

Johnston admitted that Sherman's men fought bravely at Kennesaw

Mountain, but his efforts to increase the disparity of losses between his own army and the Federal troops fell flat. The editors of the *Century* magazine contacted the inspector of the National Cemetery at Marietta who informed them that many of the men buried there had died of disease, others had fallen on fields other than that of Kennesaw Mountain, and that the burials even included some black soldiers and civilians. The editors reported all this in a footnote to Johnston's article. For some reason, Johnston even denied that McCook's and Mitchell's brigades had dug in close to Hardee's line on Cheatham's Hill. The notion "was utterly impossible," he argued. "There would have been much more exposure in that than in mounting and crossing the little rebel 'parapet.'" Johnston admitted that "a party of Federal soldiers" had dug in only seventy-five yards from the Confederates, but that was all. The magazine editors investigated this issue as well, inviting testimony from a Union soldier, Surgeon Joseph A. Stillwell of the Twenty-Second Indiana, who assured readers that two brigades of Fourteenth Corps troops had fortified securely within a few yards of the Confederate line. It is impossible to believe that Johnston was unaware of that important fact in late June 1864 and incredible that he conveniently forgot it twenty-three years later when writing his article.[45]

Regardless of the disparity of losses between Union and Confederate forces engaged on June 27, the comparative losses on that day within the context of casualties suffered during the four-month-long campaign against Atlanta are telling. Sherman's army group lost 7,530 men from June 1 to July 3, and nearly 40 percent of that number fell in the attacks of June 27. Morgan L. Smith's division of the Fifteenth Corps lost nearly one-fourth of all the casualties it suffered from May 1 to September 2 in the brief assault of June 27. Wagner's brigade of Newton's division in the Fourth Corps lost the same proportion of its total campaign casualties in the attack on Kennesaw, while the Seventy-Fourth Illinois in Kimball's brigade lost 36 percent of its campaign casualties on the morning of June 27. McCook's brigade in the Fourteenth Corps lost 37.9 percent of its campaign losses that day, but the 125th Illinois in that brigade suffered a whopping 60.1 percent of its campaign casualties in the attack. The Fifty-Second Ohio's proportion amounted to 43 percent. The 113th Ohio and 121st Ohio lost nearly half their men who were engaged for only twenty minutes because they bore the brunt of Mitchell's brigade assault. The other two regiments behind those units failed to extend the brigade line and thus were somewhat shielded from the worst of the Rebel fire by the suffering ranks of these two Ohio regiments.[46]

Captain Alexander Miller Ayers of the 125th Illinois missed the attack because of staff duties, but he visited the regiment soon after the repulse. "This has been the saddest day in the history of our Regiment," he wrote his wife late on June 27. Several companies had fewer than fifteen men left, and four companies did not have a commissioned officer on duty. "It really seems as if the Regt was nearly broken up."[47]

Oliver Otis Howard reported that his casualties were particularly high among "valuable officers," and the roll call of the fallen in Fourth Corps ranks testifies to that sad fact. Charles Harker's loss "seems irreparable," as Emerson Opdycke put it. Harker had "a presentiment in the morning that this would prove a fatal day to him." He entrusted his personal belongings to a friend before riding into the attack, and the sight of his body lying with those of many others on the field deflated the enthusiasm of Luther P. Bradley. "I felt I would as lief be there with them as not. I don't know how I escaped." Esteem for Harker extended up the chain of command in Sherman's army group to the very top. "I cannot realize that he is really gone," Howard wrote of Harker. "He used to be a member of my prayer-meeting I think, while at West Point." Harker also was in Howard's estimation "an upright, straightforward complete soldier, and a thorough gentleman." Sherman considered Harker "one of our best young generals, of rising fame, and his loss was deeply felt by me. He was universally esteemed," Sherman assured the fallen man's father, "but death, you know, chooses a shining mark."[48]

Praise mixed with grief flowed through the reports of many commanders when they wrote eloquently about the loss of valued officers that day. Lieutenant Colonel George W. Chandler of the Eighty-Eighth Illinois was "accomplished, zealous, and brave," and "no purer or more gallant spirit has fallen as a sacrifice for the honor of the Government." Howard's chief of staff, Colonel Francis T. Sherman of the Eighty-Eighth Illinois, arranged for Chandler's body to be embalmed and sent to Chattanooga where it was encased in a sealed container for shipment to Chicago. Luther Bradley praised another fallen officer, Adjutant Henry W. Hall of the Fifty-First Illinois, as "a splendid fellow in all respects" with "a perfect education, and one of the finest tempers in the world." Hall possessed a courage that "was something marvelous, for its perfect coolness and steadiness."[49]

The bodies of other favorite officers also received attention from those who were attached to their commanders. Captain Frederick W. Stegner of the Seventy-Fourth Illinois in Kimball's brigade had been killed in the attack. Two men of his company asked the Confederates for permission to retrieve his body during the truce initiated by Lieutenant Colonel Martin. The Confederates generally did not allow removal of the dead in this truce but consented only after taking Stegner's sword, belt, and pistol from his body. They left the captain's watch and pocket book, which Stegner's lieutenant kept for his family before burying the fallen officer near a Union hospital. Concerned friends were able to take Colonel Oscar Harmon's body from the bloody field on Cheatham's Hill. Alexander M. Ayers, the quartermaster of the 125th Illinois, escorted it to Big Shanty to be shipped to Chattanooga for embalming. The body of Captain William Fellows, however, lay too near the enemy position for anyone to bring it back.[50]

Dan McCook began a painful odyssey toward death when he was wounded while literally standing on the Confederate parapet at Cheatham's Hill. Transported back to a field hospital, Surgeon M. M. Hooton of the Eighty-Sixth Illinois was the first to examine him. The ball "had entered just below the clavicle on the right side of his chest," in a direction "very nearly straight toward his back. He must have been nearly facing the person that shot him," reported Hooton. The blue blouse he wore had powder burn marks from the musket discharge. The ball broke two ribs and fragmented along the way, part of it broke his collarbone and part exited from his back. McCook was transported to his brother George's house in Steubenville, Ohio, where a Dr. Pierce took up the case. Pierce probed for the fragment that had broken the collarbone but could not find it, causing added pain for the suffering man. The surgeon also flushed the wound every day to keep it clean.[51]

A message arrived at Steubenville on July 16, 1864, that McCook had been promoted to brigadier general. According to one account, he "did not seem to take much interest in it" and talked more about his old regiment, the Fifty-Second Ohio, and its history. According to another account, McCook dismissed the appointment by saying, "The promotion is too late now, return my compliments, saying 'I decline the honor.'" McCook died the next day, July 17, and was buried in Spring Grove Cemetery in Cincinnati. His brother, Colonel George W. McCook of the 157th Ohio National Guard, was then serving at Fort Delaware. He was standing before his regiment on dress parade when a telegram announcing Dan's death arrived. Upon reading it, George began to weep and told his adjutant to dismiss the regiment as he went to his quarters to deal with his grief in private.[52]

WOUNDED

Medical officers were swamped with wounded men on June 27. The flood of injured streaming into the field hospitals diminished to a trickle as the day continued, but it never stopped. Surgeon John Moore, medical director of the Army of the Tennessee, reported tending at least six hundred wounded soldiers on June 27. Most of the wounds treated in Fourth Corps hospitals had been caused by minie balls and were of the upper extremities. Surgeon Claiborne J. Walton of the Twenty-First Kentucky in Whitaker's brigade of Stanley's division shared in the work associated with treating the injured. "It was really distressing to see the ambulances coming in loaded with the wounded," he informed his wife. "We have three Operating tables in our division and we were all busy for Several hours."[53]

Lieut. Leroy S. Mayfield of the Twenty-Second Indiana was hit in the thigh with a minie ball at about 10:30 A.M. The wound bled quite a lot owing to the heat of the day and his elevated body temperature. Mayfield was transported back to Davis's division hospital by 1:00 P.M., but he could not rest comfortably all day or that night. Many wounded men were placed all around the hospital wherever there was room and had no shelter or attention from attendants.[54]

The sights, sounds, and emotions of the field hospitals were intense and seemingly never ending. Alexander Ayers, the quartermaster of the 125th Illinois, stayed at one hospital treating the wounded of McCook's brigade for three hours on June 27. The experience was "really heart sickening," Ayers told his wife. After watching so many men undergo treatment and surgery, he concluded the whole thing was "*terrible.*" Morgan's brigade also suffered casualties as it held the advanced Union line during Davis's attack, and its hospital was busy as well that day. Simeon Donelson of the Tenth Illinois suffered terribly when shell fragments lacerated his hand, but Donelson was so moved by the suffering of more seriously wounded men that he grabbed a leafy branch with his good hand and went the rounds keeping flies off of exposed flesh all day.[55]

On the Fifteenth Corps sector, Colonel Americus V. Rice of the Fifty-Seventh Ohio was brought to a field hospital for treatment of his severely injured leg. He had been shot below the right knee nearly in the same place where he had been shot during the siege of Vicksburg. In fact, Rice had been using a cane since the earlier injury. Two surgeons consulted on the case, and both agreed that the leg had to be amputated this time. Although Rice's brother-in-law objected, the wounded colonel readily agreed to the operation. By this time it was past dusk, so two men held candles for the surgeon to see properly. There was a hitch in the proceedings when the hospital steward administering the chloroform became so interested in the operation that he failed to give enough anesthetic. Near the end, when the surgeon tied up the ligatures, Rice suddenly became conscious and "clapped his hand down upon the limb, breaking the ligatures," in the words of one of the candleholders. Everyone feared it would cause serious consequences, but Rice never suffered any ill health because of the mishap.[56]

The men who were wounded on June 27 faced a trial nearly as bad as combat when Thomas ordered his medical officers to remove them within twenty-four hours to Big Shanty where they could be transported by rail northward. The rush was caused by Sherman's desire to organize a flanking movement by his entire force, cutting ties temporarily with the railroad as he swept past Johnston's flank along the route pioneered by Schofield. Surgeon George E. Cooper, Thomas's medical director, faced a daunting task. He had to move two thousand sick and wounded men from six to nine miles over dirt roads made rough by weather and constant use, requiring every wheeled vehicle he could find. Once at Big Shanty, every railroad car with any room had to be utilized to get the men northward as quickly as possible.[57]

Cooper accomplished the task but not without serious problems. Leroy Mayfield rode in a crowded ambulance that traveled over a newly cut road through the woods. It was "fill[ed] with Stumps and stone and terribly cut to pieces with artillery and wagon trains. Traveled near all night [of June 28], suffering indescribable." The wounded of the Fifteenth Corps also were shifted along this route to Big Shanty, utilizing the facilities of Thomas's Department of the Cumberland.[58]

Unfortunately, not enough food was furnished the wounded for the train trip to Chattanooga. The journey from Big Shanty to Chattanooga normally took only twelve hours, but the cars carrying the wounded encountered many delays. Some men spent thirty-six or more hours on the way, and their allotted rations soon ran out. Worse than this, many of the hospital attendants were derelict in their duties. Surgeons accompanied every train but could not go from one car to another while it was in motion. With no one watching them, many attendants refused to help the wounded, especially when they became thirsty and needed water. Only when the train waited at a siding to allow southbound cars the right of way could the surgeons go about and tend the injured. Even then it normally was during the night, and the railroad had not provided proper lanterns for the surgeons to use. As a result, many wounded men did not receive dressing changes until arrival at Chattanooga. Cooper was able to alleviate some of these problems by prevailing on the U.S. Sanitary Commission to set up refreshment stations at Kingston, Resaca, and Dalton, and their agents were diligent in providing food, coffee, and water to the wounded while trains were waiting at those places.[59]

Sanitary Commission workers also took charge of the mortally wounded Silas Miller, colonel of the 36th Illinois of Kimball's brigade. Chaplain William M. Haigh had accompanied Miller on the journey to Big Shanty and Chattanooga, but he was not able to obtain permission to go farther north. The commission agents agreed to make sure Miller was well cared for until he reached Illinois.[60]

Despite the hardships, this transfer of injured men was accomplished as quickly as one could expect under the circumstances. Ironically, there was no need for the rush. Sherman had made it clear to Thomas on the evening of June 27 that it would take a few days to stockpile supplies before the projected move toward Fulton. But he had been chastising Thomas about moving the Army of the Cumberland slowly for some time now, and Thomas imparted a sense of urgency to Cooper to show that his command could do better. It caused unnecessary suffering for the wounded; the transfer northward could have been conducted at a more leisurely pace to accommodate the delicate health of those involved.

There was an interesting accounting problem associated with the wounded of June 27. Thomas noted significant discrepancies in the reports of Fourteenth Corps losses that were forwarded to his headquarters, and he asked Palmer for an explanation. Palmer continued to support the figures forwarded by Davis as roughly accurate despite differences found in various reports. "A few men are probably treated in the hospitals for slight wounds who leave the hospitals before their names are taken," Palmer reasoned. "Other men, slightly wounded, are treated by the surgeons on the field and never go to the hospitals. Others, desperately wounded, leave their commands and die without ever reaching the hospitals. General Davis' report can be relied upon as nearly correct."[61]

The Confederate medical system was adequate to the care of Johnston's wounded on June 27 because his casualty list was much shorter than Sherman's. Thomas M. Cobb of the Second Missouri, who was severely wounded while holding Pigeon Hill against Giles A. Smith's brigade, provided an example of how individuals often pitched in to supplement the army's medical care. He was sent to a hospital at Barnesville, Georgia, where he suffered from gangrene for two months. Cobb was saved by a Mr. Elder, a wounded and disabled soldier from Tennessee, who nursed him beyond the crisis of his wound.[62]

PRISONERS

Few prisoners were taken on June 27 by either side, owing to the nature of the fighting. Davis listed only sixty-eight men as missing from among his Fourteenth Corps troops, while Howard reported eighty-three missing from the Fourth Corps units. A Confederate staff officer saw some forty prisoners taken in on the Fourth Corps sector and called them "a hard look-ing set of men." It was not uncommon for prisoners to appear this way to their captors, for shock, depression, or anger often were the normal moods associated with being taken captive. In Logan's Fifteenth Corps, only nine-teen men were reported as missing. Logan, however, claimed to take eighty-seven prisoners on June 27, all of them on the Confederate skirmish line.[63]

McCook's men captured Lieutenant James Durham West of the Thir-teenth Tennessee on the Confederate skirmish line during the initial phase of Davis's attack on Cheatham's Hill. Many of West's colleagues and men were scooped up by the Federals that morning. The officers were eventually transported to Johnson's Island in Ohio where they waited out the end of the war. West finally consented to signing a parole on June 17, 1865, before he was allowed to return to his home in Tennessee.[64]

REPORTING, BLAMING, EXPLAINING

Sherman sent his first report of the fighting to Washington at 8:00 P.M. He frankly reported lack of success and accurately estimated casualties, admit-ting that his men had damaged the Confederates very little. "The facility with which defensive works of timber and earth are constructed gives the party on the defensive great advantage," he explained to Halleck. Sherman further discussed his dilemma by pointing out that he could not turn John-ston's left flank without cutting loose from the railroad, and he did not yet have enough supplies to carry his large force through the time needed to move south without a line of communications. "I can press Johnston and keep him from re-enforcing Lee," Sherman wrote, "but to assault him in position will cost us more lives than we can spare."[65]

Sherman tried to shore up Thomas's spirits by assuring him that, if the attack had succeeded, "it would have been most decisive, but as it is our loss is small, compared with some of those East. It should not in the least discourage us." Sherman engaged in an effort to justify his decision to attack by arguing that it was sometimes necessary to do so, as at Arkansas Post, where the Federals succeeded. At other times, as on May 22, 1863, at Vicksburg, it proved a bloody failure.[66]

Johnston also informed his superiors in Richmond of the attack immediately after it ended, but his message was brief. The enemy had struck at several points along the Kennesaw Line, and "skirmishing was severe" all along the position. "Their loss is supposed to be great; ours known to be small," he wrote. The informal messages filtering into army headquarters from corps and division commanders indicated that the Federals were "severely punished." Johnston wanted to spread the news to all units of his army because he thought it "would have a good effect." Pioneer Hiram Smith Williams in Hood's Corps heard a "thousand-and-one rumors" to the effect that "the enemy were cut down by the thousand." Morale soared along the Confederate line as a result of these reports and rumors. In fact, taken in a wider perspective, the repulse of Sherman's attack on June 27 represented the high point of Confederate soldier morale during the Atlanta campaign.[67]

When news of the defensive victory on June 27 reached other parts of the Confederacy, joy and renewed confidence were the result. Dempsey Neal of the Fifty-First Tennessee in Cheatham's division was recuperating from illness at Macon when local newspapers offered glowing accounts of Johnston's victory. The "news is very good and chering," Neal wrote in his diary. When Robert E. Lee read about it in the Richmond newspapers at his Petersburg headquarters, he also felt encouraged about general strategic prospects for the Confederacy. He thought that, above and beyond "its general good effect," the victory would help the movements of Lieutenant General Jubal Early's Second Corps of the Army of Northern Virginia. Early was then operating in the Shenandoah Valley, having just cleared that strategically important area of Union troops. To pull Early back to Lee's army at Petersburg would only allow the Federals to return to the Shenandoah. Lee now favored Early's proposal to advance northward, cross the Potomac, and force Grant to weaken his posture at Petersburg to save Washington, D.C. If Johnston's victory at Kennesaw Mountain "could be united with a release of the prisoners at Point Lookout the advantages would be great," Lee thought, by creating an atmosphere of crisis to support the proposed drive toward Washington.[68]

The Federals who were trying to recover from their failed attacks concentrated on explaining and laying blame for what had happened that morning. Colonel John Henry Smith of the Sixteenth Iowa in the Seventeenth Corps wrote that "this charge was one of the follies of the war." Osterhaus was in a good position to observe the assault and spared no criticism of it in his diary. "The charge a failure—loss heavy. The whole thing utterly unprepared!" The German general had already been critical of how McPherson handled the Army of the Tennessee even before June 27 and now saw the attack on Kennesaw as further proof that the "general arrangements of Army of Tenn very poor." One of Osterhaus's men, John T. Clarke of the Thirty-First Missouri, sarcastically wrote in his diary that, "A mean, dirty rifle pit, and a few prisoners, is all we have to show for a field strewn with heroic dead & wounded."[69]

Many Fourth Corps survivors were very bitter. A corporal in the Twenty-Fourth Wisconsin noted that everyone felt angry at Newton for the way he handled his division that day. Emerson Opdycke, who commanded the skirmishers, reported that "*Miserable blunders* were made," though he did not elaborate. Opdycke later directed his anger and frustration at the Fourteenth Corps in general. "We are letting Thomas know that we think *that* Corps ought to do it's [*sic*] share of fighting," he wrote. Knowing that two brigades of Palmer's command had gone in with Newton on the morning of June 27 "suited *us*," but Opdycke still thought Howard's Fourth Corps was being called on to do more than its share of fighting and suffering. The feelings extended beyond the boundaries of Newton's division. Henry H. Maley of the Eighty-Fourth Illinois in Stanley's division informed his parents, "There has bin awful work here." In Wood's division, members of the Fifteenth Ohio felt "a general depression" over the result of the day's operations.[70]

Some newspapers took up the bitter message that Sherman had made a mistake at Kennesaw. "What was accomplished by the assault?," rhetorically asked a correspondent to the *Chicago Daily Tribune*. "Nothing," was the answer.[71]

Officers involved in the effort went to great lengths to explain why their men had been unable to puncture the Rebel line. Mitchell, who had failed to personally lead his brigade forward, argued that "the distance to be passed was too great," the heat was too intense, and he had no support on his right flank. Only the last of these three ideas bore a great deal of weight in explaining the outcome of the assault. Lieutenant Colonel Porter C. Olson of the Thirty-Sixth Illinois argued that it "was simply an impossibility" for the men of the Fourth Corps to break the enemy position, and there was no fault to be laid on the shoulders of either officers or enlisted men. Newton pinpointed several reasons why his division could not achieve Sherman's objective. The Rebel works were far too strong, they had placed many obstacles in front of them, and the "thickets and undergrowth . . . effectually broke up the formation of our columns and deprived that formation of the momentum which was expected of it." Newton also noted the volume of direct and cross fire from Confederate musketry and artillery as major factors in the defeat. Howard seconded Newton's argument in his official report as he came to the conclusion that any well-prepared defensive position such as that held by Cleburne's division on June 27 "cannot be carried by direct assault."[72]

Howard's chief of staff, Colonel Francis T. Sherman, explained at length to his father how the landscape inhibited Union army operations. "We have the worst country to fight in I ever saw," he wrote. "The forest has a dense and complete tangle of undergrowth which fills up the space beneath the large timber. The land is broken into hills, knobs, mountains, valleys, ravines, swamps, etc. When we make an advance you cannot see the length of a regiment, and as a consequence our lines become deranged and often one portion of a brigade will break off and get lost from the other in going three or four hundred yards." Francis Sherman admitted that "we were handsomely repulsed," but he refused to admit that "we are whipped."[73]

The formation of Newton's division into columns, which was adopted also by Davis in the Fourteenth Corps, played a role in discussion of the attack. Either Howard or Newton had been responsible for that decision in the Fourth Corps, but Bradley and Kimball both came to bitterly resent that they had been compelled to adopt the column formation. Thirty-one years after the battle, army officer and military theorist Arthur L. Wagner, who had not participated in the Civil War, published an influential book entitled *Organization and Tactics*. As part of his effort to inform current army officers of new developments in weaponry and tactics, Wagner solicited the opinions of Bradley and Kimball about the use of columns on June 27. He received unequivocal replies. "The assault on Kenesaw was a bad affair," Bradley wrote, "badly planned and badly timed, and the formation of our column was about the worst possible for assault on a fortified line—a column of regiments." Kimball concurred, writing that "Such formations have only the *appearance* of strength, but are really suicidal in their weakness." Arthur Wagner thought that the problem was worsened by the fact that the regiments were much reduced in strength, and the width of the column was therefore quite narrow. Because more regiments were placed in brigades now than early in the war, as a result of reduced troop strength, the column also was longer. Each brigade column "presented a narrow front and great depth," which made of them easier targets for artillery and musketry in Wagner's opinion.[74]

On the Fifteenth Corps sector, explanations for why the attack failed tended to focus on the terrain itself. Pigeon Hill and Little Kennesaw Mountain were too steep, their sides too cluttered with rock and irregularities, to make for a successful attack by any formation. "The assault failed only because the mountain was perfectly impassable," argued John T. Clarke. Fourteenth Corps troops also thought they were asked to do too much. Captain Toland Jones of the 113th Ohio in Mitchell's brigade asserted that "we had the melancholy satisfaction of knowing that we failed only because we attempted impossibilities."[75]

But some Federal commentators refused to admit that the mission was impossible. Sherman's chief engineer, Captain Orlando M. Poe, wrote privately to his wife about the failed attack. "We made a very feeble attempt to carry the rebel entrenchments by assault," he informed her without explaining why he thought the effort had been conducted without enthusiasm. According to Manning Force, Sherman confided to Leggett that his division was the only command that did well on June 27. In fact, it did more than was asked of it. In Force's words, Sherman admitted that "no other division in the army had done what he asked," a comment that echoed Poe's view of lax enthusiasm as a cause of the defeat.[76]

If Poe was unwilling to credit the attackers, those officers who commanded them certainly were not shy about praising their men. They filled official reports with references to "that ever memorable assault upon the enemy's works around Kenesaw," as Lieutenant Colonel Maris R. Vernon of the Seventy-Eighth Illinois in Mitchell's brigade put it. "Never did men fight better," asserted Colonel William L. Sanderson of the Twenty-Third Indiana in the Seventeenth Corps. Writing of his skirmish fight with the First Alabama of Quarles's brigade, Sanderson argued that, despite the disadvantages of terrain they encountered, his men "stood nobly until forced to retire, their conduct can be excelled by none; I was proud of them."[77]

Eight. Along the Kennesaw Line

The small space of red clay separating the opposing forces on Cheatham's Hill presented "a frightful and disgusting scene of death and destruction" after the end of Davis's attack. Captain James I. Hall of the Ninth Tennessee in Maney's brigade could not recall seeing any battlefield "so completely strewn with dead bodies." Yet the Federals were lodged within a few dozen feet of the Confederate line; they could not let the presence of their dead and wounded comrades interfere with efforts to exploit that close position.[1]

The survivors of McCook's and Mitchell's brigades consolidated their position on the night of June 27, deepening the hastily constructed trenches and building higher the parapets. The commanders of both brigades worked out a system of rotating regiments in and out of the front line of trenches. Dilworth, who now led McCook's battered command, moved the Eighty-Sixth Illinois forward on the morning of June 28 to relieve the 125th Illinois, which occupied the center of his advanced line, and the Fifty-Second Ohio relieved the Eighty-Sixth Illinois on the morning of June 29. Duty in the advanced line, located only 60 feet from the enemy, was difficult. The men had to sleep on their arms and be ready for anything at a moment's warning. Even in the rear line, located 215 feet from the Rebels, life was anything but pleasant.[2]

Lieutenant Colonel James W. Langley of the 125th Illinois devised a way to advance the forward line with minimal exposure. Langley and Corporal Joseph Frankenburg crawled forward to the slim protection of a tree about twenty feet ahead of the line and dug a small pit near it. When they had some degree of protection, the pair used a rope to pull empty cracker boxes to their location from the forward line. They filled these wooden boxes and used them as a parapet. More men came forward to work in the enlarging space protected by "the cracker box fortification," and before long the entire regiment advanced twenty feet.[3]

As Langley's men firmed up their position on the Federal front, the men of Mitchell's brigade fortified a picket line to screen their exposed right

165

flank. Companies A and B of the Thirty-Fourth Illinois moved silently a short distance away from Mitchell's right flank and began to dig in after dusk on June 28. At about 2:00 A.M., a group of Confederates gave a yell and advanced toward their position in the darkness. Only about half the Federals had taken their guns along, so all of them fell back to their own works, losing five men who were wounded.[4]

The Federals' creeping advance alarmed the Confederates into taking additional defensive measures. The first shipment of chevaux-de-frise arrived before the night of June 28 ended. A wooden device made of sharpened stakes slipped into holes that were drilled through a central pole, chevaux-de-frise were positioned in sections to obstruct an infantry advance. Two sections were delivered to the angle at Cheatham's Hill, and three members of the First Tennessee volunteered to place them before the works. Knowing how dangerously they would be exposed, according to Sam Watkins, the three men made out their wills before starting. They rolled the sections across the parapets and let them down the exterior slope using ropes. The sections came to rest at the foot of the parapet, and the three men secured them to the head logs with wire.[5]

The presence of the chevaux-de-frise was a sure indication that life near the angle was dangerous, tense, and exhausting. The Confederates had to maintain a vigilant watch twenty-four hours a day. It was impossible to get adequate rest in the trenches, and exposing any part of one's body above the head logs was almost certain death. Maney's brigade lost men on a regular basis to Union sharpshooters.[6]

Moreover, the smell from dozens of decaying bodies that littered the battlefield became overpowering. The Confederates in the angle lost their appetite, even though commissaries were able to provide them with adequate rations. Even farther north, along the front of Cleburne's division where Howard's Fourth Corps had attacked on June 27, the smell from dead bodies between the lines forced the Confederates to pull their pickets back into the main trench. The Rebel pickets could not "stand the stench from the Yankee dead."[7]

BURIAL TRUCE

Both sides recognized that something had to be done about the dead. Langley therefore opened communications with Colonel Horace Rice of the Twenty-Ninth Tennessee, who served as officer of the day in Vaughan's brigade, to arrange a truce. Davis, Mitchell, and other officers contributed to the negotiations, but Langley and Rice were primarily responsible for the details. They arranged for the truce to be in effect from 9:00 A.M. to 1:00 P.M. on June 29. For the poor men lodged in works only a few feet from the decaying bodies, the truce did not take place a moment too soon. A member of the First Tennessee commented that "of all the horrid stenches in the world we had it there and no relief from it."[8]

Both sides advanced a line of pickets to establish a marker along the middle of no-man's-land. Then the pickets faced toward their own works as details moved the bodies from the Confederate sector to the line. The Federals were responsible for taking care of the bodies on their side of the picket line. The truce brought out thousands of Union and Confederate soldiers from their entrenchments, and many of them crowded the pickets, causing some difficulty for officers and men of both armies to maintain the line intact. According to an officer of McCook's brigade, because the pickets were not armed, they had to use persuasion and the threat of physical restraint to keep order.[9]

James T. Holmes reported that no living men were found between the lines during the burial truce. Details counted eleven dead Federals grouped behind one tree in front of the Eleventh and Twenty-Ninth Tennessee of Vaughan's brigade. They had sought shelter there during the worst of the firing two days before. All of the bodies across the narrow space of ground separating the belligerents "were in a terrible condition," recalled Edwin Payne of the Thirty-Fourth Illinois, "and the atmosphere was almost unbearable." Hardee's artillery chief, Colonel Melancthon Smith, reported that many of the bodies had become "as black as Negroes," and were "enormously swollen, fly blown and emitting an intolerable stench." To John Hill Ferguson of the Tenth Illinois, who watched the proceedings, the dead seemed to have "swelled up as big as 4 men and black as a polished stone by laying in the sun." Flies had bothered the dead so thoroughly that "their bodies & especially their faces were a moving mass of *Maggots*," according to Alexander Miller Ayers of the 125th Illinois.[10]

Interring the dead proved difficult; the decayed condition of most of the remains forced the details to bury them on the spot in shallow graves. The Federals used shovels or the boards torn off cracker boxes to shove bodies into the holes. Nixon Stewart was one of the men detailed from the Fifty-Second Ohio, and he claimed that his comrades were able to identify all of the fallen from their regiment and mark their graves with boards. A few bodies were taken to the rear, including that of Captain Marion Lee and the "much decayed" remains of Captain William W. Fellows of the 125th Illinois. But most of the dead were interred on the Federal side of no-man's-land only a few feet from the Confederate works and extending for about one hundred yards along the length of this narrow space. Alexander Miller Ayers helped to bury three officers in holes only two feet deep in this area. He placed a blanket over each body and then piled dirt on top.[11]

While the details continued their gruesome duty, thousands of men in blue and gray took the burial truce as an opportunity to stretch, get some fresh air out of the trenches, and watch the proceedings. Ordnance officer Robert Davis Smith of Polk's brigade in Cleburne's division walked along the lines to see what was happening. The truce was effective for the sector occupied by both Davis's division and Newton's division, so peace reigned for some distance north of Cheatham's Hill. Smith noticed that men sat on top of the head logs and chatted, while officers of opposing sides mingled and conversed "as if they were the best friends in the world." Colonel George W. Gordon of the Eleventh Tennessee in Vaughan's brigade took the opportunity to ask Federal officers why their men carried loaded but uncapped guns on June 27. They told him the objective was to make sure the troops did not stop to fire before reaching the Confederate works. A Union officer told J. T. Bowden of the Twelfth Tennessee how much his men feared the possibility of a Rebel night attack on their forward position. The burial truce seems to have induced open, excessively friendly feelings among some of the belligerents.[12]

From the perspective of a man in Mitchell's brigade, however, the Confederates who came forward to chat and trade with the Yankees appeared to be "a hard looking set, dirty & raged as could be." But that did not prevent swapping of canteens and newspapers, the trading of tobacco for coffee, and the exchange of other desirable items. One Confederate soldier had left his pocketknife on a stone in front of the line several days before after killing and dressing a sheep. The Federal soldier who found the knife gave it back to him. Compliant Union men accepted messages from Confederates who wanted to communicate with friends and relatives living behind Federal lines, and promised to send them at the first opportunity. A friendly wrestling match took place when a Confederate challenged any Federal to a test of physical strength. A recruit among the Yankees accepted and threw the challenger.[13]

Many high level officers took advantage of the truce to get a close look at the enemy works and at the enemy themselves. It was the only opportunity anyone had to see the human face of his opponent. Maney, Cheatham, Cleburne, and Hindman were among the Confederate brigade and division commanders seen during the truce. Maney chatted for at least a half hour with Federal officers and meanwhile caught enough glimpses to guess the exact distance separating his line from the enemy's. When Captain William Parker of the Seventy-Fifth Illinois in Mitchell's brigade asked about his brother, who served as a major in a Confederate unit, Cleburne sent someone to locate him, and the two had a short visit while the truce lasted.[14]

Cheatham impressed many Federals. According to Robert M. Rogers, the historian of the 125th Illinois, the Rebel commander wore an "old slouch hat, a blue hickory shirt, butternut pants, and a pair of cavalry boots. The supports to his unmentionables were an old leather strap, and a piece of web, the general appearance being that of a 'johnney' gone to seed." Cheatham told Langley that he believed the war would have to end in a negotiated settlement because "neither party could conquer," as Rogers put it. "He virtually admitted that he was only fighting from principle, and not for the love of the Southern Confederacy." But some enlisted men of Polk's brigade spoke boldly to Captain Ira Beman Read of the 101st Ohio. "They were certain of success and that the North and South could never be again united."[15]

Hindman did not impress anyone on the Federal side. "In appearance he was very dressy," Rogers admitted. "His auburn hair flowed in ringlets over his shoulders, and it was stated that a light mulatto girl dressed it for him every morning." But the Federals found out that few men who wore the gray held any regard for Hindman. "He did not command the respect of his troops, and by his brother officers he was despised."[16]

Fewer high-ranking Federal officers came forth during the burial truce to observe and converse than did Confederate generals. Brigadier General James D. Morgan, one of Davis's brigade commanders, took his coat off and wore an ordinary shirt to appear to be an enlisted man. He then took a tool and pretended to be a member of a burial detail. While out, he tried to observe as much of the Rebel works as possible.[17]

During the negotiations for the burial truce, a heated disagreement developed between Langley and Rice about the disposition of the many abandoned rifles lying in no-man's-land. Dropped by the Federals when the men were shot or tried to retreat, Rice naturally argued that the weapons rightfully belonged to the Confederate army. Langley refused to comply. He argued with much conviction that no-man's-land was neutral ground, not controlled by either party. He suggested the guns be left where they were until one side or the other should gain complete control of Cheatham's Hill. Rice conceded the point, and instructions went out to all men involved not to touch the guns during the truce. To have given up the weapons at this point, Rogers pointed out, would have been to concede that the Federals had no chance of taking the hill. He estimated that something like 250 guns were at stake. Rogers also praised Rice for acting throughout the negotiations and the truce itself in a "very gentlemanly and humane" way.[18]

While most men obeyed instructions to leave the guns on the ground, a handful tried to take some of them off the field. John Hill Ferguson reported that some men "put their foot through the strap of the guns and walk slowly, dragging the gun after them."[19]

The work involved in burying remains that had lain in the hot sun for more than forty-eight hours required more time than originally planned. Langley and Rice agreed to extend the truce past 1:00 P.M. for another three hours. The work was barely finished by 4:00 P.M. when a lone sentry fired his musket into the air as a signal for all to take cover once again. Some Confederates had offered to help their enemy bury the dead, and they now threw the entrenching tools over to the Federals before returning to their own works.[20]

Disposing of the dead at Cheatham's Hill was difficult because of the narrow width of no-man's-land, which caused the opponents to be more wary of each other. But along the Fourth Corps sector just north of the hill, the lines were much farther apart. Even before the truce at Cheatham's Hill, the opponents had arranged a truce for the Federals to recover their dead along that sector. Major Luther M. Sabin of the Forty-Fourth Illinois, the officer of the day for Kimball's brigade, negotiated with Lieutenant Colonel William H. Martin of the First and Fifteenth Arkansas, who served as the officer of the day for Polk's brigade, to organize the truce. Martin was the same gallant officer who had offered the Federals an opportunity to retrieve many of their wounded from the fire on June 27. The truce went into effect on the evening of June 28.[21]

The truce gave an opportunity for George W. Parsons of the Fifty-Seventh Indiana in Wagner's brigade to recover the body of his friend, George Bowman. He and some comrades had tried to do so on the night of June 27 but failed. Parsons was grateful that the truce allowed him to honor his friend, but he noted that the Confederates had already gotten to Bowman's body and "took ever thing he had in his pockets."[22]

Fourth Corps burial details found corpses that had become so decomposed as to be unrecognizable. Some of the bodies had also been terribly burned by the fire two days before. They also were in such a condition that it was impossible to remove them to the rear for proper interment. The Federals were forced to dig shallow graves and bury them on the spot. One body, however, was in much better condition than the rest, probably because the man had lain wounded for some time before expiring. Chesley Mosman, whose pioneers were sent out to help the burial details, tried to find some indication of his identity but only came across a photograph of a young lady in the man's bible. The name of the photographer, Dillinger of Lancaster, Pennsylvania, was the only clue. When a soldier of the 100th Illinois said he thought the dead man was a member of his company, Mosman gave the photograph to him and suggested he contact "the artist to see if a clue could be obtained to the soldier's name." Mosman never found out the result.[23]

There was less spirit of cooperation between the lines along the Fifteenth Corps sector. The Federals tried to retrieve their dead on the slope of Pigeon Hill, but Confederate skirmishers stationed along the foot of the slope refused. They continued to refuse for as long as they held Pigeon Hill and Little Kennesaw Mountain. The stench and decay must have been overpowering, and still the Confederates stubbornly barred the Yankees from setting foot on the open slope. Not until the Rebels abandoned their position, nearly a week after the attack of June 27, did the Federals have an opportunity to reach their dead. They found that the enemy had taken clothing and articles of value from their pockets under cover of night but had not bothered to bury them.[24]

The burial truce at Cheatham's Hill not only eliminated a horrid spectacle and a torturing smell from no-man's-land but provided a blessed moment of relief from the cramped trenches. While many men interacted with the enemy on positive, friendly terms, others came away from the truce with negative, bitter feelings. Matthew H. Jamison of the Tenth Illinois in Morgan's brigade found some Confederates who spoke in harsh, bragging tones to the Yankees. "Rebel general seemed to enjoy our discomfiture. Reb colonel denounced Northern 'Copperheads' and New York *Herald*. Return to our line with feeling of indignation and inexpressible sorrow."[25]

NIGHT OF JUNE 29–30

Only a few hours after the end of the burial truce, the opponents occupying Cheatham's Hill engaged in one of the fiercest firefights to take place along the Kennesaw Line. The Federals tried to construct better fortifications along the picket line that shielded their right flank, filling empty cracker boxes and barrels to make a parapet. Captain Peter Ege took Companies A, B, F, and I of the Thirty-Fourth Illinois out to work on the flank, where the picket line was no more than 15 yards in front of the Union position and about 150 yards from the enemy works. They made good progress until a party of Confederates crept out of their own entrenchments and opened fire on the companies from a distance of only 20 yards at about 3:00 A.M. Much of the fire went too high, but Ege lost two men wounded during a rather hasty retreat.[26]

The incident triggered a prolonged spat of heavy firing along the lines. The Federals on Cheatham's Hill shouted "'Up! Up! Up!'" as they roused themselves with guns in their hands to repel an expected attack. Firing broke out everywhere, brightening up the area as "light as day" in the words of Styles W. Porter. Confederate artillery joined in the chorus and illuminated the hill with muzzle flashes and shell explosions. The intense firing lasted from fifteen to thirty minutes and resulted "in a heavy loss of ammunition and some swearing," according to F. M. McAdams of the 113th Ohio. On the Confederate side, Alfred Tyler Fielder of the Twelfth Tennessee described it as "a tremendous firing" that took the lives of a few men in Vaughan's brigade. In fact, a member of the Forty-Seventh Tennessee was shot accidently by his comrades because he was on the exposed line of videttes and got caught in the crossfire. The Ninety-Eighth Ohio suffered one man killed in the noisy demonstration.[27]

The sound of firing at Cheatham's Hill roused Howard's men a short distance to the north. Chesley Mosman tried to get his pioneers up and into the works "before I was half awake." He entered the entrenchments "carrying my sword and belt and my shoes in my hand." As Fourth Corps skirmishers came back to the main line, the Federals (except Wood's division on the far left of Howard's sector) opened a heavy volume of musketry into the darkness for some time to come. After a while, Mosman could tell that the enemy had no intention of attacking, and he ordered his pioneers to cease firing. The rest of the Federal line stopped soon after, but the Confederates continued firing for at least five minutes more. "The timber was 'chock full' of fireflies apparently," Mosman recorded. "The flash of their muskets reminded one of them." Most of the Rebel fire tended to be too high, "but the rear must have got plenty of lead," Mosman concluded. He was right. The Ninety-Sixth Illinois of Whitaker's brigade in Stanley's division rested to the rear and received a flight of minie balls through its bivouac area.[28]

The firing also disturbed the repose of Maney's men, for at least the First and Twenty-Seventh Tennessee and the Sixth and Ninth Tennessee had just been relieved of their perilous post on the hill. Moving to a work three hundred yards to the rear after dark on June 29, the exhausted Tennesseans had just settled down to sleep when the musketry startled them. T. H. Maney, an enlisted man in the First Tennessee, had taken off his shoes, socks, and pants and was already sound asleep when the gunfire and yells of "'Fall in, fall in, the enemy are on us!'" roused him. "Every one woke up with a start and was dazed to such a degree that we hardly knew where to go," he wrote. They were, in fact, "crazed from loss of sleep." Maney mistook his jacket for his pants and tried to put it on, but could not get his leg through the opening. Finally he realized his mistake, but could not find his pants at all in the darkness. Maney went forward to the front line ready to repel an attack dressed only in his jacket and underwear. None of his comrades noticed it, and he was able, after the scare subsided, to locate his pants. But Maney found the incident so funny he enjoyed telling everyone about it and laughing at himself for being "scared out of my pants."[29]

William Latimer of the Sixth and Ninth Tennessee also recalled that many of his comrades were so disoriented they mimicked Maney's performance. Some of them went forward "with one leg in their pants, by others with pants in hand, while others were altogether minus." The incident resulted in no casualties and therefore "furnished the boys amusement for many days."[30]

The firefight on the night of June 29–30 extended along both Cheatham's and Cleburne's division fronts. The heaviest firing took place on Cheatham's right and Cleburne's left. Polk's brigade lost two killed and three wounded, but losses in other units are unknown. It lasted up to half an hour on some parts of Cleburne's line. The Federals not inaccurately reported to Palmer and Thomas that the affair started with a Rebel advance on Mitchell's flank that was repulsed. Thomas correctly reported to Sherman that the rest of the heavy firing was not accompanied by an enemy advance. Rumors circulating within Maney's brigade had it that the entire affair started when a Yankee officer "yelled 'Forward, double-quick, charge,' just to see what would happen," as J. L. W. Blair of the First Tennessee recalled.[31]

Having twice failed to dig trenches to cover the right, Mitchell's flank remained in the air for some time to come after the night of June 29–30. The Federals continued to improve their earthworks on Cheatham's Hill for the duration of their stay, but they never again tried to dig works along Mitchell's right flank. Moreover, although several men wrote vaguely about the Yankees digging constantly and creeping ever closer to the Confederate position, the weight of evidence in personal accounts and reports indicates that they never again tried to dig closer to the enemy entrenchments than they were by June 29. Vigorous Confederate countermeasures made it too dangerous to continue advancing across the narrow, contested space that separated the belligerents. Mitchell reported that his brigade was "much annoyed by the enemy's sharpshooters," and there was a constant fear of night attacks to further impede Union activity.[32]

The lines at Cheatham's Hill rested at very close range. The Confederates insisted that the forward Union position was sixty feet from their works. J. B. Work, a veteran of McCook's brigade, measured the distance after the war and reported it was sixty-eight feet. Work also noted that thirty Federals held this advanced line while protected by cracker boxes and cartridge boxes filled with dirt. James T. Holmes also measured the distance after the war while visiting the battlefield and reported that the main Union position was ninety feet away from the Confederate line. Holmes also noted that the Union works, which were well preserved when he visited in 1897, slanted back as they extended toward the left until they were at one point 180 feet from the Confederates. Then they slanted forward again to close the distance. The hastily constructed Union works lay in contrast to the enemy entrenchments, which were uniformly laid out in a straight line.[33]

But the Confederate works, of course, were poorly placed within the context of the terrain. Standing on the ground in 1897, with an opportunity to safely observe, Holmes was struck by how the crest of the slope provided cover for the Federals after their attack failed on June 27. "It was a few inches of earth that made our sticking so close to our antagonists after the assault possible," he marveled. The ground to the rear of the Union position was open to Confederate fire and was dangerous to move across during daylight hours. But here along the narrow shelter of the crest, the Unionists clung for life and constructed a pretty impressive, impromptu system of earthworks adorned in many places with head logs.[34]

LIVING AND FIGHTING ON CHEATHAM'S HILL

"We are still here," Luther P. Bradley informed a correspondent on July 1, "under the shadow of the great Kenesaw. . . . the work being more like a siege than anything else." Speaking of the Fourteenth Corps position on Cheatham's Hill, Bradley wrote that the Federals had "to work them out of the position by slow approaches" because to attack them again would be prohibitively costly. As James T. Holmes recalled, Davis's men referred to the angle of the Confederate works on Cheatham's Hill as "Key Point."[35]

The Federals rotated units between their forward position on the hill and the rear lines. For example, Allen Fahnestock's Eighty-Sixth Illinois replaced the 125th Illinois in the forward line before dawn of June 28 and fired all day, losing one man killed and another wounded. The Fifty-Second Ohio then relieved the Eighty-Sixth the next day. Fahnestock's regiment again relieved the 125th Illinois in the front line on July 1 and was again replaced by the Fifty-Second Ohio after twenty-four hours. The regiments in Mitchell's brigade also took twenty-four shifts in the front line. Between shifts, the men of the Ninety-Eighth Ohio washed up, cleaned their clothes, and rested for one day before going back to duty. While twenty-four hours was the normal stay on the front line, the Thirty-Fourth Illinois held that position for two days near the end of the Kennesaw phase of the campaign.[36]

The Confederates could not afford to be so liberal in rotating men out of their works. The only recorded instance of this occurred when the First and Twenty-Seventh Tennessee and the Sixth and Ninth Tennessee left the hill on the evening of June 29 and slept in a rear trench. Surviving the scare afforded by the firefight that night, Sam Watkins took time to wash himself at a nearby stream. He "found my arm all battered and bruised and bloodshot from my wrist to my shoulder, and as sore as a blister," because, he estimated, he had fired 120 rounds during the attack of June 27.[37]

Duty in the works on Cheatham's Hill was dangerous and uncomfortable. While occupying the front line of Mitchell's brigade from the evening of June 30 to July 2, the Thirty-Fourth Illinois experienced the full burden of such duty. "The men in the trenches were cramped for room," wrote Edwin Payne, "and were unable to sleep except in the most uncomfortable positions. No one dared show a hand or head above the rifle-pits on either side. The hot sun beat down on them by day, and the dews of rain at night. The trenches became muddy and disgusting." Men detailed to prepare meals had to cook rations in ravines and the branch valley to the rear and then bring forward the results to those crouching in the works.[38]

W. B. Emmons of the Thirty-Fourth Illinois recorded in his diary that the trenches were barely big enough for half the men of the regiment to lay down, and "we are miserably cramped for room." Even if they had a place to curl up, they could hardly sleep because many false alarms occurred, and there was so much random firing during the night. It was "absolutely to hot to s[l]eep in the day time," Emmons wrote. The men placed poles over the trench and lay their shelter tent halves across them to provide shade during the day. Boredom, ironically enough, also was a part of life on Cheatham's Hill. "Sergt Somers is hunting the inevitable grey back from his shirt & pants by my elbow," Emmons wrote on July 2. "I must quit writing & do like wise. (Such is the every day life of the Soldier on this Campaign of Sherman's)."[39]

Emmons could not stand the trenches on the night of July 1. He was bothered greatly by a smell of death and assumed that many of the bodies buried on June 29 had been imperfectly covered up. Emmons also wondered if a few bodies had been overlooked, because the stench was nearly suffocating. The trenches also were intolerably hot. He got out of the works to find a place where he could stretch and sleep, although exposed to fire. Bullets fell within a couple of feet, but Emmons used his knapsack and haversack to protect himself, and he slept a couple of hours in the open that night.[40]

The Confederate guns positioned within Carter's brigade to the south of the angle opened a furious bombardment on the Union position on the evening of July 2, causing the men of the Thirty-Fourth Illinois to crouch ever deeper in their works. Many rounds hit the parapets and gouged chunks of red clay from them. An artillery projectile "passed within 3 feet of my head & buried its self in the bank at my side," wrote Emmons. The bombardment continued for a half hour before the Confederates ceased firing, but no one in the Thirty-Fourth Illinois was hurt. As Emmons wryly put it in his diary, there was no use to grumble at living conditions on Cheatham's Hill, "for we can plainly see that nothing short of fighting digging & hard knocks will ever end this *war*."[41]

On the afternoon of July 1, the Confederates were startled to see a Federal soldier stand up on his parapet "in plain view of our men—rubbing his eyes in a bewildering manner with a bucket on his arm," as J. T. Bowden put it. The Confederates allowed him to cross no-man's-land and took him as a prisoner into their works. What this man meant, what he tried to do, and who he was remained a mystery as far as the Rebels were concerned. Stories circulated that when he crossed the Confederate parapet, "he raised one foot & some of the boys saw them drag a cord back to their line." It seemed the man had sacrificed his freedom so that the Federals could know the exact distance between the lines because they intended to undermine the angle. Another version of the story, from the Confederate side, was that the man changed the coffee pot he held from one hand to another as he crossed the Rebel parapet, apparently as a prearranged signal to his comrades that the Rebels had not evacuated their position.[42]

But many stories circulated among the Federals also as to what this man was up to. They saw him mount the works and scramble to the enemy line carrying a bucket full of hot coffee and a mess pan, or a tin cup, depending on which version of the story one trusts. Some observers claim he dropped all his gear partway across no-man's-land and ran for his life into the arms of the Confederates, apparently a spy or a deserter. John Moore of the Fifty-Second Ohio tried to shoot him, "but he was out of sight before I could take good aim." The general opinion was that the man informed the enemy of the Federal mining project to blow up the angle.[43]

But the real story behind the man and what he did on the afternoon of July 1 is less dramatic than either the Confederate or Federal theories. Edwin Payne identified him as Private Edward O'Donnell of Company I, Thirty-Fourth Illinois. Born in Burlingay, Ireland, he was a thirty-year-old laborer when he enlisted in the Seventy-Eighth Illinois in September 1861, but O'Donnell transferred to the Thirty-Fourth Illinois in March 1864. He suffered from sunstroke early in the Atlanta campaign and had not fully recovered from its effects. On the hot afternoon of July 1, he was detailed to cook rations in the branch valley and was bringing them up to the trenches when he unaccountably walked through the entire complex of Federal works and across no-man's-land. O'Donnell was neither a spy for the Confederates nor a sacrificial lamb for the Federals; he was just a confused man who did not know where he was going. It was a miracle that he was not shot by either the Confederates or the Unionists. Nevertheless, he was listed as a deserter, for want of any better category to place him in. O'Donnell was sent to the Confederate military prison at Andersonville where he was hospitalized on July 28, 1864. He died of diarrhea on September 3, the day after Sherman captured Atlanta.[44]

SHARPSHOOTING

The musket firing across no-man's-land on Cheatham's Hill never seemed to end. Most men on both sides were fairly well protected as long as they crouched low in the trenches, but even then they were not entirely safe. Bullets sometimes glanced off the few trees that were left standing near the works and ricocheted down into the trench, hurting a few men now and then. Those trees were "clipped by bullets in a manner that is astonishing," wrote F. M. McAdams of the 113th Ohio.[45]

At such close range, any movement above the protection of the parapets could prove dangerous. When a man in the Thirty-Fourth Illinois carelessly raised his arm above the works as he shoveled dirt, he received a Rebel ball in it. When Lieutenant David F. Miser of the Fifty-Second Ohio refused to remain stooped inside the trench after refreshing himself with a cup of coffee and a hard tack, he was mortally wounded. Lieutenant Colonel Charles W. Clancy came one day to visit the Fifty-Second Ohio while he was recuperating from the contused leg he suffered in the attack of June 27. After an hour in the works, he and W. J. Funston walked along the trench to return to the rear as a Confederate sharpshooter targeted the pair. The Rebel placed bullets just behind the Federals, and Clancy told Funston to keep walking and pretend they did not notice, even though one of the rounds hit another Federal soldier in the trench. Both men survived the ordeal without a scratch, but the Fifty-Second Ohio lost a total of thirty-four men in the entrenchments from June 28 until July 2, mostly due to sharpshooting.[46]

One day the color-bearer of the Fifty-Second Ohio placed his flag on the Federal parapet. Within a relatively short time, Confederate sharpshooters shot the staff with five rounds, putting the balls "within two or three hand breadths" of each other. The Federals had to repair the staff with pieces of tin and tacks in order to continue using it.[47]

The regiments that occupied the forward Union line had orders to "keep up a constant fire," as W. B. Emmons put it. The Thirty-Fourth Illinois fired five thousand rounds, and the Fifty-Second Ohio shot thirteen thousand rounds on July 2 alone. Emmons estimated that the Confederates fired only one round for every four or five that the Federals shot on July 2. Over a period of six days, Nixon B. Stewart estimated that each man of the Fifty-Second Ohio fired two hundred rounds at the enemy. "When we could not see a Johnny to shoot at we fired away at the flag staff the rebels put up on their breast works. Several times it was shot off."[48]

A few men in McCook's brigade had earlier purchased Henry repeating rifles with their own money, and now they came in handy. One day James T. Holmes borrowed one of these advanced weapons and planted himself behind a tree that was inside the forward Union trench. He climbed on top of the parapet, believing the trunk offered adequate protection as he became absorbed with finding a target and firing toward the left. After some time he happened to glance right and had the shock of his life. He could see "the whole rebel line" in that direction and realized that the enemy could probably see him as easily if the Rebels happened to look. "The scene made cold chills run over me," he recalled many years later, "for ordinarily it was unsafe to show even a hand to that line."[49]

Specialized equipment to enhance the work of sharpshooters began to appear along the Kennesaw Line. Even before the attack of June 27, some Federals saw what came to be called "gun glasses," little mirrors about three inches square. Lieutenant E. C. Silliman of Company C, Eighty-Sixth Illinois, came across a man in the Fourth Corps who was peddling them to his comrades for their personal use in grooming. Silliman bought a number of them and gave the mirrors as gifts to his comrades in the Eighty-Sixth Illinois. Someone in McCook's brigade (Nixon B. Stewart claimed it was a man in the 125th Illinois) thought of using the mirrors to aid sharpshooting. They were framed with zinc and had a wire attached, enabling the man to tie it to the stock of a musket. It was, as Stewart put it, "so arranged that we could lie down in the trench, the rifle resting on the breast works, pointing toward the rebel head log, that you could look through the sights and with your hammer pulled back, pick off a rebel without exposing the body." Many sharpshooters used the same tree that Holmes had utilized as a post. It was, as Stewart recalled, a "large chestnut tree, hollow at the lower side," and, when used properly, could serve "as a fortress."[50]

These devices, which Lieutenant Colonel Langley of the 125th Illinois called "the refracting sight," were in use at Cheatham's Hill by June 28. "The testimony in favor of the use of this sight at short range was abundant," Langley concluded in his report. The Confederates would have readily supported his conclusion. They were fully aware of the device, catching glimpses of it now and then. The Rebels knew that it contributed to their enemy's ability to throw an inordinate amount of lead into their works with minimal exposure. Sometimes the Federal rounds glanced off the head logs on the Confederate works and ricocheted downward into the trenches, finding a human target. Actually, the unknown Federal in McCook's brigade who used the mirror first could not claim a patent on the device. Colonel Ellison Capers of the Twenty-Fourth South Carolina in Gist's brigade of Walker's division first reported the mirror being used by a sharpshooter opposite his sector of the Kennesaw Line, in the area of Gist's Salient a bit south of Pigeon Hill and well north of Cheatham's Hill. Someone in the Fourth Corps also had the idea to use these small mirrors for purposes the manufacturer had never intended.[51]

The Federals had good weapons, an unusual device for enhancing the sighting and firing, but few human targets to shoot at on top of Cheatham's Hill. Not surprisingly, they often targeted the head logs on Cheatham's works. "The boys practiced billiard tactics on the headlogs," James T. Holmes reported, and often were able to deflect their rounds into the works. After several days of such firing, the head logs were wasted, eaten away by repeated strikes of minie balls. As a member of the First Tennessee put it, they had "been literally shot to pieces." It took five days for one dedicated sharpshooter to cut a head log ten inches wide in two, according to a fascinated Rebel observer. After the campaign, visiting Federal veterans sent chunks of these decimated head logs home as souvenirs.[52]

One day, a Yankee sharpshooter forgot to take his ramrod out of the barrel before firing. This was common during pitched battles, and the man simply had to scrounge up another ramrod before continuing to fire. But this time the metal rod "struck a sapling," according to H. K. Nelson of the First Tennessee, "breaking it in two, and one piece about eight or ten inches long stuck through the leg of one of our boys and had to be pulled out."[53]

If either side dominated in the contest of sharpshooting, it probably was the Union side. The volume of fire the Yankees delivered on a regular basis and the relentless eating away of the protective head logs on the Confederate works seem to indicate that the balance tipped toward their favor. Captain James I. Hall of the Ninth Tennessee had a favorite place in the works where he felt comparatively safe. But one day while sleeping he awoke to see that a bullet had hit the post he leaned against only a few inches above his head. On the evening of June 29, after he showed an officer of a relieving unit where he might sleep, the officer was killed there twenty minutes later by a ball that glanced off the head log and hit him.[54]

The sharpshooting was less intense, but still significant, elsewhere along the line. "I always felt a little tenderfooted when getting near the works," admitted Edward Norphlet Brown of the Forty-Fifth Alabama in Lowrey's brigade. Stationed on the Fourth Corps sector, at the scene of Newton's attack on June 27, Brown felt it was "really dangerous to walk about the lines at all. The men have to lie close all the time. . . . One Minnie ball passed so close to me that it made my head dizzy. Another struck a tree just before me & another knocked up the dirt about ten feet behind me." The Confederates could joke about it, fortunately; "it was a saying among the men that it was only necessary to expose a hand to procure a furlough," wrote Hardee's artillery chief, Melancthon Smith.[55]

While the opponents along the Fourth Corps sector were not close enough to throw things at each other, the men of McCook's and Mitchell's brigades had to watch out for more than bullets. As Captain Toland Jones of the 113th Ohio put it, his men were literally "within a stone's throw of the rebel works." Rocks now and then descended on the Thirty-Fourth Illinois when it held the advanced line. While observers often thought it was done as a form of amusement, the rocks actually could do significant injury if they happened to hit someone. The Federals often retaliated by throwing them back into the Confederate works. The enemy "also threw Over Corn

Dodgers," as Allen Fahnestock recorded in his diary, "but No One was Injured by them."[56]

On the evening of June 28, members of the Fifty-Second Ohio heard a Rebel officer yell commands to "'make ready, take aim, fire!'" in order to draw the Federals together in their works. Then the Confederates threw over a fusillade of rocks, chunks of wood, and pick handles. At least three members of the regiment were seriously injured by this hail of objects and had to go to the rear for treatment.[57]

The lines were close enough on Cheatham's Hill so that the Confederates worried about a sudden attack in the night. Cheatham therefore requested that fireballs be issued to his division. These were balls of cotton that were soaked in tar, turpentine, or grease. It was not easy for Major E. B. Dudley Riley, Hardee's ordnance officer, to produce these devices. He had plenty of turpentine on hand but none of the other ingredients. Riley wrote to Colonel Moses H. Wright at the Atlanta Arsenal requesting twenty to thirty balls, but Wright was too busy making other necessary ordnance supplies to shift his crews to manufacturing them. Wright contacted the arsenals at Macon and Charleston for up to fifty fireballs. They must have arrived in time because the Confederates used many fireballs at Cheatham's Hill. They lighted the balls and threw them over the parapet to illuminate no-man's-land anytime they heard a suspicious noise in the Union works. The fireballs also hindered efforts by the Federals to dig forward under cover of darkness. The Confederates sometimes kept balls burning all night long.[58]

Hand grenades were made for just such a situation as existed on Cheatham's Hill and potentially could have been very effective. The Confederates heard rumors that Cheatham had ordered grenades to be distributed, but they apparently never were issued before the Confederates evacuated the Kennesaw Line. The Rebels did manage to gather some spare muskets from among their own dead and wounded comrades who had fallen on June 27. They loaded the weapons and fixed them along the works to be ready in case the Yankees staged a surprise attack.[59]

The fear of surprise, on both sides, dominated the waking moments of everyone. The lines were far too close for either side to establish a skirmish line, and too close even for a thin line of videttes. Both the Federals and Confederates placed one or two men along their line during the night to serve a warning to their comrades in case of an enemy advance. It was dangerous duty, to say the least.[60]

Another firefight erupted on the night of June 30–July 1 because of nervousness and false alarms. Confederate videttes along both Vaughan's and Maney's front thought they detected signs of a Federal advance. They rushed back into the trench and spread the word, which resulted in an explosion of musketry and artillery firing by the Confederates lasting half an hour. The next morning some Rebels could see Federal commissary wagons on the other side of the branch of John Ward Creek that had been shot up during the firing. Apparently the Yankees had happened to be distributing rations when the ruckus began. Wild reports spread along Confederate lines that their opponents had lost 1,100 men and 200 mules in the fight. Rumors also spread that the firing had been triggered by videttes who mistook lightning bugs for muzzle flashes and nervously began to shoot back. A similar story about lightning bugs inadvertently beginning a spate of night firing had taken place along the New Hope Church Line a month before. As Melancthon Smith put it, when the opposing forces were lodged so close to each other, false alarms easily got out of hand. Once firing started, "it moves very contagiously."[61]

MINING

Back on Cheatham's Hill, the opposing lines were close enough to allow the Federals to begin a mine designed to blow up the angle of the Confederate works. The distance was short, and the Yankees could start the underground approach in the side of the hill, just below the shallow military crest that had saved their lives when the attack broke apart on June 27. It was the first and only time in the Civil War that troops belonging to the Army of the Cumberland attempted a mining project. The only men of Sherman's army group which had experience at this unique form of warfare were members of the Army of the Tennessee, who had dug several mines during the course of the siege of Vicksburg. Johnston's Army of Tennessee had no previous experience at either mining or countermining.

Lieutenant Colonel James W. Langley of the 125th Illinois initiated the mine after he helped to push the forward Union line ahead to a distance of only a few yards from the Confederate works on June 28. As the historian of his regiment put it, Langley intended to detonate the mine on July 4 and "usher in the day by one of the grandest pyrotechnic displays that had ever occurred in those parts." Postwar measurement of what was left of the mine indicated Langley started the excavation 105 feet (35 yards) from the main Confederate line. Allen Fahnestock estimated the tunnel was 16 feet underground at its deepest.[62]

The mine "excited great interest," according to James T. Holmes, not only because it was a new experience but "because it had in it the promise of great things." If successful, the detonation would "complete the charge of June 27." But the men had to work with only "crude tools" designed for digging out trenches, not the specialized tools used by miners to work in confined spaces. Progress was slow owing to this factor, plus the men's unfamiliarity with the process of mining, but they persisted in pushing forward the gallery for many days. They carried the dirt "in sacks or baskets or buckets" along the trench line toward the left, where they dumped it at the left flank of the forward line, which happened to be 180 feet from the Confederates. The Rebels could see the fresh earth, and it was a slightly different color from the normal surface dirt, but the Federals assumed it would not arouse any suspicion.[63]

Yet the Confederates were aware that the Yankees were digging underground. When staff officer Robert Davis Smith visited the angle during the burial truce of June 29, he saw that it would be comparatively easy for the Federals to undermine the spot. Many other officers must have had the same thought. The Federals captured a few stragglers when they followed up Johnston's evacuation of the Kennesaw Line and learned from them that the Confederates had suspected mining at Cheatham's Hill. They had placed a drum on the ground with a handful of small pebbles on the surface. The vibrations of digging, even deep underground, caused the pebbles to move slightly. As Robert M. Rogers of the 125th Illinois put it, many Federals wondered "where they learned enough of philosophy to induce them to make the experiment." But this method of detecting underground mining was as old as siege warfare itself, and it is quite possible the Confederates used it at Cheatham's Hill. One of the prisoners assured his captors that "he was stationed where 'the mine would have blown him to h-ll if we'uns hadn't left.'"[64]

Langley's project neared its completion as the Fourth of July loomed on the calendar. By the night of July 2, the gallery was short of its goal by twenty to thirty feet, and the word was that higher officers had accumulated enough powder to use in it when ready.[65]

FOURTH CORPS LINE

Howard's troops continued to hold the ridge from which they had launched the attack of June 27. Brigadier General Walter C. Whitaker's brigade of Stanley's division also continued to hold the captured Confederate skirmish pits that Newton's division had cleared during the assault. Officers rotated units in and out of those pits to give them a break on a regular basis, and the men continued to improve their works. Chesley Mosman's pioneers constructed abatis using wood charred by the fire that had nearly consumed wounded men on June 27. He managed to fix sixty yards of obstructions on the night of June 30, but his clothes and hands became absolutely black from handling the material. There were frequent alarms along the Fourth Corps sector during the remainder of Howard's stay at Kennesaw.[66]

The forward Union line was close enough to the Confederate position to allow for informal truces between Howard's men and the troops of Cleburne's division. Trading tobacco for coffee was the most common element of those truces. Robert Davis Smith, the ordnance officer of Polk's brigade, noted that the pickets "have new weights & measures on our line; the Yanks give a shirt tail full of coffee for a plug of tobacco." Discussions continued unabated between the opposing forces. Federal pickets "ask all sorts of questions" of their counterparts, as Captain Samuel Foster of the Twenty-Fourth Texas Cavalry (dismounted) put it in his diary. The men were "very talkative" as a rule while doing duty on the picket line.[67]

A long truce was worked out by the major of the Forty-Ninth Illinois on July 1 that lasted twenty-four hours. It allowed the men of Kimball's and Harker's brigades to lounge outside their trenches all day. They "sit on top of the works and talk with the rebs who were seated on top of their works," recorded George Cooley of the Twenty-Fourth Wisconsin. Regimental officers of the Third Kentucky met their counterparts in no-man's-land several times to chat. "Our men sat in rows on top of our works or strolled about in the woods in the most careless manner," wrote John W. Tuttle, "and the rebs did the same in plain view of each other." Tuttle contended that "utmost courtesy and harmony characterized" all meetings of the belligerents that day. According to Cooley, however, the new rotation of officers on the picket line "gave up the truce" on July 2 and firing resumed.[68]

ALONG THE REST OF THE LINE

The positions of all units remained stable during the remainder of the time both armies spent at Kennesaw. Sixteenth Corps skirmishers had advanced their forward position during the demonstrations that supported the Fifteenth Corps attack on June 27 until they were well up the slope of Little Kennesaw Mountain. There, the Sixteenth Corps skirmish line stayed. "We are having a rough time getting into position," commented Oscar L. Jackson of the Sixty-Third Ohio when trying to take his regiment forward to that position. "We have to crawl through a dense thicket of undergrowth." Once ensconced in the advanced line, the Ohioans took cover within the rocky outcroppings that littered the side of the mountain. Confederate bullets ricocheted off the rocks and bounced "around us quite lively." Some Confederate sharpshooters were armed with Whitworth rifles, a long-range target weapon made in England and smuggled through the naval blockade into the Confederacy. When the Seventh Iowa of Sweeny's division moved forward up the slope to take its place in the skirmish line, a member of the regiment was killed by a shot from a Whitworth rifle. His comrades estimated the Rebel sharpshooter must have been upwards of a mile away at the time.[69]

Lightburn's attack on June 27 had enabled the Fifteenth Corps to establish its picket line so close to Walker's division just south of Pigeon Hill that Walker's men were unable to maintain a picket line. His troops "were constantly firing and watching" for the remainder of their stay at Kennesaw.[70]

Atop Pigeon Hill and Little Kennesaw, French's division continued to hold the high ground. French noted that the Federals seemed to "move about in a subdued manner and less lordly style" on June 28, apparently taken down a peg or two by their repulse the day before. Yet "they resent defeat by a cannonade this afternoon." Ward's battery of Storr's battalion, stationed on Little Kennesaw, fired sixty-five shells from two guns in return. The artillery fire intensified on June 29, with many fragments falling into the trenches and in camps atop Little Kennesaw as the Union gunners exploded shells high in the air despite the great height of the mountain. French was aroused by the night firing at Cheatham's Hill at 2:30 A.M. of June 30. He saddled his horse to be ready for anything, but the firing died down after about twenty minutes.[71]

On July 1, while the men of the Fourth Corps and Cleburne's division held their truce farther south, Federal guns in McPherson's Army of the Tennessee maintained a heavy fire on both Big and Little Kennesaw. As the firing continued into dusk, French could not help but admire the scene it created. He thought Big Kennesaw "now resembles Vesuvius in the beginning of an eruption." Smoke "wreathed Kennesaw in a golden thunder-cloud in the still sky, from which came incessant flashes of iridescent light from shells, like bursting stars. The canopy of clouds rolling around the peak looked softer than the downy cotton, but ever changing in color. One moment they were as crimson as the evening clouds painted by the rays of the summer setting sun, and the next, brighter than if lit by the lightning's flash, or bursting meteors." While French forgot himself for a moment in admiring the beauty of this martial scene, he reminded himself of its import. The experience "was not one of pure delight." When it ended after dark and all was silence once again, "there was no feeling of joy, only one of relief from the excitement of hope and fear ever incident to the wager of battle."[72]

The Confederates were stretched as far as they could go in their extended line at Kennesaw. Loring assured French that he had no reserve troops to send to his division, or to anyone else for that matter. He suggested that French strengthen his position with improved earthworks. Elsewhere along the line local commanders widened and deepened their trenches as a way of compensating for reduced numbers. Along Vaughan's brigade sector the trench became eight feet wide, large enough to be occupied by two lines of battle if necessary.[73]

In general, Union gunners gained the upper hand over their gray-clad opponents. "We have got their big guns on the mountain completely timidated," bragged a Union soldier in the Fourteenth Corps. Proof of that contention appeared to Hamilton Branch of the Fifty-Fourth Georgia when he walked up to the top of Little Kennesaw Mountain one day to see the sights. Confederate gunners there told him to be careful not to expose himself. Branch took one peek out of an embrasure with a field glass and saw a "puff of smoke arise" from a Federal battery. The shell exploded exactly overhead. A second round duplicated the first, and then the gunners told Branch that their lieutenant was killed on that spot a few days before. That was enough to drive Branch from the emplacement and into some bushes nearby, where he obtained a fine view of a countryside filled with Yankees. Observers who ascended Little Kennesaw reported that the Confederate gun embrasures were cut up by Union artillery fire and the Rebels had dug covered ways here and there to duck into for shelter when enemy shelling became too severe.[74]

On Hardee's part of the line, some local commanders suffered because the peculiarities of the terrain often prevented gunners from obtaining good artillery sights of the enemy. Walker's chief of artillery could not even see the Yankees because of the thick woods on one part of his division line. He asked French to send someone who knew the position to advise his men on how to reach the enemy. Llewellyn Griffin Hoxton, one of Hardee's battalion commanders, recalled that he was unable to thoroughly reply to Union artillery fire because of a shortage of ammunition. Hoxton was compelled to reserve enough rounds to repel a Federal infantry attack. Problems like these contributed to the advantage the Federal guns enjoyed along the Kennesaw Line.[75]

As the Kennesaw phase of the Atlanta campaign continued to lengthen with the onset of July, the stress and wear continued to tell on soldiers in blue and gray. "Every body is pretty well worn out by the length of the campaign," admitted George Truair of the 149th New York in Hooker's corps. Samuel McKittrick of the Sixteenth South Carolina in Gist's brigade echoed that thought. "Our Troops are so worn down by Fatigue and Hardships that many of us care but little how soon they come as we have them to fight somewhere and perhaps as well here as any where else."[76]

Nine. Flanking

On June 28, the day after the failed attacks, Sherman continued to plan his next move. "We have constant fighting along lines for ten miles, and either party that attacks gets the worst of it," he wrote to Joseph Webster in Nashville. It was obvious that Johnston would not "come out of his parapets," and turning the Confederate position involved cutting loose from the rail line that barely supplied Sherman's men with their food and other necessities. Still, Sherman could not remain idle. "It would not do to rest long under the influence of a mistake or failure," he reported to Halleck, and thus he immediately set into motion the complicated task of moving toward Johnston's left and outflanking it.[1]

Schofield's position south of Kennesaw Mountain held the key. Sherman knew that exploiting the Union advantage in that area could force Johnston to evacuate his line and either fight a major battle or retreat toward the Chattahoochee. Sherman sent Orlando M. Poe to study the road system and the topography of the area to make doubly sure that a major movement into the region would not come upon any surprises. Poe conducted his reconnaissance on June 28 and reported favorably.[2]

Preparations for the maneuver lasted several days. Thomas instructed his corps commanders to accumulate ten days' rations for men and forage for horses. Howard's chief of staff ordered John Newton to put his worsted division "in as complete state of organization as can be after your losses of yesterday." A similar message went out to Wood and Stanley as well. Sherman consulted with Thomas about the details of the move, intending to use his troops to cover McPherson's sector as the Army of the Tennessee became the first unit to pull away from Kennesaw and move south. Schofield's plan was to push the Confederates south along Sandtown Road to create more space and opportunity for McPherson's army to operate toward the railroad at Fulton. Thomas also was supposed to use Twentieth Corps troops to cover the ground vacated by Schofield. In essence, Sherman intended to use the

Army of the Cumberland to hold virtually the entire Federal position fronting the Kennesaw Line while the smaller field armies conducted the maneuver. Thomas would soon follow them.[3]

McPherson estimated on June 28 that he needed to accumulate six days' rations and five days' forage to reach Sherman's target of having ten days' worth of supplies stockpiled before starting the move. Sherman instructed him to also send back all of his wounded men. Surgeon John Moore, McPherson's medical director, shifted 1,500 men to a newly established hospital at Rome, Georgia. Moore transported beds and other essential articles for them from Huntsville, Alabama. He complained about using boxcars to transport his wounded because "the hospital train [was] being then monopolized by the Army of the Cumberland." McPherson's commissaries worked fast, reaching the ten-day target on June 29 for at least the Fifteenth and Seventeenth Corps. Brigadier General Kenner Garrard's cavalry division was responsible for patrolling the roads leading from Marietta northward to Allatoona, and for protecting the latter place as the most-forward supply depot along the railroad after the infantry moved out. Ordnance officers shipped their stores from Big Shanty to Allatoona and Resaca as well. McPherson's army also controlled a newly arrived pontoon train capable of bridging a stream up to six hundred feet wide. Sherman estimated that would be enough to span the breadth of the Chattahoochee.[4]

With high-ranking officers busily engaged in preparations, the commotion could not fail to attract attention. One of Baird's staff officers, James A. Connolly, overheard a conversation among Sherman, Thomas, Hooker, and Palmer on the morning of June 28. "I may say that something else will now be done, and if it's what I think it is, it will be one of the bold moves of the war." While Thomas faithfully participated in the preparations, Sherman recalled in his memoirs that the stolid commander of the Army of the Cumberland had his doubts about what Connolly called a bold and risky move. "General Thomas, as usual, shook his head, deeming it risky to leave the railroad," he wrote, "but something had to be done, and I had resolved on this move."[5]

It was necessary to explain the maneuver to Halleck before starting, and Sherman did so on June 29. He expected, at least, to reach the railroad at Fulton ten miles south of Marietta, but Sherman hoped that Johnston would simply fall back south of the Chattahoochee after abandoning Kennesaw. Halleck relayed word from Grant that Sherman was free to do as he thought best and need not worry any longer about pinning the Army of Tennessee in its trenches to prevent Johnston from sending troops to re-inforce Lee at Petersburg. The difficulty of supplying men in Virginia was so great, Grant thought, that the Confederates would not send large detachments to Lee from Georgia. This note of encouragement strengthened Sherman's resolve to risk the move toward Fulton.[6]

Schofield was ready to spearhead the move southward. His immediate objective was to control the crossing of Nickajack Creek, enlarging the area of Union control south of the Kennesaw Line. "I know of nothing in the way but the question of supplies," he admitted to Sherman. His troops ran out of bread on June 29, and he received only one day of extra rations of that needed staple on June 30. "Scurvy is becoming dangerously prevalent," Schofield reported. "I think it would be economy to send me some vegetables even in lieu of meat."[7]

There was no time now to deal with the scurvy problem by shipping vegetables from depots in the North. Sherman suggested that George Stoneman's cavalry, operating on Schofield's flank, could forage for "potatoes and greens for you" in the valley of the Sweetwater Creek while the move toward Fulton was taking place. Thomas began to shift troops to help the Twenty-Third Corps in its effort. Baird's division of the Fourteenth Corps replaced Geary's division so that Geary could move southward and replace Hascall's and Cox's divisions on the evening of June 30. Schofield planned to begin moving the Twenty-Third Corps at 6:00 A.M. on July 1.[8]

On the afternoon of June 30, before the move toward Fulton began and after a shower had cleared the atmosphere a bit, one of Schofield's signal officers climbed a tree on the high ground occupied by Byrd's brigade south of Olley's Creek. The officer "could distinctly see Atlanta and the smoke from the cars along the railroad." He could also see the campfires of Confederate troops outlining Johnston's position with reliable clarity. The heaviest smoke ended opposite Hascall's position, representing the end of the main Confederate line. South of that area the smoke seemed to indicate that only a picket line extended from the left flank of Hood's Corps. The signal officer saw the heaviest smoke along the sector that Thomas's troops had assaulted on June 27.[9]

At the last minute, Schofield brought up a possibility he thought worth mentioning to his superior. What if Johnston reacted to Sherman's Fulton move by remaining at Kennesaw, closing the approach to the rear of the Army of Tennessee with fortifications, and thereby making a kind of citadel based on the mountain while feeding on two to three weeks of stockpiled

supplies? Sherman was not worried about such a scenario. "I hardly think
. . . [he will] be willing to have me interpose between him and the rest of
the Confederacy. I am not bound to attack him in his position after getting below him, but may cross the Chattahoochee and destroy all his rail-
roads before he can prevent it, which will be a desperate game for us both."
Schofield hastily assured Sherman that he agreed with him, but wanted to
alert his commander to all possibilities. "I think I have contemplated every
move on the chessboard of war," Sherman assured Schofield, "but am always
much obliged for your full views."[10]

While the Federals prepared for their move toward Fulton, Johnston continued to search for ways to impair his enemy's ability to operate deep in
Georgia. The Confederate commander was eager to find ways to threaten
Sherman's tenuous supply line, and Major General Joseph Wheeler, who
commanded the Cavalry Corps of the Army of Tennessee, apparently came
up with a plan to lead a considerable force of mounted men to raid the railroad behind Sherman's army group. While no document outlining his proposal has survived, Wheeler corresponded with Hood about the proposal.
The problem was that Wheeler would need to strip the Confederate flanks
of mounted men to undertake his expedition, and Johnston was unwilling
to take that risk.[11]

If he did not possess adequate resources to interrupt Sherman's logistics, then Johnston wanted troops from other regions to help him. Unfortunately for the Confederates, there were no troops to spare from other
theaters of operations. Both Jefferson Davis and Braxton Bragg repeatedly
told Johnston that the disparity of numbers between the opposing forces in
Georgia was less than that which existed elsewhere. Major General Stephen
Dill Lee, who commanded Confederate forces in Mississippi, was in even
more desperate need of reinforcements than Johnston, and Robert E. Lee
could not spare anyone from Virginia. In fact, the Richmond authorities
tried to tell Johnston that the disparity in numbers existing in Georgia was
less than usual compared to the disparity between the Army of Tennessee and its opponents in previous campaigns. Whether that last point was
literally true or not, the message was clear; Johnston could not count on
help from anyone. Governor Joseph E. Brown of Georgia also assured the
president that he had done all he could to reinforce Johnston by mobilizing
several militia regiments, which were now on duty with the Army of Tennessee.[12]

As Sherman was well aware, Johnston did not have enough troops to hold the Kennesaw Line and protect the railroad farther south than Marietta. Writing to his wife Ellen on June 30, Sherman made it clear that he had no intention of attacking fortified lines anymore, because "at this distance from home we cannot afford the losses of such terrible assaults as Grant has made." The Federal commander felt the emotional strain of sending men to their deaths. "It is enough to make the whole world start at the awful amount of death & destruction that now stalks abroad," he wrote Ellen. "I begin to regard the death & mangling of a couple thousand men as a small affair, a kind of morning dash—and it may be well that we become so hardened. Each day is killed or wounded some valuable officers and men, the bullets coming from a concealed foe." In Sherman's view, a continuation of the static position at Kennesaw was fruitless. The only way to avoid the picking off of his men in skirmishing and sniping, and to avoid the possibility of having to attack fortified lines again, was to move toward Fulton.[13]

Just before moving, Sherman engaged in another fight with his perennial enemy, the newspaper correspondent. While reading the June 23 issue of the *New York Herald*, Thomas saw a report that Union staff officers had broken the Confederate signal code. He informed Sherman on June 29 and included his opinion that the correspondent, B. Randolph Keim, ought to be arrested and "executed as a spy." Sherman readily agreed and instructed McPherson to find Keim and send him to Thomas.[14]

Keim was personally acquainted with both McPherson and Dodge, and he often moved from one headquarters in the Army of the Tennessee to another. Keim had a good explanation for the incident. Dodge's signal officers had deciphered the Confederate code by studying Johnston's signal station on Kennesaw Mountain. An unnamed staff officer told Keim of this accomplishment, and he wrote to editor James Gordon Bennett, advising Bennett not to publish the news. Unfortunately, Keim's letter was opened by the *Herald*'s night editor when Bennett was out of the office. Without understanding the importance of confidentiality, the night editor printed the news. Bennett was upset and fired the night editor, but the damage was done.[15]

McPherson produced Keim, but Thomas was a bit confused when the correspondent reported to his headquarters on June 30. Keim was not attached to the Army of the Cumberland, so Thomas wondered whether he had any jurisdiction in his case. Moreover, Keim seemed "to be an honest-looking man." When his story was told there seemed to be no need for harsh measures. Thomas decided to "have him sent north of the Ohio River, with orders not to return to this army during the war."[16]

Final orders for the move to Fulton were issued early on July 1. They made it clear that the objective was to get away from the commanding enemy presence on Kennesaw Mountain and force Johnston "to come out of his intrenchments or move farther south." Schofield was to move so as to command the ground between Olley's Creek and Nickajack Creek. McPherson was to shift his entire army from its line on the Union left down to Schofield, positioning two corps so as to move either toward the railroad at Fulton or toward the Chattahoochee River in case Johnston decided to fall back all the way to that stream. Thomas was to cover the ground north of Olley's Creek. Kenner Garrard's division of Thomas's cavalry corps would cover the roads leading from Allatoona toward Marietta. George Stoneman's cavalry division of Schofield's Army of the Ohio and Brigadier General Edward M. McCook's division of Thomas's cavalry corps would cover the Union right flank beyond the infantry positions. "All movements must be vigorous and rapid," Sherman continued, "as the time allowed is limited by the supplies in our wagons."[17]

Hascall's division led the operation at 6:00 A.M. on the morning of July 1 by moving two miles forward from the position held by Reilly's and Cameron's brigades. Advancing south along the Sandtown Road, pushing against light resistance by Confederate cavalry, Hascall secured a vital road junction and settled in for the time being. Located near the Moss House, this intersection gave the Federals an opportunity to head northeast toward Ruff's Mill on Nickajack Creek, about two miles away. Beyond Ruff's Mill, the road led to Smyrna Station on the railroad about three miles northeast of the mill. Smyrna Station was about two miles north of Fulton Station. Cox sent troops forward to support Hascall's new position on the evening of July 1 as the Federals dug a line of earthworks to cover the important road junction. It had been a long, hot day, "unusually warm and sultry," Hascall reported, and many of his men "were sun-struck or entirely prostrated by the heat and dust. It was the hardest day's work we have endured on this campaign, and was productive of the most important results." The Federals lost about fifty troops killed and wounded in this move.[18]

Schofield extended the telegraph line southward to keep pace with Hascall's advance and report progress. Meanwhile, Sherman had instructed Thomas and McPherson to demonstrate with skirmishers and artillery that day to annoy the Confederates and divert attention from the Twenty-Third Corps. Because Schofield reported that his position was "very ex-

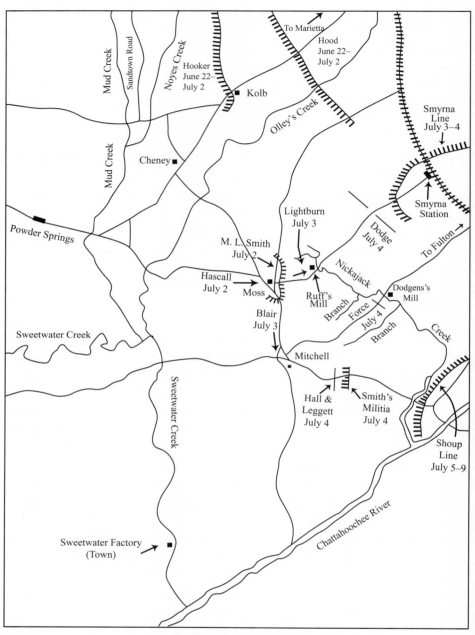

Flanking the Confederates

tended," Sherman changed his plans a bit by offering to send a division from McPherson's army ahead of the rest to help him. Schofield was happy to receive it and planned to replace Cox with the new division so that Cox could close up on Hascall's division. Sherman sent orders to McPherson to start one of his divisions southward at 4:00 A.M. on July 2.[19]

JULY 2

McPherson sent Sherman's old division, that commanded by Morgan L. Smith in the Fifteenth Corps. It was the same division that had conducted the failed attack at Pigeon Hill on June 27. Smith started his men promptly at 4:00 A.M. on July 2. The weather was just as hot and sultry as the day before, and many men suffered sunstroke during their eleven-mile march. They reached the left wing of Schofield's new position near the Moss House at 11:00 A.M. and replaced Cooper's and Strickland's brigades of Hascall's division. Smith's troops finished the new line Schofield's men had begun the night before that stretched from the Ruff's Mill Road toward the Sandtown Road. Hascall moved Cooper and Strickland farther to the left to fill up the gap between the Union line at the Moss House and that of Cox's division.[20]

Schofield now had about thirteen thousand troops dug in around the road junction at Moss House. He was four miles south of Johnston's left flank and six miles from the Chattahoochee River. Schofield now felt "really secure, for the enemy could not detach force enough to dislodge us without abandoning his position about Kenesaw and hazarding a general engagement in open field."[21]

Other Federal forces continued to demonstrate all day on July 2 to divert attention from what was taking place to the south. Acting on orders, Newton's division of the Fourth Corps opened artillery fire for half an hour at precisely 6:00 A.M. The Confederates did not reply to it. Then Newton's infantry began firing at 7:00 A.M. for ten minutes. Fourth Corps skirmishers continued to work all day. "Many had lame arms and shoulders from firing their muskets so constantly," reported the historian of the Ninety-Sixth Illinois. McPherson's artillerymen also kept up a heavier than usual fire on July 2. Forty or fifty Federal guns pounded Little Kennesaw, according to W. L. Truman of Guibor's Missouri Battery. They sprayed five hundred pounds of shell fragments "every minute for three hours," making it difficult for the Confederates to cook and eat their rations. Daniel Harris Reynolds's brigade held the sector spanning Little and Big Kennesaw; he estimated receiving 700 to 1,400 Federal artillery rounds on his position during the course of July 2.[22]

While all this heavy shelling and skirmishing took place along the Kennesaw Line, Stoneman and McCook continued to explore the territory south and west of Schofield's new position at the Moss House. The Federal horsemen had screened Schofield's right flank during Hascall's move to Moss House on July 1, but they could not find a way to cross Sweetwater Creek until early on the morning of July 2. Then they forced a crossing at Sweetwater Town, which was guarded only by a battalion of Georgia militiamen. Stoneman and McCook were then able to push south to the Chattahoochee River opposite Campbellton. The cavalry became the first Federals to see the Chattahoochee, lodged as they were fully twelve miles southwest of Schofield's position at the Moss House.[23]

McPherson's Army of the Tennessee prepared all day on July 2 for its move to the south. The army's trains set out early to get a head start. It was impossible to hide the wagons entirely from Confederate view, but the infantrymen and artillerymen tried to make arrangements so that their own evacuation of the trenches that night would be a secret. They constructed new roads leading toward the rear from the works and lay straw along the rocky parts of the roadbed to muffle the sound of wheeled vehicles. The gunners wrapped rags around the wheels of gun carriages as well.[24]

Staff officers handed out detailed instructions to unit commanders about the intent of the movement and the timing of each one's pullout. Blair's Seventeenth Corps was to withdraw first, from the far Union left, at 9:00 P.M., with each division pulling out in succession toward the right. Then Dodge's Sixteenth Corps was to withdraw, followed by Logan's Fifteenth Corps. Blair's objective was the next major road junction south of the one Schofield and Morgan L. Smith already held at the Moss House, near which the widow Mitchell made her home. He would assume the southernmost Federal infantry position thus far attained. Dodge would advance from the Moss House toward Ruff's Mill on Nickajack Creek, while Logan would constitute McPherson's reserve at the Moss House. All corps were to take along only one ammunition wagon for each regiment and battery and march quietly and quickly to its assigned position.[25]

McPherson's army began its pullout as scheduled on the evening of July 2. Thomas moved Brigadier General John H. King's brigade of the Fourteenth Corps to replace McPherson with a thin, elongated line, while Howard moved Fourth Corps troops to replace that Fourteenth Corps brigade. In fact, Howard shifted his entire corps as Stanley replaced Newton.

Thomas also positioned Colonel Benjamin Scribner's brigade of the Fourteenth Corps to refuse the far left flank of the Union line. Scribner's men worked all night on July 2 to dig a new line of works to protect the flank. Near Pigeon Hill, the Fifteenth Ohio of Howard's corps replaced a Fifteenth Corps unit in the trenches. The Ohio men found that the "ground was very filthy" and the night was very dark, but they had to make the best of their new home for the time being. Sherman had a last-minute change of mind about the massive supply depot at Allatoona. Worrying that Confederate cavalry might ride around Garrard's division and attack it as soon as they realized that McPherson had withdrawn, he ordered the accumulated stores to be moved northward as soon as possible.[26]

Kennesaw Mountain offered a superb observation platform for the Confederates, and the Federals could not hide all signs of movement from them. Reports streamed into Johnston's headquarters on July 2 that the enemy was shifting large numbers of wagons. "Every indication of move to Chattahoochee by Sherman," commented staff officer Thomas B. Mackall in his journal. Johnston knew full well that Sherman was making a major effort to pass his left flank. He also knew that Schofield was already some distance south of that flank, and he could not afford to let the enemy move even farther. Johnston decided to abandon the strong position at Kennesaw but not to go all the way to the Chattahoochee. He had in mind a new position at Smyrna Station only six miles farther south from Marietta. His headquarters issued a circular to all units at 1:30 on the afternoon of July 2. The artillery was to pull out at dusk, but the infantry of Loring's Army of Mississippi was to withdraw at 10:00 P.M., while Hardee and Hood would start their infantry at 11:00 P.M. All corps commanders were to leave a rear guard in the works until 1:00 A.M., followed by the line of skirmishers. Johnston had already issued written instructions about the lines of march and the new position to be taken up even before the circular was issued.[27]

It took some time for the circular to make its way to various units. Daniel Harris Reynolds's brigade between Little and Big Kennesaw received the word at 5:00 P.M., while French's division a bit to Reynolds's left received it two hours before. W. L. Truman in Guibor's battery was disappointed with the news. "We hate to leave our perch," on Little Kennesaw Mountain, he wrote, "it is such a lovely and exciting place, exciting to be a target up in the clouds, . . . and besides we can see and enjoy so much."[28]

Just as McPherson began his pullout, the Confederates began theirs as well. The artillery was the first to leave. George S. Storrs worked out a careful plan to extricate his guns from the top of Little Kennesaw in the dimming light of the evening on July 2. He had made certain that the military roads running down the east side of the mountain from each battery position were cleared. His gun crews worked efficiently and managed to bring every piece down without drawing attention from the enemy. This was mostly due to the fact that Storrs's crews had a habit of screening their embrasures with brush to conceal the reloading process from the watchful Federals; the brush now concealed the withdrawal of the guns. One section of Guibor's battery was located on ground so that if the gunners stood up they could be seen over the parapet. Storrs solved that problem by having the men crawl on their hands and knees to extricate the pieces with ropes.[29]

French left a handful of regiments in the works to serve as a rear guard while the other infantry units pulled out. Then he withdrew the rear guard and evacuated his skirmish line at 3:00 A.M. In Walthall's division, Daniel Harris Reynolds had difficulty taking his brigade down Little Kennesaw "owing to its being so rough."[30]

Opposite the Fourth Corps sector, Cleburne's division conducted the pullout with quiet efficiency. Captain Samuel T. Foster commanded the skirmishers of Granbury's brigade on the night of July 2. He waited until 1:00 A.M. and then began to fall back one man at a time to the empty main-line trench. There the Confederates assembled at a designated point. Foster waited another half hour after they all came in before a guide took the skirmishers to the rear, where they caught up with the brigade in motion toward Smyrna Station.[31]

Pulling away from Cheatham's Hill was more difficult than from any other part of the Confederate line. A covered way leading toward the rear, constructed since the attack of June 27, helped in this process. It was covered over with timber to make a roof, which helped to deaden the sound of troops moving toward the rear. Vaughan kept the Eleventh Tennessee behind when the rest of his brigade evacuated its works. The Tennesseans were told to "throw turpentine balls to deceive the enemy" before they followed their comrades out of the trenches.[32]

To provide extra protection, brigade commander George Maney maintained a skirmish line and a line of videttes to cover his withdrawal. Lieutenant Thomas H. Maney of Company B, First Tennessee, was put in charge of twelve videttes who were told to crawl forward into no-man's-land on their hands and knees to establish a line ten yards in front of the works. The men made their way over the parapet and through the abatis until resting uncomfortably close to the forward Union line, covered only by the dark night. Maney placed his eleven men and crawled along the line now and then to make sure everything was right. Once he got turned around in the darkness and ran into the muzzle of a musket. Hearing the hammer click, he froze as "the past life of the writer came up before him. All the mean things he ever did were passed in review in a few seconds."[33]

But Maney collected his wits and tried to find who was on the other end of the gun. He asked in a low voice for the man to identify himself but received no answer. "'If you are Federals, I am your meat,'" Maney continued. "'If you are rebs, I am your officer.'" Still no answer, and Maney sweated profusely with the strain until the muzzle of the gun slowly lowered, and Maney found out it was one of his own men who was considered to be "a little off about the head, in fact 'sorter queer.'" The man was upset that he had almost shot his own officer, and Maney had a stronger attack of nerves when he realized how close he came to being killed by this fellow, "for he had no more sense than to shoot anyhow."[34]

Despite these perils, the Confederates pulled away from Cheatham's Hill without incident. In fact, Johnston's army conducted the withdrawal from Kennesaw with consummate skill. The night was dark and cloudy, but the roads were dry and, for the most part, well known by the Confederates. Most units arrived on schedule at the new Smyrna Line where they began to dig a new system of earthworks before the Yankees made their appearance.[35]

The Federals saw indications of the Confederate pullout as early as 9:15 P.M., but they interpreted those signs as a prelude to an attack in the night. In fact, deserters told members of Osterhaus's division that Johnston intended to advance against the Federal line. McPherson instructed Logan to keep Osterhaus's and Harrow's men in their works for the time being. Dodge also received orders to keep one of his divisions in line to support Harrow. McPherson told Blair to temporarily stop the Seventeenth Corps near the threatened point of attack to provide support if needed. Sherman and Thomas thought the enemy was evacuating rather than preparing to attack, but McPherson wanted to take no chances.[36]

McPherson also was not convinced by the opinion of one of his own signal officers who reported that, just before dusk on July 2, it appeared as if the normal campfires along the Confederate line had largely disappeared. The signal officer also discovered a large column of smoke rising from Marietta, indicating that the Confederates were probably destroying something.[37]

The Federals on Cheatham's Hill received confirmation of the Rebel pullout earlier than any of their comrades. Sporadic skirmish firing continued until about 1:00 or 2:00 A.M. of July 3, followed by silence. Suddenly, according to Captain Frank James of the Fifty-Second Ohio, "we were startled by a sepulchral voice from the front, calling: 'Say, Yanks; don't shoot, will you? I want to come in, they're all gone.'" A Confederate deserter came across no-man's-land and told the Federals that his former comrades had left. Dilworth sent a company out from McCook's brigade as skirmishers to explore, and it found the Confederate line empty.[38]

Thomas informed Sherman at 2:45 A.M. that the enemy had abandoned Cheatham's Hill and that Confederate deserters had assured the Federals Johnston was falling back to a new line. He also told Sherman at 5:00 A.M. that Hooker reported the enemy gone from his front as well. Sherman was not so sure that the Confederates had fallen back. Now fearful that Johnston may have maneuvered to strike at dawn, Sherman told Logan to send a skirmish line forward up the mountain and find out for sure what was going on. The rest of McPherson's command continued to bivouac near Kennesaw for the night until developments became more clear.[39]

JULY 3

Before dawn appeared over Kennesaw on the morning of July 3, Logan's skirmishers confirmed that the formidable line of Rebel works was empty. All signs indicated a fallback toward the south. Sherman quickly issued orders to follow up the retirement. Blair and Dodge started to move south as planned, only several hours later than anticipated, while Osterhaus and Harrow began to move straight into Marietta by way of Burnt Hickory Road. Thomas's army also started toward the town by the shortest route. Sherman sent word to McPherson and Schofield that they should continue the flanking operation as planned and hit Johnston, "and if possible to catch him in the confusion of crossing the Chattahoochee."[40]

Logan moved toward Marietta early in the morning with a line of skirmishers in front of his two divisions. The troops encountered many Federal dead of June 27 that still lay between the lines because there had been no formal burial truce along the Fifteenth Corps sector after the attack. But Logan's men also captured about two hundred Confederate prisoners and stragglers along the way. Fifteenth Corps troops were the first Federals to enter the town at about 9:00 A.M. Logan established a defensive position east and south of Marietta where Osterhaus and Harrow remained until the morning of July 4. Then they started out to join Morgan L. Smith's division to the south. McPherson's chief signal officer established a station on top of Kennesaw Mountain, his men using the platform constructed by Confederate signal officers for their own work. Perched on the height, the Federals were able to flag messages between the headquarters of several army and corps commanders from July 3 to 6, until the army group became too widely separated. Catching a backward glance, the Confederate rear guard reported seeing Federal troops on top of Kennesaw Mountain as early as 5:00 A.M. From the ranks of Johnson's Fourteenth Corps division, Charles Richard Pomeroy of the Thirty-Third Ohio suddenly caught a similar sight in the first dim light of morning. "I was looking up at old Kenesaw Mt when Lo, I saw Yanky & our Flag *on the* top."[41]

Sherman liked to tell the story of the moment at which the mountain changed hands. Three months later, he chatted with Major Henry Hitchcock, a new member of his staff, about the morning of July 3. Sherman told Hitchcock he borrowed a telescope mounted on a tripod that engineer Poe had used for his own observations. Sherman gazed at the top of the mountain as dawn began to break and saw no Confederates. "Presently one [Federal] cautiously crept up," as Hitchcock recorded the story, "looked—rose, waved hat, then another came," until the top swarmed with blue coats. "I could plainly see their movements as they ran along the crest just abandoned by the enemy," Sherman recalled in his memoirs. He sent a telegram to Thomas and Schofield to break the news. "I can see our men on top both Big and Little Kenesaw."[42]

One of the first Federals to reach the top of the mountain was Andrew Hickenlooper, a member of McPherson's staff. As the rising sun lit up the countryside, Hickenlooper "had a view of the valley below, one of the most beautiful I had ever seen, and from which every movement of our troops was plainly visible." Some Sixteenth Corps troops went to the top before Dodge set out for the south that morning and were equally impressed by the view. Oscar L. Jackson thought he could see thirty miles in every direction. "Our works and the theater of the operations of both armies are spread out below like a map. . . . It looks as though they might almost have counted our men." Jackson took the time to cut a part of a hickory tree on top of the mountain that had been a visible marker for the Federals during the campaign as a souvenir.[43]

But Edwin Witherby Brown of the Eighty-First Ohio found something horrible on the mountain when he explored its slope early on the morning of July 3. Near a large, flat rock across which the Sixty-Fourth Illinois had skirmished on June 27, Brown discovered that several Union dead lying between the lines had been mutilated. "The heads had been removed from every one and rolled down to where I found them in the bushes and sensitive plants at the lower edge of the rock." Brown ascribed the most compassionate rational to the perpetrator when he wrote of his discovery long after the war. "I have always thought this mutilation was the work of some poor fellow driven to the fiendish act by the hardships of the campaign rendering him mad or insane and unaccountable for the wanton deed."[44]

Hooker prepared to push forward by 3:00 A.M., even before dawn. The men of Geary's division did not necessarily believe that the opposing trench line was empty when they received orders to get up and ready for a move forward. Stephen Pierson of the Thirty-Third New Jersey was on the skirmish line that set out before dawn, and he fully expected a battle. The line passed over the Union pickets and crossed no-man's-land noiselessly, only to find the Confederate skirmish line empty. The Federals pushed on and entered the main Rebel line without opposition. The relief was enormous. "We had wound ourselves up to the highest possible point of tension, and this sudden relief was like the snapping of a taut cable," Pierson recalled. "We laughed and cried, or hugged one another, or fell to the ground and rolled over and over in an uncontrollable hysteria of emotion. Taken altogether this was by far the hardest test in my whole army experience."[45]

Hooker pressed on through the Rebel works and toward Marietta, taking a number of prisoners. Albert M. Cook reported that "most of them were heartily sick of the war and glad to be in our hands." Many of those prisoners reported that rumors had run rampant along the Confederate line for days that the Federals were undermining the works at several points and everyone feared being blown up. Catching a glimpse of the Rebel earthworks as they passed through, Twentieth Corps men were impressed by their complexity and strength. Fronted by abatis and two rows of inclined palisades, it would have been a deadly and fruitless endeavor to attack them from the front.[46]

Howard sent a circular to his division commanders at 3:00 A.M., alerting them to the fact that the enemy seemed to have evacuated its position and instructing them to send out skirmishers at dawn. With confirmation that the opposing works were empty, Fourth Corps units set out at 7:00 A.M. with Stanley's division leading, followed by Newton and then Wood. They encountered no trouble as they reached the beautiful grounds of the Georgia Military Institute on the outskirts of Marietta by 9:00 A.M. There they found, scrawled in red pencil on a wall of the Institute, a message from a departing Rebel. "Good by Yanks—we have got sick of this country. You will find us at Cedar Bluff nine miles the other side of Atlanta. If you'uns drive us from there you will find us next time nine miles the other side of Hell."[47]

Howard's men took nearly 170 prisoners that morning as they drove toward the military institute, only to find that Hooker had reached the area a short time before them. The troops of both columns had suffered during their short march of only about three to five miles that morning. Having been immobilized for weeks in the trenches, and with a particularly hot, humid, and windless morning, the men felt baked by the rising sun and many of them dropped out of the line of march because of heat exhaustion.[48]

The Confederate withdrawal produced more general relief at Cheatham's Hill than at any other part of the Kennesaw Line. When dawn brought with it confirmation that the Rebel bastion was empty, there was loud celebration among the Federals of McCook's and Mitchell's brigades. Entering Unionists yelled at the top of their voices, and a Federal band played "Old Hundredreth" as men sang the words of the venerable hymn. Crossing the line at Cheatham Hill was a journey across the blood soaked memory of June 27 for the survivors of Davis's division. They passed through a graveyard of about a hundred comrades killed that day and buried on June 29, and the few headboards marking individual graves were riddled with bullet holes. Then they crossed the line of earthworks that had so brutally rebuffed them. The magnitude of their undertaking now sank in. The Federals "had never seen such an absolutely unassailable line of works," commented Edwin Payne of the Thirty-Fourth Illinois. Caves dug into the ground showed them how their enemy had lived during the "siege" of Cheatham's Hill. Allen Fahnestock saw that Union rifle fire had cut down some trees six inches in diameter, and the Confederate works "were almost cut to pieces with bulletts." Many Yankee generals came by "to See the Sights" before moving on that morning.[49]

Chesley Mosman's Fourth Corps pioneers were busy cutting passages through the Rebel earthworks on Howard's sector to allow artillery to move forward. While they worked, Mosman walked over to Cheatham's Hill to see the Confederate fortifications. "The effect of the musketry fire here was terrific," He wrote. "The bullets cut off good sized trees, the cheval-de-frise was shot into fibers and the Rebel head logs one half cut into on the underside, by the countless bullets that had struck it as our men fired at the only opening where a shot could do any good. The Rebels had built caves in many places to hide in from our fire."[50]

Such formidable defenses seemed immune to attack. Perhaps that is why Styles Porter of the Fifty-Second Ohio thought that mining was the only solution to the tactical stalemate on Cheatham's Hill. "If they had stayed," Porter confided to his diary, "we would have blowed them up to-morrow."[51]

Other Federal troops were astonished by the level of destruction they witnessed in the Confederate earthworks. "Oh what a sight evry bush & tree is all marked up Shell & Shot are scattered all around I never saw the ground so covered with lead," wrote Charles Richard Pomeroy in Johnson's division. Isaac Morgan discovered some artillery pieces abandoned by the Rebels. They were "struck with minies and . . . unfit for use so they left them behind," Morgan told his sister. He also found numerous graves located behind the Confederate line of works.[52]

When Davis's division finally passed over Cheatham's Hill and moved forward with the rest of Thomas's army toward Marietta, it passed by many groups of Confederate prisoners and deserters. Some of these discouraged men seemed to think that the Southern cause was lost, and they were happy to be out of the war. Lieutenant Colonel James Harrison Goodnow of the Twelfth Indiana in Harrow's division also encountered Confederate stragglers. Many of them were old soldiers who had served in the Rebel army since the beginning of the war, and they gave Goodnow the impression that the Confederacy was beginning to break up. These stragglers "thought they had no chance to Succeed. They all concur in Saying that if Johnston gives up Atlanta, that the most of his Army will leave him."[53]

Sherman rode into Marietta at 8:30 A.M., fuming at what he considered the slow pace of pursuit mounted by the infantry and by Garrard's cavalry division. He found the place nearly abandoned by the residents, and more than a mile of iron had been taken up from the railroad leading northward from town toward Johnston's old position at Kennesaw Mountain. He still hoped that Johnston would fall back across the Chattahoochee but had to await further developments before knowing for sure where his enemy would land up.[54]

For the time, Schofield operated according to plan and utilized Dodge's Sixteenth Corps divisions and Blair's Seventeenth Corps as soon as they arrived. Dodge and Blair started southward a bit after dawn on July 3 and marched well in the hot weather, arriving near the Moss House by 2:30 P.M. They rested only a few minutes before setting out on their assigned movements. Gresham's division of the Seventeenth Corps led the way toward the vital road junction at Widow Mitchell's, and Lightburn's brigade of Morgan L. Smith's Fifteenth Corps division moved northeast from the junction at the Moss House toward Ruff's Mill on Nickajack Creek.[55]

As these troops passed by Hascall's division at 3:00 P.M., McPherson chatted a while with Schofield while both men sat on their horses along the Sandtown Road. The two had been cadets together at West Point and now had a chance to catch up on many things. McPherson told Schofield of his engagement to be married and asked his friend if he thought there would be a time soon when he could obtain leave and tie the knot. Schofield thought that he would have to wait until the campaign was over and the Federals were in Atlanta before Sherman would approve a leave of absence. The two men also discussed at length the question of relative rank, an issue that was commonly discussed in Sherman's army group. They knew that Sherman tended to give preference to the man with the oldest commission when two commanders had to cooperate with each other, but McPherson and Schofield agreed that whoever held the highest command ought to be given the opportunity of temporarily commanding the other. The issue would not cause trouble between the two; while they both held a department command, they assured each other that neither had any intention of trying to take charge of their joint operations. In fact, Schofield privately was willing to defer to McPherson's orders.[56]

LIGHTBURN AT RUFF'S MILL

Even before the Sixteenth and Seventeenth Corps arrived at the Moss House, elements of Lightburn's brigade had started to move toward Ruff's Mill on July 3. Morgan L. Smith had directed Lightburn to send two regiments forward to find out exactly where the Confederates were located, and they came upon dismounted cavalry with two artillery pieces only one mile from the road junction. Lightburn advanced most of the rest of his brigade (leaving behind only the Eighty-Third Indiana) and attacked this position at 3:00 P.M. The Federals advanced at quick time through woods for three-quarters of a mile before coming upon two cornfields about half a mile across. On the other side of the open ground Nickajack Creek ran through a wooded ravine five hundred yards wide.[57]

Lightburn did not hesitate when he encountered the open ground that lay just west of Nickajack Creek. His men accelerated their tempo to double-quick time and began to cross the cornfields, pummeled all the way by the Confederate guns that had been pulled back to hastily prepared positions on the east side of the creek. Captain Edward B. Moore of the Fifty-Fourth Ohio described the experience in his diary. "The enemy shells plowing the earth in front, and in rear of us, then exploding; after which you hear the peculiar singing of the fragments as they fly on their missions of death." A section of Captain Israel P. Rumsey's Battery B, First Illinois Light Artillery, set up within range of the fight and began to support Lightburn's attack by shelling the Confederate guns. Captain Moore noticed Rumsey's fire, the Federal shells passing "but a few feet above our heads," as the infantrymen continued to push across the open space.[58]

The Federals came within the wooded bottomland of Nickajack Creek where the trees offered some degree of cover on the west side of the stream. The dismounted Confederate cavalry sheltered itself behind rail breastworks on the bottomland just east of the creek and also within tree cover. The Rebel artillery was planted three hundred yards behind the cavalry on higher ground outside the creek bottomland. The opposing sides remained in these positions for another hour, firing at each other with Ruff's Mill between the opposing forces. It consisted of both a sawmill and a gristmill with a milldam to control the flow of water along the creek. The Federals took some time to work their way across the milldam, but after they put enough force on the east side of Nickajack, the Confederates evacuated their position. At a cost of about fifty casualties, the Federals had gained a foothold across the last significant stream separating them from the railroad south of Marietta.[59]

Dodge moved his two divisions of the Sixteenth Corps to Ruff's Mill by the time Lightburn secured the area on the late afternoon of July 3. His Second Division dug works on the east side of the creek that evening and prepared for a further push toward the railroad the next day.[60]

THE ROAD TO TURNER'S FERRY

When Blair's Seventeenth Corps moved out from the road junction at the Moss House on July 3, Giles A. Smith's brigade of Morgan L. Smith's Fifteenth Corps division led the way. Smith's men pushed south along Sandtown Road toward Turner's Ferry on the Chattahoochee River, followed by Gresham's division and then the rest of Blair's command. They made good progress, shoving back Confederate cavalry outposts of William H. Jackson's division until hitting a branch of Nickajack Creek. Here the Confederates held "a very strong position," in Blair's words, and skirmishing ensued. Smith's men fired away for an hour while a brigade of Gresham's division came up and deployed. Taking over from Smith's men, the Seventeenth Corps troops mounted a push that cleared the branch crossing and continued moving south along Sandtown Road until reaching the road junction at Widow Mitchell's by 6:00 P.M. Blair was forced to pull many of his units back to the branch as that seemed to be the only available source of water in the area. He also reported that Stoneman's cavalry division of

Schofield's Army of the Ohio had cooperated closely with his right flank during the advance and had performed well.[61]

PUSHING SOUTH FROM MARIETTA

In contrast to the smooth progress of operations by McPherson, Sherman's efforts to push Thomas south of Marietta were confused and frustrating on July 3. Hooker's and Howard's columns worked at cross purposes in the area of the Georgia Military Institute. Thomas's staff officers had to stop Hooker from moving in front of Howard. This caused a delay of half an hour. Then a division of the Fourteenth Corps interfered with Howard's line of advance when it countermarched to rejoin Palmer's column. That caused another half-hour delay. When all was finally sorted out, Howard faced south on the left of Thomas's formation, with Hooker in the center and Palmer on the right. The Army of the Cumberland moved south of Marietta for six miles, skirmishing all the way, until reaching the vicinity of Johnston's new line at Smyrna Station.[62]

Sherman had to confess in his memoirs that "I had not learned beforehand of the existence of this strong place, in the nature of a *tete-du-pont*, and had counted on striking him an effectual blow in the expected confusion of his crossing the Chattahoochee, a broad and deep river then to his rear." He concluded that Johnston intended to shield his crossing of the river with this new defense line that stretched from near Nickajack Creek on the west to Rottenwood Creek on the east, straddling the railroad. He continued to criticize Thomas's slow pursuit, believing the Federals might have been able to scoop up three thousand or four thousand prisoners along the way if they had moved more aggressively.[63]

Sherman was desperate to take every advantage of Johnston's situation, with his back to a major river. In dispatches to his subordinates, he urged them to strain every effort to press the enemy to the wall on July 4. "If you ever worked in your life," he told McPherson, "work at daybreak to-morrow on that flank, crossing Nickajack somehow, and the moment you discover confusion pour in your fire." To Thomas, Sherman wrote, "We will never have such a chance again, press with vehemence at any cost of life and material." He urged the commander of the Army of the Cumberland to drop his caution. "You know what loss would ensue to Johnston if he crosses his bridges at night in confusion with artillery thundering at random in his rear." Sherman did not want to waste the rare opportunity "of a large army fighting at a disadvantage with a river to his rear."[64]

JULY 4

The eighty-eighth anniversary of Independence Day brought with it further moves that more clearly delineated Confederate positions north of the Chattahoochee. But there was no possibility of smashing Rebel troop formations or destroying Johnston's wagon trains. The Confederates were already prepared to meet their foe in another strong position.

Dodge continued measured Union efforts to locate the enemy south of Kennesaw by moving Brigadier General James C. Veatch's division of the Sixteenth Corps eastward from Ruff's Mill. Veatch advanced two miles until coming upon the left wing of Johnston's new line at Smyrna Station. He settled down into position opposite Hood's Corps and awaited the arrival of Dodge's other division, led by Brigadier General Thomas W. Sweeny, which took post to Veatch's right. Both divisions constructed earthworks.[65]

At 4:00 P.M., Dodge sent forward three regiments from each division and captured the Confederate skirmish line with 100 prisoners. Heavy fire accounted for 140 Union casualties in this maneuver, and hand-to-hand combat erupted when the Federals closed in on the enemy. Colonel Edward F. Noyes of the Thirty-Ninth Ohio was severely wounded in the leg, and he feared it would have to be amputated. Dodge spoke with him while Noyes was on his way to the rear and recalled that the colonel was worried about his new wife, "a beautiful lady in Cincinnati," in Dodge's words. "He did not seem to pay any attention to his wound but just wondered what she would think of it." The Federal loss of life was comparatively heavy for such modest gain. Years later, the historian of Fuller's Ohio Brigade commented on the casualties. "To the survivors who fought this fight to the finish, it was a momentous affair. They lost some of their best and bravest men who had served with them three years."[66]

Blair's Seventeenth Corps was very active on July 4. Two regiments from Manning F. Force's brigade moved northeastward on a road that branched off from Sandtown Road just north of Widow Mitchell's. They advanced between two branches of Nickajack Creek toward Dodgens's Mill, located on the creek itself. From Dodgens's Mill, the road continued toward Fulton on the railroad, bypassing Johnston's Smyrna Line. Force, who personally led the two regiments, crossed the creek and met resistance by Confederate cavalry. He could not locate Dodge's command and was therefore unable to connect his line to it. The gray clad troopers also put up enough fight to compel Force to retire west of the creek. Two more regiments arrived, and

Force again advanced to the east side of the stream. This time he made connection with Dodge's Sixteenth Corps troops to the left, but Blair ordered Force to retire once more. He intended to move all of Leggett's division to support Gresham in the push south along Sandtown Road. In short, Blair had decided not to pursue the line of advance toward the railroad but to concentrate on reaching the Chattahoochee instead.[67]

At the same time that Force crossed and recrossed Nickajack Creek, two regiments from Colonel William Hall's brigade of Gresham's division advanced southeast from Widow Mitchell's toward Turner's Ferry on the Chattahoochee River. They encountered Confederate cavalry with artillery about a mile from the crossroads and were stalled, forcing Hall to send three more regiments and a section of guns to the scene of action. The reinforced line drove the Confederates a mile and a half to a strong line of works that was about three miles short of the ferry.[68]

The Federals encountered elements of the Georgia Militia holding this line located three miles from Turner's Ferry. It was the first time that members of Sherman's army group confronted the state militia. Gov. Joseph E. Brown had called up the militia when Johnston retired across the Etowah River in late May, and three thousand troops assembled under Major General Gustavus W. Smith. Organized into two brigades, the militia guarded the crossings of the Chattahoochee River until Johnston moved them north of the stream to support Jackson's cavalry division on June 29.[69]

Smith found a preexisting earthwork on top of a ridge three miles north of Turner's Ferry along Sandtown Road and assumed position there, with elements of Jackson's cavalry division. The earthwork had embrasures for Captain Ruel W. Anderson's battery of four Napoleons and short connecting infantry trenches on each side, but it was not large enough to accommodate the two thousand militiamen he had moved north of the river. Moreover Smith was detached from the rest of the Confederate army and confronted by an overwhelming force of Union veterans. He took up his position on the evening of July 2, and his men improved the fortification on July 3 and much of the day on the 4th. They cut trees to enlarge the clear field of fire to the front and used the logs as well as fence rails to make breastworks. When Blair's troops neared their position, the militiamen engaged in skirmishing and endured artillery fire. For the inexperienced militiamen, the sensations of combat aroused new feelings and fears. "But I tell you minie Balls and bombshells passing over a person's head make queer music," reported P. C. Key of the Fourth Georgia Militia to his wife. Thomas J. Head of the Sixth

Georgia Militia steeled his nerves. "Sallie you cannot imagine my feelings when the bombs were bursting all around me," he wrote his wife. "I thought of *you my darling* all the time."[70]

Blair moved the rest of Gresham's division to form one thousand yards from Smith, reinforcing it with two brigades of Leggett's division. Stoneman's cavalry covered Blair's right flank during the operations of July 4, in which the Seventeenth Corps lost about forty men. The Georgia militia units also lost a few wounded during the bombardment and skirmishing, but Smith was fortunate that Blair opted for a cautious approach to his ridge-top position, allowing his green troops to stay where they were for the course of the day.[71]

Given Thomas's advance south from Marietta on July 3, there was no longer a need to retain Osterhaus's and Harrow's divisions of the Fifteenth Corps near the city, so they marched south to join McPherson early on July 4. It was an exhausting, hot march that took nearly all day. Thomas's command assumed the responsibility of provost duty in Marietta from Logan's men. Palmer chose a brigade of his Fourteenth Corps to take possession of the town.[72]

Thomas also applied pressure on the front of Johnston's Smyrna Line during the course of July 4 to draw attention from McPherson. Davis's division of the Fourteenth Corps held the extreme Union right and was available, as Sherman informed McPherson, to help the Army of the Tennessee if necessary. Howard aggressively demonstrated on the Union left, sending a heavily reinforced skirmish line from Stanley's division across a large cornfield to capture the opposing skirmish line. Stanley also advanced his main line and constructed works. Later, Newton and Wood did the same thing in an effort to snuggle the Fourth Corps troops ever closer to the Confederate position. Howard took eighty-eight prisoners and lost ninety-five men that day.[73]

Johnston's Smyrna Line was on good ground straddling the railroad and the wagon road leading toward the river, with Loring's Army of Mississippi holding the right wing east of the tracks. Hardee's Corps extended the line west of the railroad, and Hood's Corps was positioned to Hardee's left. Johnston covered his right flank with Wheeler's cavalry and his left with Jackson's cavalry and Smith's militiamen. Heavy skirmishing and artillery fire characterized the activity along the front of the line on July 4. Alfred J. Vaughan, whose Tennessee Brigade had stoutly repelled Davis's attack on Cheatham's Hill, lost a foot when a Federal shell exploded near him as he rested a couple of hundred yards behind the line. A shell fragment sliced off the foot, and surgeons trimmed the ragged stump. Vaughan was out of action for the rest of the war, but he survived his ghastly wound.[74]

Johnston had always intended his Smyrna Line as an intermediate position, well aware of the danger inherent in backing his army up against the Chattahoochee. He had already selected another position along the north bank of the river as a last stand north of the stream. Brigadier General Francis A. Shoup, his artillery chief, took on the responsibility of managing the construction of this line and designing stockades to be placed at intervals along it. These were unique features of Shoup's own creation, consisting of logs to give artillery and infantrymen added height and the opportunity to more readily fire to right and left of their position. Black laborers were used to start the construction of this line, and engineer Lemuel P. Grant, whose primary responsibility was the city defenses of Atlanta, came up to lend a hand with the Chattahoochee River Line as well.[75]

By the end of the day on July 4, Hood sent reports to army headquarters that the Federals were about to turn his left flank, testifying to the significance of Force's tentative moves at Dodgens's Mill. Johnston sent Cheatham's division from Hardee's Corps to help shore up the left. But later that evening, Smith also sent worried dispatches to army headquarters that his militiamen fronting the Federals on the line covering Turner's Ferry faced an overwhelming foe, testifying to the significance of Blair's heavy concentration of Seventeenth Corps troops on the road toward the ferry. Johnston felt compelled to evacuate the Smyrna Line on the night of July 4 and fall back to the yet incomplete Chattahoochee River Line (or, to honor the man who designed the unique stockades, the Shoup Line).[76]

JULY 5

The Federals did not learn of Johnston's move until dawn of July 5 revealed empty trenches in the Smyrna Line. Dodge followed up the pullout by advancing further, skirmishing with Stevenson's division of Loring's Army of Mississippi, which covered the Rebel withdrawal. The Sixteenth Corps troops broke contact at 1:00 P.M. and marched to Sandtown Road, where they turned south and reached the intersection at Widow Mitchell's that evening. Blair continued to advance southward along Sandtown Road toward Turner's Ferry, crossing Nickajack Creek five hundred yards from the Shoup defenses. Seventeenth Corps troops spread out to cover the left end of Johnston's Chattahoochee River Line and Stoneman extended the Union presence along the north bank of the river fifteen miles downstream from Turner's Ferry.[77]

By the end of the day, the Federals positioned themselves opposite the entire Chattahoochee River Line from Howard's left flank near Pace's Ferry down to Blair's Corps at Turner's Ferry. The Federals now occupied Vining's Station, where a particularly tall hill offered a fine view of the city of Atlanta ten miles to the south. Kenner Garrard's cavalrymen also occupied the town of Roswell, twelve miles northeast of Marietta, on July 5. Here they found an industrial complex of paper mills, flour mills, and a machine shop churning out material for the Confederate government. The Federals took into custody some four hundred female mill employees and prepared to ship them northward, closing down all operations at Roswell.[78]

The realization that Johnston was still clinging to territory north of the Chattahoochee added another burden to the emotional drain of the long drive toward Atlanta. John A. Logan confided to his wife that it seemed as if the campaign would stretch almost into infinity and result in "the destruction of one or the other of the armies." He thought it would continue "for many days or weeks yet," actually underestimating the length of time it would take to complete the conquest of the city.[79]

THE END

But weariness could not obscure the fact that Sherman's men had driven a long way from Dalton in two months, having fought many battles and pried their enemy out of several lines of earthworks. The campaign reached a watershed when the Federals touched the north bank of the Chattahoochee River and gazed upon the city of Atlanta. By July 7, work crews repaired the railroad down to a point only four miles short of the river. Although disappointed in his expectation of catching Johnston while the Confederates crossed the stream, Sherman was well pleased with his progress thus far in the campaign. As he told Stoneman, Johnston could no longer "look into our camps as he did from Kenesaw." Sherman's management of the campaign thus far, with the exception of the attack on June 27, had been very successful. "We have a nice game of war," Sherman told Stoneman, "and must make no mistakes." Atlanta was in sight, but Sherman knew "it will require hard fighting and science to take it. It must be done."[80]

Many Federals knew that the Gate City was in view from the hill at

Vining's Station, and they made a point of going there to see it. Two survivors of the Fourth Corps attack on June 27, Emerson Opdycke and Lieutenant Colonel David H. Moore of the 125th Ohio, had the privilege of walking up the hill and looking at Atlanta on the evening of July 5. "I assure you the 'Gate City' looked very inviting," Opdycke told his wife. A member of the Fiftieth Ohio in Schofield's command had an opportunity to ascend the hill and look at Atlanta's steeples, houses, and Confederate army camps through a field glass. It "was the most beautiful sight I ever saw," admitted Charles T. Kruse.[81]

Several Federals reported that the Confederates had executed a man on the hill by hanging and had left his body still swinging when they retreated. Everyone who saw the gruesome sight was haunted by it and wondered who the man was and why he had been dealt with so harshly. Long after the war ended, S. A. McNeil of the Thirty-First Ohio provided the answer to at least one of these questions. He reported that a comrade, Uriah Cahill, had searched the dead man's pockets and found a descriptive list. The paper identified him as D. P. Duncan of the Georgia Militia. Why he was executed, however, remained a mystery.[82]

The confrontation along the north bank of the Chattahoochee did not last long. Johnston pulled out of the Shoup Line on July 9 after Sherman gained control of several crossings over the river north and south of his position. But Sherman waited several days before moving across the Chattahoochee because his army group needed some time to rest. Federal quartermasters also needed to stockpile supplies for the big push south of the river.[83]

While waiting to cross the stream, Sherman once again tried to justify his decision to attack the Kennesaw Line. In essence, he sought to shore up confidence in his conduct of the Georgia campaign among his superiors in Washington. "Had the assault been made with one-fourth more vigor, mathematically, I would have put the head of George Thomas' whole army right through Johnston's deployed lines on the best ground for go-ahead, while my entire forces were well in hand on roads converging to my then object, Marietta." Sherman bemoaned the fact that Harker and McCook had been shot before they could have pushed their assaults to success, "and then the battle would have all been in our favor on account of our superiority of numbers, position, and initiative." He saw some benefit, nevertheless, in that Johnston gave up his Smyrna Line after only two days, believing the attack on June 27 had made the Confederate commander "much more cautious." Yet Sherman assured Halleck that he had no intention of trying

June 27 all over again. "I will fight any and all the time on anything like fair terms," he wrote, "and that is the best strategy, but it would not be fair to run up against such parapets as I find here."[84]

While Sherman strengthened relations with his Washington superiors, Johnston's relations with Confederate authorities reached a crisis point by the time the Army of Tennessee crossed the Chattahoochee River. Jefferson Davis was increasingly distressed at the constant fallbacks since Dalton, the lack of a general engagement to stop Sherman, and Johnston's inability to assure the politicians that Atlanta could be held. Speaking to William D. Gale, a member of Leonidas Polk's staff, Jefferson Davis poured out his fears and frustrations concerning Johnston barely a month after the Federal attack of June 27. "'I remonstrated with Genl. Johnston, urging him to give battle, telling him that if the enemy were ever permitted to cross below a certain distance, that nothing would prevent his (Sherman) sending raids through a country (Ala./& Ga/) already drained of troops and cutting his communications.'" Davis began to lose all patience as the campaign veered closer to the stream that he viewed as a kind of modern Rubicon. "At last he fell back to Kennesaw Mountain," Davis told Gale, "& then to the Chattahoochie, *There I lost all hope of a battle.*"[85]

The wheels were set in motion to give Johnston one last chance. General Braxton Bragg, Davis's chief military adviser, visited the Army of Tennessee and found in his words that the commander had no "more plan for the future than he has had in the past." Davis gave the authorization to replace him with John Bell Hood, and the transfer of authority was consummated on July 18.[86]

Johnston's Fabian strategy of remaining on the defensive culminated in the Kennesaw phase of the Atlanta campaign. That late-June phase had strained the Union invaders more seriously than at any other time of the long drive southward from Chattanooga. But it had not decisively impaired their ability to resume offensive movement. It was, in short, a failed strategy, and it drained the patience of Johnston's superiors. With Hood's appointment and the institution of an aggressive mode of defense, the campaign accelerated for a time into its bloodiest phase. In many ways, that played more into Sherman's hands than it did into Hood's.

Conclusion

Everyone recognized that the battle of Kennesaw Mountain on June 27 was a salient feature of the contest for Atlanta. Sherman called it "the hardest fight of the campaign up to that date," and Confederate trooper William E. Sloan referred to it as "the great battle" of the drive toward the Gate City. Postwar writers also pinpointed the engagement as a special event in Civil War history that added new and distinctive names to the lexicon of combat in the conflict. Even as the armies moved away from Kennesaw toward the Chattahoochee, Confederate survivors of the battle were beginning to call the salient on Cheatham's Hill the Dead Angle. Within the context of fortification terminology, that term identified a sector inadequately covered by the fire of the defender. It was applicable to Cheatham's Hill in a limited way, for an attacker was shielded only along a portion of his line of approach to the angle. The defending Confederates could cover the last few yards of the approach with their rifles and artillery. In describing the situation, Captain Peter Marchant of the Forty-Seventh Tennessee in Vaughan's brigade explained that "our fire was concentrated on that point & the havoc made amongst the enemy gave it the name of the Dead angle."[1]

Why did Sherman decide to shove his troops into the attack of June 27? The answer begs an understanding of context. Sherman was an aggressive, confident commander while on the strategic offensive, both when he had a secure line of supply (as during the Atlanta campaign) and when he conducted a strategic raid into enemy territory (as during the Meridian campaign). But he also preferred to achieve his strategic results by maneuver rather than hard fighting. Sherman conducted two failed attacks on Confederate positions prior to Kennesaw Mountain, at Chickasaw Bayou during Grant's first offensive against Vicksburg and at Tunnel Hill during the Chattanooga campaign. In both of those instances, as at Kennesaw Mountain, Sherman felt compelled to attack because of circumstances seemingly beyond his control, or he was forced to conduct the tactical offensive as a result of direct orders from his immediate superior.

215

Chickasaw Bayou was a good example of Sherman's conduct of a deep penetration of enemy territory, acting as an independent commander although under Grant's general supervision. While Grant moved overland down through central Mississippi, Sherman led about thirty thousand men from Memphis by steamer down the Mississippi River to strike at Vicksburg. The two columns were supposed to cooperate with each other, but that cooperation, loose to begin with, completely broke down when Grant concluded he could not rely on his railroad supply line and stopped further advance. Sherman was out of communication with his superior and did not know what was happening along the overland approach. He therefore felt compelled to land his troops as planned a few miles up the Yazoo River north of Vicksburg. From the river bottom, he attempted to fight his way up the steep slope of Walnut Hills to gain high ground and operate against the river city with advantage. The only alternative to attacking was to retreat. Sherman did at Chickasaw Bayou what he was to do at Kennesaw Mountain, try to find the best place to assault and make the attempt. His men did so on December 29, 1862, with disastrous results. They made no dent in the Confederate defenses, situated on good defensive ground, and lost 1,776 men in the process. Further efforts to find a better approach to the high ground failed, and rising waters in the Yazoo forced Sherman to retreat anyway. He was stung by extensive newspaper criticism of the repulse and perhaps relieved when Major General John A. McClernand soon after arrived to assume command of the expedition, and later Grant came to supersede McClernand.[2]

The situation at Tunnel Hill represented a scenario wherein Sherman had no choice but to attack a strong Confederate position on high ground. Grant was close by and in full charge of overall operations to relieve the "siege" of Chattanooga by the Army of Tennessee, then under the command of General Braxton Bragg. Cleburne's tough division stood in Sherman's way as the latter attempted to turn Bragg's right flank at Missionary Ridge. The Federals only dimly understood the topography and had little intelligence about Confederate troop positions. Yet Sherman attacked in a disjointed, hesitant way, demonstrating his lack of acumen about conducting the details of a tactical offensive. Although outnumbering Cleburne by about four to one, he was stopped cold with the loss of 1,726 men. Grant ordered Thomas's Army of the Cumberland to strike at Bragg's center along the ridge, in part to take pressure off Sherman, and the result was a magnificent victory by the troops who had been soundly defeated by Bragg's army at Chickamauga two months before.[3]

Sherman went into both attacks at Chickasaw Bayou and Tunnel Hill reluctantly, as the only alternative open to him under the circumstances, and he felt the same was true of June 27, 1864. There were few instances during the Atlanta campaign when Sherman felt under pressure to attack against his better judgment, for that long drive offered him many opportunities to maneuver to gain his strategic objective. But the Kennesaw phase of the campaign bogged his army group down in the woods of northwest Georgia, pelted by rain and dogged by the upturned red clay of newly constructed Rebel earthworks. The Confederates extended their line to keep pace with Schofield's cautious efforts to find and turn their left flank, and the campaign seemed to grind to a halt by late June.

Among the many considerations weighing on Sherman's mind, one of the most important was making sure that Johnston did not detach troops to Virginia to help Lee fight Grant. As early as April 4, a full month before the onset of the campaign, Grant made this point clear to his subordinate. Grant would do the same for Sherman, by keeping Lee so busy he could not duplicate what he had done the previous fall in detaching two divisions under Lieutenant General James Longstreet to help Bragg. Longstreet had played a key role in winning the Rebel victory at Chickamauga. Howard remembered Sherman's instructions to his subordinates in a conference held just before the start of the Atlanta campaign. He told them of the need "to keep our enemy so busy that he cannot send reinforcements elsewhere, particularly not to the East, against Grant."[4]

After the campaign began, Sherman continued to worry about this problem. He asked Halleck on May 20 to reassure Grant "that I will hold all of Johnston's army too busy to send anything against him." Again, on June 11, Sherman told the Washington authorities of his keen appreciation of this issue. "One of my chief objects being to give full employment to Johnston, it makes but little difference where he is, so he is not on his way to Virginia." He could more easily accomplish this goal by continuing the southward pace of his army group. But when progress slowed and then stopped near Kennesaw, with little immediate prospect for a quick resumption, Sherman became worried and desperate. Johnston had landed in the strongest defensive position of the campaign thus far and could have detached troops to Lee while holding the heavy earthworks with fewer men.[5]

Ironically, neither Johnston nor Lee had any intention of detaching strength to the other, but neither Sherman nor Grant could know that with certainty. Johnston was fully aware that he had selected a position that gave Sherman more trouble to approach, attack, or turn than any yet as-

sumed by his army. Both belligerents in the campaign were intensively relying on field fortifications during their every move. As a member of Alexander P. Stewart's staff put it after the war, "both armies may almost be said to
have moved behind breast works" at Kennesaw Mountain. Left to his own
thoughts, Sherman could have rested easier while taking his time to find a
viable solution to this near tactical stalemate. But the thought that Johnston may send help to Lee spurred him on to risk an attack on June 27 that
he probably would not have attempted otherwise. As Jacob Cox put it after
the war, the stalemate compelled Sherman to "break through and change
into a rout the war of positions which was too much like siege operations
to suit him." Cox, however, failed to understand that it was not mere impatience that prompted his superior to this momentous decision, but fear of
what Johnston might do if he did not distract him with aggressive moves.[6]

The attack came as a surprise to most of the Confederates who received
it. A member of the First Tennessee holding the angle on Cheatham's Hill
recalled that none of his comrades "ever entertained an idea that Sherman
would commit the folly of making such an attack, however eager they may
have been for him to make as many trials as he wished." The results of the
assault on June 27 were not surprising to careful observers, nor are they a
surprise to modern historians. It could be true, as Albert Castel has suggested, that Sherman might have had better luck by striking the Confederate right wing east of Big Kennesaw Mountain rather than frontally hitting Pigeon Hill, Cheatham's Hill, and the wooded lowland between the
latter place and Dallas Road. For that matter, stronger and more aggressive
moves to find and turn the Confederate left flank would have been a better
move than attacking frontally.[7]

The battle of Kennesaw Mountain demonstrated once again that Sherman's sense of how to conduct the tactical offensive left something to be
desired. His sense of strategic matters remained keen, however, and guided
his choice of grand tactics at Kennesaw. The attack of June 27 was unnecessary, for its chief impetus, the need to prevent Johnston from detaching
troops to Lee, was never a real option for the Confederates. Interestingly,
Sherman never mentioned this factor when explaining why he decided to
attack the Kennesaw Line. He emphasized instead the difficulties of further extending his line southward to outflank that line, and the marvelous
results that would occur if the attack was successful. Neither explanation
is convincing. Of course, the results of a successful attack held the poten-
tial to be important, but only *if* the attack succeeded. A good commander
must accurately evaluate *whether* an attack has a good chance of succeeding

rather than merely dreaming of what would happen if it worked properly. Only by accurately assessing the possibility of success can he craft an effective plan of action.

Moreover, the relative ease with which Sherman's troops completed the turning movement to pry Johnston out of the Kennesaw Line makes one wonder why Sherman would think that the attack was necessary. The Confederates knew from prior experience that the Federals would try to flank them. John Bell Hood, who latched onto any point in his feud with Joseph E. Johnston, sarcastically wrote in his memoirs that Sherman "resorted to a ruse he had learned from experience would prove effective," sending "a few troops to make a rumbling sound in our rear, and we folded up our tents, as usual, under strict orders to make no noise." The only real problem with this flanking maneuver, as far as Sherman was concerned, was that it would require him to temporarily cut his connection with the railroad and move most of his men away from their line of supply. But he had already done that when crossing the Etowah River and would do it again near the end of the Atlanta campaign, in all three cases safely and successfully. Sherman understood the need for logistical support better than any other field commander of the war, so he did not take lightly the act of letting go of that lifeline. But any reluctance he felt about marching freely through the countryside did not compel him to try attacking instead. Only the need to keep all of Johnston's troops pinned in their earthworks at Kennesaw Mountain could justify the copious shedding of blood on June 27.[8]

Confederate morale was heightened by the defensive victory of June 27, and it was not dampened by the evacuation of the Kennesaw Line. "It is wonderful how well our soldiers understand this falling back," Samuel G. French wrote in his diary on July 3. "Never before did an army constantly fight and fall back for seven weeks without demoralization, and it plainly establishes the intelligence and individuality of the men." Philip Daingerfield Stephenson of Slocomb's Fifth Battalion, Washington Artillery, thought his comrades stayed longer at Kennesaw Mountain than anyone expected. "We had indeed gotten out of the Kennesaw Line more than we could have hope[d] for, had held it far beyond anticipations. Why the heavy flanking column did not edge us out sooner, I never knew."[9]

Johnston emphasized the Kennesaw phase of the Atlanta campaign while writing postwar justifications of his military record. His mode of operation during the campaign was to act on the defensive and compel Sherman to expend blood and time in carving up territory as he approached the city. Johnston succeeded better in that strategy at Kennesaw than at any other place. The fact that Sherman lost thousands of men in an unwise assault simply reinforced Johnston's view that his Fabian strategy was working. He pointed out in his memoirs that Sherman lost more men on June 27 than did the British when attacking Andrew Jackson at the Battle of New Orleans in 1815. The Federals "had encountered *intrenched* infantry unsurpassed by that of Napoleon's Old Guard, or that which followed Wellington into France, out of Spain." But while highlighting the battle in his memoirs, Johnston made many mistakes. He termed the action on June 27 a general attack, whereas only eight of Sherman's fifty-four infantry brigades took part in it. He also characterized the heavy skirmishing by Blair's Seventeenth Corps as one of the major attacks of the day. His account of Howard's and Davis's assaults were, in the main, accurate, although Johnston incorrectly described Vaughan's brigade as being held in reserve during the battle. He also criticized Sherman's estimate of Union losses on June 27 as far too low. For a total force of 100,000 men, suffering only 3,000 losses would be "too trifling to discourage, much less defeat brave soldiers." In Johnston's view, such a low casualty rate did injustice to the quality of Sherman's rank and file and to the marksmanship of his own Confederate troops.[10]

Many Federals were critical of Sherman's decision to attack on June 27, especially members of the Army of the Cumberland. The results of June 27 tapped into simmering resentment among many in Thomas's command, resentment that troops from other departments had to rescue the Cumberland army at Chattanooga and now contributed to its further advance along the rail line toward Atlanta, a line of advance that traditionally had been the sole responsibility of the Department of the Cumberland. Moreover, the Cumberlanders seemed to resent first Grant's and then Sherman's ascendancy over their hero, George Thomas. Thomas himself set the tone for this resentment. When Grant initially arrived at Chattanooga in late October to take charge of operations designed to clean up the mess created by the army's defeat at Chickamauga, Thomas treated him coldly. His staff members understood the message well. Everyone obeyed Sherman's orders during the Atlanta campaign, but they never warmed up to their superior and waited until the war was over before launching campaigns to tarnish Sherman's record.[11]

Among the more vibrant critics of Sherman's campaign was Lieutenant Colonel Henry Van Ness Boynton of the Thirty-Fifth Ohio, who had compiled an impressive record at Chickamauga. Boynton had also been wounded in the thigh while storming Missionary Ridge on November 25,

1863, and he missed the drive toward Atlanta. That did not prevent him from severely criticizing the attack of June 27. "There was no military movement made by Sherman, from the time he began the Atlanta campaign till the end of the war, which brought such severe criticism upon him from the armies which he commanded as the assault upon Kenesaw Mountain," Boynton wrote in 1875. "By the universal verdict along the lines, it was adjudged an utterly needless move, and so an inexcusable slaughter."[12]

Captain Henry Stone, a member of Thomas's staff, also mounted a serious attack on Sherman that was published in 1910, long after the general had passed away. He called the assault of June 27 the result of "a sort of desperation" that resulted in "fruitless sacrifice." The dead and wounded on that day were "wantonly thrown away to prove the needless fact that his army could assault; as if Vicksburg and Missionary Ridge . . . had not abundantly established that truth." Stone argued that the morale of the rank and file suffered a great deal as a result of the failed assault. Their confidence in Sherman's judgment "was seriously shaken. Everybody knew that the place selected was the most unlikely of any since the first encounter at Buzzard Roost. The men in the ranks understood it perfectly; and they passed their silent and relentless sentence upon it and him."[13]

Neither Boynton nor Stone participated in the attack, and neither did other observers such as Benjamin Scribner and William B. Hazen, also members of Thomas's army. Scribner commanded a brigade in the Fourteenth Corps during the Kennesaw phase of the campaign, and Hazen led a brigade in Wood's division of the Fourth Corps. Both men criticized the attack after the war, with Scribner calling it "a desperate and disastrous assault." Writing in 1887, Scribner continued to mourn the "many gallant and choice fellows that went down that day," and "the thought sinks like a lump of lead in my heart." Hazen commented on the assault in 1885 while writing his memoirs, expressing his view that anyone who studied the operation would conclude that it was a dreadful mistake.[14]

Alexis Cope served in the Fifteenth Ohio, in Gibson's brigade of Wood's division, and he expressed his thoughts about the attack while writing the regimental history of his unit. Cope argued that "there was an undercurrent of severe criticism of General Sherman for sending our troops against works which were generally believed to be impregnable. This criticism was not softened when the General publicly assumed the responsibility." Cope, however, pointed out that initial reports exaggerated the loss of manpower on June 27, but the critics did not soften their comments after the casualty estimate was lowered to a more realistic level. Cope compared public commentary on the battle of June 27 with that of Pickett's Mill on May 27, in which the Fifteenth Ohio lost heavily. In fact, Federal casualties at Kennesaw were only twenty-one men more than Federal losses at Pickett's Mill, according to Cope, yet the public was ablaze with interest in what happened on June 27 and ignored the terrible fighting of a month before. This was due, in Cope's estimation, to the loss of well-known figures such as Harker and McCook at Kennesaw.[15]

Members of Thomas's army who participated in the attack also had dark thoughts about the wisdom of the operation, and many of their comments include bitterness toward other units within Sherman's army group. John McAuley Palmer's Fourteenth Corps sent two brigades into the attack on Cheatham's Hill, but Palmer doubted the wisdom of the move from the start. He rode over to see John A. Logan right after the attack failed to tell the Fifteenth Corps commander that it was useless to try again. Logan surprisingly told Palmer that his boys "'could go further than any live men.'" The next day, Sherman told Palmer that Logan's troops "had gone more than a hundred yards further than my men had gone." This sparked a retort from the Fourteenth Corps leader that "I had a hundred men more than I would have had if I had gone as far as Logan did; that we had all failed, and that I had no man who was not as good as he was, except that his pay was less." Logan's bombast unnecessarily hurt Palmer and denigrated the performance of McCook's and Mitchell's men, who actually had accomplished more than Logan's troops had done on June 27.[16]

Members of Harker's Fourth Corps brigade felt the sting of their costly defeat very badly. Luther P. Bradley termed the attack of June 27 "the worst piece of work we ever undertook, badly planned and badly managed, and we were terribly punished for our mistakes." Bradley blamed Sherman for the attack, but he missed an important point. While Sherman made the decision to assault, he left the choice of the target and the manner of attack up to his subordinates. Howard deserved a good deal of criticism for selecting the point of the Fourth Corps effort and for authorizing the use of columns rather than lines. R. C. Rice of Harker's brigade also blamed Sherman and no one else for the attack.[17]

The survivors of McCook's brigade more than any other Federals considered June 27 as the most important day of their war experience. Their performance entitled them to as much credit as that accorded the survivors of Pickett's Charge at Gettysburg, argued Frank B. James of the Fifty-Second

Ohio. "There is no place where we were tested that to me finds so much interest," concluded Theodore D. Neighbor of the same regiment. "Kenesaw mountain of June 27, 1864, was our golgotha and our Waterloo." In fact, Samuel Grimshaw argued that his comrades had done something on June 27 that the Federals who attacked the stone wall at Fredericksburg, the Virginians who went forth with Pickett at Gettysburg, and the Georgians and Mississippians who attacked Fort Sanders at Knoxville failed to do. "We made a lodgement and maintained our position alone and without re-inforcements until we drove the rebels out of their works July 2d to 3d."[18]

The heavy losses suffered by the brigade, especially the mortal wounding of their beloved commander, intensified the feelings of survivors about the battle of Kennesaw Mountain. They often repeated stories of McCook's wounding. R. D. McDonald spoke briefly with McCook at Nashville while taking Oscar Harmon's body back to Illinois, and he reported to his comrades after the war what their commander had told him. "McDonald, if I had not been shot, or Col. Harmon been killed, we would have gone over the rebel works in fifteen minutes more." Many members of the brigade were convinced that they could have taken the Confederate position on Cheatham's Hill if McCook had survived. Some of them even thought their superiors should have taken advantage of their close position to the Rebel works from June 27 to July 2 to mount another effort at breaking through the enemy line. "The assault, then, in our opinion, could have been made successful," wrote James.[19]

Most survivors of McCook's brigade carried for the rest of their lives the feeling that June 27 had been a horrible day. Writing in 1901, J. B. Work of the Fifty-Second Ohio asserted that "time will hardly change the conclusion then reached, that 'somebody blundered' and there had been a fearful and useless slaughter." Other men were more discrete in voicing their opinions. When James W. Langley met a group of about one hundred brigade veterans in Danville, Illinois, in 1899, the men "in low breath recalled the useless slaughter" at Kennesaw Mountain.[20]

The troops in Sherman's old command, the Army of the Tennessee, were far less critical of the attack on June 27. Captain Charles W. Wills of the 103rd Illinois in Walcutt's brigade called the assault "a rough affair, but we were not whipped." Whatever negative opinions Tennessee army men had of the operation were generally kept to themselves. They waited, as did Grenville Dodge and Edwin Witherby Brown, until they wrote their memoirs to softly voice opinions about Sherman's judgment. A salient exception was Logan himself. Forgetting his excessively boastful attitude toward Palmer, Logan had a reason for criticizing Sherman after the war ended. He held a grudge against his superior because Sherman bypassed him as permanent commander of the Army of the Tennessee to replace McPherson, who was killed in the battle of Atlanta on July 22, 1864. Although Sherman tried to assuage his feelings, Logan never forgave him for the slight. It showed in Logan's assessment of the June 27 attack, written long after the war ended. "The alacrity with which the troops moved out to an attack which was universally considered ill-advised, to say the least, was one of the strong proofs exhibited during the campaign of the complete discipline and soldierly qualities of the volunteer soldier of the Western army." Logan's wife supported her husband's views when writing her own memoirs, claiming that the attack was made "against the advice of General Logan, who considered the impossible feat little short of madness, an opinion in which General McPherson coincided."[21]

It was easier for men who had not directly participated in the attack to be more objective about it. While Jacob Cox merely criticized the use of columns instead of lines in the Fourth and Fourteenth Corps assaults, Schofield felt a personal interest in the battle. Sherman had argued in his memoirs that his subordinates all concurred in the necessity for attacking. It was true, Schofield argued in his own memoirs, that he, Thomas, and McPherson felt the lines could hardly be stretched any more without serious consequences, but they did not agree with Sherman that making frontal attacks on fortified lines was the alternative. Detaching part of the army to make a short march around the Confederate left, or moving most of it away from the railroad connection to conduct a long flanking march (as actually was started on July 1) were the true alternatives. "I did not see Thomas or McPherson for some days before the assault," continued Schofield, "but I believe their judgment like mine, was opposed to it. Undoubtedly it was generally opposed, though deferentially as became subordinates toward the commanding general. The responsibility was entirely Sherman's, as he afterward frankly stated."[22]

Schofield was equally certain that the rank and file universally opposed attacking any well-prepared positions. The assault might have been justified if the Kennesaw Line had been new and the works were not yet well developed, but it was "impregnable" by June 27. The common soldier of Sherman's army group wanted to see that he had a chance of success, in the same way that he would operate "his farm or run his sawmill" in civilian life, according to Schofield. A commander had a responsibility to maneuver and plan so as to place his men in a tactical situation where they had a chance of winning, but the situation on June 27 offered them no chance at all, according to Schofield's judgment.[23]

The consensus of opinion among historians is that the attack on June 27 was a mistake, and there is no real opportunity to dispute that judgment. But it is possible to mitigate the verdict with context. As John Schofield wisely put it in his memoirs, Sherman exhibited a high degree of prudence and caution throughout the Atlanta campaign, and he did so on June 27 as well. Schofield pointed out that the attack was not general, but strictly limited to only eight brigades out of fifty-four available to him. As Schofield put it, "the worst that could happen in that [attack] was what actually did happen, namely, a fruitless loss of a considerable number of men, yet a number quite insignificant in comparison with the total strength of his army."[24]

The attack was, in short, an experiment. The negative results of that experiment could not seriously impair Sherman's ability to continue the campaign along the more prudent lines already established. In a way, the same can be said of his attacks at Chickasaw Bayou and Tunnel Hill. In contrast to Grant's campaign in Virginia, where 64,000 men fell in the Army of the Potomac from May 4 to June 18, taking out of action half the strength of that large field army in only six weeks, Sherman's army group swallowed its modest casualties on June 27 and kept moving toward Atlanta with its level of field effectiveness undiminished. If Johnston hoped to eviscerate his enemy by enticing him into large-scale assaults on fortified positions, Sherman demonstrated at Kennesaw Mountain that, while he may be tempted to try an assault, he had no intention of wasting his manpower to the point that he could no longer sustain the strategic offensive.

"I see by the papers that too much stress was laid on the repulse of June 27," Sherman wrote to his wife on July 9. "I was forced to make the effort, and it should have succeeded, but the officers & men have been so used to my avoiding excessive danger and forcing back the Enemy by strategy." Yet, Sherman argued, attacking sometimes was needed "for its effect on the Enemy." Fourteenth Corps staff officer James A. Connolly agreed with Sherman. He also wrote his wife that the Northern public appeared to be greatly alarmed at Sherman's repulse. "Why, bless you, we didn't think anything of it here, and it has ceased to be even talked about. Everybody in this army that knew anything about it, knew that it was a kind of experiment, to try the rebel works that we have been flanking so long, to see whether they were really as strong as they appeared to be." Connolly cavalierly argued that the repulse "didn't make half as much impression on this army as two days steady rain would have made."[25]

Within three weeks following the attack at Kennesaw, Sherman's army group pursued the retreating Confederates through Marietta, forced them out of two more heavily fortified lines, and lodged securely along the north bank of the Chattahoochee River. The Federals were within six miles of Atlanta and about to knock on the door of the fortified city.

Orders of Battle

KOLB'S FARM, JUNE 22, 1864

FEDERALS

Army of the Cumberland, Maj. Gen. George H. Thomas

Twentieth Corps, Maj. Gen. Joseph Hooker

FIRST DIVISION, BRIG. GEN. ALPHEUS S. WILLIAMS

First Brigade, Brig. Gen. Joseph F. Knipe
    5th Connecticut, Col. Warren W. Packer
    3rd Maryland (detachment), Lieut. David Gove
    123rd New York, Lieut. Col. James C. Rogers
    141st New York, Col. William K. Logie
    46th Pennsylvania, Col. James L. Selfridge

Second Brigade, Brig. Gen. Thomas H. Ruger
    27th Indiana, Col. Silas Colgrove
    13th New Jersey, Col. Ezra A. Carman
    107th New York, Col. Nirom M. Crane
    150th New York, Col. John H. Ketcham
    3rd Wisconsin, Col. William Hawley

Third Brigade, Col. James S. Robinson
    82nd Illinois, Lieut. Col. Edward S. Salomon
    101st Illinois, Lieut. Col. John B. Le Sage
    45th New York, Col. Adolphus Dobke
    143rd New York, Col. Horace Boughton

Division Artillery, Capt. John D. Woodbury
    Battery I, 1st New York Light Artillery, Lieut. Charles E. Winegar
    Battery M, 1st New York Light Artillery, Capt. John D. Woodbury

SECOND DIVISION, BRIG. GEN. JOHN W. GEARY

First Brigade, Col. Charles Candy
    5th Ohio, Maj. Henry E. Symmes
    29th Ohio, Capt. Myron T. Wright
    66th Ohio, Lieut. Col. Eugene Powell
    28th Pennsylvania, Lieut. Col. John Flynn
    147th Pennsylvania, Col. Ario Pardee Jr.

Second Brigade, Col. Patrick H. Jones
    33rd New Jersey, Col. George W. Mindil
    119th New York, Capt. Chester H. Southworth
    134th New York, Lieut. Col. Allan H. Jackson
    154th New York, Maj. Lewis D. Warner
    73rd Pennsylvania, Maj. Charles C. Cresson
    109th Pennsylvania, Capt. Walter G. Dunn

Third Brigade, Col. David Ireland
    60th New York, Col. Abel Godard
    78th New York, Col. Herbert von Hammerstein
    102nd New York, Capt. Barent Van Buren
    137th New York, Lieut. Col. Koert S. Van Voorhis
    149th New York, Col. Henry A. Barnum
    29th Pennsylvania, Maj. Jesse R. Millison
    111th Pennsylvania, Col. George A. Cobham Jr.

Division Artillery, Capt. William Wheeler (killed),
Capt. Charles C. Aleshire
    13th New York Battery, Capt. William Wheeler (killed), Lieut. Henry Bundy
    Battery E, Pennsylvania Light Artillery, Capt. James D. McGill

Army of the Ohio (Twenty-Third Corps),
Maj. Gen. John M. Schofield

SECOND DIVISION, BRIG. GEN. MILO S. HASCALL

Third Brigade, Col. Silas A. Strickland
    14th Kentucky, Col. George W. Gallup
    20th Kentucky, Lieut. Col. Thomas B. Waller
    27th Kentucky, Lieut. Col. John H. Ward
    50th Ohio, Lieut. Col. George R. Elstner

CONFEDERATES

Army of Tennessee, Gen. Joseph E. Johnston

Hood's Corps, Lieut. Gen. John B. Hood

HINDMAN'S DIVISION, MAJ. GEN. THOMAS C. HINDMAN

Deas's Brigade, Brig. Gen. Zachariah C. Deas
  19th Alabama, Col. Samuel K. McSpadden
  22nd Alabama, Col. Benjamin R. Hart
  25th Alabama, Col. George D. Johnston
  39th Alabama, Lieut. Col. William C. Clifton
  50th Alabama, Col. John G. Coltart
  17th Alabama Battalion Sharpshooters, Capt. James F. Nabers

Tucker's Brigade, Brig. Gen. William F. Tucker
  7th Mississippi, Lieut. Col. Benjamin F. Johns
  9th Mississippi, Capt. S. S. Calhoon
  10th Mississippi, Capt. Robert A. Bell
  41st Mississippi, Col. J. Byrd Williams
  44th Mississippi, Lieut. Col. R. G. Kelsey
  9th Mississippi Battalion Sharpshooters, Maj. William C. Richards

Manigault's Brigade, Brig. Gen. Arthur M. Manigault
  24th Alabama, Col. Newton N. Davis
  28th Alabama, Lieut. Col. William L. Butler
  34th Alabama, Col. Julius C. B. Mitchell
  10th South Carolina, Col. James F. Pressley
  19th South Carolina, Lieut. Col. Thomas P. Shaw

Walthall's Brigade, Col. Samuel Benton
  24th and 27th Mississippi, Col. Robert P. McKelvaine
  29th, 30th, and 34th Mississippi, Col. William F. Brantly

STEVENSON'S DIVISION, MAJ. GEN. CARTER L. STEVENSON

Brown's Brigade, Brig. Gen. John C. Brown
(Col. Ed. C. Cook temporarily in command)
  3rd Tennessee, Lieut. Col. Calvin J. Clack
  18th Tennessee, Lieut. Col. William R. Butler
  26th Tennessee, Capt. Abijah F. Boggess
  32nd Tennessee, Maj. John P. McGuire
  45th Tennessee and 23rd Tennessee Battalion, Col. Anderson Searcy

Reynolds's Brigade, Brig. Gen. Alexander W. Reynolds
(Col. Robert C. Trigg temporarily in command)
  58th North Carolina, Maj. Thomas J. Dula
  60th North Carolina, Lieut. Col. James T. Weaver
  54th Virginia, Col. Robert C. Trigg
  63rd Virginia, Capt. Connally H. Lynch

Cumming's Brigade, Brig. Gen. Alfred Cumming (Col. Elihu P.
Watkins temporarily in command as Cumming led division's first line)
  34th Georgia, Maj. John M. Jackson
  36th Georgia, Maj. Charles E. Broyles
  39th Georgia, Lieut. Col. J. F. B. Jackson
  56th Georgia, Col. E. P. Watkins

Pettus's Brigade, Brig. Gen. Edmund W. Pettus (Col. Charles M. Shelley
temporarily in command as Pettus led division's second line)
  20th Alabama, Col. James M. Dedman
  23rd Alabama, Lieut. Col. Joseph B. Bibb
  30th Alabama, Col. Charles M. Shelley
  31st Alabama, Col. Daniel R. Hundley
  46th Alabama, Capt. George E. Brewer

JUNE 27, 1864

FEDERALS
MILITARY DIVISION OF THE MISSISSIPPI,
MAJ. GEN. WILLIAM T. SHERMAN

Army of the Cumberland, Maj. Gen. George H. Thomas

Fourth Corps, Maj. Gen. Oliver O. Howard

SECOND DIVISION, BRIG. GEN. JOHN NEWTON

First Brigade, Brig. Gen. Nathan Kimball
  36th Illinois, Col. Silas Miller (mortally wounded),
    Capt. James B. McNeal
  44th Illinois, Col. Wallace W. Barrett
  73rd Illinois, Maj. Thomas W. Motherspaw
  74th Illinois, Lieut. Col. James B. Kerr (mortally wounded
    and captured), Capt. Thomas J. Bryan

88th Illinois, Lieut. Col. George W. Chandler (killed),
   Lieut. Col. George W. Smith
15th Missouri, Col. Joseph Conrad
24th Wisconsin, Maj. Arthur MacArthur Jr.

Second Brigade, Brig. Gen. George D. Wagner
   100th Illinois, Maj. Charles M. Hammond
   40th Indiana, Col. John W. Blake
   57th Indiana, Lieut. Col. Willis Blanch
   28th Kentucky, Lieut. Col. J. Rowan Boone (wounded),
      Maj. George W. Barth
   26th Ohio, Maj. Norris T. Peatman (wounded), Capt. Lewis D. Adair
   97th Ohio, Col. John Q. Lane

Third Brigade, Brig. Gen. Charles G. Harker (mortally wounded),
Col. Luther P. Bradley
   27th Illinois, Lieut. Col. William A. Schmitt
   42nd Illinois, Capt. Jared W. Richards
   51st Illinois, Col. Luther P. Bradley
   79th Illinois, Capt. O. O. Bagley
   3rd Kentucky, Col. Henry C. Dunlap
   64th Ohio, Maj. Samuel L. Coulter
   65th Ohio, Lieut. Col. Horatio N. Whitbeck (wounded),
      Capt. Charles O. Tannehill
   125th Ohio, Lieut. Col. David H. Moore

Artillery, Capt. Wilbur F. Goodspeed
   1st Illinois Light, Battery M, Capt. George W. Spencer
   1st Ohio Light, Battery A, Lieut. Charles W. Scovill

Fourteenth Corps, Maj. Gen. John M. Palmer

SECOND DIVISION, BRIG. GEN. JEFFERSON C. DAVIS

Second Brigade, Col. John G. Mitchell
   34th Illinois, Lieut. Col. Oscar Van Tassell
   78th Illinois, Col. Carter Van Vleck
   98th Ohio, Lieut. Col. John S. Pearce
   113th Ohio, Lieut. Col. Darius B. Warner (wounded), Maj. Lyne S. Sullivant
   121st Ohio Col. Henry B. Banning

Third Brigade, Col. Daniel McCook (mortally wounded),
Col. Oscar F. Harmon (killed), Col. Caleb J. Dilworth
   85th Illinois, Col. Caleb J. Dilworth, Maj. Robert G. Rider
   86th Illinois, Lieut. Col. Allen L. Fahnestock

125th Illinois, Col. Oscar F. Harmon (killed), Maj. John B. Lee
22nd Indiana, Capt. William H. Snodgrass
52nd Ohio, Lieut. Col. Charles W. Clancy

Artillery, Capt. Charles M. Barnett
2nd Illinois Light, Battery I, Lieut. Alonzo W. Coe
Wisconsin Light, 5th Battery (with detachment of 2nd Minnesota Battery attached), Capt. George Q. Gardner

Army of the Tennessee, Maj. Gen. James B. McPherson

Fifteenth Corps, Maj. Gen. John A. Logan

SECOND DIVISION, BRIG. GEN. MORGAN L. SMITH

First Brigade, Brig. Gen. Giles A. Smith
55th Illinois, Lieut. Col. Theodore C. Chandler
111th Illinois, Col. James S. Martin
116th Illinois, Capt. John S. Windsor
127th Illinois, Capt. Alexander C. Little
6th Missouri, Lieut. Col. Delos Van Deusen
8th Missouri, (only Company K) Lieut. Col. David C. Coleman
57th Ohio, Col. Americus V. Rice (wounded), Lieut. Col. Samuel R. Mott

Second Brigade, Brig. Gen. Joseph A. J. Lightburn
83rd Indiana, Col. Benjamin J. Spooner (wounded), Capt. George H. Scott
30th Ohio, Col. Theodore Jones
37th Ohio, Maj. Charles Hipp
47th Ohio, Col. Augustus C. Parry (wounded), Lieut. Col. John Wallace
53rd Ohio, Col. Wells S. Jones
54th Ohio, Lieut. Col. Robert Williams Jr.

Artillery, Capt. Francis De Gress
1st Illinois Light, Battery A, Lieut. George McCagg Jr.
1st Illinois Light, Battery B, Capt. Israel P. Rumsey
1st Illinois Light, Battery H, Capt. Francis De Gress

FOURTH DIVISION, BRIG. GEN. WILLIAM HARROW

Second Brigade, Brig. Gen. Charles C. Walcutt
40th Illinois, Lieut. Col. Rigdon S. Barnhill (killed), Maj. Hiram W. Hall
103rd Illinois, Lieut. Col. George W. Wright (wounded), Capt. Franklin C. Post

97th Indiana, Lieut. Col. Aden G. Cavins
6th Iowa, Maj. Thomas J. Ennis
46th Ohio, Capt. Joshua W. Heath

CONFEDERATES

Army of Tennessee, Gen. Joseph E. Johnston

Hardee's Corps, Lieut. Gen. William J. Hardee

CHEATHAM'S DIVISION, MAJ. GEN. BENJAMIN F. CHEATHAM

Maney's Brigade, Brig. Gen. George Maney
1st Tennessee and 27th Tennessee, Col. Hume R. Feild
4th Tennessee, Lieut. Col. Oliver A. Bradshaw
6th Tennessee and 9th Tennessee, Lieut. Col. John W. Buford
19th Tennessee, Maj. James G. Deaderick
50th Tennessee, Col. Stephen H. Colms

Vaughan's Brigade, Brig. Gen. Alfred J. Vaughan Jr.
11th Tennessee, Col. George W. Gordon
12th and 47th Tennessee, Col. William M. Watkins
29th Tennessee, Col. Horace Rice
13th and 154th Tennessee, Col. Michael Magevney Jr.

CLEBURNE'S DIVISION, MAJ. GEN. PATRICK R. CLEBURNE

Polk's Brigade, Brig. Gen. Lucius E. Polk
1st Arkansas and 15th Arkansas, Lieut. Col. William H. Martin
5th Confederate, Maj. Richard J. Person
2nd Tennessee, Col. William D. Robison
35th Tennessee and 48th Tennessee, Capt. Henry G. Evans

Lowrey's Brigade, Brig. Gen. Mark P. Lowrey
16th Alabama, Lieut. Col. Frederick A. Sahford
33rd Alabama, Col. Samuel Adams
45th Alabama, Col. Harris D. Lampley
32nd Mississippi, Col. William H. H. Tison
45th Mississippi, Col. Aaron B. Hardcastle

Govan's Brigade, Brig. Gen. Daniel C. Govan
2nd Arkansas and 24th Arkansas, Col. E. Warfield
5th Arkansas and 13th Arkansas, Col. John E. Murray
6th Arkansas and 7th Arkansas, Col. Samuel G. Smith

8th Arkansas and 19th Arkansas, Col. George F. Baucum
3rd Confederate, Capt. M. H. Dixon

Army of Mississippi, Maj. Gen. William W. Loring

FRENCH'S DIVISION, MAJ. GEN. SAMUEL G. FRENCH

Cockrell's Brigade, Brig. Gen. Francis M. Cockrell
　1st Missouri and 4th Missouri, Lieut. Col. Hugh A. Garland
　2nd Missouri and 6th Missouri, Col. Peter C. Flournoy
　3rd Missouri and 5th Missouri, Col. James McCown
　1st Missouri Cavalry (dismounted) and 3rd Missouri Cavalry Battalion
　　(dismounted), Col. Elijah Gates

Division Artillery, Maj. George S. Storrs
　Alabama Battery, Capt. John J. Ward
　Brookhaven (Mississippi) Artillery, Capt. James A. Hoskins
　Missouri Battery, Capt. Henry Guibor

Appendix: Kennesaw after the War

After fourteen days of confrontation along the Kennesaw Line, the two armies moved southward to continue their struggle for control of Atlanta. The presence of something like 150,000 men near the twin-peaked eminence had transformed the rural landscape. "The country all around was cut up with entrenchments and honeycombed with rifle pits," recalled W. J. Worsham of the Nineteenth Tennessee. Vegetation in range of sharpshooters and artillerymen was devastated. Worsham described wooded stretches of ground that "looked as dreary and as desolate as if it had been swept by a tornado."[1]

Another Confederate soldier who visited Kennesaw sometime after 1869 reported that the trees were riddled, torn, and splintered for a distance of four hundred yards in front of the position held by Cleburne's division. Trees scarred by hundreds of bullets presented "the strangest and most grotesque appearance," in his view. Trunks were split for twenty feet up the trunk by the impact of artillery rounds. The unnamed veteran found one tree with a hole drilled completely through the trunk which yet was growing even though a man could thrust his arm completely through the opening until his hand appeared on the other side.[2]

Civilian visitors were keenly interested in the historic heights of Kennesaw. A minister working for the U.S. Christian Commission walked up the mountain in early August 1864 and brought back "glowing acc'ts of the scenery & extended landscape" to his colleagues working among the Union soldiers. He also picked a "specimen of cactus" and brought it from the height. Two years later, Benson J. Lossing visited Kennesaw and reported that local residents had already sold more than 200,000 pounds of spent bullets which they had dug out of the earthwork or found lying about on the ground.[3]

Most Federal veterans seemed little interested in the battlefield of Kennesaw Mountain until the 1890s, when they began to visit the quiet woods near Marietta in large numbers. Theodore D. Neighbor of the Fifty-Second Ohio toured the battlefield in 1895 and 1897 and "found everything about as we had left it" more than thirty years before. The mine shaft was still open, but many older trees had withered and died from the effects of battle. The landscape sported a new, second growth of timber. All the head logs on the Union and Confederate earthworks had long since rotted away or had been taken by local farmers, but the timber used by the Rebels to revet the interior slope of their parapets remained intact, although it had rotted. "There are young saplings six and eight inches through growing up through the works," Neighbor reported a few years later.[4]

James T. Holmes of the Fifty-Second Ohio visited the field on May 21, 1897. There was still no road leading to the top of Big Kennesaw, and the last half mile of the walk to the summit was a heroic undertaking for a man of Holmes's age. He found that by now the name Cheatham's Hill had been applied to the low eminence where the angle in the Confederate line rested. Cheatham had passed away in 1886 and, as Holmes cleverly put it, "his name very appropriately sticks, as did his troops, to this hill."[5]

The next day Holmes took a buggy tour of the battlefield with his wife, driven by Uncle Moses Bacon who ran a livery stable in Marietta. Bacon took the pair to the bivouac area of McCook's brigade on the nights of June 25–26 and then to the staging area for the attack. When he asked Holmes if he recognized the place, the veteran replied, "I *reckon* I do Uncle Mose." Holmes stepped out of the carriage and surveyed the scene. A public road ran just behind the staging area, which now was planted in cotton. Holmes walked a few paces toward the Confederate line until he could see across the branch valley. "The same sun was shining over field and wood and stream, and it was about the same hour of the morning. Cheatham hill had the same innocent, peaceful look it had on that other morning, thirty-three years ago."[6]

Holmes moved toward the objective of McCook's attack and found the trees that had once fringed the branch were gone, and the underbrush was now much lighter in growth than in 1864. "The little meadow is discernable, but somewhat effaced, so far as its lines are concerned, because the ground has been cleared half way up to our works and is now under cultivation." The Confederate skirmish pits were still there at the eastern edge of the bottomland.[7]

On the slope of Cheatham's Hill, most of the advanced Union earthworks were intact in 1897, although some had been plowed under. The trenches had filled in quite a bit with dirt and leaves, and the parapets had flattened. "Very little of grass or weeds, comparatively speaking, seems to have grown on the up-thrown earth and it lies bare and yellow, or red, distinctly defined for long distances." The entrance to the mine gallery was still open, and Holmes peered into its darkness. He could discern no sign that the gallery itself had caved in. Holmes also noted that the graves of Union dead buried between the lines on June 29 were still visible.[8]

Holmes found that a family headed by Virgil B. Channell was living on the battlefield by 1897. His home, "a comparatively modern frame house, not large, and without trees or grass about it," was located 200 yards south of Mitchell's fortifications. Channell farmed the ground from his house nearly to Mitchell's works. He told Holmes he had been born in his father's house just behind the Twentieth Corps position in 1859. Channell also pointed out to Holmes a particularly interesting oak tree that was six inches wide and about twenty feet tall. It had been hit by hundreds of balls because of its location just behind the Union line and was still living, although stunted and gnarled.[9]

Everything at Cheatham's Hill impressed Holmes. The earthworks seemed "almost untouched by the waste or change of years," except of course for natural weathering, erosion, and compacting of the red clay. Holmes told Channell that the battlefield ought to be preserved for posterity. He owned sixty-five acres, the entirety of Cheatham's Hill, and ought to give ten to fifteen acres of it for a park. Channell admitted that many people visited the site, often arriving when he was not at home and taking whatever souvenirs they could find. Before leaving, Holmes also picked up a few stray bullets that were still visible on the ground. He also purchased other souvenirs from Channell's young sons to reward the family for taking care of the battlefield. He hoped that "the tourist of 1964" would be able to understand the battle by walking about the field as well as he had done in 1897.[10]

Holmes was not alone in his concern for battlefield preservation. Other survivors of McCook's brigade had also visited the field in the 1890s and taken up the call to do something before the ground passed into less careful hands than Channell's. Lansing Dawdy Jr., who had survived his serious wound of June 27, traveled to the area in 1899 with his wife and daughter Emma. The family pretended to be tourists and drove around with Channell, Dawdy pointing out the place where he was wounded. According to a prearranged plan, Emma pretended to be struck with a spontaneous idea. "Why papa, I wish you would buy this land for me. It is so interesting." Dawdy claimed he had never thought of it before, but agreed with his daughter, and Channell seemed willing to sell. The veteran had intended to purchase only twenty acres, but before the deal was finalized he agreed to buy forty acres more. The deal was concluded on December 26, 1899.[11]

Dawdy transferred ownership of the sixty acres to Martin Kingman and John McGinnis on February 15, 1900, who then transferred it to the Colonel Dan McCook Brigade Association on August 13, 1904. Even before that last transfer, the Brigade Association had worked up interest in the land among its members. It sponsored a dedication ceremony at Cheatham's Hill on September 22, 1902, and encouraged regimental organizations to place markers on the battlefield designating where members had fallen in the failed attack. Members of the Brigade Association also created an adjunct, the Kennesaw Memorial Association, to administer the site and explore ways to restore the earthworks. The Memorial Association had difficulty raising funds and applied to the Illinois legislature unsuccessfully in 1907. A few years later, after the group changed its name to the Kennesaw Mountain Battlefield Association, the state financed the cost of raising a monument to Illinois troops involved in the attack. It was dedicated on June 27, 1914, at a cost of $25,000. Made of Georgia marble and created by a Marietta firm, the governor of Illinois presided over the dedication ceremony. Bullets previously collected from the battlefield were scattered over the ground so visiting veterans could pick them up as souvenirs after the dedication. At about this time, small markers were erected to pinpoint the spot where several members of McCook's brigade had fallen, including Sergeant Copernicus H. Coffey of Company I, Twenty-Second Indiana. Coffey was mortally wounded about fifteen paces from the Confederate line and died two days later. He was a redhaired, twenty-three-year-old farmer from Monroe County, Indiana, when he enlisted in 1861. The place where the brigade formed to attack and the entrance to the mine also were marked.[12]

The stream of veterans visiting the hill never ceased as long as any were left to make the journey, but the battlefield park had no resident caretaker until Rev. J. A. Jones was appointed in 1922. The Battlefield Association was unable to pay him a salary, but he had funds to maintain roads and was allowed to cultivate some land for his upkeep. He continued in this way until 1926.[13]

By the time Jones moved away, the Battlefield Association had succeeded, after several years of effort, in transferring control of the park to the federal government. Unable to raise enough money to properly care for the land, the Battlefield Association approached the government in 1916 and found a receptive audience. Representative Joseph G. Cannon introduced legislation and Congress passed it on February 8, 1917, authorizing the creation of the Kennesaw Mountain National Battlefield Site. But it took many years to secure clear title to the land, and the transfer of control did not take place until 1926.[14]

The federal government was interested in a greatly expanded preserve beyond the confines of Cheatham's Hill. A three-man commission (consisting of an army engineer, one Federal, and one Confederate veteran) studied the area and recommended an enlarged park of more than a thousand acres to include both Big and Little Kennesaw. Houses had already begun to appear in the area, but efforts to interest Congress in funding the enlargement of the park foundered for nine years. In the meanwhile, the War Department was in charge of the sixty acres around Cheatham's Hill. Because there still was no resident caretaker, vandals damaged the Illinois monument. This prompted Congress to fund repairs and the erection of fences and the appointment of a part time caretaker, Benjamin F. Jones, the son of J. A. Jones. He also worked for no salary but was offered a house and thirty acres of land to cultivate.[15]

The War Department transferred control of the sixty acres to the Department of the Interior in August 1933, at the start of a new era in battlefield preservation. Two years later, Congress finally appropriated funds to purchase land for an enlarged park. But local real estate agents talked landowners into allowing them to represent their interests and asked exorbitant prices for the acreage. In addition, a Delaware firm called the Kennesaw Mountain Association had purchased 450 acres of land that included both Kennesaws. This association planned an elaborate hotel complex on top of the mountain and had already begun to cut a road to the top. Plans to preserve the larger battlefield seemed almost doomed to failure, but then economic factors came to the rescue of the government. The association went bankrupt, and a court settled the value of its assets at $16,000, much less than the $80,000 association lawyers wanted. Also, the government moved in 1936 to condemn targeted land in order to purchase it at reasonable rates, thirty dollars per acre, half the price the real estate agents had initially requested.[16]

These events turned the corner in the history of Kennesaw Mountain National Battlefield Park. Selecting ground occupied by Confederate earthworks, in order to preserve the intact evidence of battle, the government purchased 2,888 acres by 1940. The secretary of the interior officially declared the park complete on October 25, 1947. The park today has more than seventeen miles of walking trails, and two additional monuments representing states with troops engaged in the battle have been erected. A visitor's center was constructed at the foot of Big Kennesaw where Federal troops advanced against the First Alabama on June 27, and the walking trail up the slope passes trenches held by the Alabamans. The walking trail continues across the top of both Kennesaw peaks and across Pigeon Hill. It then turns south along the nearly continuous line of Confederate earthworks that stretches six miles through the extent of the park, all the way to the Powder Springs and Marietta Road near Kolb's Farm.[17]

BUILDINGS

A number of historic structures associated with the Kennesaw phase of the Atlanta campaign remain intact. Andrew J. Cheney's house, constructed about 1856 and serving as Schofield's headquarters during the attempt to turn Johnston's left flank, remained standing at least until the late 1960s. The Kolb house, which was at the center of conflict on June 22, survived the war as well. Peter Valentine Kolb Sr. built the log house sometime before he passed away in 1839. His son, Peter Valentine Kolb Jr. owned it by 1851 and worked the six-hundred-acre farm with ten slaves. He died in December 1863, but his wife Eliza Gantt Kolb owned the place when Sherman's men approached in late June 1864. The family repaired the damages after the war, and the National Park Service restored the house in the 1930s.[18]

Historic Marietta includes several structures associated with the campaign. Johnston chose Fair Oaks, a house located today on Kennesaw Avenue, as his headquarters. The structure now is the home of the Marietta Garden Club. William W. Loring used Oakton, also on Kennesaw Avenue, as headquarters for the Army of Mississippi. The Marietta Country Club now occupies the grounds of the Georgia Military Institute, which had been founded by Colonel Arnoldus V. Brumby in 1851. A graduate of West Point, Brumby also served as superintendent of the institute. He made his home on Powder Springs Street, a block from the location of the school. Both the Confederates and the Federals used the institute buildings as hospitals, and the Yankees burned it on November 13, 1864, in preparation for evacuating the area prior to Sherman's March to the Sea.[19]

CEMETERIES

Like most community members who lived near a Civil War engagement, the residents of Marietta made efforts to find burial places for the dead of both sides. Henry Greene Cole, a Unionist of the city who was descended from a Northern family, donated land for a national cemetery in 1866. The Federal government collected the dead not only from the Kennesaw area but from the entire region south of the Oostanaula River. Those Federals buried north of the river were transferred to the national cemetery at Chattanooga. Ultimately, 10,132 Civil War interments took place at the Marietta National Cemetery, and 3,093 of them were unidentified. The main entrance to the cemetery is on Washington Avenue.[20]

The municipal government of Marietta set aside a section of the City Cemetery on Powder Springs and Marietta Road, across the street from the Georgia Military Institute, for Confederate burials. In 1869 local ladies took on the responsibility of raising funds and arranging for the finding, disinterment, and removal of Confederate soldiers who had been buried all the way from near the battlefield of Chickamauga down to Marietta in 1869. The work was continued after the creation of the Kennesaw Chapter of the United Daughters of the Confederacy in Marietta. Eventually, up to three thousand Confederates were buried in the Marietta Confederate Cemetery.[21]

THE KENNESAW LINE

Well-preserved battlefields serve as an outdoor classroom for the student of Civil War operations. Remnants of military features as well as the lay of the land constitute a precious resource not duplicated in official reports or personal accounts. Historians owe a huge debt to those Federal veterans and committed government officials who worked over the course of many decades to bequeath the landscape of battle on and around Kennesaw to future generations.

Indeed, no fortified position of the Atlanta campaign or in any other operation of the Western theater is as well preserved as the line at Kennesaw Mountain. It has been estimated that the Federals constructed seventy-five miles of earthworks near Kennesaw, but little of those works have survived.[22] In contrast, the visitor can walk along an almost continuous line of Confederate trench, studded with artillery emplacements, for six miles from Big Kennesaw Mountain to the Powder Springs and Marietta Road. The Rebels held this line from June 19 to July 2, improving it continually, as the red clay of northwest Georgia settled to form durable remnants. There is no better outdoor classroom to learn the intricacies of Confederate fieldwork design and construction.

BIG AND LITTLE KENNESAW

Today, one can find the remnants of four one-gun emplacements on top of Big Kennesaw, an area held primarily by Walthall's division. A trench line goes down the northwestern slope of Big Kennesaw from the top. Traverses appear about twenty paces apart from each other as the line clings to the military crest. Near the bottom, where the ground is steepest, the Confederates placed ten traverses, all of them at a forty-five-degree angle to the parapet, and each one is about seven paces from its neighbor. Only three of these ten traverses, the fifth, ninth, and tenth, extend to connect to the parapet and block the flow of movement along the trench. The natural crest lies about twenty yards to the rear of the military crest near these ten traverses.[23]

We can gain an idea of how the Confederates constructed the gun emplacements on Kennesaw by viewing a photograph exposed by George Barnard in the spring of 1866. It shows logs about ten inches in diameter that were used as revetment, held up by posts consisting of logs about six inches wide. Three embrasures are apparent, made by cutting through the log revetment to make a space for the tube to

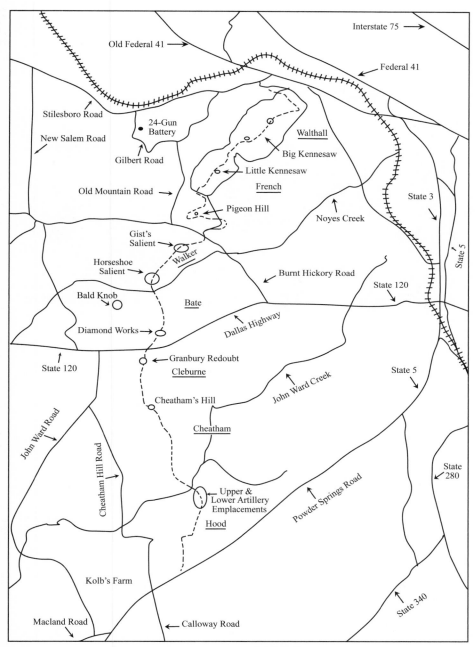

Kennesaw Mountain Today

Barnard's photograph of Confederate works on Kennesaw
(Barnard, Photographic Views, *no. 32)*

stick through. A partly disassembled window shutter leans against the inside of the parapet.

There are remnants of Federal and Confederate works on level land near Big Kennesaw Mountain that display a mix of opposing fieldworks. The Yankees reworked a line of Rebel skirmish pits for their own use, along with two emplacements for two guns each. In front of one of the emplacements, the Federals dug pits to obtain more dirt to enlarge the parapet. One section of extant trench line was initially a Confederate work but with ditches in front of only some sections of the trench. When the Federals converted it for their own use, they used the Confederate trench on the opposite side of the parapet as a ditch but did not dig out the unditched sections of the Confederate position. In other words they were willing to have a discontinuous trench. An unfinished Confederate artillery position for at least four guns was dug on a rocky bit of ground, and the many stones encountered may well explain why it was unfinished. The position is laid out in typical Confederate fashion at Kennesaw, with a curved parapet to allow the guns to fire in different directions.

Little Kennesaw Mountain, held by elements of French's division, has a well-preserved trench line running from the saddle between Big and Little Kennesaw and up its slope. It faithfully follows the military crest, but there are no remnants of traverses or in-trench flank protection today.

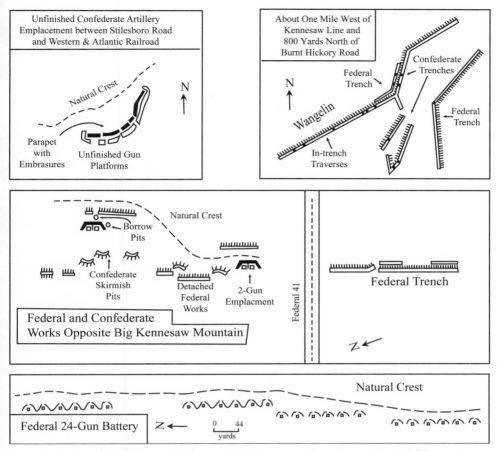

Federal and Confederate Works near Big Kennesaw (based on author's field notes)

PIGEON HILL

Pigeon Hill, occupied by Cockrell's brigade of French's division, is one-third as high as Little Kennesaw. The saddle between Little Kennesaw and Pigeon Hill is about two hundred yards from the crest of Pigeon Hill and about twenty feet lower than the crest. The hollow between the two hills is today heavily wooded. From the saddle, the ascent of Little Kennesaw is very steep and rocky. Three-fourths of the way up Little Kennesaw there is a crude line of works to cover the hollow, with no traverses or in-trench protection evident today.

The western slope of Pigeon Hill, which Giles A. Smith's brigade ascended, is quite steep. A rock outcropping appears seventy-five to one hundred yards from the bottom of the slope and is about thirty yards from the rock cap on the crest of the hill. The Confederate trench line goes from this rock outcropping south to Burnt Hickory

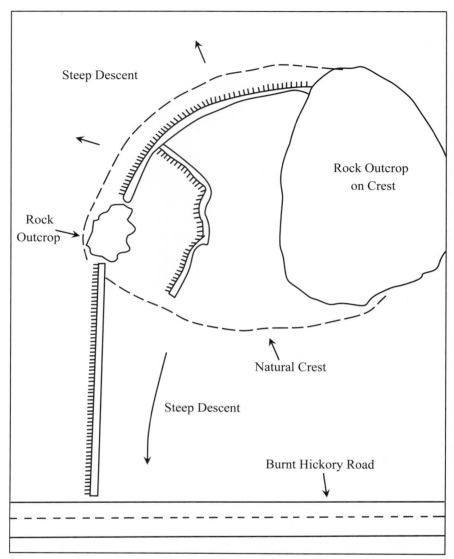

Pigeon Hill (based on author's field notes)

Road. A gap fifteen paces wide exists because of the rock outcropping; then the line continues northwest to hit the rock cap on the peak. There is a secondary line extending to the rear from this line, curving in zigzags to cover the fifteen-pace gap at the rock outcropping. Several large rocks are in the line that lies north of the rock outcropping and before it reaches the rock cap on the peak. Diggers had to move around them, and there is no ditch in front of the parapet or traverses here. Many sections of a rock breastwork that runs along and near the rock cap on the peak are gone today.

The Confederate line atop Big Kennesaw, Little Kennesaw, and Pigeon Hill forced engineers and diggers to adapt their fieldworks to high and rocky terrain. The two Kennesaws, especially, were commanding positions with narrow tops, difficult of ascent for defender and attacker alike. In these cases, the Confederates could afford to construct relatively light works of simple design. Even on Pigeon Hill, which was far less imposing, they made comparatively simple and slight works because of the rocky nature of the crest and slope. But south of Pigeon Hill the ground was much lower and blended into the surrounding countryside around the Kennesaw peaks. There was ample need for the Confederates to build more elaborate works south of the heights.

SOUTH OF PIGEON HILL

The line between Pigeon Hill and Dallas Road, held by Walker's and Bate's divisions, has many well-preserved features illustrative of Confederate earthwork construction. One hundred paces from the site of New Salem Church, which was located about eighty paces south of Burnt Hickory Road, is an emplacement for four guns. At this location, the main Confederate line lies about four hundred to five hundred yards east of the open field, which is due south of Pigeon Hill. The emplacement is on the natural crest of a shallow rise of ground; its parapet is about six feet high today. Four embrasures were cut into the parapet. There is still evidence that wooden platforms existed at the gun positions because the ground is leveled and flat. Slight ditches, one to two feet deep, front the position. The guns face northwest, while Kennesaw Mountain lies due north.

Thirty yards to the right and twenty yards behind this four-gun Confederate work is another artillery position for three guns. It is well preserved on the natural crest and has a parapet six feet high, twelve feet wide at the bottom, and four feet wide at the top. The three guns face northwest, and the ditch in front is two feet deep. This emplacement has a parapet thirty-five paces long, and there is a long traverse bank between the left and center gun positions. Moreover, the work has a refused left flank but no refused line on the right, probably because a one-gun emplacement is located to the right and a bit to the rear, which offers flank protection. This one-gun emplacement has borrow pits on both sides of the platform, made to obtain more dirt to heighten the parapet, and an embrasure in the middle of its ten-paces-long parapet.

GIST'S SALIENT

Walker's division held two prominent salients. Gist's Salient is located about 830 paces south of Burnt Hickory Road and was held by the South Carolina troops of Gist's brigade. The slope in front of the salient is gentle and long. The line forms a sharp, pointed apex toward the Federals with a one-gun emplacement in the apex. Four short secondary lines appear to the rear of the apex; one trench has a large rock, mostly underground, which blocked the progress of the diggers, so they simply stopped work and left the trench incomplete.

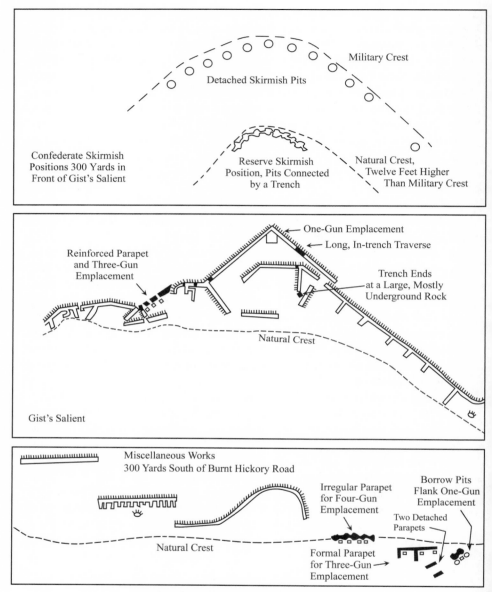

Confederate Skirmish
Positions 300 Yards in
Front of Gist's Salient

Military Crest

Detached Skirmish Pits

Reserve Skirmish
Position, Pits Connected
by a Trench

Natural Crest,
Twelve Feet Higher
Than Military Crest

One-Gun Emplacement

Long, In-trench Traverse

Reinforced Parapet
and Three-Gun
Emplacement

Trench Ends
at a Large, Mostly
Underground Rock

Natural Crest

Gist's Salient

Miscellaneous Works
300 Yards South of Burnt Hickory Road

Irregular Parapet
for Four-Gun
Emplacement

Borrow Pits
Flank One-Gun
Emplacement

Two Detached
Parapets

Natural Crest

Formal Parapet
for Three-Gun
Emplacement

Gist's Salient (based on author's field notes)

The connecting, main line of the Confederate trench that runs northward from Gist's Salient contains a number of traverses as it goes down the slope of the hill. They are placed at intervals of thirteen, twenty-eight, fourteen, and twenty-four paces, to give an example of the sequence of traverses along one segment of the line. All the traverses, interestingly, face toward the apex rather than downhill toward the right, indicating the Confederates were more worried about the enemy breaking through at the apex rather than to the north. Most of these traverses are twelve paces long, but one of them (the sixth) is twenty paces long. This particular traverse reaches back to the natural crest of the ground, which is about eight feet higher than the military crest upon which the trench line is located.

It is comparatively rare to find well-preserved skirmish pits on any Civil War battlefield, but there are some of the best examples of these kinds of works located three hundred yards in front of Gist's Salient. It is a line of detached pits along the military crest of the lower slope that fronts the apex. Each pit is about three paces long, and they are normally placed seven paces apart from each other. One of the pits, however, is twenty-three paces from its neighbor. I counted twelve pits in all and there are lots of rocks in the parapets that protect these holes. The pits are only one to two feet deep today. Reserve skirmish pits are located to the rear on the natural crest of the lower slope, which is twelve feet higher than the military crest. These reserve skirmish pits are connected by a trench.

To the left of the apex at Gist's Salient, the connecting infantry trench line goes downhill but suddenly shifts direction at a three-gun emplacement so as to allow the cannon to fire into a ravine. There are three short, straight parapets to the rear of the main trench at the jag in the line where the three-gun emplacement is located; they add strength to this odd and potentially weak angle.

HORSESHOE SALIENT

The other major salient on Walker's division line is Horseshoe Salient. It is located on a hill at least as high as Gist's Salient and about 670 paces south of Gist's position. Horseshoe Salient is about 1,500 paces south of Burnt Hickory Road.

The horseshoe in the salient is eighty paces in circumference, fifty-seven paces wide and twenty-two paces deep. It is positioned between the natural and military crest. There are three or four traverses, small and ill-preserved, located along the circumference. The semicircle is a discreet segment of trench refused on both ends, not connected to the line of trench to the left or right. Extending from near the left end of the horseshoe, the continuation of the main Confederate line runs downhill toward the bottom of Noyes Creek. It has a number of traverse ditches at regular intervals plus one in-trench traverse.

There are also some remnants of Confederate skirmish pits about forty paces in front of Horseshoe Salient and about twenty-five paces apart, some of which are dug behind boulders for added protection. These skirmish pits are on the military crest of the lower slope in front of the salient. I saw one boulder just in front of a skirmish pit that is two feet tall, two feet wide, and five feet long.

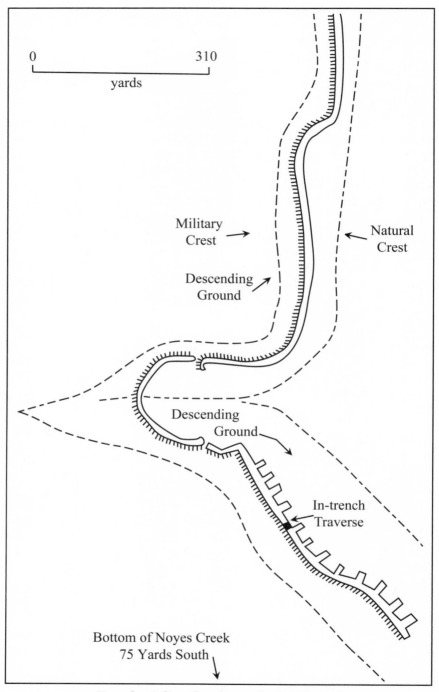

0

310

yards

Military
Crest

Natural
Crest

Descending
Ground

Descending
Ground

In-trench
Traverse

Bottom of Noyes Creek
75 Yards South

Horseshoe Salient (based on author's field notes)

Another relatively rare find on a Civil War battlefield is to discover remnants of opposing trench lines directly opposite each other. I found a Federal trench 220 paces in front of Horseshoe Salient. The Union works also appear to be the apex of a salient, or angle in the Federal line, located on ground ten feet lower than the hill on which the Horseshoe Salient rests. Another Federal angle appears sixty paces closer to Horseshoe but on lower ground than the other Union angle. There are fewer traverse ditches in the Union lines than in the Confederate works.

SOUTH OF NOYES CREEK

Noyes Creek cuts deeply into the terrain at the point where the Confederate line crosses it. South of the creek there are fascinating remnants of Rebel works with a number of unusual features, representing some of the most impressive innovations to be seen in any Civil War fieldwork system. Members of Bate's division were responsible for this segment of the Kennesaw Line.

The Confederates made a terrace of small lunettes up and down the bluff that borders the south side of Noyes Creek. Each lunette consists of two wings and thus is in the shape of a chevron. Each wing is fifteen paces long, and they are placed about eight paces apart from each other. Each parapet is about four feet lower than the previous one. There are a total of eight lunettes and the lowest one is about thirty paces from Noyes Creek.

A semicircular infantry position is located on the high ground just south of the creek. It is twenty-three paces wide at the open side, twenty paces deep, and faces west. The parapet today is three to four feet high and about the same measurement on top, twice that measurement on the bottom. An artillery position for six guns is located fifteen paces to its right. The artillery emplacement is lodged on the natural crest of the terrain. Four of the gun positions are angled toward the right, but the two on the far right are facing straight forward, or west, and have traverses for flank protection. The four on the left do not have traverses.

Farther south of this constellation of works, yet well north of Dallas Road, are two small diamond-shaped works that are incorporated into the main trench line. One is located on the first rise of ground thirty yards north of Dallas Road, and the second one is one hundred yards north of the road. Both have a triangular projection toward the Federal position. The works are fifteen paces wide and have a smaller triangular projection toward the rear. The main trench line runs directly through the works, between the two projections. The forward projection offers opportunity for angled fire along the front of the connecting infantry line, and the projection backward offers the same angled fire for the rear of that connecting line. Both of these diamond-shaped works were designed for infantry, not artillery.

North of the second diamond-shaped work, the one located one hundred yards north of Dallas Road, the main line descends toward a deep ravine. There are several traverses which are twenty paces long and placed at intervals of ten paces, and a third diamond-shaped work is located at the top of the ravine bluff. The infantry line continues north of this work but curves toward the rear as it descends the ravine slope.

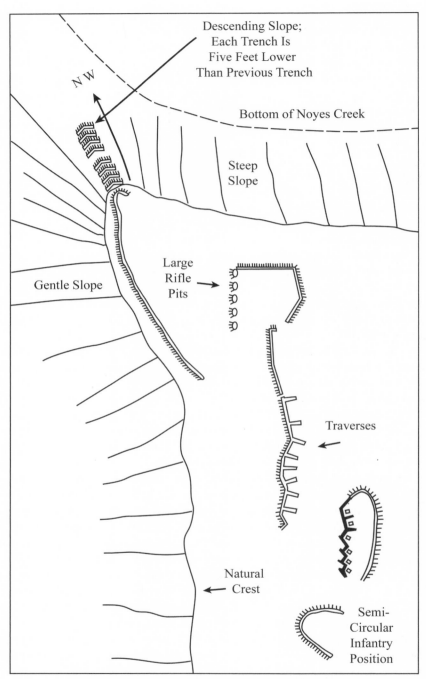

Descending Slope;
Each Trench Is
Five Feet Lower
Than Previous Trench

N W

Bottom of Noyes Creek

Steep
Slope

Large
Rifle
Pits

Gentle Slope

Traverses

Natural
Crest

Semi-
Circular
Infantry
Position

South of Noyes Creek (based on author's field notes)

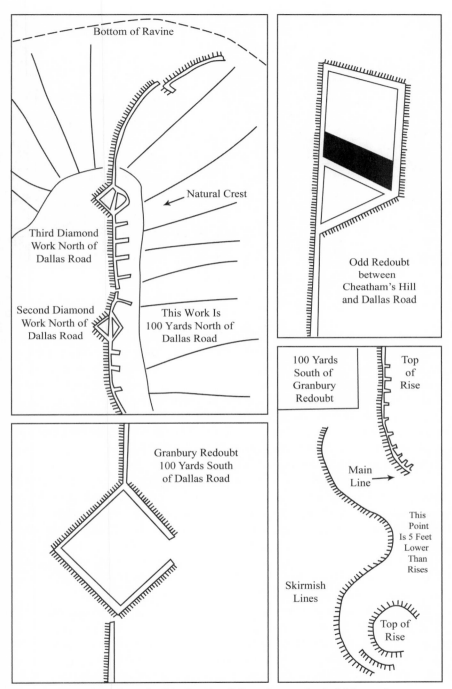

North and South of Dallas Road (based on author's field notes)

Rocky Confederate trench (Earl J. Hess)

SOUTH OF DALLAS ROAD

Cleburne's division held the line from Dallas Road to Mebane's battery emplacement near Cheatham's Hill. His men continued the quirky, innovative methods of earthwork construction displayed along Bate's line. One hundred yards south of Dallas Road, Granbury's Texas Brigade constructed a redoubt on the first high ground south of the roadway, yet it rises only about eight feet above the surrounding area. Granbury's Redoubt also is shaped like a diamond, although the main trench line connects with its flanks rather than running through its middle. An opening at the rear allows for easy entrance and exit.

South of Granbury's Redoubt, 350 yards north of Mebane's battery and 75 yards south of the Good Samaritan Marker, there is an unusual work I call the Odd Redoubt for lack of a better identifying term. It has a large traverse bank in the middle that is four to five feet tall. There are no clear remnants of artillery positions inside the work and no apparent way to get guns into it, so I conclude it is a small infantry redoubt. The work is located atop a rise of ground eight feet high with gentle slopes and is placed along the sector of Cleburne's division line that was attacked by Newton's division of the Fourth Corps on June 27.

The Confederates encountered a large rock outcropping fifty yards south of the Odd Redoubt. In fact, it was the top part of a huge rock that mostly lay underground. They dug the trench around several portions of it that stick out of the ground. One such cropping is six feet long and three feet wide. At one point the open trench exposes several feet of rock that stretches from the bottom of the trench nearly to the top of the parapet. A similar sized rock lies ten feet away from the former one, and it is located perfectly in the middle of the trench.

CHEATHAM'S HILL

One of the most interesting places at Kennesaw Mountain is Cheatham's Hill, not only for the terrible human drama that played out there on June 27 and for nearly a week after, but also because of the intricate network of Confederate earthworks that were constructed on the hill. Those earthworks, thanks to dedicated efforts by McCook's men to preserve the battlefield, are available as the main course of study in Kennesaw's outdoor classroom. It is best to see them, as is the case with all battlefields, in the late winter when the leaves are still off the trees and the weather begins to warm up.

The Confederates invested a good deal of time and energy in fortifying Cheatham's Hill, but it is not easy to determine exactly when all the earthwork remnants one can see today were built. Certainly the main line's parapet and trench were made on the night of June 20 and heavily improved during the next few days. But I do not know when the Tennesseans who held the hill constructed the secondary lines inside the angle and behind the base of the salient. The only thing certain is that what one sees there today are the eroded remnants of what the Confederates left behind when they evacuated Cheatham's Hill on the night of July 2, 1864.

Let us start our tour on the right end of the salient. Mebane's battery is a large, square work surprisingly big for only two guns. The main line continues from there in a pronounced curve to take in the top of Cheatham's Hill and conform to the shallow depression caused by a branch of John Ward Creek. The line actually faces south along the northern side of the branch. Its trench has traverses stretching toward the rear only along three segments of its length; for close to half of its length, there are no traverses at all. Moreover, there are only a handful of in-trench traverses in the main trench.

Inside the salient the Confederates eventually constructed two secondary lines. One of them goes more than halfway across the gorge of the salient, coming close to closing it off, but instead stops at the top of the natural crest of ground. The other secondary line is placed very close behind the main trench line and covers the right wing and center of the salient position. It was constructed in segments, however, not in a continuous line. Both secondary lines have numerous in-trench traverses but only one has traverses that extend backward from the trench. At only one point, where a communication trench leads back from the main line at the angle and intersects one of the secondary lines, can one gain access to the secondary line from the main trench. Otherwise, the secondary works are not connected at all with the main line.

One segment of the south-facing left wing of the salient has an interesting feature. The Confederates dug a secondary line immediately behind the main trench and began to connect it to the main line with a series of passages. These passages essentially serve as traverses, but after completing five of them and starting five more, the digging stopped. Only on one segment of this south-facing left wing of the salient can one see the evidence of a ditch in front of the main trench line.

A close examination of the ground vividly demonstrates the truth of the assertion that Confederate engineers placed the main trench line too far back to take ad-

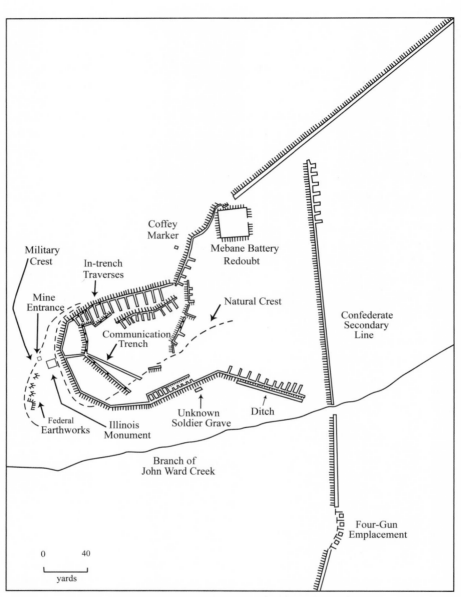

Cheatham's Hill (based on author's field notes)

Traverses at Dead Angle (Earl J. Hess)

vantage of the military crest of this shallow rise of ground. Some small remnants of Federal earthworks constructed by Mitchell's brigade remain near the military crest today, and the entrance to the Federal mine is marked, although it is obvious the mine gallery has long since collapsed. The Illinois monument stands just below the natural crest of the slope, in front of the Confederate earthworks. The marker referring to Sergeant Coffey of the Twenty-Second Indiana also remains where it had been placed by the veterans of McCook's brigade.

To the rear of the salient, a major Confederate secondary line is still intact, designed to cover the entire base of the salient. It also has numerous traverses on its far right wing. South of the branch of John Ward Creek, there is a well-preserved Confederate artillery emplacement for four guns designed to fire at the Federals as they attacked the hill. The main Confederate trench line continues south of the branch for some distance.

SOUTH OF CHEATHAM'S HILL

The highlight of a tour along the Confederate line south of Cheatham's Hill is the Upper and Lower Artillery Emplacements. Amazingly elaborate and well preserved, this collection of earthworks is a good case study of mixing large artillery concentrations with infantry works in a wooded, hilly terrain. The Upper Emplacement has eight positions for guns—some are connected, some are not, and one has a rounded mound of earth inside the parapet that separates two gun platforms. All positions except one have embrasures. Three adjacent gun positions have all the ground encompassing their collective area leveled and smoothed out, but the rest have only the individual gun position, not the area between them, leveled. A ditch three to four feet deep is in front of the guns. This Upper Emplacement occupies a high hill. Six gun emplacements point toward the northwest, and two aim at the southwest. The six that point northwest are arrayed in two lines, with three of them a few feet behind and on ground that is five feet higher than the three in the front line. There is a line of infantry trench to protect the rear of this concentration, with a ditch along part of the parapet. The infantry line runs along the military crest and is six to eight feet lower than the guns. There are two gaps in the line that are about three paces wide to allow the gunners to move cannon in and out.

The Lower Emplacement was positioned to take advantage of the available ground and support the Upper Emplacement. It is located forty-six paces southeast of the Upper Emplacement along a spur of the hill that the Upper Emplacement rests on. It is also ten feet lower than the Upper Emplacement. The Lower Emplacement has six gun positions, three of which face west, two face south, and one, in the apex, can face either way. The two positions that face south are connected, but the rest are separated by long traverses. South of the lower artillery position, an infantry trench lies about twenty-five paces from the guns and on ground that is twelve feet lower. This line has several traverses of varied lengths and some in-trench traverses. On the right, the line angles north to cover the front of the Lower Artillery Emplacement and the gap between the Upper and Lower Emplacements. This west-facing infantry trench ascends twenty-five feet in elevation from the lowest point of its line as it goes from south to north. The main Confederate trench line continues south of this infantry trench that protects the Lower Emplacement, but there is no continuation of the main line northward from the Upper Emplacement that can be seen today.

Walking north from Powder Springs and Marietta Road toward the Upper and Lower Artillery Emplacements, there is a high rise north of the first branch of John Ward Creek and south of its second branch. The Confederates planted a one-gun artillery emplacement on top, just below the peak on the north side of the rise. It is located four paces behind the infantry trench, with a gun platform behind a parapet and an embrasure in the middle of the parapet. The main line of the infantry trench has numerous traverses four paces long as well as many in-trench traverses.

FEDERAL EARTHWORKS

It is not possible to understand the Federal earthworks at Kennesaw Mountain in the same way that one can examine and explain the Confederate works. Sherman had no continuous series of high ground upon which to locate his line. The Federal position is much more irregular, with remnants existing only in segments scattered about the landscape. Those Federal remnants that are accessible tend to be uniform and unsurprising in their construction and configuration. One rarely sees anything like the quirky innovations apparent in the nearly continuous Confederate line.

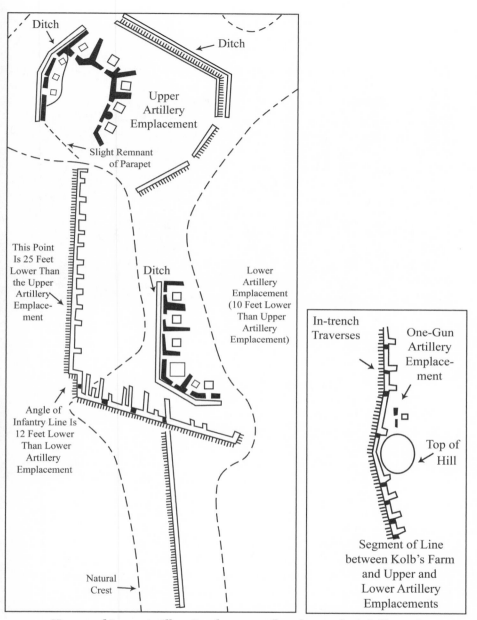

Ditch

Ditch

Upper
Artillery
Emplacement

Slight Remnant
of Parapet

This Point
Is 25 Feet
Lower Than
the Upper
Artillery
Emplace-
ment

Ditch

Lower
Artillery
Emplacement
(10 Feet Lower
Than Upper
Artillery
Emplacement)

Angle of
Infantry Line Is
12 Feet Lower
Than Lower
Artillery
Emplacement

In-trench
Traverses

One-Gun
Artillery
Emplace-
ment

Top of
Hill

Natural
Crest

Segment of Line
between Kolb's Farm
and Upper and
Lower Artillery
Emplacements

Upper and Lower Artillery Emplacements (based on author's field notes)

Barnard's photograph of Federal works near Hardage House
(Barnard, Photographic Views, *no. 31)*

The Twenty-Four-Gun Battery, however, is something of an exception to the rule. It is located on a rise opposite Little Kennesaw and consists of four segments of six guns each, to total twenty-four emplacements. Each segment of six guns lies behind a parapet about 20 paces long. The individual gun emplacements within each segment are eight paces apart from the next, all in a straight line. There is a ditch in front, and the parapet is four and a half feet tall. Every gun emplacement has an embrasure. The second segment is positioned 43 paces to the left and 10 paces in front of the first. The third segment of six guns is located 12 paces to the left and 15 paces to the front of the second segment. The fourth segment is 123 paces to the left and six feet lower than the third segment.

All segments are placed just behind the natural crest of the rise, and all guns are able to fire to the front only, not to the flanks. The third and fourth segments have connected parapets, while the first two are contiguous one-gun emplacements. In the fourth segment, the gun positions are dug deeper than in the other three, as much as three feet into the ground today, but the positions are separated by six paces of natural ground as well. The gunners had to dig deeper to obtain enough fill dirt to make their parapet continuous across the wider expanse of this fourth segment compared to the width of the other three. They did not dig a ditch, so could not obtain fill dirt from that source. There are no signs of infantry trenches anywhere near the Twenty-Four-Gun Battery today.

There is a significant cluster of earthworks located north of Burnt Hickory Road close to a mile west of Pigeon Hill. It was occupied by Colonel Hugo Wangelin's brigade of Osterhaus's Fifteenth Corps division. The cluster is important because it demonstrates that the Federals used in-trench traverses and because there is a mix of Confederate and Union earthworks here on top of a slight rise. Today there is an open field covering most of the area but the remnants are in a patch of woods. The Confederates had a line facing west here, located on the western side of the top to conform to the military crest of the rise. After they abandoned this position, the Federals built a short east-facing line immediately in front (west) of the Confederate trench. This served as a secondary, supporting position for the main Federal line which was located behind (east) of the Confederate trench. The two Union lines (the main one and the supporting line) are about thirty paces apart from each other with the top of the rise and the former Confederate works between.

George Barnard exposed a widely reproduced photograph of Federal gun emplacements located near the Hardage House along Burnt Hickory Road in the spring of 1866. The emplacement is south of the roadway, and the view takes in Pigeon Hill and Little Kennesaw Mountain. The photograph shows that the Federal gunners used a variety of readily available material to make their revetment, including saplings woven around small posts, boards, and logs. No head logs or obstructions in front of the works are apparent.

LESSONS

What conclusions can we draw from a tour of the outdoor classroom at Kennesaw Mountain? One point that impressed me during several days spent examining the line was that short fields of fire were very common. Owing to the hilly, uneven terrain, it often was not possible to take the high ground and obtain more than a clear view forty or fifty yards in front wherein one could see an approaching enemy. Civil War soldiers and their leaders did not seem to mind this very much. As long as they were alert, they could deliver enough fire to stop an attack during a relatively short approach.

Another lesson to be learned from the Kennesaw Line is that, given time and opportunity, the Confederates became very inventive in devising new forms and styles of earthwork configuration. I have never seen examples such as the diamond-shaped earthworks north of Dallas Road anywhere else on a Civil War site, and I have visited more than three hundred such sites. There are far more extant traverses stretching back from the trench at Kennesaw Mountain than anywhere else in the Western theater of operations. One would have to go to the North Anna and to Cold Harbor to see similar accumulations of traverses in the Eastern theater. Also, in-trench traverses (banks of earth that block the trench in order to provide flank protection) can be seen only in the Atlanta campaign. I have observed none of these unusual features anywhere else, east or west, and more of them can be found at Kennesaw than at any other Atlanta campaign site. The armies engaged in the drive toward Atlanta apparently were concerned about flank protection more than their comrades in other operations.

Tree growth on earthwork remnant (Earl J. Hess)

Confederate trench with no ditch (Earl J. Hess)

Also, the common form of earthwork during the Atlanta campaign was to dig a trench but rarely do much ditching in front of the work. That tended to be true of the Western campaigns in general. There was a tendency in the Eastern theater to dig ditches in front rather than to dig trenches behind the parapet. One can see many examples of this in Virginia, such as at Petersburg and at Jetersville during the Appomattox campaign. If one goes to Bentonville, North Carolina, the only extant Union earthwork that has a ditch in front and no trench is one dug by Eastern troops of the Twentieth Corps.

Another impression one gains from tramping through the woods along six miles of nearly continuous trench line is the immense amount of labor involved in building just one fortified position. The remnants today offer an opportunity to understand what was involved in terms of manually shoveling out the system with pick and spade. The entire length of the Kennesaw Line extended another two miles north of the northern boundary of the park and another two miles south of the southern boundary. Its ten-mile length represented only one of eighteen Confederate fortified lines constructed during the Atlanta campaign, and this is not to mention the digging performed by Sherman's troops. Historic photographs help a good deal to illustrate the immense amount of work by participants of both armies during the campaign, but they cannot give one the impression produced by climate, tree cover, rocks, clay bound soil, and hilly terrain that can only be had by walking extensively across the battlefield of Kennesaw Mountain.

Notes

ABBREVIATIONS

ADAH	Alabama Department of Archives and History
AHC	Atlanta History Center
AHC-UW	American Heritage Center, University of Wyoming
ALPL	Abraham Lincoln Presidential Library
ASU	Augusta State University
BC	Bowdoin College
CL-UM	William L. Clements Library, University of Michigan
CU	Cornell University
CWM	College of William and Mary
DU	Duke University
EU	Emory University
GLIAH	Gilder Lehrman Institute of American History
IHS	Indiana Historical Society
KHS	Kansas Historical Society
KMNBP	Kennesaw Mountain National Battlefield Park
LC	Library of Congress
LMU	Lincoln Memorial University
LSU	Louisiana State University
MHM	Missouri History Museum
MOC	Museum of the Confederacy
MSU	Mississippi State University
MU	Miami University
NARA	National Archives and Records Administration
NC	Navarro College
NCSA	North Carolina State Archives
NL	Newberry Library
NYSL	New York State Library
OHS	Ohio Historical Society
OR	*The War of the Rebellion: A Compilation of the Official Records of the Union and Confederate Armies*. *OR* citations take the following form: volume number(part number):page number(s)—e.g., *OR* 38(4):479–80. All citations are to series 1.
RBHPC	Rutherford B. Hayes Presidential Center
RU	Rice University
SC-SU	Stanford University

SHSI	State Historical Society of Iowa
SHSM-C	State Historical Society of Missouri, Research Center Columbia
SHSM-SL	State Historical Society of Missouri, Research Center St. Louis
SOR	*Supplement to the Official Records of the Union and Confederate Armies*. *SOR* citations take the following form: part number, volume number:page number(s)—e.g., *SOR*, Pt. 2, 46:548.
SRNB	Stones River National Battlefield
SU	Syracuse University
TC	The Citadel
TSLA	Tennessee State Library and Archives
UA	University of Alabama
UAF	University of Arkansas, Fayetteville
UGA	University of Georgia
UH	University of Houston
UI	University of Iowa
UK	University of Kentucky
UM	University of Mississippi
UMBC	University of Maryland, Baltimore County
UNC	University of North Carolina
UND	University of Notre Dame
USAMHI	U.S. Army Military History Institute
USM	University of Southern Mississippi
UTA	University of Texas, Austin
UTC	University of Tennessee, Chattanooga
UTK	University of Tennessee, Knoxville
UVA	University of Virginia
UW	University of Washington
VHS	Virginia Historical Society
VT	Virginia Polytechnic Institute and State University
WHS	Wisconsin Historical Society
YU	Yale University

PREFACE

1. Arbuckle, *Civil War Experiences*, 65.

CHAPTER ONE

1. Sherman to Halleck, September 15, 1864, *OR* 38(1):62–63.
2. Castel, *Decision in the West*, 111, 115, 121.
3. Ibid., 121, 123, 131–35, 137–38, 145–51.
4. Ibid., 152, 154, 156, 159, 160–68, 173–79, 188.
5. Ibid., 192–95, 200–202, 204–6; McMurry, *Atlanta*, 82–83.
6. Castel, *Decision in the West*, 217–21, 223, 225–26, 229–30, 233, 235, 237–41, 243–46; Howard, *Autobiography*, 1:551, 553; Hazen, *Narrative*, 257–58; Dean, "Pickett's Mill," 369, 371.
7. Castel, *Decision in the West*, 247.

8. Sherman to Halleck, September 15, 1864, *OR* 38(1):65–66; Sherman, *Memoirs*, 2:45; Osborn, *Trials and Triumphs*, 158.

9. Sherman to Halleck, June 5, 7, 8, 1864, Special Field Orders No. 21, Headquarters, Military Division of the Mississippi, June 9, 1864, *OR* 38(4):408, 428, 433, 445–46; Sherman, *Memoirs*, 2:50–51; Castel, *Decision in the West*, 264–66.

10. Castel, *Decision in the West*, 267, 269, 273; French, *Two Wars*, 201; Johnston, *Narrative*, 336; Sherman to Halleck, September 15, 1864, *OR* 38(1):67. McMurry, *Atlanta*, 103, calls the Mountain Line the First Kennesaw Line.

11. Sherman to Halleck, September 15, 1864, *OR* 38(1):67.

12. Castel, *Decision in the West*, 267, 270; Sherman to Halleck, September 15, 1864, *OR* 38(1):67; Howard to Clark, September 9, 1864, *OR* 38(3):80; Sherman to Halleck, June 13, 1864, *OR* 38(4):466; Albert Quincy Porter Diary, June 16–17, 1864, MSU; John C. Brown Diary, June 13, 1864, UI.

13. Castel, *Decision in the West*, 275–76; Sherman, *Memoirs*, 2:53.

14. Special Field Orders No. 25, Headquarters, Military Division of the Mississippi, June 14, 1864, *OR* 38(4):479–80.

15. Castel, *Decision in the West*, 278.

16. Howard to Whipple, September 18, 1864, *OR* 38(1):196; Whipple to Hooker and Howard, June 15, 1864, *OR* 38(4):483.

17. Sherman to Halleck, June 15, 1864, Sherman to Schofield, June 15, 1864, *OR* 38(4):481, 486.

18. Sherman to Halleck, June 16, 1864, *OR* 38(4):492; L. G. Bennett and Haigh, *History of the Thirty-Sixth*, 604.

19. Castel, *Decision in the West*, 280–81; Johnston, *Narrative*, 338; French, *Two Wars*, 203; McMurry, *Atlanta*, 103.

20. Byrne, *Uncommon Soldiers*, 162; Bohrnstedt, *Soldiering with Sherman*, 109; George G. Truair to father, June 17, 1864, Truair Family Papers, UTA; O'Connor to not stated, September 7, 1864, *OR* 38(2):229.

21. Sherman to Halleck, June 17, 1864, Sherman to Thomas, June 17, 1864, Whipple to Sherman, June 18, 1864, *OR* 38(4):498–99, 510–11; Castel, *Decision in the West*, 282–83; Thomas to Sawyer, July 16, 1864, Howard to Whipple, September 18, 1864, Wagner to Lee, September 10, 1864, *OR* 38(1):149, 197, 334.

22. Johnston, *Narrative*, 338.

23. Geary to Perkins, September 15, 1864, *OR* 38(2):131; Castel, *Decision in the West*, 275; Gile to not stated, June 18, 1864, David Herrick Gile Papers, YU.

24. Sherman to Thomas, June 18, 1864, Schofield to Sherman, June 18, 1864, Sherman to Schofield, June 18, 1864, *OR* 38(4):508–9, 515.

25. Sherman to [Grant], June 18, 1864, *OR* 38(4):507–8.

26. Ibid.

27. Howard to Thomas, June 18, 1864, Thomas to Howard, June 18, 1864, *OR* 38(4):512–13; Howard to Whipple, September 18, 1864, Newton to assistant adjutant general, Army of the Cumberland, September 1864, Bryan to Opdycke, September 1864, Wagner to Lee, September 10, 1864, *OR* 38(1):197, 295, 319, 334; Neal to Ra, June 20, 1864, Andrew Jackson Neal Papers, EU; French, *Two Wars*, 203.

28. Loring to French, June 18, 1864, *OR* 38(4):780.

29. Wynne and Taylor, *This War So Horrible*, 92; Johnston to Bragg, June 19, 1864, *OR* 38(4):780; Johnston to Cooper, October 20, 1864, *OR* 38(3):617; *OR Atlas*, pl. 59, no. 3; Marietta quadrant map, U.S. Department of the Interior.

30. French, *Two Wars*, 203.

31. Baumgartner, *Blood & Sacrifice*, 148, 150.

32. French, *Two Wars*, 203; Daniel Harris Reynolds Diary, June 18–19, 1864, UAF; Dacus, *Reminiscences*, unpaginated.

33. [Thomas M. Jack] to W. J. Morris, June 19, 1864, Special Orders From May 9th 1864 to June 19th 1864, Head Quarters, Army of the Mississippi, ch. 2, No. 221½, RG109, NARA; Meeker to Taylor, June 19, 1864, *OR* 38(4):529.

34. Sherman to Halleck, June 19, 1864, Sherman to Thomas, June 19, 1864, *OR* 38(4):519–20; Thomas to Sawyer, July 16, 1864, *OR* 38(1):150; John W. Tuttle Diary, June 19, 1864, UK.

35. Banning to Wilson, September 9, 1864, *OR* 38(1):702; Blair to Clark, September 12, 1864, Malmborg to Cox, June 21, 1864, *OR* 38(3):552, 559; Jackson, *Colonel's Diary*, 134; *Story of the Service of Company E*, 295.

36. Schofield to Sherman, September 10, 1864, *OR* 38(2):513; Kerr, *Fighting with Ross' Texas Cavalry*, 151; Cox, *Atlanta*, 107; Cox, *Military Reminiscences*, 2:256n; Dayton to Schofield, June 19, 1864, *OR* 38(4):529; Johnston, *Narrative*, 339.

37. Johnston, *Narrative*, 339; Castel, *Decision in the West*, 289–90; Ratchford to Hindman and Stevenson, June 19, 1864, *OR* 38(4):781.

38. Sherman to Halleck, June 19, 1864, *OR* 38(4):519; William J. Hardee to wife, June 19, 1864, Hardee Family Papers, ADAH.

39. Gates, *Rough Side of War*, 220.

40. Sherman, *Memoirs*, 2:52, 56.

41. Sherman to Thomas, June 20, 1864, *OR* 38(4):535; Sherman, *Memoirs*, 2:57; Howard, *Autobiography*, 1:580.

42. Thomas to Sawyer, July 16, 1864, Howard to Whipple, September 18, 1864, *OR* 38(1):150, 198; Whipple to Hooker, June 20, 1864, *OR* 38(4):536.

43. Howard to Whipple, September 18, 1864, Stanley to Fullerton, 1864, Whitaker to Sinclair, 1864, Fullerton, Fourth Corps Journal, June 20, 1864, *OR* 38(1):198, 223–24, 243–44, 883; Day, *Story of the One Hundred and First Ohio*, 224; Howard to brother, June 21, 1864, Charles Henry Howard Collection, BC; William J. Hardee to wife, June 21, 1864, ADAH.

44. Stanley to Fullerton, 1864, Whitaker to Sinclair, 1864, *OR* 38(1):224, 243–44; Howard to brother, June 21, 1864, Charles Henry Howard Collection, BC.

45. Stanley to Fullerton, 1864, Fullerton, Fourth Corps Journal, June 20, 1864, *OR* 38(1):224, 883; Thomas to Sherman, June 20, 1864, *OR* 38(4):534; Day, *Story of the One Hundred and First Ohio*, 224–25; Howard to brother, June 21, 1864, Charles Henry Howard Collection, BC; J. M. Raymond Diary, June 20, 1864, KHS; William J. Hardee to wife, June 21, 1864, ADAH; Yates, *Historical Guide*, 21; Howard, *Autobiography*, 1:568–69.

46. Johnston to Cooper, October 20, 1864, *OR* 38(3):617; Johnston, "Opposing Sherman's Advance," 271; Rose to [Lawton], September 14, 1864, *OR* 38(1):287; William J. Hardee to wife, June 21, 1864, ADAH.

47. French, *Two Wars*, 205; Loring to French, June 20, 1864, *OR* 38(4):782.

48. Storrs, "Kennesaw Mountain," 136–37.

49. Ibid., 138; French, "Kennesaw Mountain," 275.

50. Schofield to Sherman, June 20, 1864, Schofield to Cox, June 20, 1864, Ross to Jackson, June 20, 1864, *OR* 38(4):539–40, 783; Cox, *Military Reminiscences*, 1:257–58;

Schofield to Sherman, September 10, 1864, *OR* 38(2):513; Cox, *Atlanta*, 107–8; McMurry, "Kolb's Farm," 24; Kerr, *Fighting with Ross's Texas Cavalry*, 151.

51. Howard, *Autobiography*, 1:569–70; Howard to Whipple, September 18, 1864, Kirby to Mason, September 11, 1864, Wood to Fullerton, September 10, 1864, Hotchkiss to Bestow, September 10, 1864, Fullerton, Fourth Corps Journal, June 21, 1864, *OR* 38(1):198, 232, 380, 394, 884–85; Howard to Thomas, June 21, 1864, *OR* 38(4):546; Day, *Story of the One Hundred and First Ohio*, 226–28; J. M. Raymond Diary, June 21, 1864, KHS; Harwell, "Campaign from Chattanooga," 269.

52. Askew to McGrath, September 12, 1864, Gray to McGrath, September 15, 1864, *OR* 38(1):408–10, 414–15; Howard, *Autobiography*, 1:569–70.

53. Hooker to Whipple, June 21, 1864, *OR* 38(4):547–48.

54. Sherman to Thomas, June 21, 1864, Schofield to Cox, June 21, 1864, Cox to Campbell, June 21, 1864, *OR* 38(4):544, 552–53.

55. Whipple to Hooker, June 21, 1864, Sherman to Schofield, June 21, 1864, Schofield to Sherman, June 21, 1864, *OR* 38(4):547, 551–52; Thomas to Sawyer, July 16, 1864, Kimball to assistant adjutant general, Second Division, Fourth Corps, August 4, 1864, Bryan to Opdycke, September 1864, Bradley to Lee, September 12, 1864, *OR* 38(1):150, 303–4, 319, 354; Quaife, *From the Cannon's Mouth*, 327.

56. Johnston, "Opposing Sherman's Advance," 271; McMurry, *John Bell Hood*, 112; W. H. Brooker Diary, June 21, 1864, RU; W. B. Corbitt Diary, June 21, 1864, EU; Isaac Gaillard Foster Diary, June 20, 1864, James Foster and Family Correspondence, LSU; Jesse L. Henderson Civil War Diary, June 20–21, 1864, UM; diary, June 21, 1864, Emmett Ross Papers, MSU; Johnston, *Narrative*, 339; *OR Atlas*, Pl. 59, No. 3; Marietta quadrant map, U.S. Department of the Interior; Leggett to Alexander, June 28, 1864, *OR* 38(3):563.

57. French, *Two Wars*, 205; W. L. Truman Memoirs, June 20–21, 1864, www.cedarcroft .com; C. Wright, *A Corporal's Story*, 122; Storrs, "Kennesaw Mountain," 137–39.

58. Sears to Sanders, June 21, 1864, *OR* 38(4):784.

59. Sherman to Thomas, June 21, 1864, *OR* 38(4):546; Malmborg to Cox, June 21, 1864, *OR* 38(3):560.

60. Peter J. Osterhaus Diary, June 18–21, 1864, Osterhaus Family Papers, MHM; Merrill and Marshall, "Georgia through Kentucky Eyes," 330; Stanley to Fullerton, 1864, Kimball to assistant adjutant general, Second Division, Fourth Corps, August 4, 1864, *OR* 38(1):223, 304; L. G. Bennett and Haigh, *History of the Thirty-Sixth*, 604; John W. Tuttle Diary, June 18, 1864, UK; Ervin, "Genius and Heroism," 497; Gates, *Rough Side of War*, 219.

61. Sherman to Halleck, June 21, 1864, *OR* 38(4):544; Sherman to Halleck, September 15, 1864, *OR* 38(1):68; Sherman to Stanton, June 21, 1864, *OR* 39(2):132.

CHAPTER TWO

1. Garrett, *Confederate Diary*, 70; William Cline Diary, June 22, 1864, UND; Sherman to Thomas, June 22, 1864, Sherman to Schofield, June 22, 1864, Johnston to Bragg, June 27, 1864, *OR* 38(4):557–58, 566, 795–96; W. H. Brooker Diary, June 22, 1864, RU; Peter J. Osterhaus diary, June 22, 1864, Osterhaus Family Papers, MHM; Castel, *Decision in the West*, 290–91.

2. Hooker to Schofield, June 22, 1864, Weekly Report of Effective Force, Department

of the Cumberland, June 27, 1864, *OR* 38(4):565, 627; Castel, *Decision in the West*, 291.

3. Hooker to Whipple, June 22, 1864, Geary to Perkins, September 15, 1864, Jones to Forbes, August 1, 1864, O'Connor to not stated, September 7, 1864, *OR* 38(2):14, 132–33, 211, 229; Hooker to Whipple, June 22, 1864, *OR* 38(4):562; Spencer to Father, June 24, 1864, Israel Spencer Letters, Civil War Collection, SC-SU.

4. Quaife, *From the Cannon's Mouth*, 327; Williams to Perkins, September 12, 1864, Knipe to Pittman, September 13, 1864, Carman to Fay, September 6, 1864, Ketcham to Fay, September 6, 1864, Robinson to Pittman, July 24, 1864, *OR* 38(2):31–32, 42, 70, 79, 89; Hooker to Whipple, June 22, 1864, *OR* 38(4):562; Morhous, *Reminiscences*, 103; Cook and Benton, *"Dutchess County Regiment,"* 93–94; Morse, *Letters Written during the War*, 171–72; Irving Bronson, "Recollections of the Civil War," 42, Bruce Catton Collection, TC; Toombs, *Reminiscences of the War*, 141.

5. McMurry, "Kolb's Farm," 22, 25; D. P. Conyagham dispatch, June 22, 1864, in *New York Herald*, July 4, 1864; Carman to Gay, September 6, 1864, *OR* 38(2):70; Bauer, *Soldiering*, 129.

6. Schofield to Sherman, September 10, 1864, Hascall to Campbell, September 10, 1864, *OR* 38(2):513, 569; Hascall to Schofield, June 22, 1864, Abstract from Returns, Department of the Ohio, June, 1864, *OR* 38(4):567, 654; Schofield, *Forty-Six Years*, 135; Thoburn, *My Experiences*, 97; Cox, *Military Reminiscences*, 1:258; McMurry, "Kolb's Farm," 21.

7. Cox, *Military Reminiscences*, 1:258; Ross to Jackson, June 22, 1864, *OR* 38(4):785–86.

8. Hooker to Whipple, June 22, 1864, 12:00 P.M., *OR* 38(4):562–63; Hascall to Campbell, September 10, 1864, *OR* 38(2):569.

9. Hascall to Campbell, September 10, 1864, Strickland to Kerstetter, August 14, 1864, Gallup to not stated, August 11, 1864, *OR* 38(2):569, 646–47, 655; McMurry, "Kolb's Farm," 21–22.

10. Hascall to Campbell, September 10, 1864, Gallup to not stated, August 11, 1864, *OR* 38(2):569, 655; Morhous, *Reminiscences*, 102; Bauer, *Soldiering*, 129–33.

11. Quaife, *From the Cannon's Mouth*, 327–28; Williams to Perkins, September 12, 1864, Ruger to Pittman, September 11, 1864, *OR* 38(2):32, 61; Toombs, *Reminiscences of the War*, 140; William Merrell, "Personal Memories of the Civil War," LMU.

12. Hooker to Whipple, June 22, 1864, 3:15 P.M. and 4:00 P.M., *OR* 38(4):561.

13. Thomas to Sherman, June 22, 1864, Whipple to Hooker, June 22, 1864, 4:30 P.M. and no time, but received 7:20 P.M., *OR* 38(4):559, 562.

14. Schofield to Cox, June 22, 1864, 4:15 P.M., Schofield to Stoneman, June 22, 1864, 4:15 P.M., *OR* 38(4):568; Schofield, *Forty-Six Years*, 133.

15. Stevenson to [Ratchford], August 19, 1864, *OR* 38(3):814; Tower, *A Carolinian Goes to War*, 192; J. C. Thompson to A. P. Stewart, December 8, 1867, Joseph E. Johnston Papers, CWM; Clayton narrative, Henry DeLamar Clayton Sr. Papers, UA; McMurry, "Kolb's Farm," 21, 25; Bragg, *Joe Brown's Army*, 86, 89.

16. McMurry, *Atlanta*, 105; McMurry, "Kolb's Farm," 22; McMurry, *John Bell Hood*, 112.

17. Stevenson to [Ratchford], August 19, 1864, *OR* 38(3):814; Tower, *A Carolinian Goes to War*, 192; E. D. Willett Diary, June 22, 1862, ADAH; Willis Dunston Banks to Joe, June 24, 1864, Banks Family Papers, UGA.

18. Stevenson to [Ratchford], August 19, 1864, *OR* 38(3):815; Gallup to not stated, August 11, 1864, *OR* 38(2):655; Castel, *Decision in the West*, 294; McMurry, "Kolb's

Farm," 22. As with many Civil War engagements, the exact time of Hood's advance is a matter of opinion. The best evidence indicates that the Confederates advanced at 5:00 P.M., but other commentators indicated 3:00 P.M., 4:00 P.M., 4:30 P.M., and 5:30 P.M. See W. H. Brooker Diary, June 22, 1864, RU; Phillips, *Personal Reminiscences*, 52; Wynne and Taylor, *This War So Horrible*, 97; McMurry, "Kolb's Farm," 23; Hooker to Whipple, June 22, 1864, *OR* 38(4):563; Thomas to Sawyer, July 16, 1864, *OR* 38(1):150; Nichol diary, June 22, 1864, David Nichol Papers, Harrisburg Civil War Round Table Collection, USAMHI.

19. Stevenson to [Ratchford], August 19, 1864, *OR* 38(3):814; John Fleeman to wife, June 23, 1864, in A. L. Jordan, *Gen. Jos. E. Johnston*, 42; Bauer, *Soldiering*, 133–34; Levi Eaton to wife, July 1, 1864, Eaton Family Papers, NYSL; Alanson B. Cone Memoir, June 22, 1864, NYSL; Morhous, *Reminiscences*, 103; Castel, *Decision in the West*, 294–95.

20. Hascall to Campbell, September 10, 1864, Gallup to not stated, August 11, 1864, *OR* 38(2):569, 655; Phillips, *Personal Reminiscences*, 52.

21. Williams to Perkins, September 12, 1864, *OR* 38(2):32; Quaife, *From the Cannon's Mouth*, 328; Morse, *Letters Written during the War*, 172; Irving Bronson, "Recollections of the Civil War," Bruce Catton Collection, TC.

22. Stevenson to [Ratchford], August 19, 1864, *OR* 38(3):815; Williams to Perkins, September 12, 1864, Ruger to Pittman, September 11, 1864, Carman to Fay, September 6, 1864, *OR* 38(2):32, 61, 70; W. Walton, *Civil War Courtship*, 89; George G. Truair to father, June 28, 1864, Truair Family Papers, UTA; Bryant, *History of the Third Regiment of Wisconsin*, 247.

23. William Merrell, "Personal Memoirs of the Civil War," LMU; Knipe to Pittman, September 13, 1864, *OR* 38(2):42; Padgett, "With Sherman through Georgia and the Carolinas," 296.

24. William Merrell, "Personal Memoirs of the Civil War," LMU; Cook and Benton, *"Dutchess County Regiment,"* 94; Marvin, *Fifth Regiment Connecticut*, 317.

25. Castel, *Decision in the West*, 293–95; Quaife, *From the Cannon's Mouth*, 328, 333; Tower, *A Carolinian Goes to War*, 193; Walker, *Rolls and Historical Sketch*, 111; Mitchell, "Civil War Letters," 77; Isaac Gaillard Foster Diary, June 22, 1864, James Foster and Family Correspondence, LSU; Jesse L. Henderson Civil War Diary, June 22, 1864, UM; Robinson to Pittman, July 24, 1864, *OR* 38(2):89; Robinson to Hunt, June 24, 1864, James Sidney Robinson Papers, OHS; diary, June 22, 1864, Max Schlund Papers, NL.

26. Tower, *A Carolinian Goes to War*, 193.

27. Quaife, *From the Cannon's Mouth*, 333; Cook and Benton, *"Dutchess County Regiment,"* 96; Tower, *A Carolinian Goes to War*, 193; David Shires Myers Bodenhamer Reminiscences, unpaginated, TSLA; Willis Dunston Banks to Joe, June 24, 1864, Banks Family Papers, UGA; diary, June 22, 1864, Emmett Ross Papers, MSU; McMurry, "Kolb's Farm," 23.

28. Quaife, *From the Cannon's Mouth*, 328.

29. Geary to Perkins, September 15, 1864, Jones to Forbes, August 1, 1864, *OR* 38(2):133, 211–12; *Letters of William Wheeler*, 467–68; Mannis and Wilson, *Bound to be a Soldier*, 147; Pierson, "From Chattanooga to Atlanta," 344.

30. Bohrnstedt, *Soldiering With Sherman*, 114; Thomas to Sawyer, July 16, 1864, Howard to Whipple, September 18, 1864, Stanley to Fullerton, 1864, Stanley to Fullerton, 1864, Whitaker to Sinclair, 1864, Wagner to Lee, September 10, 1864, *OR* 38(1):150,

198, 224, 244, 334–35; Whipple to Howard, June 22, 1864, Whipple to Hooker, June 22, 1864, Howard to [Thomas], June 22, 1864, *OR* 38(4):560–61.

31. Schofield, *Forty-Six Years*, 132, 135; Schofield to Sherman, September 10, 1864, *OR* 38(2):513–14; Schofield to Sherman, June 22, 1864, Cox to Reilly, June 22, 1864, Ross to Jackson, June 22, 1864, 6:30 P.M., 9:30 P.M., *OR* 38(4):566, 568, 786–87; McMurry, "Kolb's Farm," 23; George Washington Deemer Diary, June 22, 1864, SRNB.

32. Hooker to Whipple, June 22, 1864, Carman to Fay, September 6, 1864, *OR* 38(2):15, 71; Quaife, *From the Cannon's Mouth*, 329.

33. Carman to Fay, September 6, 1864, Ketcham to Fay, September 6, 1864, *OR* 38(2):71, 79; Cook and Benton, *"Dutchess County Regiment,"* 95.

34. Williams to Perkins, September 12, 1864, Carman to Fay, September 6, 1864, *OR* 38(2):32, 71; William Merrell, "Personal Memoirs of the Civil War," LMU; Morse, *Letters Written during the War*, 172; Stevenson to [Ratchford], August 19, 1864, *OR* 38(3):815; Cook and Benton, *"Dutchess County Regiment,"* 95.

35. William Clark McLean to mother, June 23, 1864, McLean Family Papers, NYSL; McMurry, *John Bell Hood*, 113; Thomas B. Mackall Journal, June 22, 1864 (McMurry transcript), Joseph E. Johnston Papers, CWM; Stevenson to [Ratchford], August 19, 1864, *OR* 38(3):815; McMurry, "Kolb's Farm," 24; John Fleeman to wife, June 23, 1864, in A. L. Jordan, *Gen. Jos. E. Johnston*, 42–43; David Shires Myers Bodenhamer Reminiscences, unpaginated, TSLA; Harwell to J. E. Boos, February 22, 1923, J. D. Harwell Letters, USM; Phillips, *Personal Reminiscences*, 52; Richard W. Colville to father, June 26, 1864, Colville and Paine Family Letters, UTC; W. H. Brooker Diary, June 22, 1864, RU.

36. Wynne and Taylor, *This War So Horrible*, 97; Gates to wife, June 26, 1864, Luther L. Gates Letters, EU.

37. William B. Calfee to father, June 24, 1864, Calfee Papers, CWM; Joseph Hamilton Bowman Entry, Tennessee Volume, Record 28, Roll of Honour, MOC; Wysor to father, July 19, 1864, James Miller Wysor Letters, VHS.

38. Sherman to Halleck, June 23, 1864, *OR* 38(4):573; Williams to Perkins, September 12, 1864, Geary to Perkins, September 15, 1864, *OR* 38(2):32, 133; Gates to wife, June 26, 1864, Luther L. Gates Letters, EU; George G. Truair to father, June 28, 1864, Truair Family Papers, UTA.

39. McMurry, "Kolb's Farm," 24; Knipe to Pittman, September 13, 1864, Ruger to Pittman, September 11, 1864, *OR* 38(2):42, 62; record of events, 123rd New York, *SOR*, pt. 2, 46:548; Schofield to Sherman, June 22, 1864, *OR* 38(4):566.

40. Sherman to Thomas, June 22, 1864, *OR* 38(4):558.

41. Sherman to Thomas, June 22, 1864, Sherman to Hooker, June 22, 1864, *OR* 38(4):558, 561; Sherman, *Memoirs*, 2:57–58.

42. Schofield to Sherman, June 22, 1864, *OR* 38(4):566.

43. Thomas to Sherman, June 22, 1864, *OR* 38(4):560.

44. Sherman to McPherson, June 22, 1864, McPherson to Dodge, June 22, 1864, *OR* 38(4):569, 571.

45. Daniel Gishel to S. S. Miller, June 26, 1864, Thaddeus Kane Miller Papers, OHS; Richard W. Colville to father, June 26, 1864, Colville and Paine Family Letters, UTC; Quaife, *From the Cannon's Mouth*, 328–29; Hooker to Whipple, June 22, 1864, *OR* 38(4):563; Davis to wife, June 24, 1864, Leander E. Davis Letters, NYSL; Edgerton to mother, June 23, 1864, William W. Edgerton Civil War Letters, UH; William Mer-

rell, "Personal Memoirs of the Civil War," LMU; Morse, *Letters Written during the War*, 172; Marvin, *Fifth Regiment Connecticut*, 314.

46. D. P. Conyagham dispatch, June 22–23, 1864, *New York Herald*, July 4, 1864; Tower, *A Carolinian Goes to War*, 193; Thomas L. Clayton to wife, n.d., but written from headquarters of Hood's Corps, one and a half miles from Marietta on Powder Springs Road, Clayton Family Papers, UNC; Johnston to Bragg, June 24, 1864, *OR* 38(4):788; Johnston to Cooper, October 20, 1864, *OR* 38(3):617; Johnston, *Narrative*, 340; Johnston, "Opposing Sherman's Advance," 271–72; Mackall to [wife], June 26, 1864, William Whann Mackall Papers, UNC; Thomas B. Mackall Journal, June 22, 1864 (McMurry transcript), Joseph E. Johnston Papers, CWM.

47. Joseph Hamilton Bowman Entry, Tennessee Volume, Record 28, Roll of Honour, MOC; record of events, Company H, 58th North Carolina, *SOR*, pt. 2, 49:442; W. B. Corbitt Diary, June 22, 1864, EU; George Anderson Mercer Diary, June 22, 1864, UNC; Lee to Maggie Knighton, June 23, 1864, Josiah Knighton Family Papers, LSU; diary, June 22, 1864, Edwin Hansford Rennolds, Sr., Papers, UTK; William Jewel to Martha, June 23, 1864, Jewel Family Civil War Letters, SHSM-SL; David Shires Myers Bodenhamer Reminiscences, unpaginated, TSLA; Thomas L. Clayton to wife, n.d., but written from headquarters of Hood's Corps, one and a half miles from Marietta on Powder Springs Road, Clayton Family Papers, UNC; John Fleeman to wife, June 23, 1864, in A. L. Jordan, *Gen. Jos. E. Johnston*, 42; Sam L. Asbury diary, June 22, 1864, in Williamson, *Third Battalion*, 380; Harwell to J. E. Boos, February 22, 1923, J. D. Harwell Letters, USM.

48. Hood, *Advance and Retreat*, 125; S. Davis, *Atlanta Will Fall*, 82–83.

49. Tower, *A Carolinian Goes to War*, 192.

50. Ibid., 193–94; McMurry, "Kolb's Farm," 27.

51. Higdon, "Hindman's Reply to Hood," 69; Thomas L. Clayton to wife, n.d., but written from headquarters of Hood's Corps, one and a half miles from Marietta on Powder Springs Road, Clayton Family Papers, UNC; Jesse L. Henderson Civil War Diary, June 22, 1864, UM.

52. White and Runion, *Great Things*, 122–24.

53. Cox, *Military Reminiscences*, 1:261; Mattison to Elley, June 25, 1864, William N. Mattison Civil War Correspondence, AHC.

CHAPTER THREE

1. William Clark McLean to mother, June 23, 1864, McLean Family Papers, NYSL; D. P. Conyagham dispatch, June 22 and 23, 1864, *New York Herald*, July 4, 1864; W. Walton, *Civil War Courtship*, 89–90; Tappan, *Civil War Journal*, 133; Morse, *Letters Written during the War*, 172.

2. Quaife, *From the Cannon's Mouth*, 328; Gallup to not stated, August 11, 1864, *OR* 38(2):655.

3. Sherman, *Memoirs*, 2:58.

4. Ibid., 58–59; Osborn, *Trials and Triumphs*, 156.

5. Sherman, *Memoirs*, 2:59.

6. Schofield, *Forty-Six Years*, 132, 134–35.

7. Ibid., 133; Sherman, *Memoirs*, 2:57–58; McMurry, "Kolb's Farm," 24; McMurry, *Atlanta*, 106–7; Howard, *Autobiography*, 1:571–77.

8. Bauer, *Soldiering*, 135; Schofield to Sherman, September 10, 1864, Hascall to Camp-

bell, September 10, 1864, *OR* 38(2):514, 569; Frederick N. Kollock diary, June 23, 1864, Charles S. Harris Collection, UTC; Thoburn, *My Experiences*, 98; Schofield to Sherman, June 23, 1864, *OR* 38(4):576.

9. Circular, Headquarters, Hood's Corps, June 24, 1864, Ross to Jackson, June 25, 1864, Ratchford to division commanders of Hood's Corps, June 26, 1864, *OR* 38(4):789, 790, 794; Circular, June 26, 1864, General Orders and Circulars, Hood's Corps, MOC; Isaac Gaillard Foster Diary, June 24, 1864, James Foster and Family Correspondence, LSU; E. D. Willett Diary, June 23, 1864, ADAH; diary, June 23, 1864, Emmett Ross Papers, MSU; Willis Dunston Banks to Joe, June 24, 1864, Banks Family Papers, UGA; Jesse L. Henderson Civil War Diary, June 22–23, 1864, UM; J. C. Thompson to A. P. Stewart, December 8, 1867, Joseph E. Johnston Papers, CWM; John Fleeman to wife, June 23, 1864, in A. L. Jordan, *Gen. Jos. E. Johnston*, 43; McBride, *History of the Thirty-Third*, 125; Bogle, *Some Recollections*, 13.

10. Surgeon Woodruff to father, June 25, 1864, *Chicago Daily Tribune*, July 3, 1864; Stanley to Fullerton, 1864, Bryan to Opdycke, September 1864, Wagner to Lee, September 10, 1864, Blanch to Cox, September 15, 1864, *OR* 38(1):224, 319, 335, 347; Thomas to Sherman, June 24, 1864, *OR* 38(4):581; Kerwood, *Annals of the Fifty-Seventh*, 261–62.

11. Sherman to Halleck, June 23, 1864, *OR* 38(4):572–73; Stone, "Atlanta Campaign," 418, 421; Bauer, *Soldiering*, 135; Mannis and Wilson, *Bound to Be a Soldier*, 147.

12. Johnston to Bragg, June 26, 27, 1864, *OR* 38(4):792, 795–96; S. Davis, *Atlanta Will Fall*, 76–77.

13. Castel, *Decision in the West*, 285; Wood to Fullerton, September 10, 1864, *OR* 38(1):381; McMurry, *Atlanta*, 103–4; French to West, August 31, 1864, *OR* 38(3):901; Joseph Miller to Mr. Wright, June 23, 1864, VT; Naylor to Coz, June 23, 1864, James M. Naylor Papers, OHS; Jackson, *The Colonel's Diary*, 139; "Kennesaw Mountain Administrative History," www.nps.gov/kemo/; W. Kelly, *Kennesaw Mountain*, 42; Yates, *Historical Guide*, 19.

14. Reyburn and Wilson, *"Jottings from Dixie,"* 230–31; Hedley, *Marching Through Georgia*, 103; French, *Two Wars*, 203; Howard, *Autobiography*, 1:577; Jackson, *The Colonel's Diary*, 133–34.

15. Field visit to Kennesaw Mountain, December 19, 1986; Bailey, *Battles for Atlanta*, 19; Barnard, *Photographic Views*, 31–32; W. C. Davis and Wiley, *Photographic History*, 2:704.

16. Howard, *Autobiography*, 1:577–78; Howard, "Struggle for Atlanta," 310; Black, "Civil War Letters," 74; *Story of the Service of Company E*, 292; Hedley, *Marching Through Georgia*, 103; *Story of the Fifty-Fifth Regiment Illinois*, 321.

17. French, *Two Wars*, 205; French, "Kennesaw Mountain," 276; John J. Mercer Diary, June 22, 1864, AHC; W. L. Truman Memoirs, June 22, 1864, www.cedarcroft.com.

18. French, *Two Wars*, 205–6; W. L. Truman Memoirs, June 23–25, 1864, www.cedarcroft.com; A. J. Price to wife, June 26, 1864, NCSA.

19. Sherman to Halleck, September 15, 1864, *OR* 38(1):68; Barnhart, "A Hoosier Invades the Confederacy," 190; *Story of the Service of Company E*, 294–95; H. H. Wright, *History of the Sixth Iowa*, 286–87.

20. Diary, June 24–25, 1864, John Wharton Papers, MHM; Johnston, "Opposing Sherman's Advance," 274.

21. W. L. Truman Memoirs, June 25, 1864, www.cedarcroft.com.

22. Fuller to Barnes, September 12, 1864, *OR* 38(3):484; T. Brown, Murphy, and Putney, *Behind the Guns*, 96–97.

23. Field visit to Kennesaw Mountain, December 24, 1986.

24. "Battle of Kennesaw Mountain," 109–10; Cheatham recollections, *SOR*, pt. 1, 7:143; Losson, *Tennessee's Forgotten Warriors*, 152–53.

25. Cheatham recollections, *SOR*, pt. 1, 7:143; J. T. Bowden to editor, December 15, 1903, *Confederate Veteran* Papers, DU; Smith journal, *SOR*, pt. 1, 7:78; Eleazer, "Fight at Dead Angle," 312; "Battle of Kennesaw Mountain," 113–14.

26. Cheatham recollections, *SOR*, pt. 1, 7:145; "Battle of Kennesaw Mountain," 110, 113; Nelson, "Dead Angle," 321.

27. Cheatham recollections, *SOR*, pt. 1, 7:143; autobiography, 27, and diary, June 22, 1864, Edwin Hansford Rennolds, Sr., Papers, UTK; "Battle of Kennesaw Mountain," 110; Losson, *Tennessee's Forgotten Warriors*, 153.

28. Thomas to Sawyer, July 16, 1864, Howard to Whipple, September 18, 1864, *OR* 38(1):151, 198–99; Thomas to Sherman, June 23, 1864, *OR* 38(4):573; "Battle of Kennesaw Mountain," 110–11; Miles, "Col. Hume R. Feild," 326; Franklin, *Civil War Diaries*, 184; autobiography, 27–28, Edwin Hansford Rennolds, Sr., Papers, UTK; Frank Erskine to editor, June 26, 1864, *Memphis Daily Appeal*, June 29, 1864; Cheatham recollections, *SOR*, pt. 1, 7:144; Garrett, *Confederate Diary*, 71; William J. Hardee to wife, June 23, 1864, Hardee Family Papers, ADAH; Losson, *Tennessee's Forgotten Warriors*, 154.

29. Cheatham recollections, *SOR*, pt. 1, 7:144; Smith journal, *SOR*, pt. 1, 7:77–78; [Maney], "Battle of Dead Angle," 71; Franklin, *Civil War Diaries*, 184; Stewart, *Dan McCook's Regiment*, 129; Harmon, "Dead Angle," 219; Blair, "Fight at Dead Angle," 533; A. L. Jordan, "'Dead Angle' Tunneled," 601; Eleazer, "Fight at Dead Angle," 312.

30. "Battle of Kennesaw Mountain," 115–16; E. W. Payne, *Thirty-Fourth Regiment of Illinois*, 128–29.

31. "Battle of Kennesaw Mountain," 110; Blair, "Fight at Dead Angle," 533; [Maney], "Battle of Dead Angle," 71; J. T. Bowden to editor, December 15, 1903, *Confederate Veteran* Papers, DU; Marchant to Susan, July 16, 1864, Peter Marchant Civil War Correspondence, AHC.

32. J. T. Bowden to editor, December 15, 1903, *Confederate Veteran* Papers, DU; Watkins, *Co. Aytch*, 161; "View by H.M. Lynn of the Battle of Kennesaw Mountain Written after the War, Possibly for a Speech," H. M. Lynn Papers, UNC.

33. Vaughan, *Personal Record*, 34; J. T. Bowden to editor, December 15, 1903, *Confederate Veteran* Papers, DU.

34. Smith journal, *SOR*, pt. 1, 7:78; Holmes, *52d O.V.I.*, 194.

35. Barnes, "An Incident of Kenesaw," 48–49.

36. N. D. Brown, *One of Cleburne's Command*, 97; John S. Lightfoot Diary, June 26, 1864, EU.

37. Baumgartner, *Blood & Sacrifice*, 148; Byrne, *Uncommon Soldiers*, 163; Johnston to Bragg, June 26, 1864, *OR* 38(4):792; Brannock to wife, June 22, 1864, James Madison Brannock Papers, VHS; George Cooley diary, June 26, 1864, WHS; *Story of the Service of Company E*, 294.

38. Sherman to Halleck, September 15, 1864, *OR* 38(1):68; Sherman, *Memoirs*, 2:60.

39. Joseph Miller to Mr. Wright, June 23, 1864, VT; Naylor to Coz, June 23, 1864, James M. Naylor Papers, OHS; Frank P. Blair, Jr., to Apo, June 24, 1864, Breckin-

ridge Long Papers, LC; Edwin C. Obriham to sister, June 25, 1864, June and Gilbert Krueger Civil War Letters, CU.

40. Sherman to Thomas, June 24, 1864, Sherman to Halleck, June 25, 1864, *OR* 38(4):582, 589; Sherman to Halleck, September 15, 1864, *OR* 38(1):68; Sherman, *Memoirs*, 2:60; Sherman, "Grand Strategy," 252; Howard, "Struggle for Atlanta," 310; Castel, *Decision in the West*, 301–4.

41. Special Field Orders No. 28, Headquarters, Military Division of the Mississippi, June 24, 1864, *OR* 38(4):588; Castel, *Decision in the West*, 303–4.

42. Special Field Orders No. 51, Headquarters, Department and Army of the Tennessee, June 26, 1864, *OR* 38(4):605–6; Force to Mr. Soule, June 26–28, 1864, M. F. Force Papers, UW.

43. Special Field Orders No. 37, Headquarters, Fifteenth Corps, June 26, 1864, *OR* 38(4):606.

44. Cox to Reilly, June 26, 1864, Special Field Orders Number not stated, Headquarters, Department of the Cumberland, June 26, 1864, Orders Number not stated, Headquarters, Twentieth Corps, June 26, 1864, Special Field Orders No. 36, Headquarters, Army of the Ohio, June 26, 1864, *OR* 38(4):600, 602–4; Schofield, *Forty-Six Years*, 144.

45. Gates, *Rough Side of War*, 223, 225; Angle, *Three Years*, 226.

46. Sherman, *Memoirs*, 2:60; *Chicago Daily Tribune*, July 3, 1864; L. G. Bennett and Haigh, *History of the Thirty-Sixth*, 608; Sherman to Thomas, June 25, 1864, *OR* 38(4):590; Howard to Clark, September 9, 1864, *OR* 38(3):80.

47. Howard, *Autobiography*, 1:582–83; Howard to Whipple, September 18, 1864, *OR* 38(1):199; *History of the Seventy-Third*, 311; Mahan, *Advanced-Guard*, 10.

48. Palmer, *Personal Recollections*, 205.

49. Osterhaus diary, June 26, 1864, Osterhaus Family Papers, MHM; S. Bennett and Tillery, *Struggle for the Life of the Republic*, 172; Garrett, *Confederate Diary*, 71; Sherman to [Thomas], June 25, 1864, Sherman to Schofield, June 26, 1864, Schofield to Sherman, June 26, 1864, *OR* 38(4):589, 597–98; Schofield to Sherman, September 10, 1864, *OR* 38(2):514; Cox, *Military Reminiscences*, 1:263–65; Ross to Jackson, June 26, 1864, *OR* 38(4):792–93; Fout, *Dark Days*, 346.

50. S. Davis, *Atlanta Will Fall*, 86–87; Benjamin T. Smith Reminiscences, 143, ALPL.

51. Logan to Clark, June 28, 1864, [September 13, 1864], Osterhaus to Townes, September 9, 1864, Smith to Townes, June 28, 1864, Smith to Smith, June 28, 1864, Van Deusen to McAuley, September 10, 1864, Hildt to McAuley, September 9, 1864, *OR* 38(3):84, 98–99, 133, 178, 193, 206, 208; Osterhaus diary, June 26, 1864, Osterhaus Family Papers, MHM; *Story of the Fifty-Fifth*, 322; Alvah Stone Skilton speech, Skilton-Davis-Heyman Family Papers, RBHPC; "War Diary of Thaddeus H. Capron," 384.

52. Harrow to Townes, September 9, 1864, Walcutt to Wilkinson, August 10, 1864, Alexander to not stated, September 12, 1864, *OR* 38(3):279, 317–18, 337; C. W. Wills, *Army Life*, 268–69.

53. Corse to Barnes, September 8, 1864, Leggett to Alexander, June 28, 1864, *OR* 38(3):405, 563; Force to brother, July 6, 1864, in Journal and Letter Book, 511, 513, and Force to Mr. Soule, June 16–28, 1864, M. F. Force Papers, UW.

54. Maley to father and mother, July 2, 1864, Henry H. Maley Letters, UND.

55. *History of the Seventy-Third*, 311; John W. Tuttle diary, June 26, 1864, UK; diary,

December 8, 1863, Seth Abbey Papers, TSLA; Howard, *Autobiography*, 1:567, 586–87; Warner, *Generals in Blue*, 207; Comstock to Bowers, February 27, 1864, *OR* 32(2):484.

56. Thomas to Sawyer, July 16, 1864, Itinerary of the Fourteenth Army Corps, Davis to McClurg, September 1864, *OR* 38(1):151, 506, 632.

57. Aten, *History of the Eighty-Fifth Illinois*, 179–80; James, "McCook's Brigade," 256; Barnhart, "A Hoosier Invades the Confederacy," 190; diary, June 25, 1864, Allen L. Fahnestock Papers, ALPL; Holmes, *52d O.V.I.*, 177; Mitchell to Wiseman, September 4, 1864, Tassell to Wilson, September 5, 1864, Pearce to Wilson, September 9, 1864, *OR* 38(1):680, 685, 692; McAdams, *Every-Day Soldier Life*, 87.

58. Sherman to Ellen, June 26, 1864, Simpson and Berlin, *Sherman's Civil War*, 657.

59. Gordon Hickenlooper, "The Reminiscences of General Andrew Hickenlooper, 1861–1865," 54, *Civil War Times Illustrated* Collection, USAMHI; "Personal Biography of Major General Grenville Mellen Dodge 1831–1870," 1:222, Grenville Mellen Dodge Papers, SHSI; Dodge, *Personal Recollections*, 77.

60. Stewart, *Dan McCook's Regiment*, 113.

61. Dacus, *Reminiscences*, not paginated; Whitehead to Irene Cowan, June 29, 1864, Dr. P. F. Whitehead Letters, USM.

CHAPTER FOUR

1. Watkins, *Co. Aytch*, 157; Peter J. Osterhaus diary, June 27, 1864, Osterhaus Family Papers, MHM; Sherman to McPherson, June 27, 1864, Van Duzer to Eckert, June 27, 1864, *OR* 38(4):622, 626; Edge to Logan, September 12, 1864, *OR* 38(3):121.

2. C. W. Wills, *Army Life*, 269; Morgan L. Smith to Townes, June 28, 1864, French to West, August 31, 1864, *OR* 38(3):178, 901; Castel, *Decision in the West*, 307, 309.

3. Alvah Stone Skilton speech, Skilton-Davis-Heyman Family Papers, RBHPC; *Story of the Fifty-Fifth Regiment Illinois*, 322.

4. *Story of the Fifty-Fifth Regiment Illinois*, 323–24.

5. Logan to Clark, June 28, 1864, Morgan L. Smith to Townes, June 28, 1864, Lofland to Townes, September 10, 1864, *OR* 38(3):84–85, 178, 187.

6. Warner, *Generals in Blue*, 279–80.

7. Lightburn to Lofland, June 28, 1864, Jones to Lofland, September 12, 1864, Fulton to Fisk, September 8, 1864, Moore to Fisk, September 12, 1864, *OR* 38(3):221, 226, 252, 259; *Sketch of the Operations of the Forty-Seventh Ohio*, 6; Duke, *History of the Fifty-Third Regiment Ohio*, 145.

8. Duke, *History of the Fifty-Third Regiment Ohio*, 145; Morgan L. Smith to Townes, June 28, 1864, Lofland to Townes, September 10, 1864, Lightburn to Lofland, June 28, 1864, Jones to Lofland, September 12, 1864, Fulton to Fisk, September 8, 1864, Moore to Fisk, September 12, 1864, *OR* 38(3):178, 187–88, 222, 227, 252–53, 259; *Sketch of the Operations of the Forty-Seventh Ohio*, 6; Castel, *Tom Taylor's Civil War*, 132–33; W. Kelly, *Kennesaw Mountain*, 33. At least one regiment in Lightburn's brigade, the Thirtieth Ohio on the left end of the first line, started the advance north of Burnt Hickory Road and moved south of it by the right flank, after crossing the Union works and before hitting the timbered bottomland. See Hildt to McAuley, September 9, 1864, Young to Todhunter, June 28, 1864, *OR* 38(3):208–9, 913.

9. Duke, *History of the Fifty-Third Regiment Ohio*, 145–46; member of Company H,

Sixty-Third Georgia, to wife, July 1, 1864, Unidentified Soldier Letter, AHC; Castel, *Tom Taylor's Civil War*, 132; Lightburn to Lofland, June 28, 1864, Fulton to Fisk, September 8, 1864, *OR* 38(3):222, 253.

10. *Sketch of the Operations of the Forty-Seventh Ohio*, 6; Taylor to Fisk, September 10, 1864, *OR* 38(3):244; [Thomas Benton Roy], "Sketch of Lieut. [Gen] W.J. Hardee," 25, Hardee Family Papers, ADAH; "Memo Book," 74; Castel, *Tom Taylor's Civil War*, 132; W. Kelly, *Kennesaw Mountain*, 33.

11. Walker to French, June 27, 28, 1864, *OR* 38(4):799, 802; Reminiscences, 58, Joseph B. Cumming Papers, UNC; George Anderson Mercer Diary, June 27–28, 1864, UNC; Fulton to Fisk, September 8, 1864, French to West, August 31, 1864, *OR* 38(3):253, 901. An unidentified member of Company H, Sixty-Third Georgia blamed Cockrell's skirmish line for giving way before he and his comrades were driven from their skirmish pits. He told his wife that, after falling back from the skirmish line, the Sixty-Third Georgia was met by a supporting brigade which drove the Yankees away. He also claimed that the Federals "were made drunk before they started the charge." There is no supporting evidence for any of these assertions. See letter to wife, July 1, 1864, Unidentified Soldier Letter, AHC.

12. Duke, *History of the Fifty-Third Regiment Ohio*, 146; Hildt to McAuley, September 9, 1864, Jones to Lofland, September 12, 1864, Fulton to Fisk, September 8, 1864, *OR* 38(3):209, 227, 253; Castel, *Decision in the West*, 311.

13. Duke, *History of the Fifty-Third Regiment Ohio*, 146; Lightburn to Lofland, June 28, 1864, Moore to Fisk, September 12, 1864, *OR* 38(3):222, 259. A brief reference in the history of the Forty-Seventh Ohio indicates that this regiment, at least, in Lightburn's second line may have advanced to keep pace with the first line, but there is no supporting evidence for the contention. See *Sketch of the Operations of the Forty-Seventh Ohio*, 6.

14. Cockrell to Sanders, June 27, 1864, *OR* 38(3):914; Cockrell to French, [June 27, 1864], *OR* 38(4):798.

15. Cockrell to Sanders, June 27, 1864, *OR* 38(3):914; W. L. Truman Memoirs, www .cedarcroft.com.

16. Warner, *Generals in Gray*, 93–94; French, *Two Wars*, 2, 20, 81, 132.

17. French, *Two Wars*, 206, 208; French to Loring, June 28, 1864, *OR* 38(3):900. Observers in Brigadier General Matthew D. Ector's brigade on the south slope of Little Kennesaw Mountain could also see the movements of Lightburn's brigade as soon as the Federals left their own line of entrenchments. See Young to Todhunter, June 28, 1864, *OR* 38(3):913.

18. W. L. Truman Memoirs, www.cedarcroft.com.; diary, June 27, 1864, John Wharton Papers, MHM; Storrs, "Kennesaw Mountain," 138; Capers to Smith, September 10, 1864, French to Loring, June 28, 1864, *OR* 38(3):716, 900.

19. Warner, *Generals in Blue*, 456, 460.

20. Giles A. Smith to Smith, June 28, 1864, Mott to assistant adjutant general, First Brigade, Second Division, Fifteenth Corps, September 9, 1864, *OR* 38(3):194, 216.

21. Lofland to Townes, September 10, 1864, Giles A. Smith to Smith, June 28, 1864, Mott to assistant adjutant general, First Brigade, Second Division, Fifteenth Corps, September 9, 1864, *OR* 38(3):187, 194, 216; "War Diary of Thaddeus H. Capron," 384; *Story of the Fifty-Fifth Regiment Illinois*, 324–25.

22. French to Loring, June 28, 1864, *OR* 38(3):900.

23. *Story of the Fifty-Fifth Regiment Illinois*, 324–25; George W. Warren account in Bevier, *History*, 236–37; Lofland to Townes, September 10, 1864, Giles A. Smith to Smith, June 28, 1864, Mott to assistant adjutant general, First Brigade, Second Division, Fifteenth Corps, September 9, 1864, *OR* 38(3):187, 194, 216; "War Diary of Thaddeus H. Capron," 384; Castel, *Decision in the West*, 312–13.

24. Lofland to Townes, September 10, 1864, Giles A. Smith to Smith, June 28, 1864; Mott to assistant adjutant general, First Brigade, Second Division, Fifteenth Corps, September 9, 1864, *OR* 38(3):187, 194, 216; J. W. M. to *Cincinnati Commercial*, June 27, 1864, reprinted in *Cincinnati Daily Enquirer*, July 4, 1864; "War Diary of Thaddeus H. Capron," 384; *Story of the Fifty-Fifth Regiment Illinois*, 328.

25. Cockrell to Sanders, June 27, 1864, *OR* 38(3):914–15.

26. Warner, *Generals in Gray*, 57.

27. Ervin, "Perilous Undertaking," 308–9.

28. French, *Two Wars*, 208; French, "Kennesaw Mountain," 277–78; French to Loring, June 28, 1864, *OR* 38(3):900.

29. Mott to assistant adjutant general, First Brigade, Second Division, Fifteenth Corps, September 9, 1864, Cockrell to Sanders, June 27, 1864, *OR* 38(3):216, 915. George W. Warren in Cockrell's brigade reported that the fight for Pigeon Hill lasted forty-five minutes. See Bevier, *History*, 237.

30. Alvah Stone Skilton speech, Skilton diary, June 28, 1864, Skilton-Davis-Heyman Family Papers, RBHPC; Giles A. Smith to Smith, June 28, 1864, *OR* 38(3):194.

31. Mott to assistant adjutant general, First Brigade, Second Division, Fifteenth Corps, September 9, 1864, *OR* 38(3):216.

32. Alvah Stone Skilton speech, Skilton-Davis-Heyman Family Papers, RBHPC.

33. *Story of the Fifty-Fifth Regiment Illinois*, 325–27; Browne to McAuley, September 5, 1864, *OR* 38(3):201.

34. *Story of the Fifty-Fifth Regiment Illinois*, 326, 329; S. Bennett and Tillery, *Struggle for the Life of the Republic*, 172.

35. *Story of the Fifty-Fifth Regiment Illinois*, 327.

36. Ibid., 328.

37. Lofland to Townes, September 10, 1864, Hildt to McAuley, September 9, 1864, Taylor to Fisk, September 10, 1864, *OR* 38(3):188, 209, 244; *Sketch of the Operations of the Forty-Seventh Ohio*, 6.

38. Moritz to not stated, September 5, 1864, Fulton to Fisk, September 8, 1864, Moore to Fisk, September 12, 1864, Capers to Smith, September 10, 1864, *OR* 38(3):240, 253, 259, 716–17; Duke, *History of the Fifty-Third Regiment Ohio*, 146.

39. Cockrell to Sanders, June 27, 1864, *OR* 38(3):915; French, "Kennesaw Mountain," 277–78. For a different estimate of casualties suffered by the Third and Fifth Missouri, see diary, June 27, 1864, Avington Wayne Simpson Papers, UNC. A microfilm copy of the Simpson diary also is available at SHSM-C.

40. Warner, *Generals in Blue*, 535.

41. C. W. Wills, *Army Life*, 269; record of events, 103rd Illinois, *SOR*, pt. 2, 14:65; Walcutt to Wilkinson, August 10, 1864, Stewart to Upton, September 10, 1864, Alexander to not stated, September 12, 1864, *OR* 38(3):318, 324, 337.

42. C. W. Wills, *Army Life*, 268.

43. Alexander to not stated, September 12, 1864, *OR* 38(3):337; C. W. Wills, *Army Life*, 269–70.

44. Record of events, 103rd Illinois, *SOR*, pt. 2, 14:65; H. H. Wright, *History of the Sixth Iowa*, 290; Walcutt to Wilkinson, August 10, 1864, *OR* 38(3):318; Wills, *Army Life*, 269.

45. Record of events, 103rd Illinois, *SOR*, pt. 2, 14:65.

46. C. W. Wills, *Army Life*, 270.

47. Ibid.

48. Logan to Clark, [September 13, 1864], Walcutt to Wilkinson, August 10, 1864, Williston to Upton, September 9, 1864, *OR* 38(3):99, 318, 326; H. H. Wright, *History of the Sixth Iowa*, 291.

49. C. W. Wills, *Army Life*, 270.

50. French, *Two Wars*, 208; French to Loring, June 28, 1864, *OR* 38(3):901; Baumgartner, *Blood & Sacrifice*, 152.

51. Stewart to Upton, September 10, 1864, Williston to Upton, September 9, 1864, *OR* 38(3):324, 326; H. H. Wright, *History of the Sixth Iowa*, 292; C. W. Wills, *Army Life*, 268, 270–71.

52. Osterhaus to Townes, September 9, 1864, Williamson to Gordon, September 5, 1864, *OR* 38(3):133, 156; Booth, "Kenesaw Mountain: An Iowa Man Who Wants to Know Who Commanded on His Part of the Line"; Osterhaus diary, June 27, 1864, Osterhaus Family Papers, MHM; S. Bennett and Tillery, *Struggle for the Life of the Republic*, 172.

53. Oliver to Wilkinson, August 4, 1864, *OR* 38(3):341; Winther, *With Sherman to the Sea*, 115–16.

54. Loring to Mackall, July 30, 1864, French to West, August 31, 1864, *OR* 38(3):869–70, 901; Johnston, "Opposing Sherman's Advance," 271; Dodge to Clark, June 27, 1864, *OR* 38(4):623.

55. Dodge to Clark, November 25, 1864, Fuller to Barnes, September 12, 1864, Manning to not stated, July 31, 1864, *OR* 38(3):382, 484, 493; "Personal Biography of Major General Grenville Mellen Dodge 1831–1870," 1:222, Grenville Mellen Dodge Papers, SHSI.

56. Corse to Barnes, September 8, 1864, Boyd to Ellis, September 6, 1864, *OR* 38(3):405–6, 458; "Personal Biography of Major General Grenville Mellen Dodge 1831–1870," 1:222, Grenville Mellen Dodge Papers, SHSI.

57. Walthall to West, July 1, 1864, *OR* 38(3):922–23; Johnston, "Opposing Sherman's Advance," 272. O'Neal reported that Dodge's skirmishers never took his skirmish line, but the weight of evidence contradicts that assertion. See O'Neal to Barksdale, July 1, 1864, *OR* 38(3):940.

58. Dodge to Clark, November 25, 1864, Walthall to West, July 1, 1864, Reynolds to Barksdale, June 30, 1864, *OR* 38(3):381–82, 923, 934–35; Daniel Harris Reynolds Diary, June 27, 1864, UAF.

59. Blair to Clark, September 12, 1864, Gresham to Alexander, June 28, 1864, Sanderson to Cadle, June 28, 1864, *OR* 38(3):552, 577–78, 586–87; John J. Safely to Mary, June 28, 1864, McEwen Family Papers, MHM.

60. Sanderson to Cadle, June 28, 1864, Hall to Cadle, June 28, 1864, *OR* 38(3):587, 592–93; Hubbart, *An Iowa Soldier*, 49–50; O. B. Clark, *Downing's Civil War Diary*, 202.

61. Walthall to West, July 1, 1864, Quarles to Barksdale, July 1, 1864, Knox to Cox, June 30, 1864, *OR* 38(3):923, 930, 933–34; McMahon, "Samuel Knox," 89. Captain Stephen Cowley, who served as assistant inspector general on Quarles's staff, claimed

credit for saving the First Alabama from being cut off on the skirmish line. He asserted that Quarles told him "to bring that Regt out under heavy fire, I did so." There are no grounds for believing his story. Stephen Cowley to Minor, August 6, 1864, Hubbard T. Minor Papers, USAMHI.

62. Walthall to West, July 1, 1864, Quarles to Barksdale, July 1, 1864, Knox to Cox, June 30, 1864, *OR* 38(3):923, 930, 934. Knox was later wounded at Ezra Church and killed at Franklin. See McMahon, "Samuel Knox," 89.

63. Leggett to Alexander, June 28, 1864, Malloy to Douglass, September 12, 1864, *OR* 38(3):563, 574–75.

64. Leggett to Alexander, June 28, 1864, Malloy to Douglass, September 12, 1864, *OR* 38(3):563, 575; diary, June 27, 1864, George W. Modil Papers, MDAH.

65. Leggett to Alexander, June 28, 1864, Bryant to Douglass, September 11, 1864, Wiles to Douglass, September 13, 1864, Malloy to Douglass, September 12, 1864, *OR* 38(3):563, 571, 573, 575.

66. Force to Mr. Soule, June 26–28, 1864, Force to Mr. Kebler, June 29, 1864, M. F. Force Papers, UW.

67. Featherston to Johnston, November 15, 1867, *SOR*, pt. 1, 7:147–49; F. M. Cockrell to Seddon Carrington, December 14, 1900, Isaac Howell Carrington Papers, DU; Jones and Martin, *Gentle Rebel*, 37; Howard, "Struggle for Atlanta," 311; McPherson to Sherman, June 27, 1864, *OR* 38(4):623; Leggett to Alexander, June 28, 1864, *OR* 38(3):563.

68. Gordon Hickenlooper, "The Reminiscences of General Andrew Hickenlooper, 1861–1865," 54, *Civil War Times Illustrated* Collection, USAMHI; Garrard to Elliott, September 4, 1864, *OR* 38(2):804.

69. Loring to Mackall, July 30, 1864, *OR* 38(3):869–70.

CHAPTER FIVE

1. John W. Tuttle Diary, June 27, 1864, UK; Howard to Whipple, September 18, 1864, *OR* 38(1):199; Nathan Kimball letter in Wagner, *Organization and Tactics*, 91n; Howard, *Autobiography*, 1:582.

2. Luther P. Bradley and Nathan Kimball letters in Wagner, *Organization and Tactics*, 91; Howard to Whipple, September 18, 1864, Newton to assistant adjutant general, Army of the Cumberland, September 1864, Atwater to Waterman, August 12, 1864, *OR* 38(1):199, 295, 361; Howard, "Struggle for Atlanta," 311; Hardee, *Hardee's Rifle and Light Infantry Tactics*, 102–15; Shellenberger, "Kenesaw Mountain: The Causes That Led to the Repulse of Harker's Charge."

3. Wagner to Lee, September 10, 1864, Bradley to Lee, September 12, 1864, *OR* 38(1):335, 355.

4. Shellenberger, "Kenesaw Mountain: The Causes That Led to the Repulse of Harker's Charge,"; John W. Tuttle Diary, June 27, 1864, UK; Castel, *Decision in the West*, 307. Howard reported that all of Newton's brigades adopted a column of full regimental front for the attack, but Harker obviously did not. Also, while one report indicated the distance between battle lines within Harker's brigade column was at "half distance," the weight of evidence supports the contention that the lines were closed en mass. See Howard to Whipple, September 18, 1864, Clark to Waterman, September 14, 1864, *OR* 38(1):199, 364.

5. Longacre and Haas, *To Battle for God and the Right*, 189.

6. Moore to Waterman, September 12, 1864, *OR* 38(1):371; C. T. Clark, *Opdycke Tigers*, 276–77.

7. Castel, *Decision in the West*, 308, 315; Thomas to Sawyer, July 16, 1864, *OR* 38(1):151.

8. Olson to Powers, September 15, 1864, MacArthur to [Jackson], September 12, 1864, Moore to Waterman, September 12, 1864, Fullerton journal, *OR* 38(1):314, 329, 371, 887; McAdams, *Every-Day Soldier Life*, 90–91; John K. Ely Diary, June 27, 1864, Judy Beal Collection; C. T. Clark, *Opdycke Tigers*, 277; field visit to Kennesaw Mountain, December 16, 1986.

9. The seven batteries that bombarded the Confederates in preparation for the Fourth Corps attack were the Fifth Indiana Battery; Battery B, Independent Pennsylvania Light Artillery; Battery A, First Ohio Light Artillery; Battery M, First Illinois Light Artillery; Bridges's battery, Illinois Light Artillery; Sixth Ohio Battery; and Battery M, First Ohio Light Artillery. Bridges to Fullerton, September 9, 1864, *OR* 38(1):483, 487; Reyburn and Wilson, *"Jottings from Dixie,"* 232–33; Howard, "Struggle for Atlanta," 311; L. G. Bennett and Haigh, *History of the Thirty-Sixth*, 609; Sherman to Thomas, June 27, 1864, Thomas to Sherman, June 27, 1864, *OR* 38(4):607.

10. Various sources place the start of the attack at anywhere from 8:00 A.M. to 9:45 A.M., but the weight of evidence supports the earliest time. Aldrich, *Quest for a Star*, 121; Howard to Whipple, September 18, 1864, Newton to assistant adjutant general, Army of the Cumberland, September 1864, Bradley to Lee, September 12, 1864, Moore to Waterman, September 12, 1864, *OR* 38(1):199, 295, 355, 371; C. T. Clark, *Opdycke Tigers*, 277.

11. Newton to assistant adjutant general, Army of the Cumberland, September 1864, *OR* 38(1):296; John W. Tuttle Diary, June 27, 1864, UK; Holmes, *52nd O.V.I.*, 195; field visit to Kennesaw Mountain, December 16, 1986.

12. C. T. Clark, *Opdycke Tigers*, 278; Shellenberger, "Kenesaw Mountain: The Causes That Led to the Repulse of Harker's Charge."

13. Moore to Waterman, September 12, 1864, *OR* 38(1):371; Benjamin T. Smith Reminiscences, 145, ALPL; Howard, "Struggle for Atlanta," 311; C. T. Clark, *Opdycke Tigers*, 278; John W. Tuttle Diary, June 27, 1864, UK.

14. Garrett, *Confederate Diary*, 71; Benjamin T. Smith Reminiscences, 145–46, ALPL; Bradley, "Recollections of Service in the Civil War," 25–26, Luther P. Bradley Papers, USAMHI; Smith journal, *SOR*, pt. 1, 7:78.

15. Shellenberger, "Kenesaw Mountain: The Causes That Led to the Repulse of Harker's Charge."

16. Ibid.

17. Holmes, *52d O.V.I.*, 195–96; Fullerton journal, *OR* 38(1):887–88; Rice, "Kenesaw Mountain: What Troops Made the Gallant Charge June 27, 1864"; Shellenberger, "Kenesaw Mountain: The Causes That Led to the Repulse of Harker's Charge."

18. Newton to assistant adjutant general, Army of the Cumberland, September 1864, Bradley to Lee, September 12, 1864, *OR* 38(1):296, 355; Howard, "Struggle for Atlanta," 311; Benjamin T. Smith Reminiscences, 146, ALPL; Rice, "Where Harker Fell; C. T. Clark, *Opdycke Tigers*, 278; John W. Tuttle Diary, June 27, 1864, UK. There is some evidence that Harker was among members of the Forty-Second Illinois when he was shot. See Atwater to Waterman, August 12, 1864, *OR* 38(1):361; Hight, *History of the Fifty-Eighth Regiment of Indiana*, 331; Shellenberger, "Kenesaw Mountain: The Causes That Led to the Repulse of Harker's Charge."

19. Howard, *Autobiography*, 1:587; Welsh, *Medical Histories of Union Generals*, 152. Opdycke reported that Harker was shot in the left arm and that the bullet entered his side. See Longacre and Haas, *To Battle for God and the Right*, 189.

20. Bradley to Lee, September 12, 1864, Moore to Waterman, September 12, 1864, Fullerton journal, *OR* 38(1):355, 371, 888; Bradley to Buel, July 1, 1864, Luther P. Bradley Papers, USAMHI; John W. Tuttle Diary, June 27, 1864, UK.

21. Gates, *Rough Side of War*, 227.

22. Ibid.

23. C. T. Clark, *Opdycke Tigers*, 279; Moore to Waterman, September 12, 1864, *OR* 38(1):371.

24. Shellenberger, "Kenesaw Mountain: The Causes That Led to the Repulse of Harker's Charge."

25. C. T. Clark, *Opdycke Tigers*, 280, 283; Benjamin T. Smith Reminiscences, 146, ALPL; Longacre and Haas, *To Battle for God and the Right*, 189; Hight, *History of the Fifty-Eighth Regiment of Indiana*, 331; Warner, *Generals in Blue*, 208.

26. Warner, *Generals in Blue*, 533–34.

27. Wagner to Lee, September 10, 1864, Blanch to Cox, September 15, 1864, *OR* 38(1):335, 347–48; record of events, June 27, 1864, Twenty-Eighth Kentucky, *SOR*, pt. 2, 22:662; Parsons to brother, June 30, 1864, George W. Parsons Papers, IHS; Kerwood, *Annals of the Fifty-Seventh*, 263.

28. Newton to assistant adjutant general, Army of the Cumberland, September 1864, Wagner to Lee, September 10, 1864, *OR* 38(1):296, 335–36; Kerwood, *Annals of the Fifty-Seventh*, 263.

29. Newton to assistant adjutant general, Army of the Cumberland, September 1864, *OR* 38(1):296; Parsons to brother, June 30, 1864, George W. Parsons Papers, IHS; J.W.M. to editor, *Cincinnati Commercial*, June 27, 1864, in *Cincinnati Daily Enquirer*, July 4, 1864; M. Quad article in *Cincinnati Daily Enquirer*, reprinted in McAdams, *Every-Day Soldier Life*, 90.

30. Parsons to brother, June 30, 1864, George W. Parsons Papers, IHS; M. Quad article in *Cincinnati Daily Enquirer*, reprinted in McAdams, *Every-Day Soldier Life*, 90.

31. Parsons to brother, June 30, 1864, George W. Parsons Papers, IHS; Kerwood, *Annals of the Fifty-Seventh*, 263–64.

32. Thomas to Sherman, 9:00 A.M., 9:30 A.M., June 27, 1864, Sherman to Thomas, 8:50 A.M., 9:10 A.M., 9:50 A.M., June 27, 1864, *OR* 38(4):608.

33. C. T. Clark, *Opdycke Tigers*, 279–80; Fullerton journal, *OR* 38(1):888; Castel, *Decision in the West*, 316.

34. Warner, *Generals in Blue*, 267–68.

35. Kimball to assistant adjutant general, Second Division, Fourth Corps, August 4, 1864, Conrad to Jackson, September 12, 1864, MacArthur to [Jackson], September 12, 1864, *OR* 38(1):304, 326, 329; L. G. Bennett and Haigh, *History of the Thirty-Sixth*, 609; *History of the Seventy-Third Regiment of Illinois*, 312.

36. Newton to assistant adjutant general, Army of the Cumberland, September 1864, Kimball to assistant adjutant general, Second Division, Fourth Corps, August 4, 1864, Olson to Powers, September 15, 1864, Bryan to Opdycke, September 1864, Conrad to Jackson, September 12, 1864, MacArthur to [Jackson], September 12, 1864, Fullerton journal, *OR* 38(1):296, 304, 314, 319–20, 326, 329, 888; Daniel E. Barnard to sister, July 1, 1864, Howe-Barnard Family Papers, NL; Castel, *Decision in the West*, 316; *History of the Seventy-Third Regiment of Illinois*, 312; Potter, "Kene-

saw Mountain: The Great Charge on June 27, 1864." Several sources cited in this note indicate that Kimball started his attack anywhere from 8:30 to 10:30 A.M., but Kimball himself placed the time at 9:00 A.M.

37. L. G. Bennett and Haigh, *History of the Thirty-Sixth*, 609; Kimball to assistant adjutant general, Second Division, Fourth Corps, August 4, 1864, Bryan to Opdycke, September 1864, MacArthur to [Jackson], September 12, 1864, *OR* 38(1):304, 319–20, 329; *Chicago Daily Tribune*, July 6, 1864.

38. Bryan to Opdycke, September 1864, Wagner to Lee, September 10, 1864, *OR* 38(1):320, 336; Potter, "Kenesaw Mountain: The Great Charge on June 27, 1864"; Kelly, "Kenesaw Mountain: Another Account of the Famous Charge."

39. Kimball to assistant adjutant general, Second Division, Fourth Corps, August 4, 1864, Bryan to Opdycke, September 1864, Conrad to Jackson, September 12, 1864, *OR* 38(1):304, 320, 326; M. Quad article in *Cincinnati Daily Enquirer*, reprinted in McAdams, *Every-Day Soldier Life*, 91; Potter, "Kenesaw Mountain: The Great Charge on June 27, 1864."

40. Stanley to Fullerton, 1864, Kirby to Mason, September 11, 1864, Jamison to Wright, September 11, 1864, Whitaker to Sinclair, 1864, Stookey to Lawton, September 12, 1864, Hurd to Lawton, September 13, 1864, Fullerton journal, *OR* 38(1):224, 233, 236, 245, 271, 281, 888–89; J. M. Raymond Diary, June 27, 1864, KHS; Partridge, *History of the Ninety-Sixth Regiment Illinois*, 369.

41. Wood to Fullerton, September 10, 1864, Gray to McGrath, September 15, 1864, *OR* 38(1):381, 415; Cope, *Fifteenth Ohio*, 506.

42. N. D. Brown, *One of Cleburne's Command*, 97–98; R. Wills, *Old Enough to Die*, 127; Dixon diary, June 27, 1864, *SOR*, pt. 1, 7:71; Barnes, "An Incident of Kenesaw," 49; John Kern quoted in Williamson, *Third Battalion*, 207; Losson, *Tennessee's Forgotten Warriors*, 156; Miles to sister, July 4, 1864, James Jefferson Miles Letters, EU.

43. R. Wills, *Old Enough to Die*, 127; Barnes, "An Incident of Kenesaw," 49; Yates, *Historical Guide*, 21; Hulet, "Assault on Kenesaw Mountain," 340; Sutherland, *Reminiscences of a Private*, 175; John Green to mother, June 28, 1864, Benjamin and John Green Letters, UVA; Parsons to brother, June 30, 1864, George W. Parsons Papers, IHS.

44. Garrett, *Confederate Diary*, 71–72; invoice, June 30, 1864, William H. Martin service record, 1st Arkansas, M317, NARA.

45. Parsons to brother, June 30, 1864, George W. Parsons Papers, IHS.

46. Gates, *Rough Side of War*, 227; Barnes, "An Incident of Kenesaw," 49; Sutherland, *Reminiscences of a Private*, 174n; French, *Two Wars*, 211.

47. Howard to Whipple, September 18, 1864, Newton to assistant adjutant general, Army of the Cumberland, September 1864, *OR* 38(1):199, 296.

48. Letter to *Cincinnati Commercial*, printed in *Chicago Daily Tribune*, July 6, 1864.

CHAPTER SIX

1. E. W. Payne, *Thirty-Fourth Regiment of Illinois*, 130; Holmes, *52d O.V.I.*, 177; Stewart, *Dan McCook's Regiment*, 114; Styles W. Porter Diary, June 27, 1864, OHS; Griffith to Swift, September 7, 1864, Fahnestock to Swift, September 7, 1864, *OR* 38(1):718, 721.

2. Diary, June 27, 1864, Allen L. Fahnestock Papers, ALPL; Fahnestock recollections, Work, *Re-Union*, 37.

3. Davis to McClurg, September 1864, Langley to Wiseman, September 9, 1864, Cook to Swift, September 7, 1864, Holmes to Swift, September 7, 1864, *OR* 38(1):632, 710, 724, 729; McKinsay, "The Charge at Kennesaw"; Moore, "Kenesaw Mountain: The Conduct of the Fourth and Fourteenth Corps at the Charge"; Hill diary, June 27, 1864, Calvin H. Hill Papers, NC; Holmes, *52d O.V.I.*, 178, 182; Aten, *History of the Eighty-Fifth Regiment Illinois*, 181–82; Stewart, *Dan McCook's Regiment*, 115; James, "McCook's Brigade," 257. At least one source indicated that McCook's brigade deployed with intervals of only five paces between each regiment. See L. J. Dawdy recollections, Work, *Re-Union*, 35.
4. Holmes, *52d O.V.I.*, 198; Fahnestock recollections, Work, *Re-Union*, 37; diary, June 27, 1864, James Lewis Burkhalter Papers, ALPL.
5. Holmes, *52d O.V.I.*, 177, 182.
6. Warner, *Generals in Blue*, 295.
7. Grimshaw, "The Charge at Kenesaw"; Davis to McClurg, September 1864, *OR* 38(1):632; Samuel A. Harper recollections, Work, *Re-Union*, 84; Macaulay, *Critical, Historical and Miscellaneous Essays and Poems*, 765–71; Howatson, *Oxford Companion to Classical Literature*, 143–44; Ward, Heichelheim, and Yeo, *History of the Roman People*, 52–53, 69.
8. Holmes, *52d O.V.I.*, 177–78. In Stewart, *Dan McCook's Regiment*, 117, the assertion is made that McCook recited the stanza from Macaulay's poem while standing in front of the brigade. That idea is not supported by the majority of evidence.
9. J. B. Work, "Map of the 'Dead Angle,'" 1902, *Confederate Veteran* Papers, DU, provides the most detailed information on the ground covered by McCook's attack. An additional source on this topic is Holmes, *52d O.V.I.*, 178, 194. After the war, local residents called the branch that McCook crossed in his attack Big Branch. See Samuel Grimshaw recollections, Work, *Re-Union*, 43.
10. Holmes, *52d O.V.I.*, 178; James, "McCook's Brigade," 258; Mitchell to Wiseman, September 4, 1864, *OR* 38(1):680; Castel, *Decision in the West*, 308.
11. Castel, *Decision in the West*, 311; William Clark McLean diary, June 27, 1864, McLean Family Papers, NYSL.
12. "Battle of Kennesaw Mountain," 110; [Maney], "Battle of Dead Angle," 71; Cheatham recollections, *SOR*, pt. 1, 7:144.
13. Holmes, *52d O.V.I.*, 178, 182; Fahnestock to Swift, September 7, 1864, Holmes to Swift, September 7, 1864, *OR* 38(1):721, 729; Barnhart, "A Hoosier Invades the Confederacy," 190. Some sources place the start of McCook's attack at 8:30 (diary, June 27, 1864, Allen L. Fahnestock Papers, ALPL), or just before 9:00 (Davis to McClurg, September 1864, and Langley to Wiseman, September 9, 1864, *OR* 38(1):632, 710). Castel, *Decision in the West*, 311, accepts this last time estimate, but the majority of evidence coming from participants indicates that McCook started as soon as the bombardment began at 8:00 A.M. Cheatham did report in his recollections, *SOR*, pt. 1, 7:144, that the Union bombardment lasted forty minutes, which implies that there was a time lag between its start and the infantry attack, but then Cheatham also recalled that the bombardment began at 10:00 A.M., not 8:00 A.M., so his account is of dubious reliability on that point.
14. Davis to McClurg, September 1864, Langley to Wiseman, September 9, 1864, Griffith to Swift, September 7, 1864, *OR* 38(1):632, 710, 718; diary, June 27, 1864, Allen L. Fahnestock Papers, ALPL; Stewart, *Dan McCook's Regiment*, 117; Cochennour to Dawdy, December 12, 1897, Work, *Re-Union*, 121. Morgan's brigade had taken posi-

tion in the forward Union line at 6:30 A.M. that day. The Tenth Illinois alone lost five men in the process of relieving the Twenty-First Kentucky. See Jamison, *Recollections*, 247.

15. Holmes, *52d O.V.I.*, 178; James, "McCook's Brigade," 259; Aten, *History of the Eighty-Fifth Regiment Illinois*, 185; Langley to Wiseman, September 9, 1864, *OR* 38(1):710; diary, June 27, 1864, Allen L. Fahnestock Papers, ALPL; West, "Biographical Sketch," 192.

16. Holmes, *52d O.V.I.*, 178; Funston recollections, Work, *Re-Union*, 32.

17. Stewart, *Dan McCook's Regiment*, 117; Holmes, *52d O.V.I.*, 178–79.

18. Holmes, *52d O.V.I.*, 179.

19. Ibid., 179–80.

20. Ibid., 181.

21. James, "McCook's Brigade," 259.

22. Warner, *Generals in Gray*, 315–16; J. T. Bowden to editor, December 15, 1903, *Confederate Veteran* Papers, DU.

23. [Maney], "Battle of Dead Angle," 71.

24. Cheatham recollections, *SOR*, pt. 1, 7:144–45; J. T. Bowden to editor, December 15, 1903, *Confederate Veteran* Papers, DU.

25. Holmes, *52d O.V.I.*, 182–83; Holmes to Swift, September 7, 1864, *OR* 38(1):729.

26. Stewart, *Dan McCook's Regiment*, 119; Holmes, *52d O.V.I.*, 179, 181; Styles W. Porter Diary, June 27, 1864, OHS; Holmes to Swift, September 7, 1864, *OR* 38(1):729.

27. Styles W. Porter Diary, June 27, 1864, OHS; Griffith to Swift, September 7, 1864, *OR* 38(1):718; James, "McCook's Brigade," 260; Holmes, *52d O.V.I.*, 180–83; Stewart recollections, Work, *Re-Union*, 33; Stewart, *Dan McCook's Regiment*, 117–18; Gray, "Kenesaw: What the Third Brigade, Second Division, Fourteenth Corps, Did on the Eventful June 27"; E. M. Payne, "At Kenesaw: A 34th Ill. Man Tells What He Saw There."

28. Dawdy and Brubacker recollections, Work, *Re-Union*, 35, 120–21.

29. J. T. Bowden to editor, December 15, 1903, *Confederate Veteran* Papers, DU; Cheatham recollections, *SOR*, pt. 1, 7:145.

30. J. H. Brubacker letter, January 30, 1901, Work, *Re-Union*, 121.

31. S. M. Canterbury to Work, December 30, 1900, Work, *Re-Union*, 40.

32. M. M. Hooton to Work, March 27, 1901, Work, *Re-Union*, 42.

33. Samuel A. Harper to Work, January 26, 1901, Richard W. Groninger to Work, May 3, 1901, Lewis Krisher to Work, May 3, 1901, Work, *Re-Union*, 85–86.

34. Holmes, *52d O.V.I.*, 198; Stewart, *Dan McCook's Regiment*, 118; Nick B. Stewart recollections, Work, *Re-Union*, 33; Langley to Wiseman, September 9, 1864, *OR* 38(1):711.

35. Langley to Wiseman, September 9, 1864, Cook to Swift, September 7, 1864, *OR* 38(1):711, 724; Angle, *Three Years*, 228; Holmes, *52d O.V.I.*, 167, 198; Barnhart, "A Hoosier Invades the Confederacy," 190; Stewart, *Dan McCook's Regiment*, 119; Ayers to wife, June 27, 1864, Alexander Miller Ayers Papers, EU.

36. Barnhart, "A Hoosier Invades the Confederacy," 190; diary, June 27, 1864, Allen L. Fahnestock Papers, ALPL; Ayers to wife, June 27, 1864, Alexander Miller Ayers Papers, EU; E. M. Payne, "At Kenesaw: A 34th Ill. Man Tells What He Saw There."

37. Stewart, *Dan McCook's Regiment*, 119; J. T. Bowden to editor, December 15, 1903, *Confederate Veteran* Papers, DU; Allen L. Fahnestock to Work, January 29, 1901, Work, *Re-Union*, 39. Stewart, *Dan McCook's Regiment*, 118, claims that the Confed-

erates used hand grenades on June 27, and that one of them injured James Sheets of Company E, "tearing away all the flesh from his cheek." But there is no reliable evidence that hand grenades were available to Cheatham's men that day.

38. Johnson Brown to Cousin Magg, July 15, 1864, GLIAH; Holmes, *52d O.V.I.*, 183–84; Franklin, *Civil War Diaries*, 184.
39. Nick B. Stewart recollections: Sam M. Pyle to Work, April 11, 1901, Work, *Re-Union*, 33, 62; Stewart, *Dan McCook's Regiment*, 119.
40. Moore, "A Rebel Spy."
41. Neighbor, "Kenesaw Mountain: The Part Taken by McCook's Brigade in the Charge"; Styles W. Porter Diary, June 27, 1864, OHS; Holmes, *52d O.V.I.*, 184–85; Langley to Wiseman, September 9, 1864, Cook to Swift, September 7, 1864, *OR* 38(1):711, 724; James, "McCook's Brigade," 261–62; Sam M. Pyle to Work, April 11, 1901, Work, *Re-Union*, 62; Barnhart, "A Hoosier Invades the Confederacy," 190; diary, June 27, 1864, Allen L. Fahnestock Papers, ALPL; E. M. Payne, "At Kenesaw: A 34th Ill. Man Tells What He Saw"; Moore, "Kenesaw Mountain: The Conduct of the Fourth and Fourteenth Corps at the Charge"; Gray, "Kenesaw: What the Third Brigade, Second Division, Fourteenth Corps, Did on the Eventful June 27."
42. Julius Armstrong recollections, Nick B. Stewart recollections: J. T. Seay to Work, January 30, 1901, John S. Cochennour to Lansing J. Dawdy, December 12, 1897, Work, *Re-Union*, 32–33, 41, 121. Erasmus Hanson of Company A, Thirty-Fourth Illinois, in Mitchell's brigade, offered to help carry McCook to the rear but apparently his offer was not accepted. See E. W. Payne, *Thirty-Fourth Regiment of Illinois*, 131.
43. John S. Cochennour to Lansing J. Dawdy, December 12, 1897, Work, *Re-Union*, 122.
44. James Langley to Work, April 26, 1901, Work, *Re-Union*, 103–4.
45. Holmes, *52d O.V.I.*, 198; Palmer, *Personal Recollections*, 205; Jamison, *Recollections*, 247.
46. Allen L. Fahnestock recollections, Work, *Re-Union*, 37; Davis to McClurg, September 1864, *OR* 38(1):633; Holmes, *52d O.V.I.*, 184–85.
47. James, "McCook's Brigade," 262.
48. Stewart, *Dan McCook's Regiment*, 120, 122.
49. Griffith to Swift, September 7, 1864, Fahnestock to Swift, September 7, 1864, *OR* 38(1):718, 721.
50. Warner, *Generals in Blue*, 328.
51. Mitchell to Wiseman, September 4, 1864, Van Tassell to Wilson, September 5, 1864, Pearce to Wilson, September 9, 1864, Jones to Wilson, September 10, 1864, Banning to Wilson, September 9, 1864, *OR* 38(1):680, 685, 692, 697, 703; McAdams, *Every-Day Soldier Life*, 87; E. W. Payne, *Thirty-Fourth Regiment of Illinois*, 126; Payne to wife, June 28, 1864, Edwin W. Payne Papers, ALPL; Pratt, "After Assault at Kenesaw."
52. McAdams, *Every-Day Soldier Life*, 87; E. W. Payne, *Thirty-Fourth Regiment of Illinois*, 127.
53. Mitchell to Wiseman, September 4, 1864, Banning to Wilson, September 9, 1864, *OR* 38(1):680, 703.
54. Banning to Wilson, September 9, 1864, *OR* 38(1):703.
55. Blair, "Fight at Dead Angle," 532–33.
56. Mitchell to Wiseman, September 4, 1864, Van Tassell to Wilson, September 5, 1864, *OR* 38(1):680, 685–85; Robinson to Charlie, June 29, 1864, William C. Robinson Papers, ALPL; E. W. Payne, *Thirty-Fourth Regiment of Illinois*, 127–28; W. B.

Emmons Diary, June 27, 1864, UI; Pratt, "After Assault at Kenesaw." Varied estimates as to the time that Mitchell's brigade began its attack range from 8:00 A.M. to 9:00 A.M. See E. W. Payne, *Thirty-Fourth Regiment of Illinois*, 128, and Pearce to Wilson, September 9, 1864, *OR* 38(1):692. Edwin Payne became confused when writing the history of his regiment, the Thirty-Fourth Illinois; in a letter written the day after the attack, he reported to his wife that the other six companies of the regiment were placed separately from the four that constituted the first and second lines of skirmishers in front of Mitchell's brigade. They were "to support us," he reported. But in writing his regimental history (published in 1902), he asserted that the six companies were placed behind the brigade column. They would not have been in a position to support the skirmish line there. Payne also argued that, once the skirmishers took the Confederate skirmish pits, they were supposed to join the six companies behind Mitchell's column but disobeyed those instructions and pushed on toward the main Rebel line. Evidence from other, authoritative, sources strongly indicates that the six companies were placed in front of the brigade column so as to help the skirmishers if needed. See Payne to wife, June 28, 1864, Edwin W. Payne Papers, ALPL; Payne, *Thirty-Fourth Regiment of Illinois*, 126, 128; Van Tassell to Wilson, September 5, 1864, *OR* 38(1):685.

57. Pearce to Wilson, September 9, 1864, Jones to Wilson, September 10, 1864, *OR* 38(1):692, 697; McAdams, *Every-Day Soldier Life*, 87; Jamison, *Recollections*, 248; William Clark McLean Diary, June 27, 1864, McLean Family Papers, NYSL.

58. "Battle of Kennesaw Mountain," 111–12; McAdams, *Every-Day Soldier Life*, 87; Payne to wife, June 28, 1864, Edwin W. Payne Papers, ALPL; Holmes, *52d O.V.I.*, 180.

59. Mitchell to Wiseman, September 4, 1864, Pearce to Wilson, September 9, 1864, Jones to Wilson, September 10, 1864, *OR* 38(1):680, 692, 697–98.

60. Robinson to Charlie, June 29, 1864, William C. Robinson Papers, ALPL; McAdams, *Every-Day Soldier Life*, 87–89; Mitchell to Wiseman, September 4, 1864, Jones to Wilson, September 10, 1864, *OR* 38(1):680, 698; John Green to mother, June 28, 1864, Benjamin and John Green Letters, UVA.

61. Banning to Wilson, September 9, 1864, *OR* 38(1):703–4; E. W. Payne, *Thirty-Fourth Regiment of Illinois*, 128.

62. Warner, *Generals in Gray*, 210; "Battle of Kennesaw Mountain," 110–11; [Maney], "Battle of Dead Angle," 71.

63. "Battle of Kennesaw Mountain," 112–13.

64. Miles, "Col. Hume R. Feild," 326; Latimer, "Incidents Related," 167; Watkins, *Co. Aytch*, 160; Smith journal, *SOR*, pt. 1, 7:78.

65. Watkins, *Co. Aytch*, 158, 160.

66. Ibid., 157–58, 160; Nelson, "Dead Angle," 321; Marchant to wife, August 2, 1864, Peter Marchant Civil War Correspondence, AHC.

67. Watkins, *Co. Aytch*, 161.

68. Ibid., 158.

69. Latimer, "Incidents Related," 167; W. J. McDill to aunt, July 9, 1864, KMNBP; "Battle of Kennesaw Mountain," 113; Blair, "Fight at Dead Angle," 533.

70. Watkins, *Co. Aytch*, 163.

71. Fleming, *Band of Brothers*, 70–71.

72. Banning to Wilson, September 9, 1864, *OR* 38(1):703–4; John J. Mercer Diary June 27, 1864, AHC; Warfield, "Charging Kenesaw: A 121st Ohio Man Who Saw Only What Happened Near Himself."

73. Jones to Wilson, September 10, 1864, *OR* 38(1):698; McAdams, *Every-Day Soldier Life*, 88; Pearce to Wilson, September 9, 1864, *OR* 38(1):692–93.

74. E. W. Payne, *Thirty-Fourth Regiment of Illinois*, 129, 368, 370; Van Tassell to Wilson, September 5, 1864, *OR* 38(1):686.

75. Cabaniss, *Civil War Journal and Letters*, 67; Ives, "'Record That We Made,'" 334; [Maney], "Battle at Dead Angle," 72.

76. Blair, "Fight at Dead Angle," 533; [Maney], "Battle at Dead Angle," 72; E. W. Payne, *Thirty-Fourth Regiment of Illinois*, 131; Cheatham recollections, *SOR*, pt. 1, 7:145.

77. Mitchell to Wiseman, September 4, 1864, Vernon to Wilson, September 5, 1864, *OR* 38(1):680, 688; Nelson, "Dead Angle," 321; Blair, "Fight at Dead Angle," 533; [Maney], "Battle at Dead Angle," 72; Cheatham recollections, *SOR*, pt. 1, 7:144.

78. Morgan to Morrison, August 23, 1864, Cahill to Wiseman, September 8, 1864, Lum to Wiseman, August 8, 1864, *OR* 38(1):648, 661, 669; Jamison, *Recollections*, 247–48; Dewey, "The Charge at Kenesaw."

79. Thomas to Sawyer, July 16, 1864, *OR* 38(1):151; Charles Caley to Juliaette, July 1–2, 1864, Caley Family Correspondence, UND.

80. Williams to Perkins, September 12, 1864, Geary to Perkins, September 15, 1864, Jones to Forbes, August 1, 1864, *OR* 38(2):32, 134, 212; Prescott to [Houghtaling], September 5, 1864, *OR* 38(1):827; diary, June 27, 1864, Albert M. Cook Papers, SU.

81. J. T. Bowden to editor, December 15, 1903, *Confederate Veteran* Papers, DU; Castel, *Decision in the West*, 307.

82. Watkins, *Co. Aytch*, 160.

CHAPTER SEVEN

1. Cox to Reilly, June 26, 1864, Special Field Orders No. 36, Headquarters, Army of the Ohio, June 26, 1864, *OR* 38(4):600, 604; Schofield, *Forty-Six Years*, 144.

2. Ross to Jackson, June 27, 1864, 6:25 A.M., *OR* 38(4):799.

3. Sherman to Schofield, June 27, 1864, Schofield to Sherman, June 27, 1864, 1:15 P.M., Van Duzer to Eckert, June 27, 1864, *OR* 38(4):616, 618, 626.

4. Cox, *Military Reminiscences*, 1:265–66; Joyce, "Kenesaw Mountain."

5. Schofield to Sherman, June 27, 1864, 7:30 A.M., Cox to Schofield, June 27, 1864, 7:00 A.M., *OR* 38(4):616, 619; Cox, *Military Reminiscences*, 1:265–66.

6. Schofield to Sherman, June 27, 1864, 10:00 A.M., Cox to Schofield, June 27, 1864, 9:30 A.M., *OR* 38(4):616, 620; Schofield to Sherman, September 10, 1864, Hascall to Campbell, September 10, 1864, *OR* 38(2):514, 570; Fout, *Dark Days*, 346–47; Joyce, "Kenesaw Mountain."

7. Ross to Jackson, June 27, 1864, 6:25 A.M., 7:30 A.M., 8:10 A.M., *OR* 38(4):799–800; Kerr, *Fighting with Ross' Texas Cavalry*, 152–53.

8. Cox, *Atlanta*, 123.

9. Ibid., 123–24; Cox, *Military Reminiscences*, 1:266–67; Cox to Schofield, June 27, 1864, 4:30 P.M., *OR* 38(4):620–21; Fout, *Dark Days*, 349–50.

10. Schofield to Sherman, June 27, 1864, 12:20 P.M., 7:00 P.M., Cox to Schofield, June 27, 1864, 4:30 P.M., *OR* 38(4):617–18, 621.

11. Sherman to Thomas, June 27, 1864, 4:10 P.M., Sherman to Schofield, June 27, 1864, 11:45 A.M., 1:05 P.M., 4:10 P.M., *OR* 38(4):610, 616, 618; Schofield, *Forty-Six Years*, 144.

12. Sherman to Schofield, June 27, 1864, Schofield to Cox, June 27, 1864, 5:00 P.M.,

Schofield to Stoneman, June 27, 1864, 5:00 P.M., *OR* 38(4):617, 621–22; Castel, *Decision in the West*, 317–18.

13. Schofield to Sherman, June 27, 1864, Ross to Jackson, June 27, 1864, 6:30 P.M., 8:30 P.M., *OR* 38(4):617, 800–801; Sherman, *Memoirs*, 2:61.

14. Lovell to Smith, June 27, 1864, *OR* 38(4):797.

15. Cox, *Military Reminiscences*, 1:267–68.

16. Thomas to Sherman, June 27, 1864, 10:45 A.M., Stone to Palmer, June 27, 1864, 11:00 A.M., *OR* 38(4):608, 614; Fullerton journal, June 27, 1864, *OR* 38(1):888.

17. Sherman to Thomas, June 27, 1864, 11:45 A.M., 1:30 P.M., *OR* 38(4):609.

18. Thomas to Sherman, June 27, 1864, 1:40 P.M., *OR* 38(4):609.

19. Sherman to Thomas, June 27, 1864, 2:25 P.M., Thomas to Sherman, June 27, 1864, *OR* 38(4):610.

20. Stone, "Atlanta Campaign," 422; Castel, *Decision in the West*, 317.

21. Fullerton journal, June 27, 1864, *OR* 38(1):888.

22. Howard to Thomas, June 27, 1864, 2:40 P.M., Fullerton to Stanley, 2:00 P.M., Newton to Fullerton, June 27, 1864, Hooker to Whipple, June 27, 1864, Davis to Palmer, June 27, 1864, 10:30 P.M., *OR* 38(4):612, 613–15.

23. Sherman, *Memoirs*, 2:61; Sherman to Thomas, June 27, 1864, Sherman to McPherson, June 27, 1864, *OR* 38(4):611, 622.

24. Sherman to Thomas, June 27, 1864, 9:00 P.M., 9:30 P.M., 9:45 P.M., 9:50 P.M., Thomas to Sherman, [June 27, 1864], Whipple to Hooker (copies to Howard and Palmer), June 27, 1864, *OR* 38(4):611, 615.

25. C. W. Wills, *Army Life*, 271; H. H. Wright, *History of the Sixth Iowa*, 292–93; Logan to Clark, June 28, 1864, Morgan L. Smith to Townes, June 28, 1864, Lofland to Townes, September 10, 1864, Giles A. Smith to Morgan L. Smith, June 28, 1864, Jones to Lofland, September 12, 1864, Walcutt to Wilkinson, August 10, 1864, Stewart to Upton, September 10, 1864, Williston to Upton, September 9, 1864, Alexander to not stated, September 12, 1864, *OR* 38(3):85, 179, 188, 194, 222, 227, 318, 324, 326, 337; *Sketch of the Operations of the Forty-Seventh Ohio*, 6; McKittrick to wife, June 27, 1864, Samuel McKittrick Papers, TC; "War Diary of Thaddeus H. Capron," 384; *Story of the Fifty-Fifth Regiment Illinois*, 326.

26. Morgan L. Smith to Townes, June 28, 1864, *OR* 38(3):179; Alvah Stone Skilton Diary, June 27, 1864, Skilton-Davis-Heyman Family Papers, RBHPC; Edward B. Moore Diary, June 27, 1864, AHC-UW.

27. French to Cockrell, June 27, 1864, Cockrell to French, [June 27, 1864], French to Walker, June 27, 1864 Walker to French, June 27, 1864, *OR* 38(4):798–99; Renken to parents and sisters, June 28, 1864, William Augustus Renken Letters, MHM; Albert Hiffman Reminiscences, 11–12, Hiffman Family Papers, MHM; Castel, *Tom Taylor's Civil War*, 133; Wharton diary, June 27, 1864, John Wharton Papers, MHM.

28. French, "Kennesaw Mountain," 278; Renken to parents and sisters, June 28, 1864, William Augustus Renken Letters, MHM.

29. John W. Tuttle Diary, June 27, 1864, UK; Harwell, "Campaign from Chattanooga," 270; John S. Lightfoot Diary, June 27, 1864, EU; Blanch to Cox, September 15, 1864, *OR* 38(1):348; Howard, *Autobiography*, 1:585; Cope, *Fifteenth Ohio*, 507.

30. Holmes, *52d O.V.I.*, 185; William L. Kemp to friends, June 30, 1864, Scott Family Papers, SHSM-C; Pearce to Wilson, September 9, 1864, Langley to Wiseman, September 9, 1864, *OR* 38(1):693, 711; diary, June 27, 1864, Allen L. Fahnestock Papers, ALPL; Stewart, *Dan McCook's Regiment*, 122.

31. Pearce to Wilson, September 9, 1864, Banning to Wilson, September 9, 1864, Langley to Wiseman, September 9, 1864, Holmes to Swift, September 7, 1864, *OR* 38(1):693, 704, 711, 729; E. W. Payne, *Thirty-Fourth Regiment of Illinois*, 129, 131.

32. Cabaniss, *Civil War Journal and Letters*, 67; Holmes, *52d O.V.I.*, 187; Blair, "Fight at Dead Angle," 533.

33. Stewart, *Dan McCook's Regiment*, 120.

34. Dawdy recollections, Work, *Re-Union*, 35; Stewart, *Dan McCook's Regiment*, 120–22; Bostwick, "A Soldier's Gratitude"; E. W. Payne, *Thirty-Fourth Regiment of Illinois*, 130.

35. Harmon, "Dead Angle," 219; Stewart, *Dan McCook's Regiment*, 124; J. T. Bowden to editor, December 15, 1903, *Confederate Veteran* Papers, DU; Watkins, *Co. Aytch*, 162–63.

36. E. W. Payne, *Thirty-Fourth Regiment of Illinois*, 130; Banning to Wilson, September 9, 1864, *OR* 38(1):704.

37. "Battle of Kennesaw Mountain," 113; Blair, "Fight at Dead Angle," 533; Fahnestock to Work, January 29, 1901, Sam M. Pyle to Work, April 11, 1901, Work, *Re-Union*, 39, 62; Beyer and Keydel, *Deeds of Valor*, 372.

38. Holmes, *52d O.V.I.*, 183; Aten, *History of the Eighty-Fifth Regiment Illinois*, 187.

39. James, "McCook's Brigade," 261; Davis to McClurg, September 1864, Vernon to Wilson, September 5, 1864, *OR* 38(1):633, 688; Aten, *History of the Eighty-Fifth Regiment Illinois*, 187; Holmes, *52d O.V.I.*, 185.

40. "Battle of Kennesaw Mountain," 115; H. H. Wright, *History of the Sixth Iowa*, 292; Stewart, *Dan McCook's Regiment*, 124; James, "McCook's Brigade," 262–63; McAdams, *Every-Day Soldier Life*, 89; Fahnestock recollections, Work, *Re-Union*, 37–38.

41. E. W. Payne, *Thirty-Fourth Regiment of Illinois*, 130; McAdams, *Every-Day Soldier Life*, 88–89, 92.

42. Castel, *Decision in the West*, 319–20. The following sources estimate Federal losses ranging from 2,500 to 3,500, and Confederate losses from 522 to 808. See Sherman, *Memoirs*, 2:61; Sherman, "Grand Strategy," 252; Sherman to Halleck, September 15, 1864, *OR* 38(1):69; Van Duzer to Eckert, June 28, 1864, Sherman to Halleck, June 29, 1864, *OR* 38(4):633, 635; Howard, *Autobiography*, 1:586; Gordon Hickenlooper, "The Reminiscences of General Andrew Hickenlooper, 1861–1865," 54, *Civil War Times Illustrated* Collection, USAMHI; Connelly, *Autumn of Glory*, 360.

43. Sherman to Halleck, September 15, 1864, *OR* 38(1):69; Johnston, *Narrative*, 343, 580; Hardee to Davis, June 29, 1864, Crist, *Papers of Jefferson Davis*, 10:492; "Special" to editor, June 28, 1864, *Memphis Daily Appeal*, June 29, 1864; Stone, "Atlanta Campaign," 422.

44. Johnston, "Opposing Sherman's Advance," 273.

45. Ibid., 272–73. For further evidence that Johnston and other Confederates minutely studied Sherman's casualty figures on June 27, see Johnston to Cooper, October 20, 1864, Pickett to Roy, and Roy's endorsement, September 11, 1864, Loss in Engagement at Kennesaw Mountain, June 27, 1864, Loring to Mackall, July 30, 1864, French to Loring, June 28, 1864, *OR* 38(3):617, 703, 870, 901; "Battle of Kennesaw Mountain," 116.

46. Sherman, *Memoirs*, 2:63; Logan to Clark, [September 13, 1864], *OR* 38(3):113; Bryan to Opdycke, September 1864, Wagner to Lee, September 10, 1864, Mitchell to Wiseman, September 4, 1864, Jones to Wilson, September 10, 1864, Banning to

Wilson, September 9, 1864, Langley to Wiseman, September 9, 1864, Cook to Swift, September 7, 1864, Holmes to Swift, September 7, 1864, *OR* 38(1):320, 322, 336, 340, 680, 698, 704, 715–16, 725, 731; Slack to father and mother, September 10, 1864, Albert L. Slack Letters, EU.

47. Ayers to wife, June 27, July 8, 1864, diary, June 27, 1864, Alexander Miller Ayers Papers, EU.

48. Howard to Whipple, September 18, 1864, Kimball to assistant adjutant general, Second Division, Fourth Corps, August 4, 1864, *OR* 38(1):199, 304; Howard to wife, June 28, 1864, O. O. Howard Papers, BC; Longacre and Haas, *To Battle for God and the Right*, 190; correspondence of the *Cincinnati Commercial*, in *Chicago Daily Tribune*, July 6, 1864; Bradley to Buel, July 1, 1864, Luther P. Bradley Papers, USAMHI.

49. Smith to Jackson, September 10, 1864, Wagner to Lee, September 10, 1864, *OR* 38(1):323, 336; Aldrich, *Quest for a Star*, 122; Bradley to Buel, July 1, 1864, Luther P. Bradley Papers, USAMHI; Sherman to Harker, August 9, 1864, *OR* 38(5):445–46; Johnson Brown to Cousin Magg, July 15, 1864, GLIAH.

50. D. Cronemiller to Mrs. Stegner, July 2, 1864, Frederick W. Stegner Papers, NC; Ayers to wife, June 27, 1864, Alexander M. Ayers Papers, NC; Ayers to wife, July 6, 1864, Alexander Miller Ayers Papers, EU.

51. M. M. Hooton to Work, March 27, 1901, anonymous, "'Looking On' at Kenesaw," Work, *Re-Union*, 42, 83; Warner, *Generals in Blue*, 295.

52. Anonymous, "'Looking On' at Kenesaw," Work, *Re-Union*, 83; Stewart, *Dan McCook's Regiment*, 123; Souder, "Death of Gen. McCook." Word of McCook's death reached his brigade only two days after it occurred. See Ayers diary, July 19, 1864, Alexander Miller Ayers Papers, EU.

53. Benjamin T. Smith Reminiscences, 147, ALPL; Moore to Howard, September 28, 1864, *OR* 38(3):53; extracts from report by Surg. Charles W. Jones, *SOR*, pt. 1, 7:12; C. J. Walton, "'One Continued Scene of Carnage,'" 34.

54. Barnhart, "A Hoosier Invades the Confederacy," 190–91.

55. Ayers to wife, June 27, 1864, Alexander M. Ayers Papers, NC; Jamison, *Recollections*, 248–49.

56. Reese, "A Memory of the War."

57. Cooper to assistant adjutant general, Department of the Cumberland, October 11, 1864, *OR* 38(1):181–82; extracts from report by Surg. Charles W. Jones, *SOR*, pt. 1, 7:12.

58. Barnhart, "A Hoosier Invades the Confederacy," 191; *Story of the Fifty-Fifth Regiment Illinois*, 329.

59. Cooper to assistant adjutant general, Department of the Cumberland, October 11, 1864, *OR* 38(1):181–82.

60. L. G. Bennett and Haigh, *History of the Thirty-Sixth*, 610.

61. Palmer to Whipple, June 29, 1864, *OR* 38(1):509.

62. Albert Quincy Porter Diary, June 27, 1864, MSU; Cobb, "Letter," 40.

63. Howard to Whipple, September 18, 1864, Davis to McClurg, June 28, 1864, *OR* 38(1):205, 510; Garrett, *Confederate Diary*, 72; Logan to Clark, June 28, [September 13], 1864, French to Loring, June 28, 1864, Cockrell to Sanders, June 27, 1864, *OR* 38(3):85, 99, 901, 915.

64. West, "Biographical Sketch," 192–93.

65. Sherman to Halleck, June 27, 1864, 8:00 P.M., *OR* 38(4):607.

66. Sherman to Thomas, June 27, 1864, *OR* 38(4):611.

67. Johnston to Bragg, June 27, 1864, Johnston to Wheeler, June 27, 1864, *OR* 38(4):796; Thomas B. Mackall Journal, June 27, 1864 (McMurry transcript), Joseph E. Johnston Papers, CWM; Wynne and Taylor, *This War So Horrible*, 99; Johnston to Cooper, October 20, 1864, Loring to Mackall, July 30, 1864, French to West, August 31, 1864, *OR* 38(3):617, 870, 901; M'Neilly, "Great Game of Strategy," 380; French, *Two Wars*, 209; McKittrick to wife, June 28, 1864, Samuel McKittrick Papers, TC; John Kern diary, June 27, 1864, in Williamson, *Third Battalion*, 207; Bell to wife, June 30, 1864, A. W. Bell Papers, DU; Hamilton M. Branch to mother, June 28, 1864, Branch Family Papers, UGA; Joseph E. Johnston to Wigfall, June 28, August 27, 1864, Louis Trezevant Wigfall Family Papers, LC; Markham to mother, June 30–July 4, 1864, Thomas R. Markham Papers, LSU; Jim Huffman, comp. "Pre- & Civil War Letters of Lt. Col. Columbus Sykes 16th [*sic*] Regiment, Mississippi Infantry," 70, MDAH; Dan to Cousin Lou, June 30, 1864, Avie Honnoll Papers, MSU; Mitchell to wife, July 2, 1864, Robert Goodwin Mitchell Papers, UGA; Clampitt, *Confederate Heartland*, 67.

68. Neal diary, June 28, 1864, Dempsey Neal Papers, NC; Lee to Davis, June 29, 1864, *OR* 37(1):769.

69. D. M. Smith, "Civil War Diary," 147; "War Diary of Thaddeus H. Capron," 384; Peter J. Osterhaus diary, June 24, 27, 28, 1864, Osterhaus Family Papers, MHM; Jim to brother, July 1, 1864, Giaque Family Papers, UI; Clarke, "With Sherman in Georgia," 361; Newell to Kate, June 28, 1864, William McCulloch Newell Papers, NC.

70. *History of the Seventy-Third Regiment of Illinois*, 313; Benjamin T. Smith Reminiscences, 160, ALPL; Daniel, *Days of Glory*, 410; George Cooley Diary, June 27–28, 1864, WHS; Longacre and Haas, *To Battle for God and the Right*, 190–91; Maley to father and mother, July 2, 1864, Henry H. Maley Letters, UND; Cope, *Fifteenth Ohio*, 513.

71. Blake dispatch to editor, June 30, 1864, *Chicago Daily Tribune*, July 3, 1864.

72. Howard to Whipple, September 18, 1864, Newton to assistant adjutant general, Army of the Cumberland, September 1864, Olson to Powers, September 15, 1864, Mitchell to Wiseman, September 4, 1864, *OR* 38(1):199, 296, 314, 680; Howard, "Struggle for Atlanta," 311.

73. Aldrich, *Quest for a Star*, 121–22.

74. Wagner, *Organization and Tactics*, 91, 91n.

75. Logan to Clark, June 28, 1864, Walcutt to Wilkinson, August 19, 1864, *OR* 38(3):85, 318; Dodge to Clark, June 27, 1864, *OR* 38(4):623; Clarke, "With Sherman in Georgia," 361; Morgan to Drane, July 2, 1864, Isaac N. Morgan Papers, NC; Jones to Wilson, September 10, 1864, *OR* 38(1):698.

76. Poe to wife, June 28, 1864, Orlando Metcalfe Poe Papers, LC; Force to brother, July 6, 1864, Journal and Letter Book, 515, M. F. Force Papers, UW.

77. Davis to McClurg, September 1864, Vernon to Wilson, September 5, 1864, *OR* 38(1):633, 688; Sanderson to Cadle, June 28, 1864, *OR* 38(3):587.

CHAPTER EIGHT

1. Fleming, *Band of Brothers*, 71.

2. James, "McCook's Brigade," 262; Langley to Wiseman, September 9, 1864, *OR* 38(1):711; J. B. Work, "Map of the 'Dead Angle,'" 1902, *Confederate Veteran* Papers, DU; Davis to McClurg, September 1864, *OR* 38(1):633; Payne, "At Kenesaw: A 34th

Ill. Man Tells What He Saw"; Gray, "Kenesaw: What the Third Brigade, Second Division, Fourteenth Corps Did in the Eventful June 27."

3. Rogers, *125th Regiment Illinois*, 98; Nelson, "Dead Angle," 321.

4. W. B. Emmons Diary, June 29, 1864, UI; Banning to Wilson, September 9, 1864, *OR* 38(1):704.

5. J. T. Bowden to editor, December 15, 1903, *Confederate Veteran* Papers, DU; Watkins, *Co. Aytch*, 161–62; Holmes, *52d O.V.I.*, 197; Aten, *History of the Eighty-Fifth Regiment Illinois*, 189; Shellenberger, "Kenesaw Mountain: The Causes That Led to the Repulse of Harker's Charge."

6. Blair, "Fight at Dead Angle," 533; [Maney], "Battle at Dead Angle," 72.

7. [Maney]. "Battle at Dead Angle," 72; Garrett, *Confederate Diary*, 72; John Batchelor Diary, June 28, 1864, ALPL.

8. Rogers, *125th Regiment Illinois*, 99; Philip R. Ward Diary, June 29, 1864, Charles S. Harris Collection, UTC; [Maney], "Battle at Dead Angle," 72; McAdams, *Every-Day Soldier Life*, 92; John J. Mercer Diary, June 28–29, 1864, AHC; John S. Lightfoot Diary, June 28, 1864, EU; Cheatham recollections, *SOR*, pt. 1, 7:145; Aten, *History of the Eighty-Fifth Regiment Illinois*, 187; Langley to Wiseman, September 9, 1864, *OR* 38(1):711; [Maney], "Battle at Dead Angle," 72. Some sources indicate different times for the start and end of the burial truce. See Styles W. Porter Diary, June 29, 1864, OHS; Ellison, *On to Atlanta*, 55; John Batchelor Diary, June 29, 1864, ALPL.

9. Latimer, "Incidents Related," 167; E. W. Payne, *Thirty-Fourth Regiment of Illinois*, 133–34; James, "McCook's Brigade," 263; Carroll Henderson Clark Memoirs, 42, TSLA.

10. Holmes, *52d O.V.I.*, 187; "Battle of Kennesaw Mountain," 115–16; E. W. Payne, *Thirty-Fourth Regiment of Illinois*, 133; Jamison, *Recollections*, 249; Smith journal, *SOR*, pt. 1, 7:78; Ellison, *On to Atlanta*, 56; Ayers to wife, June 29, 1864, Alexander Miller Ayers Papers, EU.

11. J. T. Bowden to editor, December 15, 1903, *Confederate Veteran* Papers, DU; Watkins, *Co. Aytch*, 159; E. W. Payne, *Thirty-Fourth Regiment of Illinois*, 134; Stewart, *Dan McCook's Regiment*, 126; Cheatham's recollections, *SOR*, pt. 1, 7:145; Holmes, *52d O.V.I.*, 188, 197; Ayers to wife, June 28, 29, 1864, and diary, June 29, 1864, Alexander Miller Ayers Papers, EU. Some Confederates attempted to fix the number of Federal dead that were buried on June 29 at absurdly high figures, from 800 to 925. See "Battle of Kennesaw Mountain," 114–16.

12. Garrett, *Confederate Diary*, 72; "Battle of Kennesaw Mountain," 115–16; John S. Lightfoot Diary, June 29, 1864, EU; J. T. Bowden to editor, December 15, 1903, *Confederate Veteran* Papers, DU; J. M. Raymond Diary, June 29, 1864, KHS.

13. Philip R. Ward Diary, June 29, 1864, Charles S. Harris Collection, UTC; Morgan to Drane, July 2, 1864, Isaac N. Morgan Papers, NC; Nelson, "Dead Angle," 321; Harwell, "Campaign from Chattanooga," 270–71; Stewart, *Dan McCook's Regiment*, 127; Ellison, *On to Atlanta*, 55; E. W. Payne, *Thirty-Fourth Regiment of Illinois*, 134; Styles W. Porter Diary, June 29, 1864, OHS; George Cooley Diary, June 29, 1864, WHS; J. T. Bowden to editor, December 15, 1903, *Confederate Veteran* Papers, DU.

14. James, "McCook's Brigade," 263, 274; E. W. Payne, *Thirty-Fourth Regiment of Illinois*, 134; Ayers to wife, June 29, 1864, Alexander Miller Ayers Papers, EU.

15. Rogers, *125th Regiment Illinois*, 99; Bishop, "Twenty-Ninth Tennessee Infantry," 436–37; Harwell, "Campaign from Chattanooga," 271.

16. Rogers, *125th Regiment Illinois*, 99.

17. Ellison, *On to Atlanta*, 55; Jamison, *Recollections*, 249–50; Holmes, *52d O.V.I.*, 188.

18. Rogers, *125th Regiment Illinois*, 99; diary, June 29, 1864, Allen L. Fahnestock Papers, ALPL. Some observers contended that Davis and Dilworth had a hand in refusing to give up the abandoned muskets in no-man's-land. See Fahnestock recollections, Work, *Re-Union*, 38, Aten, *History of the Eighty-Fifth Regiment Illinois*, 188.

19. Ellison, *On to Atlanta*, 55.

20. E. W. Payne, *Thirty-Fourth Regiment of Illinois*, 134; "Battle of Kennesaw Mountain," 115; diary, June 29, 1864, Calvin H. Hill Papers, NC; Garrett, *Confederate Diary*, 72; Aten, *History of the Eighty-Fifth Regiment Illinois*, 189; *History of the Seventy-Third Regiment of Illinois*, 314.

21. Whitaker to Sinclair, 1864, Kimball to assistant adjutant general, Second Division, Fourth Corps, August 4, 1864, *OR* 38(1):245, 304; Partridge, *History of the Ninety-Sixth Regiment Illinois*, 370–71; Harwell, "Campaign from Chattanooga," 270; Kerwood, *Annals of the Fifty-Seventh*, 264; Laird to mother, June 29, 1864, John McNickle Laird Collection, UTK; J. M. Raymond Diary, June 28, 1864, KHS; Potter, "Kenesaw Mountain: The Great Charge on June 27, 1864."

22. Parsons to brother, June 30, 1864, George W. Parsons Papers, IHS.

23. John W. Tuttle Diary, June 29, 1864, UK; John K. Ely Diary, June 28, 1864, Judy Beal Collection; Gates, *Rough Side of War*, 228.

24. *Story of the Fifty-Fifth Regiment Illinois*, 330; Hawthorn to sister, June 26–July 9, 1864, John Hawthorn Papers, NC; Hamilton M. Branch to mother, July 2, 1864, Branch Family Papers, UGA.

25. Jamison, *Recollections*, 250.

26. Diary, June 29, 1864, Allen L. Fahnestock Papers, ALPL; Cheatham's recollections, *SOR*, pt. 1, 7:145–46; W. B. Emmons Diary, June 30, 1864, UI; Aten, *History of the Eighty-Fifth Regiment Illinois*, 190; E. W. Payne, *Thirty-Fourth Regiment of Illinois*, 133; Franklin, *Civil War Diaries*, 185; Van Tassell to Wilson, September 5, 1864, *OR* 38(1):686; E. M. Payne, "At Kenesaw: A 34th Ill. Man Tells What He Saw."

27. James, "McCook's Brigade," 265; Styles W. Porter Diary, June 30, 1864, OHS; McAdams, *Every-Day Soldier Life*, 92–93; Franklin, *Civil War Diaries*, 185.

28. Gates, *Rough Side of War*, 229; Cope, *Fifteenth Ohio*, 514; Partridge, *History of the Ninety-Sixth Regiment Illinois*, 371–72; John W. Tuttle Diary, June 30, 1864, UK; Harwell, "Campaign from Chattanooga," 271.

29. [Maney], "Battle at Dead Angle," 72–73.

30. Latimer, "Incidents Related," 167–68.

31. Smith journal, Cheatham's recollections, *SOR*, pt. 1, 7:78, 146; Garrett, *Confederate Diary*, 72; N. D. Brown, *One of Cleburne's Command*, 99; Thomas B. Mackall Journal, June 30, 1864 (McMurry transcript), Joseph E. Johnston Papers, CWM; Thomas to Sherman, June 29, 1864, Palmer to Whipple, June 30, 1864, *OR* 38(4):636, 642; Thomas to Sawyer, July 16, 1864, Vernon to Wilson, September 5, 1864, Pearce to Wilson, September 9, 1864, *OR* 38(1):151, 688, 693; Blair, "Fight at Dead Angle," 533; E. W. Payne, *Thirty-Fourth Regiment of Illinois*, 133; Mulligan [ed.], *Badger Boy in Blue*, 106–7; diary, June 30, 1864, Charles Richard Pomeroy Papers, DU; Thomas Moore Woods to father and mother, June 30, 1864, Woods and Young Family Papers, UA; Jones and Martin, *Gentle Rebel*, 42; Alexander Dobbin Diary, June 30, 1864, EU; Hight, *History of the Fifty-Eighth Regiment of Indiana*, 331.

32. Mitchell to Wiseman, September 4, 1864, *OR* 38(1):680; J. T. Bowden to editor, December 15, 1903, *Confederate Veteran* Papers, DU.

33. Cheatham recollections, *SOR*, pt. 1, 7:146; Nelson, "Dead Angle," 321; "A Rash Deed at Dead Angle," 394; J. B. Work, "Map of the 'Dead Angle,'" 1902, *Confederate Veteran* Papers, DU; Llewellyn Griffin Hoxton Reminiscences, unpaginated, UVA; Holmes, *52d O.V.I.*, 191–92.

34. Holmes, *52d O.V.I.*, 185, 192.

35. Bradley to Buel, July 1, 1864, Luther P. Bradley Papers, USAMHI; C. J. Walton, "'One Continued Scene of Carnage,'" 34; Holmes, *52d O.V.I.*, 188.

36. James, "McCook's Brigade," 262; diary, June 28–29, July 1–2, 1864, Allen L. Fahnestock Papers, ALPL; Van Tassell to Wilson, September 5, 1864, Pearce to Wilson, September 9, 1864, *OR* 38(1):686, 693; Philip R. Ward Diary, June 30, July 1–2, 1864, Charles S. Harris Collection, UTC; Pratt, "After the Assault at Kenesaw."

37. Watkins, *Co. Aytch*, 159–60.

38. E. W. Payne, *Thirty-Fourth Regiment of Illinois*, 134.

39. W. B. Emmons Diary, July 1–2, 1864, UI.

40. Ibid., July 2, 1864.

41. Ibid., July 1–2, 1864; E. W. Payne, *Thirty-Fourth Regiment of Illinois*, 135.

42. J. T. Bowden to editor, December 15, 1903, *Confederate Veteran* Papers, DU; Nelson, "Dead Angle," 322; Nelson, "Dead Angle Again," 32.

43. Stewart, *Dan McCook's Regiment*, 128; Aten, *History of the Eighty-Fifth Regiment Illinois*, 189; Moore, "A Rebel Spy"; James, "McCook's Brigade," 264; Jamison, *Recollections*, 249.

44. Affidavit by Joseph Teeter, May 27, 1865, Casualty Sheet, undated, Inventory of Effects Sheet, undated, Memorandum From Prisoner of War Records, undated, Muster Cards, Edward O'Donnell service record, Thirty-Fourth Illinois, NARA; E. W. Payne, *Thirty-Fourth Regiment of Illinois*, 134.

45. Fahnestock to Swift, September 7, 1864, *OR* 38(1):721; E. W. Payne, *Thirty-Fourth Regiment of Illinois*, 135; McAdams, *Every-Day Soldier Life*, 92.

46. W. B. Emmons Diary, July 1, 1864, UI; Holmes, *52d O.V.I.*, 186; W. J. Funston recollections: Sam M. Pyle to Work, April 11, 1901, Work, *Re-Union*, 32, 62; Stewart, *Dan McCook's Regiment*, 128.

47. Holmes, *52d O.V.I.*, 186.

48. W. B. Emmons Diary, July 2, 1864, UI; Stewart, *52d. O.V.I.*, 128; Morgan to Drane, July 2, 1864, Isaac N. Morgan Papers, NC. Styles W. Porter Diary, July 2, 1864, OHS, indicates that the Fifty-Second Ohio fired eighteen thousand rounds that day rather than thirteen thousand.

49. Aten, *History of the Eighty-Fifth Regiment Illinois*, 191; Holmes, *52d O.V.I.*, 186.

50. Allen L. Fahnestock recollections, Samuel Grimshaw recollections, J. B. Work recollections, Work, *Re-Union*, 38, 43, 121; Stewart, *Dan McCook's Regiment*, 127; Grimshaw, "The Charge at Kenesaw."

51. Samuel Grimshaw recollections, Work, *Re-Union*, 43; Langley to Wiseman, September 9, 1864, *OR* 38(1):711; Watkins, *Co. Aytch*, 164; Capers to Smith, September 10, 1864, *OR* 38(3):716.

52. Holmes, *52d O.V.I.*, 187; "Battle of Kennesaw Mountain," 115; Cabaniss, *Civil War Journal and Letters*, 67; Allen L. Fahnestock recollections, Work, *Re-Union*, 39.

53. Nelson, "Dead Angle," 322.

54. Fleming, *Band of Brothers*, 72.

55. Brown to Fannie, July 2, 1864, Edward Norphlet Brown Letters, ADAH; Smith journal, *SOR*, pt. 12, 7:7.

56. Jones to Wilson, September 10, 1864, *OR* 38(1):698; Ives, "'Record That We Made,'" 334; *History of the Seventy-Third Regiment of Illinois*, 314; Fleming, *Band of Brothers*, 118; Poe to wife, July 1, 1864, Orlando Metcalfe Poe Papers, LC; diary, July 1, 1864, Allen L. Fahnestock Papers, ALPL.

57. Stewart, *Dan McCook's Regiment*, 126; Grimshaw, "The Charge at Kenesaw."

58. Riley to Moses H. Wright, June 30, 1864, E. B. Dudley Riley service record, M331, NARA; Wright to Hypolite Oladowski, June 30, 1864, Moses H. Wright service record, M331, NARA; Aten, *History of the Eighty-Fifth Regiment Illinois*, 189; James, "McCook's Brigade," 263; Fleming, *Band of Brothers*, 71, 118–19; Cabaniss, *Civil War Journal and Letters*, 67; J. T. Bowden to editor, December 15, 1903, *Confederate Veteran* Papers, DU; Grimshaw, "The Charge at Kenesaw"; A. L. Jordan, "'Dead Angle' Tunneled," 601; diary, July 1, 1864, Allen L. Fahnestock Papers, ALPL. Only one source, a Confederate account, indicates that the Federals used turpentine balls at Cheatham's Hill. There is no other evidence to support that contention. See Harmon, "Dead Angle," 219.

59. Nelson, "Dead Angle," 321; James, "McCook's Brigade," 262.

60. James, "McCook's Brigade," 265.

61. N. D. Brown, *One of Cleburne's Command*, 99; Taylor, "Why Firing Occurred," 77; Eleazer, "Fight at Dead Angle," 312; Nelson, "Dead Angle," 321; Harris, "Dead Angle," 560; Carroll Henderson Clark Memoirs, 42, TSLA; Smith journal, *SOR*, pt. 1, 7:78–79.

62. Rogers, *125th Regiment Illinois*, 98; Styles W. Porter Diary, June 28, 1864, OHS; diary, June 29, July 3, 1864, Allen L. Fahnestock Papers, ALPL; Holmes, *52d O.V.I.*, 187; Otho Herron Morgan, "Home Letters," 225, AHC; J. B. Work, "Map of the 'Dead Angle,'" 1902, *Confederate Veteran* Papers, DU; Theodore D. Neighbor to Work, February 5, 1901, Work, *Re-Union*, 34.

63. Holmes, *52d O.V.I.*, 187, 192; Aten, *History of the Eighty-Fifth Regiment Illinois*, 190; James, "McCook's Brigade," 264.

64. Garrett, *Confederate Diary*, 72; Rogers, *125th Regiment Illinois*, 98–99; Stewart, *Dan McCook's Regiment*, 128. If the Confederates had any doubt that a mining project had been underway at Cheatham's Hill, the truth was revealed to them after the campaign ended. When Hood took the Army of Tennessee northward to threaten Sherman's rail line after the fall of Atlanta, the troops briefly stopped at Kennesaw and explored the area around Cheatham's Hill. Now, for the first time, they could see the mine entrance. J. T. Bowden to editor, December 15, 1903, *Confederate Veteran* Papers, DU; A. L. Jordan, "'Dead Angle' Tunneled," 601.

65. Holmes, *52nd O.V.I.*, 187; James, "McCook's Brigade," 264. Chaplain John J. Hight of the Fifty-Eighth Indiana claimed Federal diggers tunneled only about fifteen feet into Cheatham's Hill by the end of the campaign. See Hight, *History of the Fifty-Eighth Regiment of Indiana*, 335.

66. Whitaker to Sinclair, 1864, Taylor to Mason, September 15, 1864, *OR* 38(1):245, 247; Gates, *Rough Side of War*, 230–31.

67. Taylor to Mason, September 15, 1864, *OR* 38(1):247; N. D. Brown, *One of Cleburne's Command*, 98–99; Garrett, *Confederate Diary*, 72; Morgan to Drane, July 2, 1864, Isaac N. Morgan Papers, NC.

68. George Cooley Diary, June 30–July 2, 1864, WHS; John W. Tuttle Diary, June 30–July 1, 1864, UK.

69. Jackson, *The Colonel's Diary*, 137; Ackley to wife, July 1, 1864, Charles Thomas Ackley Civil War Letters, UI.

70. Capers to Smith, September 10, 1864, *OR* 38(4):717.

71. French, *Two Wars*, 210; "Report of Engagement of Wards Battery on Little Kennesaw Mountain June 28th," George S. Storrs Papers, ASU.

72. French, *Two Wars*, 210.

73. West to French, June 28, 1864, *OR* 38(4):802; autobiography, 28, Edwin Hansford Rennolds, Sr., Papers, UTK.

74. Morgan to Drane, July 2, 1864, Isaac N. Morgan Papers, NC; Hamilton M. Branch to mother, July 2, 1864, Branch Family Papers, UGA; C. Wright, *A Corporal's Story*, 121–22.

75. Walker to French, June 28, 1864, *OR* 38(4):802; Llewellyn Griffin Hoxton Reminiscences, unpaginated, UVA.

76. George G. Truair to father, June 28, 1864, Truair Family Papers, UTA; McKittrick to wife, June 28, 1864, Samuel McKittrick Papers, TC.

CHAPTER NINE

1. Sherman to Webster, June 28, 1864, *OR* 38(4):629; Sherman to Halleck, September 15, 1864, *OR* 38(1):69.

2. Sherman to McPherson, June 28, 1864, Sherman to Schofield, June 28, 29, 1864, Schofield to Sherman, June 29, 1864, *OR* 38(4):631, 638; diary, June 28, 1864, Orlando Metcalfe Poe Papers, LC; Cox, *Military Reminiscences*, 1:269.

3. Fullerton to Newton, June 28, 1864, Sherman to Thomas, June 28, 29, 1864, Schofield to Thomas, June 30, 1864, *OR* 38(4):630, 636, 646.

4. Sherman to McPherson, June 28, 30, 1864, McPherson to Sherman, June 28, 29, 30, 1864, Baylor to Dayton, June 30, 1864, *OR* 38(4):631, 639, 641–642,646–47; Moore to Howard, September 28, 1864, Reese to Poe, September 14, 1864, Kossak to Reese, September 10, 1864, *OR* 38(3):53, 65–66, 68; Sherman, *Memoirs*, 2:61.

5. Angle, *Three Years*, 229; Sherman, *Memoirs*, 2:61–62.

6. Halleck to Sherman, June 28, 1864, Sherman to Halleck, June 29, 1864, *OR* 38(4):629, 635.

7. Schofield to Sherman, June 30, 1864, *OR* 38(4):645.

8. Thomas to Schofield, June 30, 1864, Schofield to Hascall, June 30, 1864, Sherman to Schofield, June 30, 1864, McClurg to Baird, June 30, 1864, *OR* 38(4):641, 643, 645–46; Jones to Forbes, August 1, 1864, *OR* 38(2):212; itinerary, June 30, 1864, Numa Barned Papers, CL-UM.

9. Schofield to Sherman, June 30, 1864, *OR* 38(4):645.

10. Schofield to Sherman, June 30, 1864, Sherman to Schofield, June 30, 1864, *OR* 38(4):643–44, 646.

11. Wheeler to Hood, June 29, 1864, Ratchford to Wheeler, June 30, 1864, Hood to Wheeler, June 30, 1864, Johnston to Wheeler, June 30, 1864, *OR* 38(4):805–6.

12. Brown to Davis, June 28, 1864 Davis to Brown, June 29, 1864, *OR* 52(2):680–81; Bragg to Davis, June 29, 1864, *OR* 38(4):805.

13. Sherman to Ellen, June 30, 1864, Simpson and Berlin, *Sherman's Civil War*, 660–61.

14. Thomas to Sherman, June 29, 1864, Sherman to Thomas, June 29, 1864, Sherman to McPherson, June 29, 1864, *OR* 38(4):637.

15. "Personal Biography of Major General Grenville Mellen Dodge 1831–1870," 1:219–20, Grenville Mellen Dodge Papers, SHSI.

16. Thomas to McPherson, June 30, 1864, *OR* 38(4):642.

17. Special Field Orders No. 31, Headquarters, Military Division of the Mississippi, July 1, 1864, *OR* 38(5):14; Sherman to Schofield, June 30, 1864, *OR* 38(4):644–45.

18. Special Field Orders No. 40, Headquarters, Army of the Ohio, June 30, 1864, *OR* 38(4):649; Schofield to Sherman, September 10, 1864, Hascall to Campbell, September 10, 1864, *OR* 38(2):514, 570–71; Schofield to Sherman, July 1, 1864, *OR* 38(5):9; Kerr, *Fighting with Ross' Texas Cavalry*, 153–54.

19. Sherman to Thomas and McPherson, July 1, 1864, Schofield to Sherman, July 1, 1864, 3:00 P.M. and 9:45 P.M., Sherman to Schofield, July 1, 1864, Schofield to Hascall, July 1, 1864, Van Duzer to Eckert, July 1, 1864, *OR* 38(5):5, 8–9, 11, 14.

20. Castel, *Tom Taylor's Civil War*, 134; Saunier, *History of the Forty-Seventh Regiment Ohio*, 266; Taylor to Fisk, September 10, 1864, *OR* 38(3):245; Schofield to Sherman, September 10, 1864, Hascall to Campbell, September 10, 1864, *OR* 38(2):514, 571; Sherman to Schofield, July 2, 1864, Schofield to Sherman, July 2, 1864, *OR* 38(5):20.

21. Schofield to Sherman, September 10, 1864, *OR* 38(2):515; Castel, *Decision in the West*, 329.

22. *History of the Seventy-Third Regiment of Illinois*, 314; John W. Tuttle Diary, July 2, 1864, UK; Partridge, *History of the Ninety-Sixth Regiment Illinois*, 372; French, *Two Wars*, 212; W. L. Truman Memoirs, July 1–2, 1864, www.cedarcroft.com.; Daniel Harris Reynolds Diary, July 2, 1864, UAF.

23. Schofield to Sherman, September 10, 1864, *OR* 38(2):514–15.

24. John Moore to Howard, September 28, 1864, *OR* 38(3):53; Gordon Hickenlooper, "The Reminiscences of General Andrew Hickenlooper, 1861–1865," 54, *Civil War Times Illustrated* Collection, USAMHI.

25. Peter J. Osterhaus diary, July 2, 1864, Osterhaus Family Papers, MHM; Special Field Orders No. 57, [Headquarters, Army of the Tennessee], July 2, 1864, *OR* 38(5):28–29.

26. Blair to Clark, September 12, 1864, *OR* 38(3):552; Sherman to Thomas, July 2, 1864, Thomas to Sherman, July 2, 1864, Whipple to Howard, July 2, 1864, Whipple to Palmer, July 2, 1864, Sherman to Schofield, July 2, 1864, *OR* 38(5):16–17, 20; Stanley to Fullerton, 1864, *OR* 38(1):224; Scribner, *How Soldiers Were Made*, 303; Cope, *Fifteenth Ohio*, 514–15.

27. Thomas B. Mackall Journal, July 1, 2, 1864 (McMurry transcript), Joseph E. Johnston Papers, CWM; Johnston, *Narrative*, 345; Johnston to Cooper, October 20, 1864, *OR* 38(3):617; Johnston to Bragg, July 3, 1864, circular, Headquarters, Army of Tennessee, July 2, 1864, 1:30 P.M., *OR* 38(5):860.

28. Daniel Harris Reynolds Diary, July 2, 1864, UAF; W. L. Truman Memoirs, July 2, 1864, www.cedarcroft.com.

29. Storrs, "Kennesaw Mountain," 139; diary, July 2, 1864, John Wharton Papers, MHM.

30. French, *Two Wars*, 215; Daniel Harris Reynolds Diary, July 2, 1864, UAF.

31. N. D. Brown, *One of Cleburne's Command*, 99.

32. Harmon, "Dead Angle," 219; Franklin, *Civil War Diaries*, 185.

33. [Maney], "Battle at Dead Angle," 73–74.

34. Ibid., 74.

35. Wynne and Taylor, *This War So Horrible*, 100; John S. Lightfoot Diary, July 3, 1864, EU; Hamilton M. Branch to mother, July 3, 1864, Branch Family Papers, UGA; George Anderson Mercer Diary, July 2, 1864, UNC; diary, July 2, 1863, Edwin Hansford Rennolds, Sr., Papers, UTK.

36. McPherson to Logan, July 2, 1864, 9:15 P.M., John Alexander Logan Family Papers,

LC; Albert Hiffman reminiscences, 12, Hiffman Family Papers, MHM; Thomas to Sherman, July 2, 1864, Sherman to Thomas, July 2, 1864, *OR* 38(5):15–16.

37. Howard to Clark, September 9, 1864, *OR* 38(3):80.

38. Diary, July 2, 1864, Allen L. Fahnestock Papers, ALPL; E. W. Payne, *Thirty-Fourth Regiment of Illinois*, 135; James, "McCook's Brigade," 265–66; Stewart, *Dan McCook's Regiment*, 129.

39. Sherman to Schofield, July 2, 1864, Thomas to Sherman, July 3, 1864, 2:45 A.M., 5:00 A.M., Sherman to Thomas, 4:00 A.M., *OR* 38(5):23, 29; Dodge to Clark, November 25, 1864, *OR* 38(3):382; Howard, *Autobiography*, 1:591; William Cline Diary, July 3, 1864, UND.

40. Logan to Clark, [September 13, 1864], *OR* 38(3):100; Sherman to Halleck, September 15, 1864, *OR* 38(1):69.

41. Logan to Clark, [September 13, 1864], *OR* 38(3):100; Hawthorn to sister, June 26–July 9, 1864, John Hawthorn Papers, NC; Peter J. Osterhaus diary, July 3, 1864, Osterhaus Family Papers, MHM; Goodnow to wife, July 5, 1864, James Harrison Goodnow Papers, LC; Osterhaus to Townes, September 9, 1864, *OR* 38(3):133; H. H. Wright, *History of the Sixth Iowa*, 298; Howard to Clark, September 9, 1864, *OR* 38(3):80; Thomas B. Mackall Journal, July 3, 1864 (McMurry transcript), Joseph E. Johnston Papers, CWM; diary, July 3, 1864, Charles Richard Pomeroy Papers, DU.

42. Howe, *Marching with Sherman*, 52; Sherman to Thomas, copy to Schofield, July 3, 1864, *OR* 38(5):30; Sherman, *Memoirs*, 2:62; Sherman to Halleck, September 15, 1864, *OR* 38(1):69.

43. Gordon Hickenlooper, "The Reminiscences of General Andrew Hickenlooper, 1861–1865," 54, *Civil War Times Illustrated* Collection, USAMHI; Jackson, *Colonel's Diary*, 139.

44. Edwin Witherby Brown, "Under a Poncho with Grant and Sherman," 91–92, MU.

45. John Michael Tomey Diary, July 3, 1864, IHS; Pierson, "From Chattanooga to Atlanta," 345.

46. Cook to Fred, July 7, 1864, Cook diary, July 3, 1864, Albert M. Cook Papers, SU; Toombs, *Reminiscences of the War*, 144. A member of Osterhaus's division also noted that the Confederate works were fronted by three rows of sharpened stakes, slanted at a forty-five-degree angle. See Hawthorn to sister, June 26–July 9, 1864, John Hawthorn Papers, NC.

47. John W. Tuttle diary, July 3, 1864, UK; Fullerton to Stanley, July 3, 1864, Howard to Thomas, July 3, 1864, *OR* 38(5):31; Taylor to Mason, September 15, 1864, *OR* 38(1):247–48; J. M. Raymond Diary, July 3, 1864, KHS; P. D. Jordan, "Forty Days," 139.

48. Howard, *Autobiography*, 1:591–93; Gates, *Rough Side of War*, 233; J. M. Raymond Diary, July 3, 1864, KHS; Bauer, *Soldiering*, 138; Jamison, *Recollections*, 250.

49. W. B. Emmons Diary, July 3, 1864, UI; Stewart, *Dan McCook's Regiment*, 129; E. W. Payne, *Thirty-Fourth Regiment of Illinois*, 135; Fahnestock recollections, Work, *Re-Union*, 39; diary, July 3, 1864, Allen L. Fahnestock Papers, ALPL; Pratt, "After Assault at Kenesaw"; Hight, *History of the Fifty-Eighth Regiment of Indiana*, 333–34; *Letters of Captain Henry Richards*, 39–40.

50. Gates, *Rough Side of War*, 233.

51. Styles W. Porter Diary, July 2 [sic, really July 3], 1864, OHS.

52. Diary, July 3, 1864, Charles Richard Pomeroy Papers, DU; Morgan to sister, July 6, 1864, Isaac N. Morgan Papers, NC.

53. W. B. Emmons Diary, July 3, 1864, UI; Styles W. Porter Diary, July 3, 5, 1864, OHS; Goodnow to wife, July 5, 1864, James Harrison Goodnow Papers, LC.

54. Sherman to Halleck, September 15, 1864, *OR* 38(1):69; Sherman, *Memoirs*, 2:65; Sherman to Halleck, July 3, 1864, *OR* 38(5):29.

55. Sherman to Schofield, July 3, 1864, McPherson to Sherman, July 3, 1864, *OR* 38(5):34, 36; Force to Mr. Kebler, July 9, 1864, Force to brother, July 6, 1864, Journal and Letter Book, 515, M. F. Force Papers, UW; diary, July 3, 1864, George W. Modil Papers, MDAH; Ackley to wife, July 6, 1864, Charles Thomas Ackley Civil War Letters, UI.

56. Schofield to Sherman, September 10, 1864, *OR* 38(2):515; Schofield, *Forty-Six Years*, 136–37.

57. Jones to Lofland, September 12, 1864, Taylor to Fisk, September 10, 1864, Fulton to Fisk, September 8, 1864, *OR* 38(3):227, 245, 253; Duke, *History of the Fifty-Third Regiment Ohio*, 147; Saunier, *History of the Forty-Seventh Regiment Ohio*, 267; Edward B. Moore Diary, July 3, 1864, AHC-UW.

58. Lofland to Townes, September 10, 1864, Hildt to McAuley, September 9, 1864, Jones to Lofland, September 12, 1864, Taylor to Fisk, September 10, 1864, Moore to Fisk, September 12, 1864, *OR* 38(3):188, 209, 227, 245, 259; Edward B. Moore Diary, July 3, 1864, AHC-UW.

59. Lofland to Townes, September 10, 1864, Hildt to McAuley, September 9, 1864, Jones to Lofland, September 12, 1864, *OR* 38(3):188, 209, 227; Edward B. Moore Diary, July 3, 1864, AHC-UW; Castel, *Tom Taylor's Civil War*, 134.

60. Dodge to Clark, November 25, 1864, *OR* 38(3):382; "Personal Biography of Major General Grenville Mellen Dodge 1831–1870," 1:227, Grenville Mellen Dodge Papers, SHSI; Ackley to wife, July 6, 1864, Charles Thomas Ackley Civil War Letters, UI; Naylor to Coz Sallie, July 16, 1864, James M. Naylor Papers, OHS.

61. Lofland to Townes, September 10, 1864, Blair to Clark, July 3, 1864, Blair to Clark, September 12, 1864, Gresham to Alexander, 1864, *OR* 38(3):188, 541, 552, 579; Newell to Kate, July 4, 1864, William McCulloch Newell Papers, NC.

62. Howard, *Autobiography*, 1:593.

63. Sherman, *Memoirs*, 2:65; Sherman to Halleck, September 15, 1864, *OR* 38(1):69; Sherman to McPherson, July 3, 1864, *OR* 38(5):36–37.

64. Sherman to Thomas, July 3, 1864, Sherman to McPherson, July 3, 1864, *OR* 38(5):30–31, 36–37.

65. Dodge to Clark, November 25, 1864, *OR* 38(3):382; Naylor to Coz Sallie, July 16, 1864, James M. Naylor Papers, OHS; Edwin Witherby Brown, "Under a Poncho with Grant and Sherman," 93, MU.

66. Dodge to Clark, November 25, 1864, *OR* 38(3):382; "Personal Biography of Major General Grenville Mellen Dodge 1831–1870," 1:227–29, Grenville Mellen Dodge Papers, SHSI; C. Wright, *A Corporal's Story*, 116; C. H. Smith, *Fuller's Ohio Brigade*, 158, 160.

67. Blair to Clark, July 4, September 12, 1864, *OR* 38(3):541–42, 553; Force to brother, July 6, 1864, Journal and Letter Book, 517, M. F. Force Papers, UW.

68. Blair to Clark, July 4, September 12, 1864, *OR* 38(3):542, 552; Hubbart, *An Iowa Soldier*, 50–51.

69. Johnston, *Narrative*, 344; G. W. Smith, "Georgia Militia," 331–32; Smith to Hood, September 15, 1864, *OR* 38(3):970; [P. C. Key] to wife, July 2, 1864, Key Family Civil War Letters, UGA; Scaife and Bragg, *Joe Brown's Pets*, 29.

NOTES TO PAGES 204–9 : 299

70. G. W. Smith, "Georgia Militia," 332–33; Hess, "Civilians at War," 335–36; Daniel to Girls, July 3, 1864, George Hewitt Daniel Civil War Correspondence, AHC; Wood to Family, July 6, 1864, Robert T. Wood Papers, UGA; P. C. Key to wife, July 5, 9, 1864, Key Family Civil War Letters, UGA; Scaife and Bragg, *Joe Brown's Pets*, 31; Thomas J. Head to Sallie, July 7, 1864, Earl J. Hess Collection.

71. Blair to Clark, July 4, September 12, 1864, Gresham to Alexander, 1864, *OR* 38(3):542, 552, 579; Thomas J. Head to Sallie, July 7, 1864, Earl J. Hess Collection.

72. Dayton to Thomas, July 4, 1864, Whipple to Palmer, July 4, 1864, *OR* 38(5):43; Goodnow to wife, July 5, 1864, James Harrison Goodnow Papers, LC; Hawthorn to sister, June 26–July 9, 1864, John Hawthorn Papers, NC; Peter J. Osterhaus diary, July 4, 1864, Osterhaus Family Papers, MHM; Osterhaus to Townes, September 9, 1864, *OR* 38(3):133.

73. Howard to Thomas, July 4, 1864, Sherman to McPherson, July 4, 1864, *OR* 38(5):43, 46.

74. Johnston, *Narrative*, 345; Vaughan, *Personal Record*, 86; Johnston to Bragg, July 5, 1864, *OR* 38(5):865.

75. Johnston, *Narrative*, 345.

76. Ibid., 346; Mackall to [wife], July 5, 1864, William Whann Mackall Papers, UNC; Sherman to Halleck, September 15, 1864, *OR* 38(1):69.

77. Thomas to Sherman, July 5, 1864, McPherson to Sherman, July 5, 1864, 11:30 A.M., 9:00 P.M., Stoneman to Sherman, July 5, 1864, *OR* 38(5):50, 55–56, 60–61; "Personal Biography of Major General Grenville Mellen Dodge 1831–1870," 1:228, Grenville Mellen Dodge Papers, SHSI; Naylor to Coz Sallie, July 16, 1864, James M. Naylor Papers, OHS; Blair to Clark, September 12, 1864, Gresham to Alexander, 1864, *OR* 38(3):553, 579.

78. Sherman to McPherson, July 5, 1864, Garrard to Dayton, July 5, 1864, *OR* 38(5):59–60.

79. Logan to wife, July 5, 1864, John Alexander Logan Family Papers, LC.

80. Sherman to Stoneman, July 5, 1864, Sherman to McPherson, July 7, 1864, *OR* 38(5):60–61, 80.

81. Longacre and Haas, *To Battle for God and the Right*, 193; Kruse to parents, July 9, 1864, Charles T. Kruse Letters, NL. For other men who went up the hill at Vining's Station to see Atlanta, consult George Cooley Diary, July 6, 1864, WHS; John Batchelor Diary, July 5, 1864, ALPL; diary, July 5, 1864, Allen L. Fahnestock Papers, ALPL.

82. J. M. Raymond Diary, July 6, 1864, KHS; McNeil, "It Gives Some Light."

83. Sherman to Halleck, July 9, 1864, *OR* 38(5):91–92.

84. Ibid. Sherman continued to explain the attack for some time that summer. See Sherman to Ellen, July 9, 1864, Sherman to Ewing, July 13, 1864, Simpson and Berlin, *Sherman's Civil War*, 663–65; Sherman to Harker, August 9, 1864, *OR* 38(5):445; Sherman to Halleck, September 15, 1864, *OR* 38(1):69.

85. Transcript of Davis interview with William D. Gale, July 30, 1864, Crist, *Papers of Jefferson Davis*, 10:570.

86. Bragg to Davis, July 15, 1864, *OR* 38(5):881.

CONCLUSION

1. Sherman, *Memoirs*, 2:61; William E. Sloan Diary, June 27, 1864, Civil War Collection, TSLA; *"Southern Battlefields,"* 15; "View by H.M. Lynn of the Battle of Kennesaw Mountain Written after the War, Possibly for a Speech," H. M. Lynn Papers, UNC; Marchant to Susan, July 16, 1864, Peter Marchant Civil War Correspondence, AHC.

2. Sherman to Rawlins, January 3, 1863, return of casualties, Chickasaw Bayou, *OR* 17(1):605–10, 625.

3. Sherman to Rawlins, December 19, 1863, *OR* 31(2):581; Cozzens, *Shipwreck of Their Hopes*, 154–55, 205–43.

4. Sherman, *Memoirs*, 2:25–26; Sherman to Comstock, April 5, 1864, Grant to Sherman, April 19, 1864, *OR* 32(3):262, 409; "Personal Recollections: Strategy and battles of Sherman & Johnston illustrated in active campaigns," unpaginated, box 5, folder 3, Oliver Otis Howard Papers, LMU. As Orlando Poe told his wife in mid-July, "This was not a campaign for the capture of Atlanta, so much as it was to prevent any of Johnston's force going east." Poe to Nell, July 18, 1864, Orlando Metcalfe Poe Papers, LC.

5. Sherman to Halleck, May 20, June 11, 1864, *OR* 38(4):260, 455; Sherman to Ellen, June 30, 1864, Simpson and Berlin, *Sherman's Civil War*, 660.

6. J. C. Thompson to Alexander P. Stewart, December 8, 1867, Joseph E. Johnston Papers, CWM; Seay to Gray, August 5, 1864, *OR* 38(3):170; Cox, *Military Reminiscences*, 1:257. A member of the Twenty-Fourth Kentucky in Cox's division echoed Cox's view that Sherman's attack grew out of impatience and frustration. See Joyce, "Kenesaw Mountain."

7. "Battle of Kennesaw Mountain," 114; Castel, *Decision in the West*, 343.

8. Hood, *Advance and Retreat*, 125; Sherman, *Memoirs*, 2:61.

9. French, *Two Wars*, 215; Hughes, *Civil War Memoir*, 202.

10. Johnston, *Narrative*, 341–44.

11. Cozzens, *Shipwreck of Their Hopes*, 45–46.

12. Budd to Beatty, November 30, 1863, *OR* 31(2):538; Boynton, *Sherman's Historical Raid*, 107.

13. Stone, "Atlanta Campaign," 420, 422.

14. Scribner, *How Soldiers Were Made*, 300–2; Hazen, *Narrative*, 265.

15. Cope, *Fifteenth Ohio*, 507.

16. Palmer, *Personal Recollections*, 205.

17. "Recollections of Service in the Civil War," 25–27, Luther P. Bradley Papers, USAMHI; Rice, "Where Harker Fell."

18. James, "McCook's Brigade," 267–68; Theodore D. Neighbor letter, February 5, 1901, Samuel Grimshaw recollections, 1901, Work, *Re-Union*, 35, 44; Neighbor, "Kenesaw Mountain: The Part Taken by McCook's Brigade in the Charge"; Moore, "Kenesaw Mountain: The Conduct of the Fourth and Fourteenth Corps at the Charge."

19. R. D. McDonald article in unidentified newspaper, Work, *Re-Union*, 55; James, "McCook's Brigade," 269–70.

20. James W. Langley to Work, August 21, 1900, J. B. Work, "The Assault on Kenesaw, Was It Necessary?," Work, *Re-Union*, 33, 137; James, "McCook's Brigade," 273.

21. C. W. Wills, *Army Life*, 271; "Personal Biography of Major General Grenville Mellen

Dodge 1831–1870," 1:223, Grenville Mellen Dodge Papers, SHSI; Edwin Witherby Brown, "Under a Poncho with Grant and Sherman," 92, MU; Logan, *Volunteer Soldier*, 683; Mrs. John A. Logan, *Reminiscences*, 155–56.

22. Cox, *Atlanta*, 129; Schofield, *Forty-Six Years*, 142–44.

23. Schofield, *Forty-Six Years*, 144–45.

24. Woodworth, *Nothing but Victory*, 525; Castel, *Decision in the West*, 320–21; S. Davis, *Atlanta Will Fall*, 87; McMurry, *Atlanta*, 108–9; Daniel, *Days of Glory*, 409–10; Schofield, *Forty-Six Years*, 340.

25. Sherman to Ellen, July 9, 1864, Simpson and Berlin, *Sherman's Civil War*, 663–664; Angle, *Three Years*, 236.

APPENDIX

1. Worsham, *Old Nineteenth Tennessee*, 123.

2. M. Quad article in *Cincinnati Daily Enquirer*, reprinted in McAdams, *Every-Day Soldier Life*, 91. The Confederate soldier discussed here was an anonymous veteran of Cleburne's division who had been interviewed by Charles Bertrand Lewis (pen name M. Quad), for the *Cincinnati Daily Enquirer*.

3. P. D. Jordan, "Forty Days," 150–51; Lossing, *Pictorial Field Book*, 3:402. Local efforts to promote Kennesaw Mountain as a tourist magnet included the distribution of photographs highlighting the historic features of the place. See four photographs in box 2, folder 13, Samuel G. French Papers, MDAH, and two photographs in Photography Collection, UMBC.

4. Theodore D. Neighbor letter, February 5, 1901, Work, *Re-Union*, 34.

5. Holmes, *52d O.V.I.*, 169–70, 176.

6. Ibid., 176–77.

7. Ibid., 191.

8. Ibid., 190–92, 196.

9. Ibid., 190, 192–93.

10. Ibid., 191, 195–96, 198.

11. "Buys a Battlefield," *Peoria Herald Transcript*, December 10, 1899, clipping in Lansing Dawdy, Jr., Papers, ALPL.

12. "Kennesaw Mountain Administrative History," www.nps.gov/kemo; circular, Headquarters, Col. Dan McCook's Brigade, August 14, 1902, Allen L. Fahnestock Papers, ALPL; circular letter by Dawdy, February 15, 1907, Lansing Dawdy, Jr., Papers, ALPL; field visit to Cheatham's Hill, December 16, 1986; C. H. Coffey pension record, NARA.

13. A. L. Jordan, "'Dead Angle' Tunneled," 601; "Kennesaw Mountain Administrative History," www.nps.gov/kemo.

14. "Kennesaw Mountain Administrative History," www.nps.gov/kemo.

15. Ibid.

16. Ibid.

17. Ibid.; Yates, *Historical Guide*, 21; park information on www.nps.gov/kemo.; W. Kelly, *Kennesaw Mountain*, 42. For modern photographs of Cheatham's Hill, see D. Kelly, "Atlanta Campaign," 50–51.

18. McMurry, "Kolb's Farm," 24; Yates, *Historical Guide*, 23. For a modern photograph of the restored Kolb house, see W. Kelly, *Kennesaw Mountain*, 30. Photographs of

the progress of the Kolb House restoration during the 1930s can be found on the Library of Congress Prints and Photographs website, www.loc.gov.

19. W. Kelly, *Kennesaw Mountain*, 44; Yates, *Historical Guide*, 40, 43–44.

20. Yates, *Historical Guide*, 38; W. Kelly, *Kennesaw Mountain*, 44.

21. W. Kelly, *Kennesaw Mountain*, 44; "The Work of Kennesaw Chapter," 621; Yates, *Historical Guide*, 43.

22. Johnson and Hartshorn, "Development of Field Fortification," 593.

23. My discussion of fortification remnants at Kennesaw Mountain is based on field visits to the park, December 16, 19, 24, 30, 31, 1986, and January 31, 1987, and Barnard, *Photographic Views*, nos. 31, 32.

Bibliography

ARCHIVES

Abraham Lincoln Presidential Library, Springfield, Illinois
  John Batchelor Diary
  James Lewis Burkhalter Papers
  Lansing Dawdy Jr. Papers
  Allen L. Fahnestock Papers
  Edwin W. Payne Papers
  William C. Robinson Papers
  Benjamin T. Smith Reminiscences
Alabama Department of Archives and History, Montgomery
  Edward Norphlet Brown Letters
  Hardee Family Papers
  E. D. Willett Diary
Atlanta History Center, Atlanta, Georgia
  George Hewitt Daniel Civil War Correspondence
  Peter Marchant Civil War Correspondence
  William N. Mattison Civil War Correspondence
  John J. Mercer Diary, Antebellum and Civil War Collection
  Otho Herron Morgan. "Home Letters"
  Unidentified Soldier Letter, Co. H, 63rd Georgia, Antebellum and Civil War
    Collection
Augusta State University, Special Collections, Augusta, Georgia
  George S. Storrs Papers
Judy Beal Collection, Harrogate, Tennessee
  John K. Ely Diary
Belleville Public Library, Belleville, Illinois
  Peter Joseph Osterhaus. "What I Saw of the War"
Bowdoin College, Special Collections, Brunswick, Maine
  Charles Henry Howard Collection
  O. O. Howard Papers
The Citadel, Archives and Museum, Charleston, South Carolina
  Irving Bronson, "Recollections of the Civil War," Bruce Catton Collection
  Samuel McKittrick Papers
College of William and Mary, Special Collections, Williamsburg, Virginia
  Calfee Papers
  Joseph E. Johnston Papers

Cornell University, Division of Rare and Manuscript Collections, Ithaca, New York
    Edwin C. Obriham Letters, June and Gilbert Krueger Civil War Letters
Duke University, Rare Books, Manuscripts, and Special Collections, Durham,
    North Carolina
    A. W. Bell Papers
    Isaac Howell Carrington Papers
    Confederate Veteran Papers
    Charles Richard Pomeroy Papers
Emory University, Manuscript, Archives, and Rare Books Library, Atlanta, Georgia
    Alexander Miller Ayers Papers
    W. B. Corbitt Diary, Confederate Miscellany Collection, Series 1
    Alexander Dobbin Diary
    Luther L. Gates Letters
    John S. Lightfoot Diary
    James Jefferson Miles Letters
    Andrew Jackson Neal Papers
    Albert L. Slack Letters
Gilder Lehrman Institute of American History, New York
    Johnson Brown Letter
Earl J. Hess Collection, Knoxville, Tennessee
    Thomas J. Head Letters
Indiana Historical Society, Indianapolis
    George W. Parsons Papers
    John Michael Tomey Diary
Kansas Historical Society, Topeka
    J. M. Raymond Diary
Kennesaw Mountain National Battlefield Park, Kennesaw, Georgia
    W. J. McDill Letter
Library of Congress, Manuscript Division, Washington, D.C.
    James Harrison Goodnow Papers
    John Alexander Logan Family Papers
    Breckinridge Long Papers
    Orlando Metcalfe Poe Papers
    Louis Trezevant Wigfall Family Papers
Lincoln Memorial University, Abraham Lincoln Library and Museum, Harrogate,
    Tennessee
    Oliver Otis Howard Papers
    William Merrell, "Personal Memoirs of the Civil War"
Louisiana State University, Louisiana and Lower Mississippi Valley Collections,
    Baton Rouge
    James Foster and Family Correspondence
    Josiah Knighton Family Papers
    Thomas R. Markham Papers
Miami University, Special Collections, Oxford, Ohio
    Edwin Witherby Brown, "Under a Poncho with Grant and Sherman"
Mississippi Department of Archives and History, Jackson
    Samuel G. French Papers

Jim Huffman, comp. "Pre- & Civil War Letters of Lt. Col. Columbus Sykes 16th
  [*sic*] Regiment, Mississippi Infantry"
George W. Modil Papers
Mississippi State University, Special Collections, Starkeville
  Avie Honnoll Papers
  Albert Quincy Porter Diary
  Emmett Ross Papers
Missouri History Museum, St. Louis
  Hiffman Family Papers
  McEwen Family Papers
  Osterhaus Family Papers
  William Augustus Renken Letters
  John Wharton Papers
Museum of the Confederacy, Richmond, Virginia
  General Orders and Circulars, Hood's Corps
  Tennessee Volume, Record 28, Roll of Honour
National Archives and Records Administration, Washington, D.C.
  RG109, War Department Collection of Confederate Records
    Special Orders From May 9th 1864 to June 19th 1864, Head Quarters, Army
      of the Mississippi, ch. 2, No. 221½
  C. H. Coffey pension record, 22nd Indiana
  Edward O'Donnell service record, 34th Illinois
  William H. Martin service record, 1st Arkansas, M317, Compiled Service Records
    of Confederate Soldiers Who Served in Organizations from the State of Arkansas
  Moses H. Wright service record, M331, Compiled Service Records of Confederate
  General and Staff Officers, and Non-Regimental Enlisted Men
Navarro College, Pearce Civil War Collection, Corsicana, Texas
  Alexander M. Ayers Papers
  John Hawthorn Papers
  Calvin H. Hill Papers
  Isaac N. Morgan Papers
  Dempsey Neal Papers
  William McCulloch Newell Papers
  Frederick W. Stegner Papers
Newberry Library, Chicago
  Howe-Barnard Family Papers
  Charles T. Kruse Letters
  Max Schlund Papers
New York State Library, Albany
  Alanson B. Cone Memoir
  Leander E. Davis Letters
  Eaton Family Papers
  McLean Family Papers
North Carolina State Archives, Raleigh
  A. J. Price Letter
Ohio Historical Society, Columbus
  Thaddeus Kane Miller Papers

James M. Naylor Papers
Styles W. Porter Diary
James Sidney Robinson Papers
Rice University, Woodson Research Center, Houston, Texas
W. H. Brooker Diary
Rutherford B. Hayes Presidential Center, Fremont, Ohio
Skilton-Davis-Heyman Family Papers
Stanford University, Special Collections, Stanford, California
Israel Spencer Letters, Civil War Collection
State Historical Society of Iowa, Des Moines
Grenville Mellen Dodge Papers
State Historical Society of Missouri, Research Center Columbia
Scott Family Papers
Avington Wayne Simpson Diary
State Historical Society of Missouri, Research Center St. Louis
Jewel Family Civil War Letters
Stones River National Battlefield, Murfreesboro, Tennessee
George Washington Deemer Diary
Syracuse University, Special Collections, Syracuse, New York
Albert M. Cook Papers
Tennessee State Library and Archives, Nashville
David Shires Myers Bodenhamer Reminiscences, Civil War Collection
Carroll Henderson Clark Memoirs, Civil War Collection
William E. Sloan Diary, Civil War Collection
U.S. Army Military History Institute, Carlisle, Pennsylvania
Luther P. Bradley Papers
Gordon Hickenlooper, ed., "The Reminiscences of General Andrew Hickenlooper,
1861–1865," *Civil War Times Illustrated* Collection
Hubbard T. Minor Papers
David Nichols Papers, Harrisburg Civil War Round Table Collection
University of Alabama, W. Stanley Hoole Special Collections Library, Tuscaloosa
Henry DeLamar Clayton Sr. Papers
Woods and Young Family Papers
University of Arkansas, Special Collections, Fayetteville
Daniel Harris Reynolds Diary
University of Georgia, Hargrett Rare Book and Manuscript Library, Athens
Banks Family Papers
Branch Family Papers
Key Family Civil War Letters
Robert Goodwin Mitchell Papers
Robert T. Wood Papers
University of Houston, Special Collections, Texas
William W. Edgerton Civil War Letters
University of Iowa, Special Collections, Iowa City
Charles Thomas Ackley Civil War Letters
John C. Brown Diary
W. B. Emmons Diary
Giaque Family Papers

University of Kentucky, Special Collections and Digital Programs, Lexington
    John W. Tuttle Diary
University of Maryland, Baltimore County, Special Collections, Baltimore
    Photography Collection
University of Michigan, William L. Clements Library, Ann Arbor
    Numa Barned Papers, James M. Schoff Civil War Collections
University of Mississippi, Archives and Special Collections, Oxford
    Jesse L. Henderson Civil War Diary
University of North Carolina, Southern Historical Collection, Chapel Hill
    Clayton Family Papers
    Joseph B. Cumming Papers
    H. M. Lynn Papers
    William Whann Mackall Papers
    George Anderson Mercer Diary
    Avington Wayne Simpson Papers
University of Notre Dame, Rare Books and Special Collections, South Bend, Indiana
    Caley Family Correspondence
    William Cline Diary
    Henry H. Maley Letters
University of Southern Mississippi, Archives, Hattiesburg
    J. D. Harwell Letters
    Dr. P. F. Whitehead Letters
University of Tennessee, Special Collections, Chattanooga
    Colville and Paine Family Letters
    Frederick N. Kollock Diary, Charles S. Harris Collection
    Philip R. Ward Diary, Charles S. Harris Collection
University of Tennessee, Special Collections, Knoxville
    John McNickle Laird Collection
    Edwin Hansford Rennolds Sr. Papers
University of Texas, Dolph Briscoe Center for American History, Austin
    Truair Family Papers
University of Virginia, Special Collections, Charlottesville
    Benjamin and John Green Letters
    Llewellyn Griffin Hoxton Reminiscences
University of Washington, Special Collections, Seattle
    M. F. Force Papers
University of Wyoming, American Heritage Center, Laramie
    Edward B. Moore Diary
Virginia Historical Society, Richmond
    James Madison Brannock Papers
    James Miller Wysor Letters
Virginia Polytechnic Institute and State University, Blacksburg
    Joseph Miller Letter
Wisconsin Historical Society, Madison
    George Cooley Diary
Yale University Library, New Haven, Connecticut
    David Herrick Gile Papers, Civil War Manuscript Collection

NEWSPAPERS

Chicago Daily Tribune
Cincinnati Daily Enquirer
Memphis Daily Appeal
National Tribune
New York Herald

WEBSITES

"Kennesaw Mountain Administrative History." www.nps.gov/kemo
W. L. Truman Memoirs. www.cedarcroft.com

ARTICLES AND BOOKS

Aldrich, C. Knight, ed. *Quest for a Star: The Civil War Letters and Diaries of Colonel Francis T. Sherman of the 88th Illinois*. Knoxville: University of Tennessee Press, 1999.

Angle, Paul M., ed. *Three Years in the Army of the Cumberland: The Letters and Diary of Major James A. Connolly*. Bloomington: Indiana University Press, 1959.

Arbuckle, John C. *Civil War Experiences of a Foot-Soldier Who Marched with Sherman*. Columbus, Ohio: n.p., 1930.

"Arkansas' Work on Kennesaw Mountain." *Confederate Veteran* 19 (1911): 206–7.

Aten, Henry J. *History of the Eighty-Fifth Regiment, Illinois Volunteer Infantry*. Hiawatha, Kans.: Henry J. Aten, 1901.

Bailey, Ronald H. *Battles for Atlanta: Sherman Moves East*. Alexandria, Va.: Time-Life Books, 1985.

Barnard, George N. *Photographic Views of Sherman's Campaign*. New York: Dover, 1977.

Barnes, W. T. "An Incident of Kenesaw Mountain." *Confederate Veteran* 30 (1922): 48–49.

Barnhart, John D., ed. "A Hoosier Invades the Confederacy: Letters and Diaries of Leroy S. Mayfield." *Indiana Magazine of History* 39 (1943): 145–91.

"Battle of Kennesaw Mountain." In *The Annals of the Army of Tennessee and Early Western History*, ed. Edwin L. Drake, 109–17. Nashville: A. D. Haynes, 1878.

Bauer, K. Jack, ed. *Soldiering: The Civil War Diary of Rice C. Bull, 123rd New York Volunteer Infantry*. San Rafael, Calif.: Presidio Press, 1977.

Baumgartner, Richard A., ed. *Blood & Sacrifice: The Civil War Journal of a Confederate Soldier*. Huntington, W.V.: Blue Acorn Press, 1994.

Bennett, L. G., and William M. Haigh. *History of the Thirty-Sixth Regiment Illinois Volunteers, during the War of the Rebellion*. Aurora, Ill.: Knickerbocker and Hodder, 1876.

Bennett, Stewart, and Barbara Tillery, eds. *The Struggle for the Life of the Republic: A Civil War Narrative by Brevet Major Charles Dana Miller, 76th Ohio Volunteer Infantry*. Kent, Ohio: Kent State University Press, 2004.

Bevier, R. S. *History of the First and Second Missouri Confederate Brigades, 1861–1865*. St. Louis: Bryan, Brand, and Company, 1879.

Beyer, W. F., and O. F. Keydel, eds. *Deeds of Valor: How America's Heroes Won the Medal of Honor*. Detroit: Perrien-Keydel, 1905.

Bishop, W. P. "Twenty-Ninth Tennessee Infantry." In *The Military Annals of Tennessee, Confederate*, ed. John Berrien Lindsley, 433–41. Nashville: J. M. Lindsley, 1886.

Black, Wilfred W., ed. "Civil War Letters of George M. Wise." *Ohio Historical Quarterly* 65, no. 1 (January 1956): 53–81.

Blair, J. L. W. "The Fight at Dead Angle." *Confederate Veteran* 12 (1904): 532–33.

Bogle, Joseph. *Some Recollections of the Civil War*. Dalton, Ga.: Dalton Argus, 1911.

Bohrnstedt, Jennifer Cain, ed. *Soldiering with Sherman: Civil War Letters of George F. Cram*. DeKalb: Northern Illinois University Press, 2000.

Booth, W. H. "Kenesaw Mountain: An Iowa Man Who Wants to Know Who Commanded on His Part of the Line." *National Tribune*, August 11, 1892.

Bostwick, S. H. "A Soldier's Gratitude." *National Tribune*, October 18, 1883.

Boynton, H. V. *Sherman's Historical Raid: The Memoirs in the Light of the Record*. Cincinnati: Wilstach, Baldwin, 1875.

Bragg, William Harris. *Joe Brown's Army: The Georgia State Line, 1862–1865*. Macon, Ga.: Mercer University Press, 1987.

Brown, Norman D., ed. *One of Cleburne's Command: The Civil War Reminiscences and Diary of Capt. Samuel T. Foster, Granbury's Texas Brigade, CSA*. Austin: University of Texas Press, 1980.

Brown, Thaddeus S. C., Samuel J. Murphy, and William G. Putney. *Behind the Guns: The History of Battery I, 2nd Regiment, Illinois Light Artillery*. Carbondale: Southern Illinois University Press, 1965.

Bryant, Edwin E. *History of the Third Regiment of Wisconsin Veteran Volunteer Infantry, 1861–1865*. Madison, Wis.: Veteran Association of the Regiment, 1891.

Byrne, Frank L., ed. *Uncommon Soldiers: Harvey Reid and the 22nd Wisconsin March with Sherman*. Knoxville: University of Tennessee Press, 2001.

Cabaniss, Jim R., ed. *Civil War Journal and Letters of Serg. Washington Ives, 4th Florida C. S. A.* N.p.: n.p., 1987.

Castel, Albert. *Decision in the West: The Atlanta Campaign of 1864*. Lawrence: University Press of Kansas, 1992.

———. *Tom Taylor's Civil War*. Lawrence: University Press of Kansas, 2000.

Clampitt, Bradley R. *The Confederate Heartland: Military and Civilian Morale in the Western Confederacy*. Baton Rouge: Louisiana State University Press, 2011.

Clark, Charles T. *Opdycke Tigers: 125th O. V. I.* Columbus, Ohio: Spahr and Glenn, 1895.

Clark, Olynthus B., ed. *Downing's Civil War Diary*. Des Moines: Homestead, 1916.

Clarke, John T. "With Sherman in Georgia." *Bulletin of the Missouri Historical Society* 8, no. 4 (July 1952): 356–70.

Cobb, Thomas M. "Letter." *Confederate Veteran* 2 (1894): 40.

Connelly, Thomas Lawrence. *Autumn of Glory: The Army of Tennessee, 1862–1865*. Baton Rouge: Louisiana State University Press, 1971.

Cook, S. G., and Charles E. Benton, eds. *The "Dutchess County Regiment": (150th Regiment of New York State Volunteer Infantry) in the Civil War*. Danbury, Conn.: Danbury Medical Printing, 1907.

Cope, Alexis. *The Fifteenth Ohio Volunteers and Its Campaigns*. Columbus: Edward T. Miller, 1916.

Cox, Jacob Dolson. *Atlanta*. New York: Charles Scribner's Sons, 1882.

———. *Military Reminiscences of the Civil War*. 2 vols. New York: Charles Scribner's Sons, 1900.

Cozzens, Peter. *The Shipwreck of Their Hopes: The Battles for Chattanooga.* Urbana: University of Illinois Press, 1994.

Crist, Lynda Lasswell, ed. *The Papers of Jefferson Davis.* 17 vols. Baton Rouge: Louisiana State University Press, 1971–2008.

Dacus, Robert H. *Reminiscences of Company "H," First Arkansas Mounted Rifles.* Dayton, Ohio: Morningside Bookshop, 1972.

Daniel, Larry J. *Days of Glory: The Army of the Cumberland, 1861–1865.* Baton Rouge: Louisiana State University Press, 2004.

Davis, Stephen. *Atlanta Will Fall: Sherman, Joe Johnston, and the Yankee Heavy Battalions.* Wilmington, Del.: Scholarly Resources, 2001.

Davis, William C., and Bell I. Wiley, eds. *Photographic History of the Civil War.* 2 vols. New York: Black Dog and Leventhal, 1994.

Day, L. W. *Story of the One Hundred and First Ohio Infantry.* Cleveland: W. M. Bayne, 1894.

Dean, Jeffrey S. "The Forgotten 'Hell Hole': The Battle of Pickett's Mill." In *The Campaign for Atlanta and Sherman's March to the Sea*, vol. 2, ed. Theodore P. Savas and David A. Woodbury, 343–73. Campbell, Calif.: Savas Woodbury, 1994.

Dewey, L. H. "The Charge at Kenesaw." *National Tribune*, January 29, 1885.

Dodge, Grenville M. *Personal Recollections of President Abraham Lincoln, General Ulysses S. Grant and General William T. Sherman.* Denver: Sage Books, 1965.

Duke, John K. *History of the Fifty-Third Regiment Ohio Volunteer Infantry, during the War of the Rebellion, 1861 to 1865.* Portsmouth, Ohio: Blade Printing, 1900.

Eleazer, W. D. "Fight at Dead Angle, in Georgia." *Confederate Veteran* 14 (1906): 312.

Ellison, Janet Correll, ed. *On to Atlanta: The Civil War Diaries of John Hill Ferguson, Illinois Tenth Regiment of Volunteers.* Lincoln: University of Nebraska Press, 2001.

Ervin, W. J. "Genius and Heroism of Lieut. K. H. Faulkner." *Confederate Veteran* 14 (1906): 497–98.

———. "Perilous Undertaking of Two Brothers." *Confederate Veteran* 15 (1907): 308–9.

Fleming, James R. *Band of Brothers: Company C, 9th Tennessee Infantry.* Shippensburg, Pa.: White Mane, 1996.

Fout, Frederick W. *The Dark Days of the Civil War, 1861 to 1865.* N.p.: F. A. Wagenfuehr, 1904.

Franklin, Ann York, compiler. *The Civil War Diaries of Capt. Alfred Tyler Fielder, 12th Tennessee Regiment Infantry, Company B, 1861–1865.* Louisville, Ky.: Ann York Franklin, 1996.

French, S. G. "Kennesaw Mountain." *Southern Bivouac* 1, no. 7 (March 1883): 273–80.

———. *Two Wars: An Autobiography.* Nashville: Confederate Veteran, 1901.

Garrett, Jill K., ed. *Confederate Diary of Robert D. Smith.* Columbia, Tenn.: Capt. James Madison Sparkman Chapter, United Daughters of the Confederacy, 1975.

Gates, Arnold, ed. *The Rough Side of War: The Civil War Journal of Chesley A. Mosman, 1st Lieutenant, Company D, 59th Illinois Volunteer Infantry Regiment.* Garden City, N.Y.: Basin Publishing, 1987.

Gilson, L. W. J. "Walcutt's Charge at Little Kenesaw." *National Tribune*, May 31, 1883.

Gray, I. M. "Kenesaw: What the Third Brigade, Second Division, Fourteenth Corps, Did on the Eventful June 27." *National Tribune*, November 15, 1894.

Grimshaw, S. "The Charge at Kenesaw." *National Tribune*, January 15, 1885.

Hardee, W. J. *Hardee's Rifle and Light Infantry Tactics.* New York: J. O. Kane, 1862.

Harmon, B. H. "Dead Angle." *Confederate Veteran* 11 (1903): 219.

Harris, George W. "Dead Angle—Georgia Campaign." *Confederate Veteran* 11 (1903): 560.

Harwell, Richard B., ed. "The Campaign from Chattanooga to Atlanta as Seen by a Federal Soldier." *Georgia Historical Quarterly* 25, no. 3 (September 1941): 262–78.

Hazen, W. B. *A Narrative of Military Service.* Boston: Ticknor, 1885.

Hedley, F. Y. *Marching through Georgia.* Chicago: Donohue, Henneberry, 1890.

Hess, Earl J. "Civilians at War: The Georgia Militia in the Atlanta Campaign." *Georgia Historical Quarterly* 66, no. 3 (Fall 1982): 332–45.

Higdon, J. C. "Hindman's Reply to Hood." *Confederate Veteran* 8 (1900): 69.

Hight, John J. *History of the Fifty-Eighth Regiment of Indiana Volunteer Infantry.* Princeton, [Ind.]: Clarion, 1895.

A History of the Seventy-Third Regiment of Illinois Infantry Volunteers. N.p.: Regimental Reunion Association, 1890.

Holmes, J. T. *52d O.V.I.: Then and Now.* Columbus, Ohio: Berlin Printing, 1898.

Hood, J. B. *Advance and Retreat: Personal Experiences in the United States and Confederate States Armies.* Philadelphia: Burk and M'Fetridge, 1880.

Howard, Oliver O. *Autobiography.* 2 vols. New York: Baker and Taylor, 1907.

———. "The Struggle for Atlanta." In *Battles and Leaders of the Civil War*, vol. 4, ed. Robert Underwood Johnson and Clarence Clough Buel, 293–325. New York: Thomas Yoseloff, 1956.

Howatson, M. C., ed. *The Oxford Companion to Classical Literature.* 2nd ed. New York: Oxford University Press, 1991.

Howe, M. A. DeWolfe, ed. *Marching with Sherman: Passages From the Letters and Campaign Diaries of Henry Hitchcock, Major and Assistant Adjutant General of Volunteers, November 1864–May 1865.* Lincoln: University of Nebraska Press, 1995.

Hubbart, Phillip A., ed. *An Iowa Soldier Writes Home: The Civil War Letters of Union Private Daniel J. Parvin.* Durham, NC: Carolina Academic Press, 2011.

Hughes, Nathaniel Cheairs, Jr., ed. *The Civil War Memoir of Philip Daingerfield Stephenson, D. D.* Conway: University of Central Arkansas Press, 1995.

Hulet, C. C. "The Assault on Kenesaw Mountain." *Confederate Veteran* 35 (1927): 339–40.

Ives, W. M. "'The Record That We Made.'" *Confederate Veteran* 31 (1923): 334.

Jackson, Oscar L. *The Colonel's Diary.* N.p.: n.p., 1922.

James, F. B. "McCook's Brigade at the Assault upon Kenesaw Mountain, Georgia, June 27, 1864." In *Sketches of War History, 1861–1865: Papers Prepared for the Ohio Commandery of the Military Order of the Loyal Legion of the United States, 1890–1896*, 4:255–77. Wilmington, N.C.: Broadfoot, 1991.

Jamison, Matthew H. *Recollections of Pioneer and Army Life.* Kansas City, Mo.: Hudson Fields, [1911].

Johnson, W. C., and E. S. Hartshorn. "The Development of Field Fortification in the Civil War." *Professional Memoirs, U.S. Army and Engineer Department at Large* 7 (September–October 1915): 570–602.

Johnston, Joseph E. *Narrative of Military Operations, Directed, during the Late War between the States.* New York: D. Appleton, 1874.

———. "Opposing Sherman's Advance to Atlanta." In *Battles and Leaders of the Civil War*, vol. 4, ed. Robert Underwood Johnson and Clarence Clough Buel, 260–77. New York: Thomas Yoseloff, 1956.

Jones, Mary Miles, and Leslie Jones Martin, eds. *The Gentle Rebel: The Civil War Let-*

ters of 1st Lt. William Harvey Berryhill Co. D, 43rd Regiment Mississippi Volunteers. Yazoo City, Miss.: Sassafras Press, 1982.

Jordan, A. L. "'Dead Angle' Tunneled." *Confederate Veteran* 17 (1909): 601.

———. *Gen. Jos. E. Johnston: A Review of His Military Career.* Pulaski, Va.: B. D. Smith, [1907].

Jordan, Philip D., ed. "Forty Days with the Christian Commission: A Diary by William Salter." *Iowa Journal of History and Politics* 33, no. 2 (April 1935): 123–54.

Joyce, John A. "Kenesaw Mountain." *National Tribune,* November 29, 1883.

Kelly, Dennis. "Atlanta Campaign: Mountains to Pass, a River to Cross." *Blue and Gray* 6, no. 5 (June 1989): 8–30, 46–58.

Kelly, Walden. "Kenesaw Mountain: Another Account of the Famous Charge." *National Tribune,* November 13, 1890.

———. *Kennesaw Mountain and the Atlanta Campaign: A Tour Guide.* Atlanta: Susan Hunter Publications, 1990.

Kerr, Homer L., ed. *Fighting with Ross' Texas Cavalry Brigade, C. S. A.: The Diary of George C. Griscom, Adjutant, 9th Texas Cavalry Regiment.* Hillsboro, Tex.: Hill Junior College Press, 1976.

Kerwood, Asbury L. *Annals of the Fifty-Seventh Regiment Indiana Volunteers.* Dayton, Ohio: W. J. Shuey, 1868.

Latimer, William. "Incidents Related by William Latimer, of Sumner, Tex." *Confederate Veteran* 25 (1917): 167–68.

Letters of Captain Henry Richards of the Ninety-Third Ohio Infantry. Cincinnati: Wrightson, 1883.

Letters of William Wheeler of the Class of 1855, Y.C. Cambridge, Mass.: H. O. Houghton, 1875.

Logan, John A. *The Volunteer Soldier of America.* Chicago: R. S. Peale, 1887.

Logan, Mrs. John A. *Reminiscences of a Soldier's Wife: An Autobiography.* Carbondale: Southern Illinois University Press, 1997.

Longacre, Glenn V., and John E. Haas, eds. *To Battle for God and the Right: The Civil War Letterbooks of Emerson Opdycke.* Urbana: University of Illinois Press, 2003.

Lossing, Benson J. *Pictorial Field Book of the Civil War: Journeys through the Battle-fields in the Wake of Conflict.* 3 vols. Baltimore: Johns Hopkins University Press, 1997.

Losson, Christopher. *Tennessee's Forgotten Warriors: Frank Cheatham and His Confederate Division.* Knoxville: University of Tennessee Press, 1989.

Mahan, D. H. *An Elementary Treatise on Advanced-Guard, Out-Post, and Detachment Service of Troops, and the Manner of Posting and Handling Them in Presence of an Enemy.* New Orleans, Louisiana: Bloomfield and Steel, 1861.

[Maney, T. H.] "The Battle of Dead Angle on the Kennesaw Line, near Marietta, Georgia." *Southern Bivouac* 3, no. 2 (October 1884): 71–74.

Mannis, Jedediah, and Galen R. Wilson, eds. *Bound to Be a Soldier: The Letters of Private James T. Miller, 111th Pennsylvania Infantry, 1861–1864.* Knoxville: University of Tennessee Press, 2001.

Marvin, Edwin E. *The Fifth Regiment Connecticut Volunteers.* Hartford, Conn.: Wiley, Waterman, and Eaton, 1889.

McAdams, F. M. *Every-Day Soldier Life; or, A History of the One Hundred and Thirteenth Ohio Volunteer Infantry.* Columbus, Ohio: Charles M. Colt, 1884.

McBride, John Randolph. *History of the Thirty-Third Indiana Veteran Volunteer Infan-*

try during the Four Years of Civil War, from September 16, 1861 to July 21, 1865.
Indianapolis: William R. Burford, 1900.

Macaulay, Thomas Babington. *Critical, Historical and Miscellaneous Essays and Poems.*
3 vols. New York: A. L. Burt, n.d.

McKinsay, H. "The Charge at Kenesaw." *National Tribune*, December 25, 1884.

M'Mahon, G. W. "Samuel Knox—a Patriot." *Confederate Veteran* 32 (1924): 89.

McMurry, Richard M. "The Affair at Kolb's Farm." *Civil War Times Illustrated* 7, no. 8
(December 1968): 20–27.

———. *Atlanta 1864: Last Chance for the Confederacy.* Lincoln: University of Nebraska
Press, 2000.

———. *John Bell Hood and the War for Southern Independence.* Lexington: University
Press of Kentucky, 1982.

———. "Kennesaw Mountain." *Civil War Times Illustrated* 8, no. 9 (January 1970):
19–34.

McNeil, S. A. "It Gives Some Light." *National Tribune*, December 16, 1886.

M'Neilly, James H. "A Great Game of Strategy." *Confederate Veteran* 27 (1919): 377–84.

"Memo Book: William O. Norrell—Co. B, 63d Ga. Regt. Vols. Mercer's Brigade, Walker's
Division Hardee's Corps Army of Tennessee." *Journal of Confederate History* 1, no. 1
(Summer 1988): 49–82.

Merrill, James M., and James F. Marshall, eds. "Georgia through Kentucky Eyes: Letters Written on Sherman's March to Atlanta." *Filson Club History Quarterly* 30,
no. 4 (October 1956): 324–39.

Miles, Charles W., Sr. "Col. Hume R. Feild." *Confederate Veteran* 29 (1921): 325–26.

Mitchell, Enoch L., ed. "The Civil War Letters of Thomas Jefferson Newberry." *Journal
of Mississippi History* 19, no. 1 (January 1948): 44–80.

Moore, John. "Kenesaw Mountain: The Conduct of the Fourth and Fourteenth Corps at
the Charge." *National Tribune*, April 3, 1890.

———. "A Rebel Spy." *National Tribune*, November 14, 1895.

Morhous, Henry C. *Reminiscences of the 123d Regiment, N.Y.S.V.* Greenwich, N.Y.:
People's Journal, 1879.

Morse, Charles F. *Letters Written during the Civil War, 1861–1865.* Boston: T. R. Marvin
and Sons, 1898.

Mulligan, William H., Jr., [ed.] *A Badger Boy in Blue: The Civil War Letters of
Chauncey H. Cooke.* Detroit: Wayne State University Press, 2007.

Neighbor, T. D. "Kenesaw Mountain: The Part Taken by McCook's Brigade in the
Charge." *National Tribune*, December 25, 1890.

Nelson, H. K. "Dead Angle, or Devil's Elbow, Ga." *Confederate Veteran* 11 (1903): 321–22.

———. "Dead Angle Again." *Confederate Veteran* 12 (1904): 32.

Osborn, Hartwell. *Trials and Triumphs: The Record of the Fifty-Fifth Ohio Volunteer
Infantry.* Chicago: A. C. McClurg, 1904.

Padgett, James A., ed. "With Sherman through Georgia and the Carolinas: Letters of a
Federal Soldier." *Georgia Historical Quarterly* 32 (1948): 284–322.

Palmer, John M. *Personal Recollections.* Cincinnati: Robert Clarke, 1901.

Partridge, Charles A., ed. *History of the Ninety-Sixth Regiment Illinois Volunteer Infantry.* Chicago: Brown, Pettibone, 1887.

Payne, E. M. "At Kenesaw: A 34th Ill. Man Tells What He Saw There." *National Tribune*,
May 25, 1893.

Payne, Edwin W. *History of the Thirty-Fourth Regiment of Illinois Volunteer Infantry.* Clinton, Iowa: Allen, 1902.

Phillips, Brenda D., ed. *Personal Reminiscences of a Confederate Soldier Boy: Robert M. Magill, Co. F, 39th Ga. Reg. Inf.* Milledgeville, Ga.: Boyd Publishing, 1993.

Pierson, Stephen. "From Chattanooga to Atlanta in 1864—A Personal Reminiscence." *Proceedings of the New Jersey Historical Society* 16, no. 3 (July 1931): 324–56.

Potter, A. M. "Kenesaw Mountain: The Great Charge on June 27, 1864." *National Tribune,* November 6, 1890.

Pratt, Henry C. "After Assault at Kenesaw." *National Tribune,* July 28, 1910.

Quaife, Milo M., ed. *From the Cannon's Mouth: The Civil War Letters of General Alpheus S. Williams.* Detroit: Wayne State University Press, 1959.

"A Rash Deed at Dead Angle." *Confederate Veteran* 12 (1904): 394.

Reese, C. D. "A Memory of the War." *National Tribune,* June, 1879.

Reyburn, Philip J., and Terry L. Wilson, eds. *"Jottings from Dixie": The Civil War Dispatches of Sergeant Major Stephen F. Fleharty, U. S. A.* Baton Rouge: Louisiana State University Press, 1999.

Rice, R. C. "Kenesaw Mountain: What Troops Made the Gallant Charge June 27, 1864." *National Tribune,* October 9, 1890.

———. "Where Harker Fell." *National Tribune,* June 8, 1905.

Richards, Henry. *Letters of Captain Henry Richards, of the Ninety-Third Ohio Infantry.* Cincinnati: Wrightson, 1883.

Richardson, Eldon B. *Kolb's Farm: Rehearsal for Atlanta's Doom.* N.p.: n.p., 1979.

Rogers, Robert M. *The 125th Regiment Illinois Volunteer Infantry.* Champaign, Ill.: Gazette Steam Print, 1882.

Said, Abner. "A Picnic on the Skirmish Line." *National Tribune,* April 16, 1903.

Saunier, Joseph A. *A History of the Forty-Seventh Regiment Ohio Veteran Volunteer Infantry.* Hillsboro, Ohio: Lyle Printing, [1903].

Scaife, William R., and William Harris Bragg. *Joe Brown's Pets: The Georgia Militia, 1861–1865.* Macon, Ga.: Mercer University Press, 2004.

Schofield, John M. *Forty-Six Years in the Army.* New York: Century, 1897.

Scribner, B. F. *How Soldiers Were Made; or, The War as I Saw It.* Chicago: Donohue and Henneberry, 1887.

Shellenberger, John L. "Kenesaw Mountain: The Causes That Led to the Repulse of Harker's Brigade." *National Tribune,* December 11, 1890.

Sherman, William T. "The Grand Strategy of the Last Year of the War." In *Battles and Leaders of the Civil War,* vol. 4, ed. Robert Underwood Johnson and Clarence Clough Buel, 241–59. Eds. New York: Thomas Yoseloff, 1956.

———. *Memoirs.* 2 vols. New York: D. Appleton, 1875.

Simpson, Brooks D., and Jean V. Berlin, eds. *Sherman's Civil War: Selected Correspondence of William T. Sherman, 1860–1865.* Chapel Hill: University of North Carolina Press, 1999.

A Sketch of the Operations of the Forty-Seventh Ohio Volunteer Infantry. Cincinnati: George P. Houston, 1885.

Smith, Charles H. *The History of Fuller's Ohio Brigade, 1861–1865.* Cleveland: A. J. Watt, 1909.

Smith, David M., ed. "The Civil War Diary of Colonel John Henry Smith." *Iowa Journal of History* 47, no. 2 (April 1949): 140–70.

Smith, Gustavus W. "The Georgia Militia about Atlanta." In *Battles and Leaders of the*

Civil War, vol. 4, ed. Robert Underwood Johnson and Clarence Clough Buel, 331–35. New York: Thomas Yoseloff, 1956.

Smith, H. I. *History of the Seventh Iowa Veteran Volunteer Infantry during the Civil War.* Mason City, Iowa: E. Hitchcock, 1903.

Souder, J. B. "Death of Gen. McCook." *National Tribune,* June 18, 1885.

"Southern Battlefields": A List of Battlefields on and near the Lines of the Nashville, Chattanooga & St. Louis Railway and Western & Atlantic Railroad. Nashville: Nashville, Chattanooga & St. Louis Railway, n.d.

Stewart, Nixon B. *Dan McCook's Regiment, 52nd O.V.I.* Alliance, Ohio: Review Print, 1900.

Stone, Henry. "The Atlanta Campaign." In *The Mississippi Valley, Tennessee, Georgia, Alabama, 1861–1864. Papers of the Military Historical Society of Massachusetts,* 8:341–492. Boston: Military Historical Society of Massachusetts, 1910.

Storrs, George S. "Kennesaw Mountain." *Southern Bivouac* 1, no. 4 (December 1882): 135–40.

The Story of the Fifty-Fifth Regiment Illinois Volunteer Infantry in the Civil War, 1861–1865. Clinton, Mass.: W. J. Coulter, 1887.

Story of the Service of Company E, and of the Twelfth Wisconsin Regiment, Veteran Volunteer Infantry, in the War of the Rebellion. Milwaukee: Swain and Tate, 1893.

Supplement to the Official Records of the Union and Confederate Armies. 100 vols. Wilmington, N.C.: Broadfoot Publishing, 1993–2000.

Sutherland, Daniel E., ed. *Reminiscences of a Private: William E. Bevens of the First Arkansas Infantry, C. S. A.* Fayetteville: University of Arkansas Press, 1992.

Tappan, George, ed. *The Civil War Journal of Lt. Russell M. Tuttle, New York Volunteer Infantry.* Jefferson, N.C.: McFarland, 2006.

Taylor, T. L. "Why Firing Occurred at Dead Angle at Night." *Confederate Veteran* 15 (1907): 77.

Thoburn, Lyle, ed. *My Experiences during the Civil War.* Cleveland: n.p., 1963.

Toombs, Samuel. *Reminiscences of the War.* Orange, N.J.: Journal Office, 1878.

Tower, R. Lockwood, ed. *A Carolinian Goes to War: The Civil War Narrative of Arthur Middleton Manigault, Brigadier General, C. S. A.* Columbia: University of South Carolina Press, 1983.

Tritsch, John W. "Honor between Soldiers in Service." *Confederate Veteran* 15 (1907): 539.

Vaughan, A. J. *Personal Record of the Thirteenth Regiment, Tennessee Infantry.* Memphis: Burke's Book Store, n.d.

Wagner, Arthur L. *Organization and Tactics.* New York: B. Westermann, 1895.

Walker, C. I. *Rolls and Historical Sketch of the Tenth Regiment, So. Ca. Volunteers, in the Army of the Confederate States.* Charleston, S.C.: Walker, Evans & Cogswell, 1881.

Walton, Claiborne J. "'One Continued Scene of Carnage': A Union Surgeon's View of War." *Civil War Times Illustrated* 15, no. 5 (August 1976): 34–36.

Walton, William, ed. *A Civil War Courtship: The Letters of Edwin Weller from Antietam to Atlanta.* Garden City, N.Y.: Doubleday, 1980.

"War Diary of Thaddeus H. Capron, 1861–1865." *Journal of the Illinois State Historical Society* 12 (1919–20): 330–406.

The War of the Rebellion: A Compilation of the Official Records of the Union and Confederate Armies. 70 vols. in 128. Washington, D.C.: Government Printing Office, 1880–1901.

Ward, Allen M., Fritz M. Heichelheim, and Cedric A. Yeo. *A History of the Roman People*. 3rd ed. Upper Saddle River, N.J.: Prentice-Hall, 1999.

Warfield, C. R. "Charging Kenesaw: A 121st Ohio Man Who Saw Only What Happened near Himself." *National Tribune*, September 6, 1864.

Warner, Ezra J. *Generals in Blue: Lives of the Union Commanders*. Baton Rouge: Louisiana State University Press, 1964.

———. *Generals in Gray: Lives of the Confederate Commanders*. Baton Rouge: Louisiana State University Press, 1959.

Watkins, Sam R. *Co. Aytch: A Side Show of the Big Show*. New York: Collier, 1962.

———. "Dead Angle, On the Kennesaw Line." *Confederate Veteran* 25 (1917): 166–67.

Welsh, Jack D. *Medical Histories of Union Generals*. Kent, Ohio: Kent State University Press, 1996.

West, Elizabeth Howard. "Biographical Sketch of the Reverend James Durham West, D.D." *Tennessee Historical Magazine* 7, no. 3 (October 1921): 191–93.

White, William Lee, and Charles Denny Runion, eds. *Great Things Are Expected of Us: The Letters of Colonel C. Irvine Walker, 10th South Carolina Infantry, C. S. A.* Knoxville: University of Tennessee Press, 2009.

Williamson, David. *The Third Battalion Mississippi Infantry and the 45th Mississippi Regiment: A Civil War History*. Jefferson, N.C.: McFarland, 2004.

Wills, Charles W. *Army Life of an Illinois Soldier: Including a Day by Day Record of Sherman's March to the Sea*. Washington, D.C.: Globe Printing, 1906.

Wills, Ridley, II, ed. *Old Enough to Die*. Franklin, Tenn.: Hillsboro Press, 1996.

Winther, Oscar Osburn, ed. *With Sherman to the Sea: The Civil War Letters, Diaries & Reminiscences of Theodore F. Upson*. Bloomington: Indiana University Press, 1958.

Woodworth, Steven E. *Nothing but Victory: The Army of the Tennessee, 1861–1865*. New York: Alfred A. Knopf, 2005.

Work, J. B., ed. *Re-Union of Col. Dan McCook's Third Brigade, Second Division, Fourteenth A. C., "Army of the Cumberland": Assault of Col. Dan McCook's Brigade on Kenesaw Mountain, Ga., June 27, 1864/August 27th and 29th, 1900*. Chicago: Allied, 1901.

"The Work of Kennesaw Chapter." *Confederate Veteran* 16 (1908): 620–21.

Worsham, W. J. *The Old Nineteenth Tennessee Regiment, C. S. A., June, 1861–April, 1865*. Knoxville: Paragon, 1902.

Wright, Charles. *A Corporal's Story: Experiences in the Ranks of Company C, 81st Ohio Vol. Infantry, during the War for the Maintenance of the Union, 1861–1864*. Philadelphia: James Beale, 1887.

Wright, Henry H. *A History of the Sixth Iowa Infantry*. Iowa City: State Historical Society of Iowa, 1923.

Wynne, Lewis N., and Robert A. Taylor, eds. *This War So Horrible: The Civil War Diary of Hiram Smith Williams*. Tuscaloosa: University of Alabama Press, 1993.

Yates, Bowling C. *Historical Guide for Kennesaw Mountain National Battlefield Park and Marietta, Georgia*. N.p.: n.p., 1976.

Index

Sears, Claudius W., 26
Shellenberger, John K., 97, 101, 111
Sherman, Francis T., 163
Sherman, William T.: Atlanta campaign,
    1–15; attack of June 27, 62–63, 66,
    69–70, 106, 138–42, 144–47, 153,
    155, 160–64, 213–14; battle of Kolb's
    Farm, 42–43, 47–49; criticism of,
    220–24; confronting Kennesaw Line,
    xiii–xiv, 6, 17–19, 24–27, 215; decision
    to attack at Kennesaw Mountain, 215,
    226; flanking Kennesaw Line, 188,
    201, 204–5, 207
Skilton, Alvah Stone, 71, 82
Smith, Giles A., 71–72, 78–79
Smith, Melancthon, 167, 182
Smith, Morgan L., 72, 78
Smith, Robert Davis, 110, 168, 183
Smyrna Line, 208–11
Sloan, William E., 215
Stanley, David S., 109
Stegner, Frederick W., 155–56
Stevenson, Carter L., 33–35, 37, 40, 46
Stewart, Nixon B., 70, 122, 127, 150, 178
Stone, Henry, 221
Storrs, George S., 22, 25–26, 53–55, 197

Tennessee units
    1st, 133
    32nd, 41
Thomas, George H., 11, 14–15, 32–33, 43,
    192, 210; at Kennesaw Mountain, 58,

66, 106, 144–47, 151, 158–60, 173,
    189
Truman, W. L., 56, 197
Tuttle, John W., 102, 148, 184

Vaughan, Alfred J., 120, 210–11
Vernon, Maris R., 164
Vining's Station, 212–13, 300 (n. 81)
Virginia units
    54th, 41

Wagner, Arthur L., 163
Wagner, George D., 104–5, 108
Walcutt, Charles C., 85
Walker, C. Irvine, 46
Walker, W. H. T., 75
Walton, Claiborne J., 157
Warren, George W., 79
Watkins, Sam R., 132–33, 136, 151, 175
Webber, Alonzo P., 151
West, James Durham, 160
Wheeler, William, 39
Whitesides, Edward G., 102–3
Williams, Alpheus S., 28–29, 32, 36,
    38–40, 43
Williams, Hiram Smith, 15, 41, 161
Wills, Charles W., 68, 86–87, 223
Wisconsin units
    24th, 107–8
Work, J. B., 174, 223
Worsham, W. J., 235
Wright, Henry, 55